D1597176

THE NASTY FOOTBALL HISTORY OF MICHIGAN vs MICHIGAN STATE

Why Every Game Drew Blood from 1898 to 2020

Barry Gallagher

Power Group Publishing

Aurora, Illinois

Barry Gallagher/Go Blue Publishing
2748 Kirk Road, Suite 106, #165
Aurora, Illinois 60502
www.PowerGroup@comcast.net
Book Layout ©2017 BookDesignTemplates.com

Ordering Information:
Quantity sales. Special discounts are available on quantity purchases by corporations, associations, and others. For details, contact the "Special Sales Department" at the ad-dress above.

The Nasty Football History of Michigan vs Michigan State/Barry Gallagher —1st ed.

ISBN 978-1-7344313-3-9

CONTENTS

FOREWORD

Back in the fall of 1973 my good friend Jim Carlson talked me into officiating a youth football game. I never imagined that the "officiating bug" would bite me and I'd go on to officiate high school varsity, NCAA D3 and then have the opportunity to work twenty years in the Big 10 Conference. (Including 15 bowl games, a national championship [Auburn/Oregon], and the amazing Fiesta Bowl between Boise State & Oklahoma.) In 2007, I was fortunate to officiate games in Japan and later in Africa and Mexico. Yes, officiating allowed me to see America and the world and make new friends who love this game as much as I do. Now, to close out this career, I'm honored to work for ESPN these past eight years as an on-air rules analyst.

I was quoted in an interview during my last year on the field that the five games I officiated between Michigan and Michigan State were more intense than any of the six games times I officiated between UM and OSU, including 2006 when they were #2 and #1 in the country. That surprised several sports writers and obviously got Barry's attention.

Part of our weekly routine as officials always involved us doing our homework on game tapes and reviewing questions that coaches always send in on the other team. Our prep time averages ten to fifteen hours. Once we arrived the night before the game, we had a pre-game meeting to discuss team tendencies, the game day schedule, and other somewhat generic routines except for UM vs MSU games. The number one topic during the week and at our pre-game meeting was "game control." The intensity of this game began the moment we went on the field sixty minutes before kickoff and lasted until the game clock hit 0:00 in the fourth quarter. Other rivalry games like UM/OSU, Iowa/Iowa State or Indiana/Purdue were intense. However, after each team had a possession on offense, the teams usually dropped the rivalry intensity and just played football. Not so in Ann Arbor or East Lansing! It didn't matter the score of the game or the team rankings. We always had to concentrate on every play, but with UM and MSU we had to be what we call the best "dead ball officials" in the game. We had to be that police officer with presence, ready to get between players, ready to manage, and prevent things from getting out of hand.

As you read this account of what Barry describes as "The Nasty Football History of Michigan vs Michigan State, you might agree with me that "Nasty" may be an understatement. Without being a spoiler, I learned that in the early days of college football, college teams sometimes played not only "small" college teams but also high school teams. Albion College played Michigan twelve times and actually beat UM once…much to the delight of my daughter who attended Albion.

I had no idea that my remarks about UM and MSU in 2014 would result in a book about the greatest college football story never told—until now. Enjoy!

Bill LeMonnier
Big Ten Referee (Retired)
ESPN Rules Analyst

DEDICATION

This book is dedicated to all Michigan and Michigan State football players who have played in the Mitten State rivalry. Thanks to their efforts, it is now one of the greatest rivalries in the history of college football.

INTRODUCTION

I became a college football fan in 1962 when my parents brought home a program from a Michigan Wolverine football game. I fell in love with the famous winged football helmets. Yes, my favorite team has always been the Michigan Wolverines. Of course, one of the teams that Michigan played every year was the Michigan State Spartans. When I was a Sophomore in high school, I had an English teacher who was a Michigan graduate and a BIG Wolverine football fan. Mr. Hill always had something interesting to say about the annual football brawl between the two schools. Yes, he described it as a very intense rivalry.

The Spartans usually beat Michigan in the 1960s. After losing his first game against Duffy Daugherty's Spartans, Bo Schembechler changed that! He won seventeen of the next twenty games from 1970 to 1989. Yes, that was a good time to be a Michigan football fan! As the years went on, I continued to follow my beloved Wolverines and became a season ticket holder in the late Eighties.

Things changed in our family when our second son became a MSU Spartan in 1993. Yes, our household was officially a "house divided" and our youngest son also became a Spartan in 2000. Michigan vs Michigan State football games took on a whole new meaning in our family with these split loyalties. My first and third sons were strong Wolverine backers while Mom and our Spartan sons backed the Green and White. Our daughter did not really cheer for either team in those days, she just wanted everybody to get along! Things never get out of control when we are watching the Paul Bunyan game together, or from afar. But it is always interesting!

I continued to be a huge Michigan fan, but also learned to cheer for the Spartans when they were not playing the Wolverines. It was the least that a good father/husband could do, right? Over the years, I read many books about Michigan Wolverine football history and their rivalries with Ohio State and Notre Dame. However, there were no books about the Mitten State football rivalry.

In July 2014, I read an interesting article about a retiring Big Ten football referee named Bill LeMonnier. Mr. LeMonnier served as a Big Ten official for over twenty-years. He saw a lot of football in his time, but one thing he said he never saw was a rivalry more intense than Michigan vs Michigan State. I found that hard to believe, but I understood completely after he clarified his remarks later in the article. Yes, he officiated many famous battles between Michigan and Ohio State. Of course, this annual classic was ranked by ESPN as the "greatest North American sports rivalry" in 2000. (*"The 10 greatest rivalries". ESPN. January 3, 2000.*)

Bill LeMonnier said that Michigan vs Michigan State was different because the intensity of this game started before the game began, carried on through every play, and even spilled over to post-game "activities." He felt that it was always a difficult game to work because he had to keep his officiating crew on their toes for the entire day.

After reading the article, I decided to find out why these two teams hated each other so much. I learned that the football games are merely the "tip of the iceberg" in this rivalry. Yes, they have played 113 games, but there are so many "off-the-field" disputes, slights and put-downs that have happened over the years. It is not just one thing, or one game, that sparked this legendary rivalry. Instead, it is a lot of big, and little, things that have happened over eighteen decades. Yes, this rivalry has longevity since the "bad history" goes all the way back to the 1850s. It also has story after story that you cannot make up. Folks, this stuff really happened. You are about to learn why this rivalry is so "nasty" and why every game drew blood starting in 1898.

I also want to share what I learned about football rivalries, especially "in-state" rivalries like Michigan and Michigan State. When you lose a game to a rival from your same state you actually lose four times because: 1) You lose a game 2) You lose a rival game 3) You lose bragging rights for a year 4) You lose state recruiting advantages for a year. Of course, if you are in the same conference, like UM and MSU, you also lose a Big Ten game (5). Finally, if a trophy is involved like one called Paul Bunyan you lose again (6) if you don't win the game. Yes, that's six losses in one day. This is why there is nothing better than winning the annual game between Michigan and Michigan State. Of course, there is nothing worse than losing this all-important football matchup Now you know why there is always a lot riding on the outcome of this "nasty" football get together!

Documenting the complete history of Michigan vs Michigan State took longer than I anticipated, but I thoroughly enjoyed the journey. You will notice that I referenced many books (twenty to be exact) as well as hundreds of newspaper articles. It was fun to see the rivalry unfold through the words of my favorite *Detroit Free Press* writers (I delivered the *Free Press* for a few years when I was growing up) as well as reporters from many other fine newspapers. My wife, and my Spartan sons, encouraged me to tell this story objectively and that is what I tried to do. I am happy to declare that there is finally a book that documents one of the most colorful and intense rivalries in the history of college football. I hope you enjoy reading this book as much as I enjoyed writing it. Thank you!

CHAPTER 1

In the Beginning 1817 to 1897

Why is the football rivalry between The University of Michigan and Michigan State University so intense and so nasty? To answer that question, we must go back to the origins of both institutions. Indeed, the rivalry goes back to a time when football was not even played in the great state of Michigan. Yes, the bad feelings between the two schools began before students ever set foot on either campus.

On August 26, 1817, The University of Michigan was officially founded as the "Catholepistemiad of Michigania." It was part of an aggressive, and visionary, effort to upgrade education in the Michigan territory. William G. Scheller, author of *The University of Michigan Story: Hail to the Victors,* explained that "Catholepistemiad" is a word derived "…from Catholepistemia which meant "universal science." (Scheller, Page 11) The territorial act of 1817 called for President and Vice-President of the Catholepistemiad to control the university as well as other colleges, schools, libraries, and other entities dedicated to the betterment of cities, towns, counties, and townships throughout the entire Michigan territory. Construction began in September and within one year a primary school and a classical academy were fully functioning. The university, however, was an institution in name only. (Scheller, Page 11)

The "Catholepistemiad" part of the universities name was removed in April 1821 when the Territorial Act of 1817 was repealed. A new territorial act changed the name of the "paper" institution to the "University of Michigan." A Board of Trustees (numbering 20 people) took charge of the "mythical" university. After Michigan became a state on January 26, 1837, things changed again. On March 20, 1837, the new state legislature re-created The University of Michigan. (Scheller, Page 11)

Version two of the university called for a twelve-person Board of Regents. According to Mr. Scheller, The University of Michigan was instructed to occupy a site or lot of ground "...not less than forty acres in a thriving community called Ann Arbor." (Scheller, Page 11) Interestingly, some businessmen in Ann Arbor had set land aside to win a bid for the state capital. Obviously, the state capital did not go to the Tree City. Instead, it went to a city located to the north called Lansing, Michigan. Yes, the land that did not host the state capital would now serve as the location of the states' first university. Nobody knew it at the time, but a "rivalry" was born and there would be other things to fight for, and about, for many, many years to come!

TIME FOR SOME ACADEMIC CONTROVERSY!

The paper-based University of Michigan moved from Detroit (where it never existed) to Ann Arbor in 1837. The Board of Regents held their first meeting in Ann Arbor on June 5th of that eventful year. The regents set out to build and organize the first university in the newest state in the union. After a humble start, formal classes began in 1841. Henry Tappan, the first university president, modeled Michigan's curriculum after a German research model. However, he "...strongly supported the expansion beyond the classical subject matter into the rapidly developing sciences." (Scheller, Page 14) Michigan's first graduating class (eleven men) earned their degrees in 1845. The College of Literature, Science and the Arts became the first college in the system with the School of Medicine becoming the second in 1850. The university grew steadily and, in time, became one of the largest in the Midwest. The Ann Arbor campus served the region and the people well. However, Michigan was not serving the state's farmers or the agriculture industry.

Article 13, Section 11 of Michigan's State Constitution of 1850 directed that the legislature would "...provide for the establishment of an agricultural school." The constitution also stated that an "agricultural school" could be part of The University of Michigan or become an entirely new and independent institution. The constitution even referred to a tract of local land that could be used for a new school in the Lansing area. Eventually, the disgruntled farming community pushed for a new agriculture school in Michigan. When the call for an agriculture institution came forth, they were strongly opposed by The University of Michigan. Keith Widder, author of *Michigan Agricultural College: The Evolution of a Land-Grant Philosophy 1855-1925*, stated that "A fierce battle ensued over the next four years to determine the disposition of Michigan's Agricultural College." (Widder, Page 24)

University President Henry Tappan did everything in his power to stop the founding of a separate "agriculture school" in Michigan. He opposed the idea of an agricultural college because he believed that all higher education within Michigan should take place in Ann Arbor, as outlined in the state constitution. Tappan took steps to offer agricultural studies at Michigan in hopes of appeasing the farming community. Kim Clarke, editor of *Always Leading, Forever Valiant: Stories of The University of Michigan, 1817-2017,* wrote about Tappan's failed efforts. She detailed Tappan's efforts in her University of Michigan Heritage Project article titled, *Seeds of Discontent.* President Tappan thought he would win the day with the hiring of Charles Fox, a respected agriculture expert, to become the first Professor of Agriculture in the State of Michigan. Sadly, within one month of his hiring Fox died of cholera. (Clark, *Seeds of Discontent*, Chapter 4)

Professor Fox was only thirty-eight years old when he died. Technically, the death of Professor Fox was also the death of Presidents Tappan's bid for his agricultural school. John C. Holmes, Secretary of the Michigan Agricultural Society, was the man who led the effort for a separate agricultural college in Michigan. While Henry Tappan of The University of Michigan was happy with a Department of Agriculture in Ann Arbor, Holmes wanted more! Yes, Holmes and his supporters wanted more than books and lectures. They wanted a school with a "model farm" that would allow for agricultural experimentation and testing instead of just theory. Ultimately, Holmes and his practical approach won the day over Tappan's theoretical plan. (Widder, Page 29)

It took many years of political infighting and numerous frustrations, but the Agricultural College of the State of Michigan was officially founded in 1855. Yes, Holmes, and his supporters, accomplished a "first" that enabled them to better serve the interests of Michigan's farmers. (Widder, Page 29) The birth of the Agricultural College of the State of Michigan was significant in the Mitten State and America as well. Michigan's newest institution of higher learning was the first agricultural college in the history of the United States. It also paved the way for the Land Grant College concept.

A RIVAL IS BORN

The Agricultural College of the State of Michigan (ACSM) opened in 1857 with 63 students attending in the first year. Because of continued opposition from Tappan and his supporters, the young agricultural school struggled from 1855 to 1860. ACSM was officially renamed the State Agricultural College (SAC) in 1861. On July 2, 1861, President Abraham Lincoln signed the Morrill Bill into law. (Widder, Page 47)

The Morrill Act provided a huge boost to the folks in East Lansing when SAC became one of the first Land Grant Colleges in the nation. In addition to the prestige that this brought, there was a generous donation of land. Other federal support allowed the agricultural school to forge ahead in their efforts to build a more practical college program than the one being developed in Ann Arbor. Land grant schools were chartered with a mission of what I call the "Labor Arts" in contrast to the "Liberal Arts" focus of schools like the University of Michigan. The two schools clearly differed in their vision and their purpose. However, both academic "rivals" found ways to serve the people of Michigan, the region and eventually the world!

MICHIGAN FOOTBALL: THE EARLY YEARS

The University of Michigan was the first team in the State of Michigan to play another school in the emerging game of football. In fact, they were the first school west of the Allegheny Mountains to play America's newest game. Michigan played a "two game" season in 1879— some ten years after Rutgers and Princeton played the first ever college football game at New Brunswick, New Jersey in 1869. Michigan's first football game (it resembled rugby more than the American football we know today) was played against Racine College from Wisconsin on May 30, 1879. It took place on a field located in what is now Millennium Park in Chicago. The Wolverines were victorious by a score of 1-0. The second game of the season was against The University of Toronto in Detroit on November 1, 1879. The game ended in a 0-0 tie.

The early Wolverine football teams played without coaches. The teams were led by player captains, who organized the team, set practice schedules, and arranged for contests against anyone who would play them. Michigan's captains led the football charge for the first eleven seasons. The captains worked hard to get Michigan football off to an excellent start. They posted a record of 23 wins, 10 losses, and 1 tie for a winning percentage of almost seventy percent (.691). Michigan finally hired two coaches (Frank Crawford and Mike Murphy) in 1891 and fired them at the end of the season after they only won 4 of 9 games.

Things improved with the next few hires and Michigan posted thirty-one wins over the next four years and lost ten games. The Michigan footballers played for sixteen seasons and accumulated eighty-five games of experience before the men from East Lansing ever set foot on a football field. In November 1895, Michigan's record for the first sixteen seasons of football stood at 58 wins, 25 losses, and 2 ties (Winning percentage of .694). Michigan's outstanding record allowed them to be called the best team in the State of Michigan. They were also one of the few Midwest teams to regularly challenge the powerhouse teams from the east like Harvard, Yale, Princeton, and Cornell. Michigan played many football games against in-state schools from 1883 to 1897. In fact, they played thirty-one games against ten different Michigan based teams during this time. The chart on the next page provides a summary of those games against in-state opponents.

The Wolverines posted an outstanding record of 29 wins, 1 loss and 1 tie for a winning percentage of just over ninety-five percent (.952). Historically, Michigan used the "in-state" games as "scrimmage" games to get ready for the "Big Boys" like Wisconsin, Minnesota, Illinois in the west and Harvard, Cornell, and Pennsylvania in the east. So, that is where Wolverine football stood before their first game against State Agricultural College (SAC) in 1898.

4

Michigan's Early In-State Rivals

School/Team	Games	Won	Lost	Tied
Adrian College	1	1	0	0
Albion College	12	11	1	0
Ann Arbor High School	1	1	0	0
Detroit Athletic Club	5	5	0	0
Detroit Independents	1	1	0	0
Grand Rapids High School	1	1	0	0
Michigan Athletic Association	2	2	0	0
Michigan Military Academy	3	2	0	1
Michigan Normal	3	3	0	0
Olivet College	2	2	0	0
Total	31	29	1	1

STATE AGRICULTURAL COLLEGE FOOTBALL: THE EARLY YEARS

The State Agricultural College played their first inter-collegiate football season in 1896. Like the Wolverines, there was no coach that first year. Instead, some students got together and organized four games and got the ball rolling in East Lansing (pun intended!). The Aggies posted a record of 1 win, 2 losses, and 1 tie for that inaugural season.

Harry Keep was hired in 1897 to be the first paid coach in SAC history. Mr. Keep did better than the first paid coaches in Ann Arbor since he posted a winning record of 4 wins, 2 losses, and 1 tie. The upstart State Agricultural College football team only had two years of experience when they decided to challenge the Wolverines footballers from Ann Arbor.

The chart on the next page shows the number of in-state teams that State Agricultural College played before their first game against the University of Michigan in 1898. Yes, they also played against a high school team in the early years, it was just the way things were in the early years. Notice, however, that they played fewer total teams and a lot less games against their Mitten State rivals.

State Agricultural College's Early In-State Rivals

School	Games	Won	Lost	Tied
Alma College	4	2	1	1
Kalamazoo College	2	0	2	0
Lansing High School	2	2	0	0
Olivet	2	1	0	1
Total	10	5	3	2

THE STAGE IS SET

The early years of college football were interesting to say the least. The players loved this wild and crazy game. Fans were becoming more appreciative of the athleticism and raw brutality with each passing season. College football was here to stay. The game continued to gain popularity despite criticism that called for an end to the game because of the deaths and serious injuries that took place in some games. By the end of the 1897 season Michigan and SAC had vastly different experiences on the football field. Michigan was an established "western" power and the Aggies were definitely the "new kids" on the block. Here is what the football records of the two schools looked like at the end of the 1897 season:

School	Seasons	Games	Won	Lost	Tied	Win %
Michigan	18	103	73	27	3	.723
SAC	2	11	5	4	2	.545

The Wolverines had an eighteen-year track record of success before they agreed to meet SAC on the football field. The Aggies only had two years of competitive football experience. By all accounts Michigan was the "older" institution with considerably more football experience. State Agricultural was younger and less experienced. Already the comparisons of "older brother" vs "younger brother" and "big brother" vs "little brother" were probably in someone's head, but not Mike Harts since he was not born yet!

Yes, there was some serious drama between the two cities and institutions before the first game. The bad feelings and discord that grew out of the early fights and disagreements between the University of Michigan and the State Agricultural College formed the basis of an enduring rivalry. The establishment of the state capital and the State Agricultural College of Michigan was history. Now, it was time for East Lansing and Ann Arbor to fight about something else. The years of "off the field" drama, would soon be played out on the football field. Of course, lots of interested people wanted to see how it would develop. The rest, as they say, is history.

Game On! 1898

Michigan was definitely the best team in the State of Michigan at the start of the 1898 season. They were also the most experienced with eighteen seasons under their football belt. As we learned in Chapter One, their record against in-state teams was stellar (29 wins, 1 loss and 1 tie). It is unclear why Michigan scheduled a game with State Agricultural College for the first time in 1898. However, another team to feast on probably seemed like a good idea at the time. Scheduling the Aggies reduced travel time and expenses. It was also a good way to get some work in before facing the "Big Boys" from the Western Conference. Hopefully, they could win some more games and maybe create interest in the sport of football in the State of Michigan.

ABOUT THE GAME OF FOOTBALL IN 1898

As I mentioned in Chapter One, the early game of college football (1869 to 1879) was much more like rugby than the game we know today. The field was much bigger (70 yards wide by 120 yards long), the ball was more like a rugby ball (a large leather egg), and teams had twenty-five players per side. It was crazy!

The game evolved rapidly, and changes were made almost every year. Former Yale Player, Walter Camp, was instrumental in creating a more modern game with changes that he initiated in the 1880s. According to James E. Herget, author of *American Football: How the Game Evolved*, many significant changes took place from 1880 to 1898. As the twentieth century approached, the game looked less like rugby and more like the game we know as American football.

7

By the time Michigan and SAC met on the football field in 1898 there were many changes. The field was smaller and resembled the field that is used today. Teams now had eleven players on a side, goal posts with crossbars were positioned at both ends of the field and teams had three downs to move the ball five yards or they gave up possession of the ball. Rules concerning eligible players and substitutions often had to be ironed out before kick-off. However, much progress had been made prior to the turn of the century. Most games were played in two twenty-minute halves and scoring was as follows in 1898:

- Touchdowns = 5 points (changed from 4 points in 1896)
- Field Goals = 5 points (no change from 1897)
- Safety   = 2 points (no change from 1897)
- Extra Point = 1 point (was 2 points in 1896) (Herget, Pages 47-48)

Game #1: October 12, 1898 at Regents Field in Ann Arbor

BACKGROUND INFORMATION:

The first game between Michigan and the State Agricultural College (SAC) took place at Regent's Field in Ann Arbor on Wednesday, October 12th. (Yes, they played games in the middle of the week in those days.) This game marked the first, and only, time that coaches Gustave Ferbert of Michigan and Harry Keep of SAC faced each other. Both coaches were gone before the next game was played.

This contest was the third game of Michigan's ten game season. Michigan defeated Michigan Normal (21-0) and Kenyon (29-0). The Wolverines entered the game undefeated and unscored upon. The State Agricultural College of Michigan had one game under their belt— an 11-6 win over a team from Ypsilanti. Other than the rivalry issues already discussed in Chapter One, there were no other new issues that added to the storyline of this much anticipated football encounter. Obviously, there was plenty of intensity about this contest in East Lansing and Ann Arbor. In addition, many people from around the state were keenly interested in the outcome of this contest. It was hard to tell at the time, but this first game would be the start of something special between the two schools. Game on!

GAME SUMMARY: SAC 0 UM 39

The first game between the Mitten State rivals went as expected considering the experience levels of the two teams. Game number one was played in two twenty-minute halves. The story headline in the *Detroit Free Press (DFP)* read: "Michigan Practices on the S.A.C. For a Fair Total." (DFP, 10/13/1898, Page 6) As it turned out, Michigan treated the first series game as a scrimmage or a practice game.

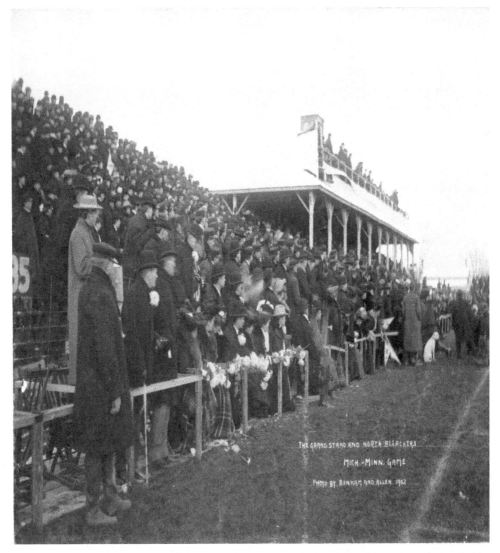

Image 1 This is what historic Regents Field looked like in 1898 at the birth of this rivalry. (Permission: Bentley Historical Library at The University of Michigan, See Page 369)

The Wolverines looked like the better drilled and more seasoned team because they were better drilled and much more experienced. Coach Ferbert was probably not too concerned about the outcome since he substituted players freely throughout the game. The Aggies put up their best fight, but they could not overcome the Wolverines. Charles Widman scored two touchdowns and Clayton Teetzel, Cliff Barabee, Alan Steckle and Fred Hartzburg each scored one touchdown for the victors. Leo Keena kicked a 23-yard field goal and two extra points. Teetzel also kicked two Points After Touchdown (PATs). (*DFP.* 10/13/1898, Page 6). The Aggies probably had a long ride back to East Lansing. Game number one was in the books and the seeds for a rivalry were planted. Would the two teams play again, or would the Spartans be content to play less successful teams from the state in the future?

SERIES UPDATE:

Every story starts at the beginning. The football story about Michigan and Michigan State began on October 12, 1898. The game went as expected. Michigan took the series lead with a record of 1 win, 0 losses, and 0 ties. Of course, the Aggies had a record of 0 wins, 1 loss and 0 ties after one game.

SERIES MILESTONES:

I will highlight some of the major milestones in the series as we go through each game. Obviously, the October 1898 matchup was the first game of the series. It was also the first and only game of the nineteenth century between the two schools. This inaugural game also marked the first series game in Ann Arbor and produced Michigan's first win and their first shutout of the Aggie footballers. In contrast, it also marked SAC's first loss against Michigan and their first scoreless game of the series. It was also the first series game to be played on a Wednesday. Clayton Teetzel may have scored the first series touchdown, but I am not certain about that. I am certain that Leo Keena's 23-yard field goal was the first one recorded in the series. I am also certain that Michigan lineman William Cunningham was the first All-American to play in this series. According to the Bentley Historical Library archives, the mid-week contest drew a crowd of two-hundred twenty-eight people. Humble beginnings for sure!

SEASON SUMMARIES:

The Aggies finished with a winning record for the second consecutive season (4-3-0). They lost to Notre Dame (53-0), won three straight games against Albion, Olivet, and Ypsilanti again, but lost the season finale at Kalamazoo (17-0).

Michigan dominated everyone else on their schedule for the rest of the season including their conference rivals. Their final record was perfect—10 wins 0 losses and 0 ties. The Wolverines also won their first Western Conference Championship. Of course, the post-game celebration inspired a famous fight song. The Wolverines also celebrated their first All-American player, Center William Cunningham. By all measures it was a successful football season in Ann Arbor.

DECADE AND SERIES SUMMARY:

The teams did not play in 1899. The first "decade" of football between the Wolverines and Aggies numbered one game. Starting now, I will summarize the results of each decade and the series status at the end of each chapter. This information will provide an up-to-date summary about how the series was going for both teams.

Decade and Series Summary 1890 to 1899

Series Games	UM Won-Lost-Tied	SAC Won-Lost-Tied
1	1-0-0	0-1-0

PROGRAM SUMMARIES:

Once again, Michigan had much more experience at playing and winning than did the Aggies. Of course, SAC had to start somewhere. The chart below gives the reader a look at some key numbers for both teams. At the end of the nineteenth century the gap between the two schools was BIG! The Aggies had some work to do, but they also had a model to follow. Michigan had one of the best programs in the "west." The eastern football experts were starting to take notice. If the Aggies wanted to play with the "Big Boys" they needed to get on Michigan's schedule as often as possible. Yes, they would probably take some lumps along the way, but the Aggie path to football excellence would have to travel through Ann Arbor.

Program Summaries 1890 to 1899

Statistical Area	UM	SAC
Number of Head Coaches	1	1
Games Played	94	25
Wins	72	11
Losses	20	11
Ties	2	3
Winning Percentage	.777	.500
Winning Seasons	9	2
Losing Seasons	1	2
Even Seasons	0	0
National Championships	0	0
All-American Players	1	0

CHAPTER 3

Looking for a Rival 1900 to 1909

The Michigan Wolverines continued to play at a very high level at the start of the 20th Century. The Wolverines won seven games in 1900 and kicked into overdrive in 1901. Fielding H. Yost hit Ann Arbor and the Midwest like a hurricane. Michigan won all eleven games in 1901 and shut out every opponent. Yost's "Point-a-Minute" team outscored their opponents by a margin of 550 to 0 in that dominating season. They were still rolling when they faced off against the Aggies in Ann Arbor in 1902. In fact, the best team in the State of Michigan was now the best team in the Western Conference and the defending national champions when the second game of the series took place in October 1902. The State Agricultural College started wearing uniforms with MAC emblems sewn on as early as 1900 even though the school was not officially designated as Michigan Agricultural College until June 1909. Regardless of what their official name was, the question was "Would the Aggies be ready for Yost and his footballers?"

Game #2: October 8, 1902 at Regents Field in Ann Arbor.

BACKGROUND INFORMATION:

There were no significant changes in the way college football was played prior to the 1902 season. The previous efforts to reduce the injuries that occurred because of the "mass" plays were only mildly successful. Unfortunately, more blood had to be shed and more lives had to be lost before any more revolutionary rules were adopted.

The second game between Michigan and the State Agricultural College (SAC) was scheduled for Regent's Field in Ann Arbor on Wednesday, October 8th. This game marked the first time that Fielding Yost faced a team from SAC. It was also the first series game for third year Aggie coach George Denman.

The Aggies were still looking for respect on the football field and Michigan was looking to keep rolling over every team that dared to step on the same field. Yost had already earned a reputation for running up the score on his opponents with the worst being a 128-0 whipping of Buffalo in 1901. The MAC footballers probably arrived in Ann Arbor with high hopes, but also with some trepidation. Would they be able to stop, or at least slow down, Yost's "point-a-minute" juggernaut?

This contest was the third game of Michigan's eleven game season in 1902. Michigan had already defeated Albion and Case by a combined score of 136 to 6. The Wolverines went into the second series game with a thirteen-game winning streak. MAC lost their first game against Notre Dame (33-0) but won against Detroit (11-0). Were the Aggies ready to compete with the mighty Wolverines?

GAME SUMMARY: SAC 0 UM 119

The second series game turned out worse than expected for the Aggies, much worse! The Aggie players were probably relieved, and maybe hopeful, when they learned that two Wolverine stars (Willie Heston and Everett Sweely) would not play that day. Unfortunately for the Aggies, it did not matter. The Wolverine substitutes stepped up nicely and contributed to a display of "fast break" football that had never been seen in the State of Michigan. The Aggie players may have thought that their chances for an upset were slim, but the final score of 119-0 was quite a shock! Just like that, Michigan handed their rivals from East Lansing the worst defeat in their young football history!

It would be hard to know how much blood was shed that day, but it is probably a good bet that the Aggies gave more than the Wolverines that day, a lot more! As bad as the game turned out, it could have been worse! The rules of the day called for the game to be played in a pair of twenty-minute halves. Yost and Denman agreed to halt the game with two minutes remaining. Michigan's "Point-a-Minute" team scored 119 points in thirty-eight minutes. Yes, the high scoring Wolverines averaged 3.1 points per sixty-seconds in this game—ouch! Also, a touchdown was only worth five points at this time but increased to six points in 1912. If the scoring rule had changed sooner the final score would have been 139-0!

Eight different Michigan players scored at least one touchdown and kicker James Lawrence probably had a sore toe after kicking 19 extra points. Albert Herrnstein (7) Herb Graver (3) and Paul Dickey (3) each had more touchdowns than the Aggies had first downs (3). It was just ugly. (*DFP*, 10/09/1902, Page 6)

Team	1st Half	2nd Half	Final
SAC	0	0	0
UM	71	48	119

SERIES UPDATE:

Michigan now led the series with a record of 2-0-0. Of course, the Aggies were stuck at 0-2-0. After two games Michigan had outscored the Aggies by a margin of 159 to 0. It was a rough start for the boys from East Lansing. The Aggies had to be wondering if they would ever be able to match the mighty Wolverines on the football field.

SERIES MILESTONES:

Game number two was the first meeting of the Twentieth Century between the two schools. It was also the first series game for Coach Yost and his first series victory. It was the first and only series game for Coach Denman who was fired at the end of the season. Michigan Halfback Albert Herrnstein became the first player in series history to return a kickoff for a touchdown. He also claimed a special place in series history as the only player to score seven touchdowns in a series game. Michigan kicker James Lawrence became the first and only player to kick nineteen extra points in a series game. This was the last time the teams played at Regents Field and the last time they played on a Wednesday. Yes, this was the most lopsided game in the history of the two-game series, but it would never again be this bad for the Aggies. Some tough games were still to come, but the State Agricultural College would make some changes and come back for more. Defeated, yes!, Discouraged, no!

SEASON SUMMARIES:

The remainder of the Aggies season was better than the loss to Michigan, but not that much better. They were able to bounce back nicely form the Michigan loss and win two straight games, but the second game was against the Michigan freshman team. SAC defeated the Wolverine Freshman team by a score of 2-0. (Note-The game does not count in the overall "series" results, but a win is a win, right?) The Aggies lost three of their last four games and finished the season with a record of 4 wins and 5 losses.

The Wolverines romped through their remaining games and finished the season with another perfect record of 11 wins, 0 losses and 0 ties. Although the Aggie game was their season scoring high, they did score 107 points against Iowa and hammered Ohio State by a score of 86-0. Michigan scored 644 points and only allowed 12 points during the 1902 season. They won their second straight conference championship and were also named national champions. Fielding Yost was on a roll and some people wondered if Michigan would ever lose another game.

Game #3: October 12, 1907 at Ferry Field in Ann Arbor

BACKGROUND INFORMATION:

Several significant rules changes occurred since the Aggies and Wolverines last met in 1902. First, the scoring rules changed again in 1904 and this would be the first game where they affected the "varsity" game between Michigan and MAC. The new rules resulted in the following point values:

- Touchdowns = 5 points
- Field Goals = 4 points (was 5 points in 1903)
- Safety   = 2 points
- Extra Point   = 1 point (Herget, Pages 47-48)

Image 2 The "checkerboard" look at Ferry Field in 1907.
(Permission: Bentley Historical Library at The University of Michigan, See Page 369)

Second, the markings on the field were quite different when the Aggies and Wolverines squared off in Ann Arbor in 1907. The field now resembled a giant checkerboard with the traditional yard lines being intersected by another set of lines that were parallel to the sidelines. The new lines were five yards apart and ran the length of the field. The lines were added to help officials apply a 1903 rule that allowed a player to receive the snap and run with it if he was five yards to the right or left of the spot from where the ball was snapped. The picture above shows you what it looked like. Of course, this is where the term "gridiron" originated. The "checkerboard" playing field will be forever linked to the game of American football.

Third, the forward pass was legalized in 1906 to "open up" the game and get away from the "mass" rushing plays that had been responsible for so many deaths and injuries in the early years of college football. Although it did not change the game immediately, the forward pass was an important addition that eventually changed the game forever. The size of the ball, some interesting restrictions on the pass and severe penalties for incompletions caused coaches to embrace this idea cautiously. (Herget, Page 91)

Finally, "the Intercollegiate Athletic Association of the United States (IAAUS) was founded on March 31, 1906. This action was in direct response to the mayhem that was injuring and killing players on college football fields around the country. The mission of IAAUS was simple: reform the rules and regulations of college sports. (Library of Congress Post, pulled 8/24/2021)

The embarrassing loss to Michigan in 1902 was cause for alarm in East Lansing. According to Steve Grinczel, author of *Michigan State Football: They Are Spartans,* SAC President Jonathan L. Snyder declared that "If we are to have football, I want the kind that wins." (Grinzel, Page 9) Synder's remarks triggered some dramatic changes in the direction of the football program at State Agricultural College.

First, Coach George Denman was replaced by Chester Brewer. Brewer was a four-sport star at Wisconsin, but football was his best sport. He earned All-Western honors in football during the 1896 season. Brewer was considered a defensive genius which promised to be a good thing, especially against Michigan. Second, the Aggies chose not to play Yost's varsity team from 1903 to 1905. Instead, they scheduled the Michigan Freshman team and defeated them three straight times. Again, none of these games counted in the "series" history. However, they were confidence builders since the Aggies won all three games without allowing a Wolverine point. (11-0, 39-0 and 24-0). Finally, Coach Brewer immediately established a winning tradition at MAC. He posted four winning seasons in his first four years.

Brewer's first four teams posted an outstanding record of 30 wins, 6 losses and 3 ties. His winning percentage of almost eighty-one percent (.807) was very impressive and easily the best record in the short history of the Aggie football program. The Aggies entered game three of the series on a two-game winning streak by virtue of their victories over Detroit (17-0) and Michigan School of the Deaf (40-0). Things were looking up in East Lansing. Maybe they were ready for a better showing against the bullies from Ann Arbor!

Meanwhile, back in Ann Arbor, Coach Yost and his footballers continued to win at an extremely high rate. Michigan posted an incredible record of 37 wins, 2 losses and 1 tie from 1903 to 1906. Yost's winning rate was almost ninety-four percent (.937). Yes, beating Michigan in 1907 was still going to be a challenge for Coach Brewer. The 1907 season was Michigan's first season as an "independent" since they left the Western Conference over some eligibility, scheduling, and training table issues. Games were much harder to find since the other conference teams were boycotting the renegades from Ann Arbor. Mr. Yost and his players were probably happy to play the Aggies in 1907.

The Wolverines had one game under their belts before they hosted the Aggies. Michigan defeated Case at Regent's Field by a score of 9-0 on October 5, 1907. The Case game was usually a warm-up game for Michigan and previous victories were by much larger margins. Either Case was getting better, or Michigan was getting worse. It was time to find out how good the Wolverines were in 1907.

GAME SUMMARY: SAC 0 UM 46

Game number three was better for the Aggies because they only lost by 46 points instead of 119 points. Of course, the Wolverines probably looked at it as a step back since they did not come close to the blowout win that they had achieved in 1902. The game was played in two twenty-minute halves and it did not end early this time. Technically, it was "over" by the end of the first half.

Coach Yost was not interested in running up the score again on the Aggies. Apparently, he was saving some plays for tougher opponents down the road. Three different players scored touchdowns on this day. Team captain Paul Magoffin made five trips to the end zone, Walt Rheinschild made two trips and Jack Loell scored once. Michigan kicker "Octy" Graham booted eight extra points. (*DFP*, 10.13/1907, Page 17) Once again, the Wolverines won another "practice game."

Team	1st Half	2nd Half	Final
MAC	0	0	0
UM	24	22	46

SERIES UPDATE:

After three games, Michigan had scored 204 points and could, and probably did, boast that the farmers from East Lansing had yet to score a single series point! Yes, scoring continued to be a problem and the Aggies did not even manage to gain a first down during the game. Michigan's record improved to 3-0-0. Chester Brewer's teams made a lot of progress in four years. Unfortunately, this game clearly demonstrated that there was still more work to do. Michigan was simply the dominant team in the State of Michigan. Coach Brewer knew that there was plenty of room for improvement in all three phases of SAC's game.

SERIES MILESTONES:

The third series game marked the first rivalry contest that was ever played on a Saturday. It was also the first time that the game was ever played at Michigan's newly constructed Ferry Field. This was also the first series game for Coach Chester Brewer and his first series loss. Finally, this marked the first time that a series game was played on a "checkerboard" field. I am certain that it was quite a sight to behold!

SEASON SUMMARIES:

After losing to Michigan, the Aggies defeated Wabash and Olivet and tied Alma before losing their last game against the Detroit Athletic Club. State Agricultural College ended another successful season and posted their fifth consecutive winning campaign under Coach Brewer. The Aggies finished with a final record of 4 wins, 2 losses and 1 tie.

The Wolverines rolled through the rest of their season, shutting out Wabash, Ohio State and Vanderbilt. Michigan's last game of the season saw Pennsylvania turn the tables on Yost's footballers. The Quakers scored the only touchdown allowed the entire season and defeated the Wolverines by a score of 6-0 in Ann Arbor. Michigan finished the season with a record of 5 wins, 1 loss and 0 ties. Of course, there was no conference championship for Yost's "independent" football team.

Game #4: October 10, 1908 at Old College Field in East Lansing

BACKGROUND INFORMATION:

There were no significant rules changes for the 1908 season. Scoring was still the same, the forward pass was still legal and the checkerboard field, or gridiron, was still in place. Some big changes were being discussed, but they would come later.

Series game number four was much anticipated. Aggie fans and players felt that this was their year. Michigan backers were expecting another "ho hum" pre-season win before they started battling the east coast "Big Boys." Coaches Yost and Brewer were getting ready for their second football encounter. Yost's record against the Aggies was perfect at 2 wins, 0 losses and 0 ties. Brewer lost his first and game against Michigan, but expectations were still high for the Aggie football leader. For the first time, the game would be played in East Lansing.

The Wolverines entered the game with a win under their belts, having defeated Case by a score of 16-6 the week before. Michigan had previously defeated the Case team by some large margins. People were wondering if this might be a "down" year for the Wolverines. The fourth game of the series was the first one on the 1908 schedule for the Aggies. Brewer's team was untested, but eager to measure themselves against the Wolverines. Hopes were high in East Lansing and a victory over Michigan could make this season something special.

GAME SUMMARY: UM 0 SAC 0:

The fourth series game produced a surprise: a 0-0 tie! If there is anything that could be described as an "upset tie," this was it! Michigan. Of course, heavily favored Michigan, did not win the game, but they did not lose either. Everyone wearing Maize and Blue treated this game as a loss. There was no way that the farmers from East Lansing could stand "toe-to-toe" with the Mighty Wolverines. How did this happen?

Well, it happened for a lot of reasons. First, it was the first time the Aggies had ever hosted the Wolverines on their home field. Second, there was a large crowd, estimated at six thousand people, and a lot of them were Aggie fans. In short, the Aggies were "fired up!" Finally, it did not help that Michigan played without their Captain and All-American center, Germany Schultz, plus two other star players. Of course, Michigan fans let it be known that this must be the reason for the closeness of the game, not the fact that SAC gave a good effort.

19

This started a trend that continues to annoy Aggie/Spartan fans to this day. Michigan seemed to be quite adept at explaining away any SAC success that came at the expense of the Wolverines. The fact was that both teams put forth spirited efforts. The longer the Aggies held the famous Yost offense, the more optimistic the farmers became. They started to believe that they could play with the Wolverines for the entire game and they did!

Game number four turned out to be a "good news, bad news" story for both teams. Michigan was disappointed that they did not win, but relieved that they did not lose. If there was ever a "moral" victory in the brief history of Aggie football, this was it! The Aggies were thrilled that they did not lose again and shaking their heads that they did not win.

SAC's outstanding halfback/kicker Parnell McKenna had three failed "dropkicks" and any one of them could have won the game and honored his name forever in Aggie football lore. The East Lansing footballers had their chances, but just could not find a way to put some points on the scoreboard. The game was played in two twenty-five-minute halves and both teams battled hard to the last second of the game. There was probably a lot of blood spilled by both teams on this day and probably in equal amounts!

The box score was nothing special, just a bunch of zeros, but that was fine with the Aggie faithful. The folks in East Lansing celebrated as if they had won the game! A *Detroit Free Press* writer penned that Aggie fans "went wild with delight" when the game ended. No such descriptions were written about the Wolverine faithful that day. (*DFP*, 10/11/1908, Page 22)

Team	1st Half	2nd Half	Final
UM	0	0	0
SAC	0	0	0

SERIES UPDATE:

The "series" numbers did not change much after game number four of the series. Michigan owned a record of 3-0-1 while the Aggies had one that read 0-3-1. The Wolverines had scored 204 points and SAC had yet to cross the Wolverine goal line or even kick a field goal. The Aggies did manage to stop Yost's powerful offense. This was not one of Yost's best teams, but the Aggies stepped up and played some incredibly good football. Coach Brewer's defense lived up to expectations. Oh, what might have been if the offense could have made a few plays and put some points on the scoreboard!

SERIES MILESTONES:

Game four of the series produced a few historic milestones. First, it was the first series game ever played in East Lansing. Second, it was the first series tie. Third, it was also the first time that the game was ever played at SAC's College Field. Finally, the gathering of 6,000 Michiganders made it the largest crowd in series history. Yes, this game between two hated rivals was generating a lot of interest in Michigan!

SEASON SUMMARIES:

The Wolverines won the next four games. Unfortunately, they lost badly to Pennsylvania (29-0) and Syracuse (28-4) to finish the season with a final record of 5 wins, 2 losses and 1 tie. It was the worst finish in Yost's eight year run at Michigan.

The Aggies used the momentum of the Michigan "tie" to post their first undefeated season in history. They won almost every game, most by decisive margins. The only bump in the road was another scoreless tie with DePaul in the middle of the season. SAC posted their sixth consecutive winning season under Coach Brewer and finished with a record of 6 wins, 0 losses and 2 ties.

DECADE AND SERIES SUMMARY:

There were three times as many games between Michigan and MAC in the second decade of competition as there were in the first decade. Michigan still held the advantage in Decade Two, but the Aggies were making progress. Remember, the margin of victory in the first game of the decade was 119 points and the last game of the decade was even. Aggie fans were hopeful that a victory would come sooner than later. Wolverine fans were yearning for more decisive victories over the farmers from East Lansing.

Decade and Series Summary 1898 to 1909

Time Frame	UM Won-Lost-Tied	SAC Won-Lost-Tied
1900-1909	2-0-1	0-2-1
1898-1909	3-0-1	0-3-1

PROGRAM SUMMARIES:

Michigan was a superior team from 1900 to 1909. They won four straight national championships and dominated the Western Conference for the first half of the decade. Their abrupt departure from the conference affected them more than most people thought it would. By the end of the decade, the Wolverines were living in their "Decade of Defiance" and searching for an identity.

Chester Brewer put SAC football on the regional map—period! His teams became known for their strong defensive style, but they also scored a lot of points. This dangerous combination produced an impressive body of work in East Lansing. The Aggies posted some outstanding numbers in the last seven years of the decade and people were starting to take notice.

Both teams made great strides in the first decade of the Twentieth Century. Michigan went from being a "western power" to four-time national champions! Their winning percentage improved from over seventy-seven percent (.777) to almost ninety percent (.898). They were as good as anyone in the country from 1900 to 1909!

The Aggies made an impressive improvement in their winning rate by going from fifty percent (.500) to almost seventy-two percent (.715). Coach Brewer made significant gains in the football program. His Aggies were starting to earn respect in the State of Michigan and the Midwest. Well, probably everywhere but Ann Arbor.

Respect was something that came grudgingly from the folks in the Tree City and that was not going to change anytime soon. It was obvious that the Wolverines ended the decade on a low note, while the Aggies were coming on strong. Fans from both schools were optimistic about the next decade.

Program Summaries 1900 to 1909

Statistical Area	UM	MAC
Number of Head Coaches	2	2
Games Played	93	86
Wins	82	58
Losses	8	21
Ties	3	7
Winning Percentage	.898	.715
Winning Seasons	10	7
Losing Seasons	0	3
Even Seasons	0	0
National Championships	4	0
All-American Players	4	0

CHAPTER 4

A One-Way Rivalry 1910 to 1919

Fielding Yost's football teams continued to play some very good football as the first decade of the Twentieth Century ended. However, they were not the dominant team they were in Yost's first five years. The Wolverines struggled with the realities of life without the Western Conference. Scheduling remained a significant problem since conference teams were boycotting the Wolverines. Michigan had to go "east" to some interesting places to create a competitive schedule for most of the decade.

The Aggies continued to play a better brand of football and their improved play made them more competitive in the State of Michigan and in the Midwest. Michigan Agricultural College needed to play Michigan and beat them sooner than later to earn the respect they felt they deserved in the football world. The Wolverines needed to play the Aggies because they needed the games and the gate revenue. Even though Michigan was a reluctant rival, they played the annoying farmers every year from 1910 to 1919. Things were about to get more interesting and more intense in the Mitten State football series!

Game #5: October 15, 1910 at Ferry Field in Ann Arbor

BACKGROUND INFORMATION:

College football experienced more rules changes in 1910 than any other season since 1880. One scoring rule took place in 1909, but the teams did not play that season. The field goal was reduced from four points to three points so that was the first change that affected the game in 1910. All other scoring rules remained in place. In addition, a total of six sweeping changes were made in the way the game was played. Clearly, American football was defining a unique place in the sports world. Now, it was only a distant cousin of that roughhouse game of rugby that it resembled at the turn of the century. Here is a quick summary of the 1910 changes that were detailed in James E. Herget's excellent book titled *American Football-How the Game Evolved:*

1) Seven men now had to be on the line of scrimmage at the snap of the ball.
2) Players were restricted from pushing or pulling on a ball carrier on their own team to advance him and the ball. The interlocking of hands and arms was also outlawed to end the violent "mass" plays that had been killing and injuring players since 1869.
3) The timing and organization of the game also changed. College football would now be played in four quarters of fifteen minutes each.
4) Players could now pass or run to the left or right from any point upon receiving the snap. There was no need for the five-yard lines that ran parallel to the sidelines. The checkerboard field was gone—forever!
5) One backfield player could be in motion before the snap of the ball, but he could not be moving toward the line of scrimmage, only parallel or away. Once again, a direct effort to stop the "mass" plays.
6) The forward pass now had to be released from five yards behind the line of scrimmage. It could not travel any farther than twenty yards down the field. (Herget, Pages 104-105)

Although there were other proposed changes, these rules were the ones that were put in place in 1910. The intent of the rule makers was to eliminate the violence in the game by taking away the "mass" rushing plays. They also wanted to open the game a bit more by making it easier to run sweep plays to the right or left of center. It was hoped that speed would soon matter as much as size on the gridiron. Finally, the forward pass was still in place, but it was an advance that was getting mixed reviews. The teams in the east were not too excited about it, but many western teams embraced the idea. One final note to mention was that the National Collegiate Athletic Association (NCAA) became what was the Intercollegiate Athletic Association of the United States. The NCAA was now in charge of all rules in football, baseball, track and basketball too! (Library of Congress Post, pulled 8/24/2021)

Another name change also took place in East Lansing. The State Agricultural College (SAC) was renamed Michigan Agriculture College (MAC) in 1909. The Aggies entered series game five on a two-game winning streak by virtue of their victories over the Detroit Athletic Club (35-0) and Alma (11-0). The Aggies now enjoyed a streak of seven consecutive winning seasons under Coach Brewer. Yes, expectations were higher than ever in East Lansing. Would this be the year that Chester Brewer's footballers defeated mighty Michigan?

Michigan's game against MAC was the second game on the 1910 schedule. The Wolverines were still reeling from a surprising tie against Case (3-3). This was the first time they had not won a season opening game in fifteen years. The last tie (12-12) at the start of a season was in 1894 against Michigan Military Academy. People in Ann Arbor were shocked at the unexpected outcome of Yost's first game in 1910. Nobody really knew what to expect when the Wolverines faced off against the Aggies.

GAME SUMMARY: MAC 3 UM 6

Game number five was absolute torture for the Aggies. They blocked two Michigan punts and kept the Wolverines in their own end for most of the game. They scored their first points of the series (a 21-yard field goal) and led for most of the second half. The Wolverines used the forward pass late in the game to key their victory. Michigan Quarterback Shorty McMillan completed a long pass to Stan Borleske who was tackled at the Aggie fifteen-yard line. Halfback Don Green advanced the ball twelve more yards to the Aggie three-yard line as the clock ticked. The MAC defense stopped the Wolverines on the next play. It appeared that Michigan would attempt a field goal and settle for a tie. Instead, they faked the kick and Don Green scampered into the end zone for the precious five-point touchdown. Fred Conklin kicked the extra point. Michigan won a close one by a final score of 6 to 3 over the disheartened Aggies. (*DFP*, 10/16/1910, Page 15 & 21)

It was the closest game of the series that did not end in a tie. Oh boy, the Aggies claimed that they were robbed because they had a touchdown (on a seventy-yard punt return) called back after Coach Yost pointed out a holding play to one of the officials. They also questioned the legality of the long pass that put Michigan in position to eventually win the game. Of course, the actual end of the game was disputed by the Aggies as well. Apparently, the Michigan timekeeper signaled that the game was over, but the Aggie "clock man" said seven minutes remained to be played. Since it was in Ann Arbor, the officials ignored the MAC timer. Game over! Wow, no wonder that the Aggies had trouble accepting this bitter defeat! (*DFP*, 10/16/1910, Page 15 & 21)

Team	1st	2nd	3rd	4th	Final
MAC	0	0	3	0	3
UM	0	0	0	6	6

This was another small step in the right direction for the Aggies. Not quite the moral victory that they enjoyed with the 0-0 tie, but it was certainly better than losing a forty-point blowout! Fielding Yost was gracious in victory and spoke highly of the Aggies. Coach Brewer's teams continued to show significant improvements on defense and special teams. If the offense could find a way to get into the Wolverine end zone, the future would be very bright for the Aggies.

SERIES UPDATE:

Five series games were now in the books and Michigan was still undefeated. The Wolverines upped their record to 4 wins, 0 losses, and 1 tie. The Aggies managed to score their first points of the series which was a plus. However, they still had not crossed Michigan's goal line and that was not good. Coach Yost must have been scratching his head about the next step for his Wolverines.

SERIES MILESTONES:

There were several milestones in game five of the series. First, this was the first time that MAC and Michigan met on the football field after SAC changed their name. Second, MAC finally scored when they kicked their first field goal of the series. Leon "Bubbles" Hill was in the series history book for his three-point field goal that put the Aggies in the lead in the third quarter. Third,, this was also the first series game ever played at Michigan's newly constructed Ferry Field. Fourth, it was the first series contest to be played in four quarters of fifteen minutes each. Finally, this was the first series game to be decided on the last play of the game, but it would not be the last!

SEASON SUMMARIES:

The Aggies finished strong and did not lose a game the rest of the season. They posted their first win ever win against Notre Dame by a score of 17-0. The victory over the Irish proved to be the highlight of an excellent season for MAC. They outscored their last four opponents by a score of 119 to 2! The Aggies finished with a record of 6 wins and 1 loss. That made it eight straight winning seasons for Coach Brewer and that would be the end of Coach Brewers first tenure of fun at MAC. He accepted a coaching job at the University of Missouri. Just like that, Coach Brewer was gone!

The Wolverines continued a pattern that developed over the first two games of the season. The pattern was simple: tie a game and then win the next one. This pattern was repeated three times so Michigan finished with an interesting record of 3 wins (MAC, Syracuse, and Minnesota), 0 losses and 3 ties (Case, Ohio State, Pennsylvania). Yost's team did not score like some of his earlier teams, but they scored enough to win three games. In fact, Michigan only scored 29 points for the entire season, but only allowed three field goals. Coach Yost's early teams would score 29 points in the first 29 minutes of play. This was not a typical Fielding Yost team. However, their undefeated record combined with a difficult schedule earned them recognition as the champions of the west for the 1910 season. Two Michigan players (Guard Al Benbrook and End Stanfield Wells) earned first-team All-American honors.

Game #6: October 14, 1911 at Old College Field in East Lansing

BACKGROUND INFORMATION:

There were no significant rules changes for the 1911 season. The scoring rules remained the same and the forward pass was still legal and now easier to manage with the elimination of the "five yard behind the line" and the twenty-yard maximum passing rules. The checkerboard field was also eliminated. (Herget, Page 104)

Michigan was not as good as they were in the early years of Fielding Yost's tenure, but he was still perfect against the Aggie (3 wins, 0 losses, and 1 tie). Once again, the Wolverines entered the Aggie game with a victory under their belts. They defeated Case by a score of 24-0 in Ann Arbor to get their 1911 season off to a good start. Case had a strong team in 1910 and they were expected to be competitive again in 1911. Michigan appeared to win easily over a competitive team. The Aggies had to be wondering just how good the Yost men would be in the sixth game of the series.

Aggie fans spent most of the off-season time in 1911 wondering if MAC could overcome the loss of their first great coach. To make matters worse, the man who was eventually selected to lead the Aggies was the third choice. Hugo Bezdek and Jess Harper were both offered the job before Macklin and both men denied the fine folks in East Lansing. Finally, John Farrell "Big John" Macklin, a relative unknown, said "Yes" to MAC. He was coaching prep school football in New York before he became the fifth coach in Aggie football history. In an interesting side note, when the Aggies could not close the deal on their first two coaching options, MAC President John Snyder reached out to an old friend named Mike Murphy.

Murphy, then an athletic trainer at Pennsylvania, was one of the most renowned trainers and track coaches in the nation. He was also a co-coach/athletic trainer on the 1891 Michigan football team. Mr. Murphy's strong recommendation sealed the deal for the young Macklin and that is how the Aggies found their fifth football coach. Despite the uncertainty about their new coach, Aggie fans could not help but feel optimistic about the upcoming season. Yes, they had an unproven new coach, but many of the team's best players were returning from an outstanding squad in 1910. Aggie fans were hoping that things would be different against Michigan in 1911.

Like Michigan, the Aggies entered the Wolverine game with a perfect record of 1 win, 0 losses and 0 ties. Coach Macklin won his debut with a 12-0 win over Alma. He worked hard to prepare his Aggies for a great effort against the Wolverines.

Macklin's practices were long and intense. He did not want to leave anything to chance. Game six had all the signs of a special game. Would the teams be able to play their best amid all the hype? The UM vs MAC game would be played in East Lansing for only the second time in the series. Could the Aggies take advantage of the home field environment and send the Wolverines home with a loss?

GAME SUMMARY: UM 15 MAC 3

Game six of the Michigan vs Michigan Agricultural College series produced another win for the Wolverines and more disappointment for the Aggies. Once again, the Aggies proved that they could play with the Wolverines and battled them to a scoreless tie at halftime. Michigan had numerous scoring opportunities in the first half, but the Aggie defense intercepted a pass, stopped the Wolverines on downs, and saw a short field goal attempt miss the mark. (*DFP*, 10/15/1911, Page 23)

The Aggies opened the scoring with a thirty-five-yard field goal by their excellent halfback/kicker Leon "Bubbles" Hill. For the second game in a row the Aggies had taken the lead, but could their defense hold the determined Wolverines? It did not take long for Michigan to answer the question. They used the forward pass to set up Captain Fred Conklin's 20-yard field goal that tied the game just before the end of the third quarter. (*DFP*, 10/15/1911, Page 23) The Wolverines took control of the game in the final quarter. Stanfield Wells finished a 63-yard drive with a five-yard trip to the end zone to make the score 8-3 in favor of Michigan and Conklin kicked the extra point to put the Wolverines ahead by six points (9-3). Later in the game, Michigan fullback George "Bubbles" Thomson scored on a 35-yard run and Conklin's kick finished the scoring and sealed a 15-3 victory for Michigan. (*DFP*, 10/15/1911, Page 23)

27

Team	1st	2nd	3rd	4th	Final
UM	0	0	3	12	15
MAC	0	0	3	0	3

The 5,000 fans who watched the game saw another intense gridiron battle that was not decided until late in the game. Clearly, Coach Macklin's team was one to be respected. Michigan knew that they were fortunate to leave East Lansing with a victory. Apparently, days of blowout wins over the Aggie were history. The farmers from MAC could play and the Wolverines left town knowing that the Aggies would be back for more in 1912.

SERIES UPDATE:

The "series" numbers continued to grow in favor of the Wolverines. Michigan's record against MAC remained perfect (5 wins, 0 losses, and 1 tie). The Wolverines had now outscored the Aggies by a margin of two hundred twenty-five to six. (225-6). Yes, it was still ugly. Even though Michigan's scoring was "down" for three straight games, they still had not tasted defeat at the hands of the fighting farmers. The Aggies had to find a way to score more than field goals in order to defeat the Wolverines on the football field.

SERIES MILESTONES:

The sixth game of the series produced three more series firsts. First, John Macklin coached his first game of the series. Second, Macklin lost his first game. Finally, MAC's loss was the first time the Aggies had been defeated at Old College Field. Certainly, an inauspicious start for the Macklin Era at Michigan Agricultural College.

SEASON SUMMARIES:

The Wolverines finished another successful season in November 1911. After the Aggie game, they posted victories Ohio State Vanderbilt and Pennsylvania. Michigan tied Syracuse and Nebraska and lost at Cornell by a score of 6-0. Michigan's final record finished at 5 wins, 1 loss, and 2 ties. The Wolverines scored a total of ninety-points and only allowed thirty-eight. For the eleventh straight season, Fielding Yost's team ended with a winning record. Michigan was still one of the power teams in the west and Coach Yost was intent on keeping it that way in the future!

The resilient Aggies bounced back from the Michigan loss to win four straight games and finish the season with a final record of 5 wins and just 1 loss. They only allowed fifteen points in their last four games and only one game, a 6-0 win over DePauw was even close. The Aggies scored a total of ninety-three points for the season and only allowed thirty-points. These numbers were remarkably close to the numbers that Michigan posted. The Aggies finished strong. Coach Macklin must have been optimistic about the team's prospects for the 1912 season.

Game #7: October 12, 1912 at Ferry Field in Ann Arbor

BACKGROUND INFORMATION:

The 1912 season was the last season for so many significant changes to the game of American football. After that, there was always some "tweaking," but the game as we know it was pretty much in place by September 1912. A total of seven important changes were made in the way the game would be played. Clearly, the rules makers were intent on opening the game and eliminating the "mass" plays forever! Once again, James E. Herget's excellent book titled *American Football-How the Game Evolved* provided valuable insight into these "game changing" rules as follows:

1) A touchdown was now worth six points—double the value of the field goal!
2) Technically, the playing field was reduced in length—going from 110 yards to 100 yards, but end zones that were ten yards deep were added to each end of the field. So, the playable field expanded to 120 yards. (Note-it was decided that the goalposts would still be located on the goal line.)
3) To balance offense and defense, a fourth down was added to give the offense one more chance to gain ten yards.
4) The kickoff point was moved back from the 55-yard line to the kicking team's forty-yard line.
5) The twenty-yard limitation on passing distance was eliminated.
6) A pass could now be caught in the end zone for a touchdown.
7) The size of the ball was greatly reduced to make it easier to throw, even by a quarterback with smaller hands. (Herget, Page 106)

Yes, these rules changes were designed to change the game and that is what they did! Fielding Yost was already a strong proponent of the forward pass, but now he would embrace it more fully. Coach Macklin and his Aggies also made it a priority in their offensive game planning. Things were starting to get more interesting and more explosive in the game of American college football.

Michigan and Michigan Agricultural College played for the seventh time in 1912. Both teams had successful seasons in 1911. In fact, they both won five games and only lost one game. The Wolverines also tied two games.

Coach Macklin was in his second year and his system was successful in year one. Michigan Agricultural College now had nine consecutive winning seasons in the books. John Macklin also had many returning players and expectations were high for the Aggies! The Aggies opened their season with a solid win over Alma by the score of 14-3.

The Wolverines kicked off their season against Case for the seventh consecutive year in Ann Arbor. The final score was 34-0 in favor of Michigan. It appeared to the "experts" that Michigan could have an outstanding team in 1912 based on the first game result.

GAME SUMMARY: MAC 7 UM 55

Game number seven was a huge setback for the Aggies. The *Detroit Free Press* headline summarized the game perfectly: "Yost's Men Run Up High Score Against Aggies." (*DFP*, 10/13/1912. Page 17) Not only did they lose again to the hated Wolverines, but the score indicated that they might be headed back to the earlier days of Wolverine domination. It is certain that this loss did not set well with anyone in East Lansing! Fortunately, for Coach Macklin, he was able to continue coaching the Aggies.

The game started well for the Aggies. They scored first in the very first quarter. Not only did they score first, but they also scored their first touchdown of the series on an eighty-five-yard interception return by Blake Miller. Oh boy, would this be the year that MAC finally beat Michigan?

The Wolverines tied the game in the second quarter and then put the game away in the second half with a forty-eight-point outburst! The Wolverines crossed the Aggie goal line eight times. Halfbacks Jimmy Craig and Tommy Hughitt both scored two touchdowns and Captain George Thomson, Herb Huebel, Charles Barton, and Tom Bushnell each scored once. Kicker George Paterson kicked seven of eight extra points to complete the rout. (*DFP*, 10/13/1912. Page 17)

Since the game was not that close, there were no post-game protests by the Aggies like in 1911. The game probably did not end soon enough for the Aggies and their fans!! This game belonged to Michigan and it was back to the drawing board for the farmers.

Team	1st	2nd	3rd	4th	Final
MAC	7	0	0	0	7
UM	0	7	14	34	55

SERIES UPDATE:

After seven series games Michigan's record remained perfect. The Wolverines had 6 wins, 0 losses, and 1 tie. The Aggies, of course, were now saddled with a record of 0 wins, 6 losses, and 1 tie. The progress that had been made in the three previous games seemed to be lost. Was Aggie football headed in the wrong direction? And the bigger question was: "Would this losing to Michigan ever end?"

SERIES MILESTONES:

Game seven produced more series milestones. First, Blake Miller scored the first Aggie touchdown in the series which was a good thing for MAC! Second, Miller's interception was first "pick six" in series history. Third, it was also the first game played under the six-point touchdown rule, the four-down rule, and the newly "dimensioned" field. Finally, it was the first game played with the smaller, passer friendly, football.

SEASON SUMMARIES:

The Aggies recovered nicely after the Michigan loss and blasted Olivet by a score of 52-0. They defeated DePauw, Ohio Wesleyan, Mt. Union, and Wabash by at least twenty-four points each. Then, John Macklin engineered one of the biggest wins in Aggie football history. The Macklin Men were on a five-game winning streak when they rolled into Columbus, Ohio for a Thanksgiving Day finale against Ohio State.

They left "Buckeye Land" with their first victory over a Western Conference team. Final Score: MAC 35 and OSU 20! The Aggies finished the 1912 season on a huge upswing. Coach Macklin did a masterful job of helping his team "get over" the disappointing loss at Michigan. Instead, he made sure that everyone else on the schedule "paid" for the loss. John Macklin's record at MAC stood at 12 wins and only 2 losses (both to Michigan) after his first two seasons. His job was to get his 1913 team ready for something special—period!

The Wolverines won three of their last five games to finish the season with a record of 5 wins and 2 losses. They lost to eastern powers Syracuse (18-7) and Pennsylvania (27-21) but did manage to defeat a good Cornell team by a score of 17-0. Michigan scored a lot of points in 1912, but their defense was one of the weakest in the Yost Era. The final stats looked like this for the Wolverines: 158 points scored, and 65 points allowed. Not a bad season for many teams, but not good enough for the hyper-competitive Yost. Michigan would have to be better in 1913!

Game #8: October 18, 1913 at Ferry Field in Ann Arbor

BACKGROUND INFORMATION:

College football did not experience any significant rules changes for the 1913 season. Instead, the rules makers decided it was time to get the coaches out of the "rule books" and back into their "play books." Coaches had the entire off-season from December 1912 to the September 1913 to design passing plays that worked. Of course, everyone had to design defenses that would keep their opponents from making their passing plays work on them!

The Michigan game was the third game of the season for Michigan Agricultural College in 1913. The Aggies appeared to be strong after two dominating wins to start the season. Game one was a 26-0 win over Olivet and the next one was even more decisive—a 57-0 shellacking of Alma. The Aggies were on an eight-game winning streak dating back to their early season loss to the Wolverines in 1912. Even more impressive, six of those wins were shutouts! Would this be the year that the Aggies finally beat the Wolverines at their own game?

Series game number eight was also the third game on Michigan's schedule in 1913. Coach Yost was entering his thirteenth year at the helm of the Wolverines. As always, he had high hopes for his Maize and Blue footballers. Coach Yost had a strong cast of returning lineman, but his backfield lacked experience. Yost was concerned about scoring enough points. Despite his concerns, Yost's Wolverines looked surprisingly good in their first two games against Case and Mount Union. Both teams left Ann Arbor without scoring a point while Michigan put sixty-two points on the scoreboard. So far, so good.

31

GAME SUMMARY: MAC 12 UM 7

Game number eight was one that Aggie fans had been waiting for since 1898! The Aggies came to Ferry Field on a mission. The *New York Times* headline read: "Michigan Suffers Defeat: State Agricultural Team Outplays University Men 12 to 7." This was a score heard around the state, around the Midwest and around the nation. The farmers from East Lansing had finally defeated Mighty Michigan! (*NYT*, October 19, 1913, Page 29) Fred W. Stabley, author of *The Spartans: Michigan State Football,* quoted Detroit newsman Eddie Batchelor who stated, "This must be ranked among the biggest upsets in all college football history." (Stabley, Page 37)

It was another titanic struggle between two very good football teams in front of the largest crowd (8,509 people) ever to watch the two beams battle. The Aggies capitalized on a pinpoint passing attack and a stout defense that thwarted Michigan's offense time after time. One of the Aggie stars was George Gauthier, a shifty, but small (5 feet 6 inches tall and 133 pounds) quarterback. Macklin's "Wolverine Killer" completed seven of nineteen passes for one hundred yards and kept the Aggie offense moving most of the afternoon. MAC fullback "Carp" Julian scored on a three-yard run to put the Aggies up 6-0 in the first quarter. The Aggies suffered a huge setback late in the first half when their star halfback Blake Miller was seriously injured. Apparently, a late Wolverine "piled on" the downed Miller, injuring his neck and sending him to the hospital. To make matters worse, the Wolverine player was not even penalized. Yes, the Aggies were pretty fired up about the play.

The MAC used the incident to fuel another half of strong play that saw the Aggies score on a 46-yard fumble return to take a 12-0 lead in the third quarter. (They missed the extra point again.) The touchdown was scored by Hewitt Miller, Blake's brother. The Wolverines replicated the second Aggie score in the fourth quarter when Clyde Bastian recovered an MAC fumble near midfield and rumbled 45-yards and a touchdown. George Paterson kicked the extra point. Michigan Agricultural College still led by a score of 12-7. Late in the game, Michigan used the forward pass to advance the ball deep into Aggie territory. However, the game ended when a thirty-five-yard pass fell incomplete as time expired. (*Lansing State Journal*, 10/20/1913, Page 5)

Team	1st	2nd	3rd	4th	Final
MAC	6	0	6	0	12
UM	0	0	0	7	7

Aggie fans (estimated at one thousand) were not very gracious in victory. The *Detroit Free Press* reported that two Aggie fans were arrested and jailed for "throwing bottles" and other rowdy behavior. (*DFP*, 10/19/ 1913, Page10)

To make matters worse, the bombastic MAC ROTC Cadet Band had the audacity to parade through the Ann Arbor playing "The Victors." Of course, you probably knew that MAC did not have a fight song of their own at the time. So, they had to play something. Oh my, that must not have set very well with anyone in the Tree City! Yes, MAC probably "over-celebrated." Can you blame them?

The "farmers" waited a long time to get a measure of revenge against the hated Wolverines. This series event established a pattern that continues to this day. A Michigan victory is the biggest prize a MAC/MSU football team can claim. However, Michigan has bigger fish to fry like Ohio State and Notre Dame. So, a Wolverine victory over Aggie/Sparty just does not seem to carry as much weight in Ann Arbor. This was a huge step in the right direction for the Aggies. It was so much more than any moral victory that they enjoyed previously. Playing to a tie or playing a close game before losing by a few points was no longer good enough. The bar had been raised. Victory over Michigan was the new standard. If they did it once, they could do it again, right? Suddenly, it was a great time to be an Aggie. According to Fred Stabley, this is what columnist Edgar Guest wrote a few days later in the *Detroit Free Press:*

The MAC Grad

I met him on the street this morn;
His smile was good to see;
He walked about with chest puffed out
As proud as he could be. (Stabley, Page 38)

SERIES UPDATE:

After eight games, the series records looked different. Finally, the Aggies had a number in the win column! Yes, Michigan still had a big series advantage, but it was good for the MAC footballers to have a record of 1 win, 6 losses, and 1 tie. Of course, the Aggies had more football o play in 1913, but this achievement would live in Aggie football history forever!

SERIES MILESTONES:

There were a few important milestones in game eight of the UM vs MAC football series. First, it was the first win for the Aggies. Second, it was the first time that an African American player (Sophomore lineman Gideon Smith) ever played in the series. Third, it was the first time that a fumble was returned for a touchdown and it happened twice—one by each team! Fourth, it was the largest crowd in the history of the series with over eight thousand (8,509) fans in attendance. Finally, it was John Macklin's first series win and the first series loss for Coach Yost and Michigan.

SEASON SUMMARIES:

The Aggies followed up their upset win over Michigan with an equally impressive victory over a heavily favored Wisconsin team by the same 12-7 score that downed Michigan. The Aggies went on to defeat Akron (41-0), Mount Union (13-7), and South Dakota (19-7). MAC finished the season with a perfect record of 7 wins, 0 losses, and 0 ties—the first perfect season in MAC football history! The stingy MAC defense posted three shutouts during the season and with the excellent work of the offense, they outscored opponents by a margin of 180-28! The Aggies were riding an impressive winning streak of thirteen games over two seasons. Respect for Aggie football was slow in coming but continued to grow every year!

The Wolverines proved to be a strong team for the remainder of the 1913 season. They finished the season with four straight wins over some good teams and ended with an impressive record of 6 wins and 1 loss. It was the first time that the Wolverines ever defeated three eastern teams (Syracuse, Cornell, and Pennsylvania) in the same season. The Wolverines outscored their opponents by a margin of 175 points to 21 for the season. Indeed, the 12 points scored by the Aggies were more than half the total allowed for the entire season. Two Michigan players (Tackle Miller Pontius and Halfback James Craig) earned first-team All-American honors.

Game #9: October 17, 1914 at Old College Field in East Lansing

BACKGROUND INFORMATION:

The 1914 season only saw two "tweaks" to the rules and a new penalty. All of them involved the ever-evolving passing game. First, intentional grounding was prohibited. Second, any pass that was thrown out of bounds was simply declared a "dead" ball with no penalty. Previously, an overthrown pass that traveled out of bounds resulted in a loss of possession. A new penalty was instituted for "roughing the passer." Yes, the rules makers were intent on the success of the passing game. Remember, I said passing the ball was a risky venture in 1906. In the early years, six things could happen when a team passed the ball and five of them were bad! The new rules were three more small steps that advanced the passing game a little bit more. (Herget, Page 111)

Michigan, in a slight departure from previous years, scheduled the Aggies a week later and added an extra game in September and a mid-week game to get four games in before they played the Aggies in 1914. They entered the MAC game with a perfect record of 4 wins and 0 losses, or ties. They had outscored their opponents (DePauw, Case, Mount Union, and Vanderbilt) by a margin of 177 to 10! If the Wolverines were not ready to play some good football against the Aggies by October 17, 1914, they would never be ready. Game on!

Aggie fans probably spent the off-season gloating over their history-making victory in 1913. Coach Macklin knew that the victory was a wonderful thing, but that Aggie fans would want another one in 1914. He probably started preparing for Michigan the day after the season ended in 1913. The 1914 game would be the third game on the Aggie schedule that season. MAC appeared ready for the Michigan game as they easily defeated Olivet (35-7) and Alma (60-0) to start the season. Bring on the Wolverines!

GAME SUMMARY: UM 3 MAC 0

The ninth game of the Mitten State football series was another hard-fought, physical game from start to finish. Michigan was intent on getting back on the winning side of the ledger against MAC and the Aggies wanted to prove that their 1913 victory was no fluke!

Team	1st	2nd	3rd	4th	Final
UM	0	0	0	3	3
MAC	0	0	0	0	0

The 8,934 fans who watched the game saw another intense gridiron battle that was not decided until the last quarter. Clearly, Coach Macklin's defense played well enough to earn a victory, but the offense did not do their part. To Michigan's credit, their defense was strong and the offense did just enough to eke out another victory. The only score of the game came in the fourth quarter on a twenty-yard field goal by Michigan kicker Laurence Splawn. That was all the scoring and another bitter battle between UM and MAC was in the books. (*DFP*, 10,18,1914, Page 17)

SERIES UPDATE:

The "series" numbers continued to favor Michigan, but the tenor of the games was changing with each passing season. The Aggies were not a team that Michigan could take lightly. The Wolverine continued to enjoy the advantage in the series with a record of 7-1-1.

SERIES MILESTONES:

The ninth game of the series only produced a couple of notable milestones. First, it was the largest crowd (8,934) to ever watch the two teams battle for Mitten State football supremacy. Second, it was the first time that the game had been decided by a score of 3-0.

SEASON SUMMARIES:

The Aggie game seemed to take a lot out of the Wolverines who slipped badly after their victory over MSC. Their final four games were against eastern teams and they lost three of them (Syracuse, Harvard, and Cornell). Michigan managed to defeat Pennsylvania by a score of 34-3. Yost's team finished with a final record of 6 wins, 3 losses, and 0 ties which made it the worst record of any Yost team so far. The only real bright spot for the season was the inspired play of halfback John Maulbetsch who was named All-American at the end of the season.

The Michigan loss was another bitter disappointment for the Aggies. The loss halted MAC's fifteen game winning streak (the longest in school history) and may have affected their play in the next game against Nebraska. The Huskers defeated MAC by a score of 24-0! Coach Macklin got the Aggies back on track and they finished the season with three straight victories. The final game was a historic win over Penn State (6-3) because it was the first inter-sectional win for the Aggies over an eastern power. The MAC footballers finished with a final record of 5 wins, 2 losses and, 0 ties which was still a winning season, but also the "worst" season in Coach Macklin's four-year tenure.

Game #10: October 23, 1915 at Ferry Field in Ann Arbor

BACKGROUND INFORMATION:

Once again, no significant rules changes framed the 1915 season although a uniform "recommendation" was made for all programs to consider. The rules makers made it an option for teams to display uniform numbers on the backs of player jerseys for the 1915 season. MAC opted in on the numbers, but Michigan did not for series game number ten. The good news for college football was that the game was becoming much less violent and more entertaining.

The forward pass increased the excitement of the game and it was becoming an integral part of every team's offensive arsenal. Scoring was up, serious injuries were down, and attendance was growing astronomically. American football had taken the nation's hearts and pocketbooks. College football was becoming a BIG business!

Coach Macklin's Aggies rolled through the first three games of the 1915 and seemed well-prepared for their trip to Ann Arbor. Teams from Olivet (35-7), Alma (77-12) and Carroll (56-0) were no match for the fighting farmers from MAC. Maybe the Wolverines would provide a better test for the powerful Aggies.

Michigan, once again, lined up four games to get them ready for the Aggies. The Wolverines shutout Lawrence (39-0) and Mount Union (35-0) in the first two games of the season. They pounded Marietta (28-6) and defeated a spirited Case team by the score of 14-3. The Wolverines appeared ready for the last half of the 1915 season.

GAME SUMMARY: MAC 24 UM 0

Series game number ten proved to be an Aggie classic—period! The determined Aggies outplayed the Wolverines in front of a series record crowd (21,000) in Ann Arbor. MAC's dominating victory was the second worst home loss in Coach Yost's career. Only the Pennsylvania loss in 1908 (29-0) was this bad. Coach Yost recognized the outstanding play of Aggie fullback Nino "Jerry" DaPrato by giving him the game ball after the game.

It was a genuinely nice gesture by Yost because DaPrato had put on an All-American performance that day (rushing for 153 yards and scoring all 24 points in the game: three touchdowns, three extra points and 1 field goal). In addition to leading this game in scoring, De Prato also led the nation in scoring for the 1915 season. That man knew how to get points on the board! (*DFP*, 10/24/1915, Page 19) The Aggies had many stars that day, but three men stood out. Of course, DaPrato was the best player on the field that day, but Captain Blake Miller also had many strong runs. MAC quarterback Bob "Hub" Huebel also played an excellent game. In an interesting turn of events, he played for Michigan in 1914, but decided to transfer to MAC for the 1915-16 school year. It turned out well for him and the Aggies.

The MAC defense had many stars as well since they completely shut down Michigan's offense that was led by Captain John Maulbetsch, who was an All-American in 1914. The primary reason that Maulbetsch failed to get into the end zone was a man named Gideon Smith. You may remember that Smith was the first African American to play at MAC and this was his final season. Nobody on Michigan's line could block Mr. Smith. Eddie Batchelor, a reporter for the *Detroit Times* wrote that "Gideon Smith, the big MAC tackle, was far and away the best man in the game." (Stabley, Page 47)

Team	1st	2nd	3rd	4th	Final
MAC	7	7	7	3	24
UM	0	0	0	0	0

Of course, Aggie fans (3,000 strong) relished the historic win and celebrated to the max. All the fine folks from Ann Arbor could do was sit and watch the farmers carry on. Apparently, someone at MAC was working on a "fight song" for the Aggies, but it was not finished in time for the big win. Fortunately, the MAC ROTC Cadet Band knew the "*The Victors*." Once again, the cadets played the only fight song they knew for their "conquering heroes." Talk about adding insult to injury! Are you getting a sense of the "little things" that are adding up over the years to make this such a "nasty" rivalry? The annals of Aggie football history call this game "The Slaughter." It was simply a dominating performance by MAC and plenty of Wolverines gave blood to a losing cause on this day!

SERIES UPDATE:

Even with the bitter defeat, Michigan still held the series advantage with a record of 7-2-1. However, the Aggies earned bragging rights for the next year. MAC fans did not have a lot of years of practice in "series bragging," but they would figure it out.

SERIES MILESTONES:

There were numerous significant milestones in the tenth series game. First, it was the first shutout victory for the Aggies and easily their largest margin for an Aggie victory so far in the series. Second, it was the first time that Aggie players wore numbers in the series, but only on the backs of their jersey. Third, the crowd of 21,000 people made it the largest gathering to witness a UM vs MAC series game in Ann Arbor and in series history. Fourth, it was the first time that an Aggie All-American played in a series game (Two to be exact - Halfback Jerry DaPrato and End Blake Miller). Fifth, it was tenth game of the series with Michigan still holding the advantage. (7-2-1). Sixth, it was the first time that a series team (MAC) scored in every quarter of a series game. Finally, John Macklin's second series win was also his last. He ended his series "career" with a record of 2 wins and 3 losses.

SEASON SUMMARIES:

The Aggies followed up their upset win over Michigan with an embarrassing Homecoming loss to Oregon State (20-0). Maybe they "over-celebrated" or maybe Oregon State was simply the better team that day. The Aggies took their frustrations out on poor Marquette a week later. Final score: MAC 68 and Marquette 6! MAC finished the season with a record of 5 wins and 1 loss. John Macklin left MAC in March to return to his roots in Pennsylvania and work in the coal mining industry. Respect for Aggie football was at an all-time high when John Macklin left the banks of the Red Cedar River. Macklin's tenure was the best in Aggie football history! His five-year run at MAC resulted in a record of 29 wins, 5 losses and 0 ties. His winning percentage of almost eighty-six percent (.853) is still the second best in Aggie/Spartan football history. Thanks to Macklin, the Aggies were the best football team in Michigan from 1911 to 1915.

The Wolverines finished the 1915 season as an average team. Their final record was 4 wins, 3 losses, and 1 tie. Either the Aggie loss took the wind completely out of their sails, or maybe they were not that good of a football team to begin with. After MAC halted their winning streak, the Maize and Blue lost to Syracuse (14-7) and Cornell (34-7) before finishing the season on a low note with a scoreless tie (0-0) at Pennsylvania.

It was the second straight three-loss season for the Wolverines another "first" and last for a Yost coached Wolverine team. This would never happen again in Yost's tenure. He was probably preparing for the 1916 season on the train ride back to Ann Arbor in November 1915.

It is interesting to note that Michigan's record from 1911 to 1915 (Macklin vs Yost) finished with 26 wins, 10 losses and 3 ties for a winning percentage of .705. Of course, Yost held the advantage in head-to-head games against Macklin and MAC during this era winning three of the five series games played. It is probably a good guess that Mr. Yost was glad to see "Big John" Macklin leave the State of Michigan in 1916.

Game #11: October 21, 1916 at Ferry Field in Ann Arbor

BACKGROUND INFORMATION:

The biggest rules change in the 1916 season dealt with defining "forward progress" and clarifying where a ball was "downed" on a given play. Before the 1916 season, a ball carrier could be pushed backward by the defensive players until the ball touched the ground. This resulted in all sorts of mayhem and player injuries. Starting in 1916, the ball was considered "down" and would be spotted where a player's forward progress had stopped. (Herget, Page 113)

Although MAC lost John Macklin in 1915, they did gain a fight song. The Aggie spirit song was written by a student Yellmaster named Francis Erving Lankey in 1915. For some reason, it was not sung by the victorious Aggies in their 1915 win in Ann Arbor. Maybe nobody knew the words or maybe it was not completed until after the teams met in 1915.

The Aggies opened their season with a new coach. Frank Sommers, like Macklin, hailed from Pennsylvania. He came to East Lansing with three years of coaching experience: one year at Colgate (5-2-0) and two years at Villanova (10-4-1). He was an unknown in Aggie circles, but Macklin had left many good players for Coach Sommers to work with. Aggie fans were probably expecting another winning season and maybe another win over Michigan. Hopefully, the ROTC band knew the Aggie fight song by now. All the MAC footballers had to do was defeat Michigan for the second straight season and the band would let it rip!

The Wolverines kicked off their 1916 pigskin campaign successfully with a 38-0 win over Marietta College. They also defeated Case (19-3) before rolling over Carroll (54-0) and Mount Union (26-0). It appeared that the Wolverines were ready for the second half of their season. Their first big test would be against the fighting farmers from East Lansing.

GAME SUMMARY: MAC 0 UM 9

Game number eleven was another rough, tough, physical battle between two incredibly good football teams. The largest crowd in series history (22,000) braved cold and rain for this Great Lakes State "grudge match." Both defenses were strong, and the tackling was heavy. Gaining yards was a difficult task on this day and scoring points was even harder.

The Wolverines finally prevailed by a score of 9-0. *Detroit Free Press* writer E. A. Batchelor's headline read: "Michigan Defeats Plucky MAC Team." *(DFP, 10/22/1916, Page 19)* It was not a pretty win for the Wolverines, but it still counted.

This hard-earned victory was highlighted by one of the strangest plays in series history. Cliff Sparks, a first year starting quarterback, was the holder who lined up to get the ball down for a thirty-two-yard field goal attempt by Captain John Maulbetsch. The ball was snapped so high that Sparks had to leap to catch it. Then, as if he had done it a thousand times, he drop-kicked the ball through the uprights for a Michigan score! (Perry, Page 88) That first quarter effort put the Wolverines up by a score of 3-0. Sparks was a strong ground gainer for the Wolverines during the game along with Maulbetsch. The game remained close until Maulbetsch scored on a two-yard run to make the final score 9-0 in favor of Michigan. *(DFP, 10/22/1916, Page 19)*

The Michigan Daily, obviously tired of the Aggie braggarts who were still chirping about the 1915 game, had this to say about the Wolverine victory. "Michigan's Varsity pushed the Farmers right off the top of the proud and elevated pedestal that they have occupied for the past season and the resounding thump as they struck the cold, soggy ground was music to the ears of the majority of the 22,000 spectators who defied the elements and saw one of the most interesting battles that has claimed a Ferry Field setting for many a moon." (*Michigan Football: From the Pages of the Michigan Daily*, Page 26) There is no mention of the MAC ROTC Cadet Band playing "*The Victors*" after the game which makes sense. There was nothing for the Aggies to celebrate!

Team	1st	2nd	3rd	4th	Final
MAC	0	0	0	0	0
UM	3	0	0	6	9

SERIES UPDATE:

After eleven series games Michigan still held a decided advantage in what was now becoming an annual event in the State of Michigan. The Wolverines now owned a series record of 8 wins, 2 losses, and 1 tie. Yost's record was now an impressive 7 wins, 2 losses and 1 tie. The Aggies remained an extremely dangerous and competitive team since the blowout loss (55-7) in 1912. In fact, they were even with the Wolverines in the last four games (2 wins, 2 losses, and 0 ties). The BIG questions were: "Where is this series going?" and "Is it a true rivalry between equal foes, or would one team exert itself and assume a dominant role?"

SERIES MILESTONES:

The eleventh game of the now annual fall "blood-letting" ritual between the Aggies and the Wolverines produced quite a few interesting milestones. First, the series attendance record now stood at twenty-two thousand people (22,000) which eclipsed the old record by about one thousand. Second, it was the first series game for Coach Sommers and his last. It was also his first and only loss in the series. Finally, it marked the tenth series game for Coach Fielding Yost of Michigan, easily the most games coached by one man in the series so far.

SEASON SUMMARIES:

The Aggies recovered nicely after the Michigan loss and easily defeated North Dakota State (30-0). They tied South Dakota the next week (3-3) before losing the Homecoming finale to Notre Dame by a score of 14-0. The good news for the Aggies was that they finished with a winning record of 4 wins, 2 losses, and 1 tie. That made it fourteen consecutive winning seasons for the Aggies! The bad news was that, like the four men who preceded him, Coach Frank Sommers lost his first encounter against the Wolverines. Unfortunately for Sommers it would be his first and last series game. Although he had a winning season a record of 4 wins, 2 losses and 1tie was not good enough. Frank Sommers was gone by the new year and things would look different in the fall of 1917, but not totally.

The Wolverines won the next two games against Syracuse (14-13) and Washington University of St. Louis (66-7) before being stopped by two brick walls. Eastern powers Cornell and Pennsylvania both bested Michigan and the Wolverines finished with a final record of 7 wins, 2 losses, and 0 ties. This was the first season without three losses in three years which was a good thing for Michigan fans. However, the relentless Yost was hoping for something better. No doubt, "Hurry Up" Yost was back to the drawing board in the off-season trying to figure out ways to return to the glory days of his first five years at Michigan.

Game #12: October 20, 1917 at Ferry Field in Ann Arbor

BACKGROUND INFORMATION:

The 1917 did not see any rules changes for the first time in many years. The game of American football, as we know it, was done making revolutionary changes. Fine tuning and minor changes would remain a part of the game, but the game had not changed in any way from the 1916 season. Finally, the coaches, could focus on their playbooks instead of the rulebooks.

The University of Michigan and Michigan Agricultural College played for the twelfth time in 1917. Both teams posted winning records in 1916. Expectations were high for both squads in 1917 despite some player shortages caused by World War I. The question in the State of Michigan was, "Who would have the better team this year?"

Michigan Agricultural College experienced another change in their football program with the departure of Frank Sommers. However, instead of going back to Pennsylvania to find another coach, they contacted an old friend, Chester Brewer, the winningest coach in Aggie football history, about returning to East Lansing. Brewer had left Missouri after three seasons and finished with a Missouri Valley Conference title (1913) and an overall record of 14 wins, 8 losses, and 2 ties. He had been out of coaching for three years but was eager to return to the Aggie program. I am certain that Coach Brewer and the Aggie faithful were hoping that he would pick up right where he left off. The Aggies opened their season with disappointing home losses to Alma (14-7) and Kalamazoo (7-3). The young Aggies had lost a significant number of experienced players to the war effort and it was obvious that they would have trouble in 1917. I doubt if the Aggies were looking forward to the Michigan game.

A big change occurred in Ann Arbor because the Wolverines were back in the Big Ten (Western Conference) after their ten-year absence. Due to scheduling challenges, the Wolverines only played one conference game in 1917. Michigan was "officially" welcomed back to their conference family on November 24, 1917 when they were beaten by Northwestern (21-12). Fielding Yost compiled a record of 52 wins, 16 losses and 7 ties as a reluctant independent. Coach Yost was all about winning championships. Getting back into the Western Conference would give him the opportunity to do that every season, starting in 1918! The Wolverines rolled to four straight victories over Case (41-0), Western State (17-3), Mount Union (69-0), and Detroit (14-3). They outscored their foes by a margin of 141-6. It appeared that the Yost's footballers were ready for the Aggies and everyone else on their schedule.

GAME SUMMARY: MAC 0 UM 27

Game number twelve was all about the Michigan Wolverines Yost's team scored in the first, third and fourth quarters to win going away. The Wolverines were strong on offense, defense, and special teams. Tad Wieman, future Captain (1918) and Wolverine Head Coach (1927-28), ran for three touchdowns. Halfback Archie Weston also scored on a fifteen-yard run in the first quarter. The Aggies had no answer for Michigan's strong running attack and failed to muster any sort of offense. (*DFP*, 10/21/1917, Page 19) I am sure that it was a long ride back to East Lansing for the Aggie team.

Team	1st	2nd	3rd	4th	Final
MAC	0	0	0	0	0
UM	6	0	7	14	27

SERIES UPDATE:

After a dozen series games Michigan was still a tough team for the Aggies to beat. The Wolverines now had a series record of 9 wins, 2 losses, and 1 tie. The Aggies, of course, were now saddled with a record of 2 wins, 9 losses and 1 tie. The progress that had been made in the three previous games seemed to be lost. Was Aggie football headed in the wrong direction?

SERIES MILESTONES:

Chester Brewer was back in East Lansing again which made him the first coach in series history to have two different tenures. As it turned out the result was the same. His record against Michigan's varsity now stood at 0 wins, 3 losses, and 1 tie. The crowd of 9,038 was not a record breaker, but still impressive since it came during a war year.

SEASON SUMMARIES:

The Aggies never recovered from the Michigan loss. The farmers lost all their remaining games and finished with their first and only winless season (0 wins, 9 losses, and 0 ties) in Aggie football history. In an ironic turn of events, the winningest coach in the history of Aggie football was winless in his return to East Lansing. It would be long off-season for the Aggies and many questions needed to be answered before the start of the 1918 season. Of course, the first question that drove all the rest was: "Who would coach the Aggie football team in 1918?"

The Wolverines won three more games against Nebraska, Kalamazoo and Cornell before the wheels fell off in road contests at Pennsylvania and Northwestern. The Wolverines finished with an excellent record of 8 wins, 2 losses, and 0 ties. Michigan also had three players who earned All-American honors in 1917—Guards Ernest Allmendinger and Frank Culver and Fullback Cedric Smith. The Wolverines lost their only conference game and finished in a tie for 8th place. However, the good news for Yost and Michigan is that they were back in the Western Conference!

Game #13: November 23, 1918 at Ferry Field in Ann Arbor

BACKGROUND INFORMATION:

Once again, there were no significant rules changes for the 1918 season. The game was "opening up" and teams were starting to show creativity in the passing game. It was a good time for American college football.

The 1918 college football season was greatly affected by America's involvement in World War 1. Both Michigan and MAC lost many excellent players to military service. The Aggies and the Wolverines also played fewer games that season because of war-time travel restrictions. To make matters worse, a deadly flu epidemic that killed over 600,000 Americans caused the cancellation of many games for each team. Yes, it was a terrible time for everyone in America and the world. Sound familiar?

The thirteenth series game between the Aggies and the Wolverines was played in Ann Arbor for the tenth time in 1918. This game began a Ferry Field "home" streak that reached six games before the series returned to East Lansing. Up to this point, only three games had been played in Aggie "land" (1911, 1914 and 1917).

For the third straight year, the Aggies opened their season with a new coach. George Gauthier, a former quarterback under John Macklin, was selected as the seventh man to lead the Aggie football program. Coach Gauthier knew the expectations were high, certainly much higher than in 1917. The forgettable 1917 campaign was the worst in Aggie history. Gauthier wanted to lead MAC to a much better showing in 1918.

The Aggies started out very well under George Gauthier. They won their first three games against Albion (21-6), Hillsdale (66-6), and Western State (16-7), but lost to a strong Purdue team (14-6). They pulled off a huge upset the following week against a heavily favored Notre Dame team (13-7) coached by a young fellow named Knute Rockne. George Gauthier knew what it took to beat Michigan because he was on the first team to defeat the Wolverines in 1913. He would have his team ready for a big effort for their trip to Ann Arbor the following week.

Michigan began the 1918 football season on October 5th at home against Case. The result was a 33-0 win for the Wolverines. Since the next three games were cancelled, the Wolverines did not play another game until November 9th when they traveled to Chicago to take on the Maroons. Michigan was able to win their first conference game of the season by a score of 13-0 over Stagg's footballers. The Wolverines defeated Syracuse (15-0) the next week and appeared ready to play their best against the Aggies.

GAME SUMMARY: MAC 6 UM 21

The Aggie-Wolverine game drew the largest crowd of the 1918 season (15,000) in Ann Arbor. Once again, the teams slugged it out in a very physical contest. Accounts of the game highlighted the strong play of Michigan's offensive and defensive lines. Halfback Abe Cohen, fullback Frank Steketee and quarterback Ken Knode ran hard all day. Cohen and Knode both scored touchdowns. Angus Goetz, who captained the 1919 team, also returned an Aggie fumble for a touchdown. (*DFP*, 11/24/1918, Page 21) Steketee, kicked all three extra points. The Wolverine defense played strong all day and only allowed a late touchdown when the game was already decided.

Team	1st	2nd	3rd	4th	Final
MAC	0	0	0	6	6
UM	0	14	7	0	21

SERIES UPDATE:

The Wolverines remained large and in charge after thirteen series games. Michigan increased their series advantage to 10 wins, 2 losses, and 1 tie. Yost's record against the Aggies improved to 9 wins, 2 losses, and 1 tie. The Aggies continued to be a competitive team, but it was difficult to assess where the MAC football program was going. Coach Gauthier made it three coaches in three years for the Aggies while Yost had been on the job in Ann Arbor for seventeen straight winning seasons. Too many coaching changes usually do not bode well for a football program, regardless of the era. Since the abrupt departure of John Macklin, MAC was struggling to find the right man to lead the Aggie football program back to prominence. What would happen after the 1918 season?

SERIES MILESTONES:

The thirteenth game of the series produced a few interesting milestones. First, this was the first series game ever played in the month of November. Second, this was the first, and only, time that the Aggie vs Wolverine game was played on a Homecoming Weekend in Ann Arbor. Third, it was the first series game where freshmen were eligible to play because of the shortage of players due to the war effort. Fourth, it was the tenth series game ever played in Ann Arbor and Michigan's tenth series win. Fifth, it was the first time that a MAC alumnus (George Gauthier) ever led his Aggies against the Wolverines. Finally, it was Coach Gauthier's first series game, his first series loss, and his last series game.

SEASON SUMMARIES:

MAC's football season ended the next week in Madison with a tough loss at Wisconsin (7-6) on Thanksgiving Day. After winning their first three games under Coach Gauthier, the Aggies lost three of the next four and finished at 4-3-0. The only highlight was the stunning win against Notre Dame in November. Like I said earlier, the questions surrounding the Aggie football program centered around who would lead them into the future. That question was partially answered when George Gauthier's employment at MAC was terminated. Who would become the next Aggie football coach?

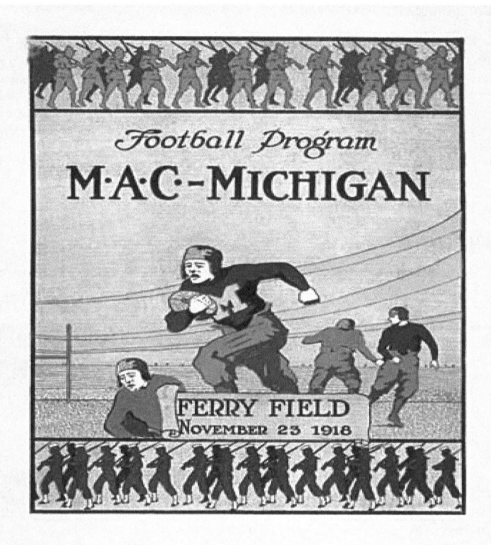

Image 3 Series Game #13 was played during the Spanish Flu Pandemic in 1918.
(Permission: Bentley Historical Library at The University of Michigan, See Page 369)

The Wolverines won their fifth and final game the next week against Ohio State. They ended the season with a record of 5 wins, 0 losses, and 0 ties. The season was low on quantity since three games were cancelled in October, but high in quality. Michigan shutout every opponent except the Aggies and finished with a positive point differential of ninety-points (96 points scored versus 6 points allowed). Yost's footballers finished in first place in the Big Ten Conference with a record of 2 wins and 0 losses and were declared National Champions for the fifth time in Fielding Yost's seventeen-year tenure at Michigan. Finally, Frank Steketee (fullback and kicker) was named a consensus All-American at the end of the season. All in all, a great season for the Wolverines during an exceedingly difficult time in America's history.

Game #14: October 18, 1919 at Ferry Field in Ann Arbor

BACKGROUND INFORMATION:

In a pattern that continued for the next few years, there were no rules changes or tweaks for the 1919 season. Coaches continued to refine their passing games and probably spent equal amounts of time trying to design defenses that could stop the pass. Every team in college football had adopted the forward pass and it was like a two-edged sword—something that could really help or hurt you on game day.

Once again, the fourteenth series game was played again Ann Arbor. Now that Michigan was back in the Western Conference they did not have as much "need" to schedule the Aggies. The series would continue as a "one-way" rivalry which meant that the Aggies had to show up in Ann Arbor or they might not get on the schedule.

As it turned out that was not the worst thing for the Aggies since they had never won in East Lansing (only a tie). Of course, they owned two victories in Ann Arbor. Besides, the crowds were usually double in size in Ann Arbor so the payout for the trip was usually quite good for MAC's athletic department budget. With the end of World War I, every college team had a huge influx of returning players eager to play again. Both Michigan and MAC benefitted from the return of many excellent players to their programs. In the end, it turned out that things might have helped MAC a little bit more than Michigan, but neither team would have a season to write home about.

For the fourth straight year, the Aggies began their season with a new coach. Alumnus George Gauthier was gone after one season making him the second "one-and-done" coach in the last three seasons. The Aggies asked Chester Brewer, to return to East Lansing and get the MAC football program back on track. The Aggies used a scheduling trick from the Michigan "play book" and played three games in eight days to start the season.

MAC opened with wins over Albion (14-13) and Alma (46-6) before losing to Western State by a score of 16-7. Coach Brewer probably did not really know how good his Aggies would be in 1919, but he found out quickly.

The Wolverines started the 1919 football with another easy win over Case (34-0). Michigan would find out very quickly how good the season would go when the Fighting Farmers showed up in Ann Arbor. Yost's footballers were looking to defend their Western Conference Championship and the National Championship too!

GAME SUMMARY: MAC 0 UM 26

The Aggie-Wolverine game attracted another excellent crowd (21,000), but it was not a record breaker. Harry Bullion, writing for the *Detroit Free Press,* summed up the game as follows: "M.A.C. came, saw and was conquered this afternoon on Ferry Field...." (DFP, 10/19/1919, Page 21) In another fiercely contested game, the Wolverines scored the most and sent the Aggies home to ponder things like offense, defense, and special teams.

Michigan halfback Archie Weston led the scoring with two touchdowns and Duke Dunn caught a five-yard scoring pass from Cliff Sparks. Lineman Frank Czyz also recovered an Aggie fumble in the end zone for six more Wolverine points. Sparks also kicked two extra points. Michigan's defense was strong for the entire game and kept the Aggies out of the end zone for the third time in the last four seasons. (*DFP*, 10/19/1919, Page 21)

Team	1st	2nd	3rd	4th	Final
MAC	0	0	0	0	0
UM	0	6	7	13	26

SERIES UPDATE:

Once again, Michigan was the better team in all three phases of the game. The Wolverines pushed their series advantage to 11 wins, 2 losses, and 1 tie. Yost improved his series record to 10 wins, 2 losses, and 1 tie. Things were not looking good for the Aggies at this point, but Wolverine fortunes looked bright!

SERIES MILESTONES:

As usual, game number fourteen game of the UM vs MAC series also produced a few more milestones. First, it was the first decade where a series game was played every year between the two rivals. Second, Fielding Yost became the first coach to win ten series games. Third, it was also the final series game, really, for Chester Brewer. He is the first and only man to lead a team in three different tenures in the series. Brewer's teams faced off against the Wolverines in five games, but the best they could do was a tie (0-0) in 1908. Chester Brewer's final record in the series finished at 0 wins, 4 losses, and 1 tie. It was time to find a new leader for the MAC football program. Hopefully, someone who would stick around, win a lot of games, and beat those hated Wolverines!

SEASON SUMMARIES:

The Aggie season was not a disaster, but it was not good enough for Coach Brewer to continue coaching the team. After the Michigan loss, the Aggies bounced back with a nice win over DePauw (27-0) before losing to Purdue by a score of 13-7. They won against South Dakota (13-0), lost to Notre Dame (13-0), and tied Wabash (7-7). The final record in Coach Brewers last season at MAC ended at 4 wins, 4 losses, and 1 tie. It was not a winning season, it was not a losing season, it was just a season. Like the Wolverines, the Aggies would have to go back to the drawing board for the 1920 season, but first they would have to find a coach. I am certain that this was getting old for Aggie fans and players!

After defeating the Aggies, Michigan's seven game winning streak (from 1918 to 1919) came to a screeching halt in Ann Arbor with a 13-3 loss to Ohio State. They managed to defeat Northwestern the following week by a score of 16-13. Then the wheels fell off as they lost to Chicago, Illinois, and Minnesota. It ended as a "no" season in Ann Arbor since there was "no" Western Conference Championship, "no" National Championship and "no" All-Americans. The mighty Wolverines hit the ground on November 22, 1919 with a mighty thud! Michigan ended the season with a final record of 3 wins, 4 losses, and 0 ties—the first, and only, losing season in Coach Yost's brilliant Michigan career. It was an ugly time in Ann Arbor, but I am certain that Aggie fans were not feeling sorry for the Wolverines!

DECADE AND SERIES SUMMARY:

As I said earlier, this was the first decade in which a series game was played every season between the two in-state rivals. Michigan still held the upper hand, but the Aggies had made some progress, at least until the middle of the decade. A series of coaching changes did not help the Aggie football fortunes and Yost and his Wolverines took advantage of the coaching "turmoil" in East Lansing.

Although both programs ended the decade on a low note, the Wolverines still held the upper hand. Even though he had a losing season, Fielding Yost was not going anywhere. Meanwhile, the Aggies had to find another leader. They had to find someone like Macklin who would stay and win for a very long-time! How hard could that be?

Decade and Series Summary 1898 to 1919

Time Frame	UM Won-Lost-Tied	MAC Won Lost-Tied
1910-1919	8-2-0	2-8-0
1898-1919	11-2-1	2-11-1

PROGRAM SUMMARIES:

During the third decade of the series, Michigan, again, was the better team, but not by much! Their decision to leave the Western Conference in 1907 affected Michigan in more ways than they probably thought they would. The Wolverines finally got back into the conference after a ten-year hiatus, but the independent years took a toll. Michigan bounced back nicely in 1918 with their championships. Unfortunately, they ended the decade on a sour note with their first losing season since 1891. Coach Yost was intent on proving that the 1919 season was a fluke, an aberration, something that would never happen again on his watch. He would work tirelessly in the off-season to bring Michigan back to prominence in 1920 and position the Wolverines for continued greatness.

Program Summaries 1910 to 1919

Statistical Area	UM	MAC
Number of Head Coaches	1	4
Games Played	76	73
Wins	52	47
Losses	18	24
Ties	6	2
Winning Percentage	.724	.658
Winning Seasons	9	8
Losing Seasons	1	1
Even Seasons	0	1
National Championships	1	0
All-American Players	9	1

Coach John Macklin took Aggie football where it had never been before. He put them on the college football map. Then, just as quickly, the Aggies got lost and nobody could find them! Michigan Agricultural College finished the decade on a low note with too many coaches and too few victories, especially against Michigan! The first seven seasons of the decade were exceptionally good for MAC. Coaches Brewer and Macklin produced a winning percentage (.806) that eclipsed Yost's achievements (.722) at Michigan. However, Yost still won more of the series games so the Aggies could not brag too much. With that said, it was clear that they were a rising program and a force to be reckoned with in the State of Michigan. Everything changed in the last three years of the decade when coaches changed as often as the seasons! Michigan Agricultural college was looking for an identity at the end of the 1919 football season and still looking for a leader of their program.

CHAPTER 5

Wolverine Perfection 1920 to 1929

Questions, questions, and more questions. Yes, there were many questions surrounding the UM and MAC football programs in 1920. Would the Aggies find a coach who could compete with Yost and Michigan? Would Fielding Yost return the Wolverine footballers to their winning ways, or would there be another losing season? Fans in Ann Arbor wanted a return to the glory years that marked the turn of the century. Aggie fans just wanted a coach who could win more games especially against the Maize and Blue bullies from Ann Arbor. Let us take a closer look at how the Mitten State football rivalry evolved in the "Roaring Twenties."

Game # 15: October 16, 1920 at Ferry Field in Ann Arbor

BACKGROUND INFORMATION:

The college rules makers knew a good thing when they saw it and they chose, again, not to fix something that was not broken! College football was growing everywhere. Injuries were down, attendance was up—college football was on a roll and there was no end in sight. Coaches were innovating, as coaches always do, and players were playing with more skill and determination than ever. It was a good time to be a coach, a player, and a fan!

Michigan and Michigan Agricultural College began the decade in vastly different ways. Fielding Yost returned to the sidelines for his twentieth season in Ann Arbor. MAC welcomed a new coach for the fifth straight season. George "Potsy" Clark, an All-American quarterback who played for the legendary Bob Zuppke at Illinois, was chosen to lead the Aggie football team for the twenty-fifth season of Aggie football. Clark would be the fifth coach in ten years. Would Coach Clark be the man who would stay awhile and build something special?

Potsy Clark's football team played four games before they met Michigan in Ann Arbor. Game one did not go well as the Aggies lost to Kalamazoo by a score of 21-2. The next two games went better against Albion (16-0) and Alma (48-0). The Aggies lost the next game to a strong Wisconsin (27-0) team which evened their record at 2-2-0. Game five would probably set the course for the rest of the 1920 season. An upset over the Wolverines might propel the Aggies to an excellent pigskin campaign. Another loss to Michigan would probably send them into a tailspin that might not end very well.

Michigan played, and won, their only game before their now annual matchup with MAC. Case, once again, provided a nice "warm up" game for Yost's gridders. Final score: Michigan 35 and Case 0. This would not be enough information to determine how the season might go since the Wolverines defeated Case by a score of 34-0 in 1919 and then finished with 3 wins and 4 losses. Maybe the Aggies would give Yost a better idea of how the season could develop.

GAME SUMMARY: MAC 0 UM 35

Mitten State series game number fifteen was another easy win for Michigan. It was their fifth straight win over the Aggies and their fourth shutout in the last five games. Nothing went right for MAC after the opening kickoff. Another year, another loss to Michigan. This had to be getting really, really old for the Aggies and their fans. Did anyone contact John Macklin to see if he would return to East Lansing and fix this football mess?

According to Detroit Free Press reporter K. W. Hall's headline: "Michigan Outplays Farmers at All Stages of Annual Gridiron conflict on Historic Ferry Field." (DFP, 10/17/1920, Page 21) The Wolverine lineman dominated their Aggie counterparts on both sides of the ball. Michigan took a 7-0 lead into the locker room thanks to a first quarter touchdown run by halfback John Perrin and an extra point kick by Frank Steketee. (*DFP*, 10/17/1920, Page 21)

Although nothing went right for MAC in the first half, they were still in the game. Would they be able to come back and beat hated Michigan? Unfortunately, for the Aggies, the Wolverines had other plans. Ed Usher and Abe Cohn each ran for a touchdown in the third quarter. Both Jack Dunne and Usher scored in the final quarter. Steketee kicked four more points after touchdown in the second half. The game ended at 35-0 in favor of Michigan. (*DFP*, 10/17/1920, Page 21)

Team	1st	2nd	3rd	4th	Final
MAC	0	0	0	0	0
UM	7	0	14	14	35

The Wolverines totaled 410-yards of offense compared to just 67-yards for the Aggies. Michigan earned fifteen first downs and MAC only totaled four. Clark's quarterbacks went 0-10 in the Aggie passing attack. Unfortunately, they did complete five passes to the Wolverine defense which is never good!

SERIES UPDATE:

Fifteen games were now in the series history book and Michigan still controlled the series. The Wolverines now owned an excellent record of 12 wins, 2 losses, and 1 tie. The disheartened Aggies were now sitting on a disappointing record of 2 wins, 12 losses, and 1 tie. Things were about as bad as they could be in East Lansing. Ugh!

SERIES MILESTONES:

Game number fifteen produced some new milestones. First, this game tripled as Coach Clark's first game, his first loss and his last series game. Second, it was also the first time that a defense (Michigan) picked off five passes in a series game. Of course, this meant that it was also the first time that series team MAC) threw five interceptions. Finally, this loss meant that it was another Michigan victory, another MAC defeat, and another MAC coaching change on the horizon. Maybe things would be different in 1921 or, maybe not!

SEASON SUMMARIES:

The Aggies followed up their loss to Michigan with a listless performance in East Lansing. Marietta College came to town and left with a surprising victory (23-7) over the Aggies. MAC took their frustrations out on poor Olivet College the next week. Final score: MAC 109 and Olivet 0! They followed that historic win with another blow-out victory over Chicago YMCA (81-0) on Homecoming. The Aggies had 4 wins and 4 losses going into the final two games. Maybe they would turn things around and finish on a high note.

Coach Clark's footballers played a couple of "toughies" at the end of the season. Nebraska (35-7) and Notre Dame (25-0) felt no shame in defeating the "Fighting Farmers." The Aggies had not won their last game of the season since 1915 and it did not happen in 1920 either. MAC finished the season with 4 wins, 6 losses, and 0 ties. That kind of record usually finishes a coach's career and that is what happened to George "Potsy" Clark in East Lansing. Another "one and done" coach had come and gone, along with the hopes of Aggie football fans. What now?

Michigan began their conference season the next week with a one-point loss against Illinois (7-6). They defeated Tulane the next week (21-0) and won two of their last three games to finish with an overall record of 5 wins, 2 losses, and 0 ties. Certainly, a winning record and a better season than 1919, but not what Yost was hoping for. The Wolverines finished in the middle of the Big Ten with a record of 2 wins and 2 losses. It was back to the drawing board for the relentless Yost who lived for wins and championships!

Game # 16: October 15, 1921 at Ferry Field in Ann Arbor

BACKGROUND INFORMATION:

Once again, the rules makers let the game grow. No rules "tinkering" took place for the fifth consecutive year. The game was doing fine. Some minor tweaks were on the horizon, but no changes were made for the 1921 season.

For the seventh straight season, the Mitten State mauling game was played at Ferry Field. This was the twelfth game in Ann Arbor compared to only four in East Lansing. However, that was not really a big deal since the Aggies were 0-3-1 vs Michigan in East Lansing. Playing in Ann Arbor was not the worst thing that could happen to the Aggies. After all, both MAC series wins took place at Ferry Field!

The Aggies opened the season with a different coach for the seventh straight season. Legend has it that the Aggies had inked Knute Rockne to a contract for the 1921 season, but the deal fell through and so did some interesting prospects for the future of Aggie football. (Stabley, Pages 53-54) A man like Rockne roaming the sidelines in East Lansing could have been a wonderful thing, but it was not meant to be!

As usual, the Aggies failed to get their first choice. Instead, they settled for a man named Frank Barron. Like Macklin and Sommers before him, Barron was a Pennsylvania native. The MAC school administrators probably hoped that Mr. Barron might be able to bring some winning "eastern" football to East Lansing. Aggie fans did not really know what to expect, but sports fans are generally optimistic at the start of a new season. Maybe Mr. Barron could get things going in the right direction. His Aggies began the season with a nice win over Alma (28-0) but lost to Albion (24-7) in East Lansing. The Aggies would find out very quickly how the season would go when they squared off against the Wolverines in Ann Arbor.

The Wolverines warmed up with two easy wins over Mount Union (44-0) and Case (65-0). Coach Yost was probably feeling good about his team. Wolverine fans had high hopes for their Maize and Blue men and things were setting up nicely for another special season. MAC was the last non-conference game of the season. It was time to chalk up another win and get ready for the conference "Big Boys."

GAME SUMMARY: MAC 0 UM 30

The Wolverines prevailed again in series game number sixteen and it was not that close. For the second straight season, the Aggies were only down by seven points at halftime. Michigan was outplaying Barron's men, but they could not stop throwing the ball to the Aggies. Then, things changed for the worse for MAC. Richard N. Heath of the *Detroit Free Press* summed up the game with this headline: "Farmers Crumple After Great Fight." (*DFP*, 10/16/1921, Pages 23-24) Harry Kipke, who was born in East Lansing, made life miserable for the Aggies by scoring three touchdowns and punting the Aggies into bad field position all day long! Paul Goebel also starred with two fumble recoveries that set up easy scores. He also blocked a punt and returned it for a touchdown. (*DFP*, 10/16/1921, Pages 23-24)

Team	1st	2nd	3rd	4th	Final
MAC	0	0	0	0	0
UM	7	0	14	9	30

Once again, the Aggies left Ann Arbor with frowns on their faces, bruises on their bodies and more blood lost! Yes, losing to Michigan was getting old, incredibly old. This loss made it six straight wins for Michigan, which set a new series record.

SERIES UPDATE:

Michigan's series record grew to 13 wins, 2 losses, and 1 tie. That made it three straight series shutouts for the Wolverines. MAC had only scored six points since their last win in 1915. It is hard to win a football game, let alone compete with a hated rival, if you cannot score points. The Aggies had to figure this out.

SERIES MILESTONES:

Game number sixteen did not produce any notable milestones. Albert Barron became the ninth straight SAC/MAC coach to lose his first series game to Michigan. Yes, it was starting to feel like "Groundhog Day" in East Lansing:

- Travel to Ann Arbor
- Fail to score and lose again in Ann Arbor
- Return home with a frown
- Hope to win next year!

SEASON SUMMARIES:

Coach Albert Barron's Aggies bounced back from their Michigan loss with a win over Western State (17-14) but lost the next game to Marquette (7-0). Barron's men made the Aggie fans smile on Homecoming Day with a shutout win over South Dakota (14-0). Unfortunately, they finished "weak, not strong" with two straight losses to Butler (3-2) and Notre Dame (48-0). Coach Barron's first year in East Lansing was a disappointment. A final record of 3 wins and 5 losses does not inspire optimism for the future!

The Wolverines hosted the Ohio State Buckeyes the next week in the "biggest" game of the year and came up flat. Final score: Buckeyes 14 and Wolverines 0. This was not the way Coach Yost wanted his rising Wolverines to play in front of a Homecoming Crowd in Ann Arbor! The Wolverines went on to defeat Illinois (3-0), tie Wisconsin (7-7) and beat Minnesota (38-0). Michigan finished their season with a record of 5 wins, 1 loss, and 1 tie. Paul Goebel (End) and Ernie Vick (Center) were named All-Americans for their strong play. It was a good season, but not good enough for the indefatigable Yost!

Game # 17: November 4, 1922 at Ferry Field in Ann Arbor

BACKGROUND INFORMATION:

Once again, there were no major rules changes for the 1922 season. However, there were two tweaks. The first change moved the spot for the point after touchdown to the five-yard line and allowed teams to kick, run, or pass for the extra point. The second change was about substitutions. Players who left the game in the first half could not return until the second half and players who left in the second half were out for the rest of the game! (Herget, Page 167)

The seventeenth game of the in-state series was played in Ann Arbor for the eighth straight season. It was also the second November game of the series. Instead of being an early season "warm up" game the Aggies provided a "break" right in the middle of Michigan's conference schedule.

The good news in East Lansing was that MAC began the 1922 season with the same coach for the first time in eight years. The bad news was that Coach Barron's Aggies were not off to a stellar start. The farmers were not showing a lot of "fight" in the first five games. The Aggies had a record of 2 wins, 2 losses, and 1 tie heading into the Michigan game. They knew that Michigan was rolling, but the big questions was, "Could the Aggies stop the Wolverine football machine?"

Michigan was off to an exceptional start when they faced off against MAC in November. The Wolverines were undefeated in four games (3-0-1) and had outscored their opponents by a margin of 91-0. There was no doubt that this would be one of Yost's better teams in recent memory. The Wolverines were ready for the Aggies. The real question was "Were the Aggies be ready for Michigan?"

GAME SUMMARY: MAC 0 UM 63

Once again, Michigan defeated the Aggies, and it was ugly! Michigan showed up, but many of the Aggies must have missed the train to Ann Arbor. This was clearly a case of two football teams going in completely different directions. Michigan was heading for a conference championship and national prominence. Michigan Agricultural College was a team, a program, in disarray—a football entity that needed a new direction, and fast!

The Wolverines played flawlessly and showed the farmers how the game of football should be played in 1922. Yost's footballers dominated every phase of the game and scored in every quarter. It was Michigan's second largest victory margin over MAC. The *Battle Creek Enquirer and Evening News* (*BCEEN*) summed it up in one telling headline: "Michigan Walks Away in a Hurry With Aggies by a Score of 63-0." (*BCEEN*, 11/5/1922. Page 19)

Michigan scored nine touchdowns, one field goal and six points after touchdown. The Wolverines rushed for five touchdowns, passed for three more and returned an interception for a score. Michigan completed 17 passes on 33 attempts and kept the Aggie defense off-balance the entire game. It was hard for Aggie fans to watch, but Wolverine fans loved it!

Team	1st	2nd	3rd	4th	Final
MAC	0	0	0	0	0
UM	14	19	9	21	63

SERIES UPDATE:

This game was another huge setback for the Aggie football program. They probably lost a lot of hope after this game as well as some more blood. Michigan extended their series winning streak to seven games and increased their overall record to 14-2-1. During the Wolverine winning streak the Aggies had been outscored by a whopping margin of 211 to 6. Sadly, MAC had not scored a point since 1918!

SERIES MILESTONES:

The one-sided game in Ann Arbor set a new series attendance record (42,000) that almost doubled the previous record. As it turned out, Frank Barron coached his second and final game against the Wolverines and left the series with a record of 0 wins, 2 losses, and 0 ties. Next man up for the Aggies! Wow, this had to be getting old for MAC fans. Finally, this was the first game that the Wolverines scored in every quarter.

SEASON SUMMARIES:

For the second straight season, Coach Albert Barron and his Aggies finished with a losing record. After their devastating defeat at Michigan, MAC lost two more games to Ohio Wesleyan and Creighton before defeating Massachusetts State (45-0) on Homecoming Day. They tied St. Louis (7-7) to finish with a final record of 3 wins, 5 losses, and 2 ties. Unfortunately, Albert Barron could not get the Aggie football program back on track. Who would lead the farmers back to football respectability?

The Wolverines finished their seventh undefeated season in the Yost Era. Victories over Wisconsin (13-6) and Minnesota (16-7) allowed Michigan to finish with a final record of 6 wins, 0 losses, and 1 tie. They were Big Ten Conference co-champions once again. Harry Kipke, Michigan's outstanding halfback, kicker, and punter, was named All-American for his excellent all-around play in 1922. This was one of Fielding Yost's most satisfying seasons and prospects looked bright with many excellent players returning for the 1923 season.

Game # 18: October 27, 1923 at Ferry Field in Ann Arbor

BACKGROUND INFORMATION:

Once again, the college football rules makers chose not to make any new rules or subtle changes for the 1923 season. They were still watching the impact of the "modifications" from the 1922 season and that is all they planned to do this season. College football continued to grow exponentially. Schools were building new stadiums, or planning to, and the press loved the game. It was a good time for college football in America.

Like every season, the 1923 version was full of hope and promise in East Lansing and Ann Arbor. Fielding Yost returned for his twenty-third season in Ann Arbor and was looking forward to his sixteenth game in the series.

Meanwhile, back in East Lansing another coach (Barron) had come and gone, and a new man was selected to lead the Aggies for the 1923 season. Ralph Young, who had played a season of football for that guy named Yost was the next man up for the Aggies. Mr. Young was the sixth different Aggie coach in the last nine seasons. Would he be the one to put some "fight" back in the farmers and string together some winning seasons? Of course, it would be nice if Coach Young could engineer some wins over Michigan too!

The 1923 Aggie football schedule was one of the more difficult schedules in recent years. Ralph Young's record was even going into the Michigan game. His farmers had a record of 2 wins, 2 losses, and 0 ties. They defeated Lake Forest (21-6) and Albion (13-0) but lost to Chicago (34-0) and Wisconsin (21-0). The Spartans were probably underdogs going into the Ann Arbor matchup with the hated Wolverines. Ralph Young knew what it would take to steal a victory against Michigan. The question was, "Did the Aggies have a chance?"

Michigan had some strong players back for another year including Lansing native, and team captain, Harry Kipke. Once again, expectations were extremely high for Captain Kipke (an All-American in 1922) and his teammates. Michigan was undefeated (3 wins, 0 losses, and 0 ties) and unscored upon when they hosted the Aggies in late October. The Wolverine stars had come out to shine in the first three games and everyone expected them to do the same against MAC.

GAME SUMMARY: MAC 0 UM 37

Game number eighteen of the Mitten State pigskin series resulted in another Michigan victory. The Wolverines chalked up their fifteenth series win thanks to another strong game by Kipke and his teammates. Michigan extended the winning streak over the Aggies to eight games. It was also their fifth straight shutout.

Not a lot of good news here for the Aggies. In fact, there was not any good news other than the money they received for coming to Ann Arbor for another "beat down" in front of a bunch of Wolverine fans. This game made the front page of the Detroit Free Press on Sunday, October 28, 1923. The headline read: Maize and Blue Crushes Over-Matched Aggies in Annual Game, Score 37-0." (*DFP*, 10/28/1923, Page 20) Harry Kipke opened the scoring in the first quarter with one of his two touchdowns. Jack Miller, Charles Grube. Fred Parker and Ernie Vick added touchdowns to the Michigan scoresheet. Apparently, every player on the Michigan roster saw action, good action, in the game. (*DFP*, 10/28/1923, Page 20)

Team	1st	2nd	3rd	4th	Final
MAC	0	0	0	0	0
UM	12	7	7	18	37

SERIES UPDATE:

After eighteen games it continued to look like a very one-way (fourteen games in Ann Arbor) and one-sided (fifteen wins for UM and only two for the Aggies with one tie) football event. The Wolverines owned an outstanding record of 15 wins, 2 losses, and 1 tie. The over-matched Aggies were now sitting on a disappointing record of 2 wins, 15 losses, and 1 tie. The good news for the Aggies was that things could not get much worse, or could they?

SERIES MILESTONES:

Ralph Young became the ninth straight coach to lose his first game against the Maize and Blue bullies. Like his mentor, Fielding Yost, Coach Young would spend his off season trying to figure out a way to win more games, especially against Michigan!

SEASON SUMMARIES:

The MAC footballers lost their next two games to Ohio Wesleyan (19-14) and Creighton (27-7) before ending the misery with a narrow win over Detroit (2-0). The Aggies finished the 1923 season with a record of 3 wins, 5 losses, and 0 ties. That made it four straight losing seasons. Ugh! The Ralph Young Era in East Lansing was off to a shaky start. However, the likeable coach was given a chance to make things right the next season. So, that is what he set out to do!

Fielding Yost's football machine gathered more momentum after their win over MAC and they kept rolling through the rest of their schedule. They defeated three more conference teams (Iowa, Wisconsin, and Minnesota) and hammered the Quantico Marines (26-6). The Wolverines ended with a perfect record of 8 wins, 0 losses, and 0 ties. Michigan scored one-hundred and fifty points during the season and only allowed twelve. Their dominating season enabled them to win the Big Ten Conference Championship and the national championship as well. This was Coach Yost's sixth national championship and certainly one of his most satisfying since it came after some "down" years. Yes, "the old man" could still coach at a high level. Center Jack Blott was named All-American for his stellar season. It was the third straight year that Michigan had at least one All-American player.

Game # 19: October 11, 1924 at College Field in East Lansing

BACKGROUND INFORMATION:

Once again, the rules makers made a conscious effort to let the game go and just let it grow. There were no new rules or changes in the game for the 1924 season.

The biggest change for the nineteenth game of the UM vs MAC series was the absence of Fielding Yost as the "official" head coach of the Michigan football team. It seems that the long time Michigan coach thought that he could give up coaching his beloved Wolverines to devote his full-time efforts to his duties as athletic director. Yost wanted to build a new stadium in Ann Arbor and wanted to have the time to do it right and do it BIG!

George Little, Fielding Yost's trusted assistant for the last two seasons, was the Michigan head coach for the 1924 season. Michigan fans were wondering how it would all turn out for the defending national champions. Mr. Yost had a difficult time tearing himself away from his beloved football team. He was frequently seen at practices and on the field during many of the games. He was probably around more than Coach Little desired, but that is another story.

Another big change was the fact that the game would be played in East Lansing in a new stadium that had not been "officially" dedicated even though it was a year old. The Aggies played at "new" College Field for the entire 1923 season and posted a record of 2-2-0. However, the Aggies wanted to christen College Field against their in-state rivals from Ann Arbor.

Yost, who was now the Michigan athletic director, graciously accepted MAC's "invitation" to participate in the dedication game. Coach Ralph Young was preparing his team for a better result this season and hopefully, a victory in the special series game. The Wolverines entered the nineteenth series game with a record of 1 win, 0 losses, and 0 ties. They defeated Miami of Ohio by a score of 55-0. It appeared that Michigan was ready for the Aggies.

Ralph Young had his Aggies off to strong start. They won their first two games against North Central College of Illinois (59-0) and Olivet (54-3). MSC looked like they might be ready for the hated invaders form Ann Arbor. The big question was, "Were the Aggie warm up games against two smaller schools enough to get the farmers ready for Michigan?"

GAME SUMMARY: MICHIGAN 7 MAC 0

The fired-up Aggies gave the Wolverines all they could handle in this classic in-state battle. As always, the tackling was hard, the emotions were high and plenty of blood was spilled to "officially" christen "new" College Field. Both defenses were strong, especially against the run. Michigan guard Edward "Butch" Slaughter was particularly effective on both sides of the ball. He was the only player on the field that day to earn All-American honors at the end of the season.

Michigan only earned three first downs during the game and one was on a penalty. The Aggies fared slightly better with four first downs. MAC had some good scoring opportunities, but they all end in missed field goals. An Associated Press story that ran in the *Battle Creek Enquirer and Evening News (BCEEN)* summed it up nicely: "One lone touchdown scored in the closing minutes of play, won for Michigan here this afternoon in one of the hardest battles ever staged between the state university and the state agricultural college." *(BCEEN,* 10/12/1924, Page 12)

With two minutes to play, the Wolverines turned to the pass even though they had already thrown three interceptions to Aggie defenders. Michigan claimed victory on a 45-yard pass-and-run play from Freddy Parker to team captain Herb Steger. This was the official end to the dedication festivities as the Wolverines spoiled this special day in Aggie football history. Another reason for the Aggies and their fans to really, really hate Michigan! *(BCEEN,* 10/12/1924, Page 12)

Image 4 The "dedication" game in 1924 was an important day in MAC football history. (Permission: Bentley Historical Library at The University of Michigan, See Page 369)

Team	1st	2nd	3rd	4th	Final
UM	0	0	0	7	7
MAC	0	0	0	0	0

SERIES UPDATE:

For the record, Michigan upped their series slate to 16-2-1. Once again, the Wolverines left East Lansing with another victory. However, I am sure they were exhausted from the effort. Michigan knew they were lucky to win and were relieved that another game against the Aggies was over. The Wolverines did not come to East Lansing very often, but every trip had earned them a victory (3) except for the tie in 1908.

The devastated Aggies must have been wondering why Michigan kept winning these series games. The good news was that it was not a "blow out", but it was still a shutout—the sixth straight for Michigan. The farmers from East Lansing showed a ton of "fight" in this game. However, until they could score some points, the best they could ever hope for was a tie. Ralph Young had to put this game out of his mind since he had a game to play next week. Finding a way to score and win against Michigan would be on his mind for a long time.

SERIES MILESTONES:

Obviously, the dedication of College Field was the big news in this game, but so was the crowd! (Note: although the stadium did not have an official name, it was referred to as College Field in the dedication game program according to author Steve Grinczel in *Michigan State Football-They are Spartans*. (Grinczel, Page 24) A huge gathering (20,500) shattered the old East Lansing series attendance record by almost twelve-thousand people. The Aggies also made it even more special by making it a Homecoming encounter as well. This would be the first and only time that this series game was held on a Homecoming weekend in East Lansing. The historic series game was the first series game to be "called" on the radio as Jimmy Hasselman described the pigskin action on local station WKAR. (Grinczel, Page 24) It was also the first series game for Coach George Little and his first, and last, series win. He was the third straight Michigan coach to win against the Aggies in his first try.

SEASON SUMMARIES:

The Wolverines traveled to Champaign, Illinois for their second straight dedication game the following week. Unfortunately, the Illinois game did not go as well for the Wolverines. Coach Bob Zuppke turned a football force named Harold "Red" Grange loose against the Wolverines. It was ugly! Grange returned the opening kickoff for a touchdown and proceeded to run over, around and through the Michigan defense all day long. When it was over, Grange had scored five touchdowns, earned the nickname "Galloping Ghost," and captured a place in college football history—forever! Illinois demolished Michigan by a score of 39-14. It was one of the worst road losses in the history of Michigan football.

Coach Little's team came back strong the next four games by posting shutout wins against Wisconsin, Minnesota, Northwestern, and Ohio State. However, they lost the season finale on Homecoming Day to Iowa (9-2). George Little finished with a record of 6 wins and 2 losses. In January 1925, Little moved on to Wisconsin and became the Badger Athletic Director and Head Football Coach. Yost would return to the sidelines at Michigan in 1925 with the same two titles.

Coach Ralph Young's Aggies were disappointed and probably mad when they took the field the next week. The poor lads from Chicago YMCA paid the price as the Aggies pounded them by a score of 34-3. The Aggies lost another tough game to Northwestern (13-9) but came back to defeat Lake Forest of Illinois (42-13). They split their final two games by losing to St. Louis (9-3) and finishing with a win over South Dakota State (9-0). MAC finished with a winning record of 5 victories and 3 defeats. It was the first winning season in East Lansing since 1918. The farmers displayed a lot of "fight" in 1924 and gave their fans some hope that things would continue to improve.

Game # 20: October 3, 1925 at Ferry Field in Ann Arbor

BACKGROUND INFORMATION:

Believe it or not, there would be no significant rules changes for the 1925 season. The game of American college football was in a good place and there was no need to change anything for now.

Three BIG changes marked the 1925 game between the hated pigskin rivals from East Lansing and Ann Arbor. First, Michigan Agricultural College (MAC) was now called Michigan State College of Agriculture and Applied Science (MSC for short). Second, the mascot changed from Aggies to Spartans. Third, Coach Ralph Young was back for his third season.

The newly named Spartans played one game before their trip to Ann Arbor. Adrian proved to be a good "warm up" game since the MSC footballers won by a score of 16-0. Coach Young's third season was off to a good start. Of course, a win over the Wolverine tormentors would make it a "great" start to the 1925 season!

For the first time in series history, Michigan began the season with a game against their rivals from East Lansing. There were no "warm up" games this time—it was simply game on! The Wolverines had several strong players back for another year. And, by the way, they had a man named Yost on the sidelines once again. Yes, expectations were high again in Ann Arbor.

GAME SUMMARY: MSC 0 UM 39

The annual in-state pigskin battle drew the largest crowd (30,000) for a season opening game in Michigan football history! Previous season openers saw less than half that total. Once again, interest throughout the state caused the large crowd. All Spartan fans in attendance were hoping to be "dancing" in the streets after another upset victory.

The Wolverines quickly extinguished any thoughts of a Spartan upset win right from the start. Michigan scored two touchdowns and one extra point after touchdown in the first quarter and led by a score of 13-0 at halftime. They really poured it on in the third quarter with a twenty-six-point outburst. When it was over the scoreboard showed 39 points for Michigan and 0 for MSC. (*DFP*, 10/4/1925, Page 21)

Once again, Michigan's "stars" came out to shine in this game. Center Robert Brown and tackles Thomas Edwards and Harry Hawkins were impressive on offense and defense. All three men were named All-Americans at the end of the season. Two more players, quarterback Benny Friedman and end Bennie Oosterbaan also impressed the fans and the sportswriters with their marvelous play. The "Benny-to-Bennie" passing combination became famous and enabled the Wolverines to win many, many games over two seasons. Friedman ran for one touchdown and threw for two more while Oosterbaan caught two touchdown passes. Bruce Gregory, Dick Babcock, and Louis Gilbert also scored touchdowns for Michigan. Unfortunately, the Spartans had no answer for Michigan's "stars" and could not score either. Not a good day for Sparty! (*DFP*, 10/4/1925, Page 21)

SERIES UPDATE:

The most recent Wolverine victory looked a lot like the six previous wins over the victims from East Lansing. It was another shutout, which made it seven straight scoreless games for the Aggie/Spartans. Even worse, it was also Michigan's tenth consecutive series victory! So, the Wolverine advantage over the Aggie/Spartans now stood at 17 wins, 2 losses, and 1 tie.

Team	1st	2nd	3rd	4th	Final
MSC	0	0	0	0	0
UM	13	0	26	0	39

SERIES MILESTONES:

The 1925 version of the in-state series game produced several notable milestones. First, this was the twentieth game of the series. Second, as already mentioned, it was the first time in the series that it was the season opener for a Michigan football team. Third, this was the first series game between The University of Michigan and Michigan State College of Agriculture and Applied Science. Fourth, as already stated, the MSC mascot was now a Spartan, not an Aggie. Hopefully, the footballers could take on a new persona that would aid their football cause. Spartans just sounds a lot more intimidating than Aggies and better than the "Michigan Staters", which almost became the nickname, can you imagine that? Finally, this was the first time that five All-Americans, all from Michigan, played in a series game.

SEASON SUMMARIES:

Unfortunately, the first season of MSC Spartan football history did not end so well in East Lansing. Ralph Young's team had a few "ups" during the season but more "downs" which is why they ended the season with a record of 3 victories and 5 defeats. The Spartans managed to defeat Centre College in week four by a score of 15-13. Unfortunately, they lost three of the final four games of the season. Fortunately, they were able to win big in their Homecoming Game against Toledo (58-0). The Homecoming win over Toledo was probably the highlight of the season. Coach Ralph Young knew he had a lot of work to do, and the likeable coach was hoping that he would be around the next season to make some improvements to Spartan football.

The Wolverines used the momentum of their big win over MSC to roll through their next four opponents without allowing a point. Michigan's winning streak came to a sloppy, sudden halt when they went to Northwestern to play the Wildcats in a miserable, rainy mess in Evanston. No touchdowns were scored but Northwestern kicked a field goal which trumped Michigan's safety. Final score: Wildcats 3 and Michigan 2. The Wolverines shutout Ohio State (10-0) and Minnesota (35-0) to finish with a final record of 7 wins and 1 loss.

Michigan scored two hundred and twenty-seven points and only allowed three for the season. The Aggies probably felt no shame for not scoring against the Wolverines. Michigan finished first in the Big Ten Conference with a record of 5 wins and 1 loss and tied Alabama for the title of second-best team in the nation, just behind Dartmouth. Many year's later Fielding Yost called the 1925 team "my greatest eleven." (Perry, Page 117) However, Yost stuck to his guns with his claim and never wavered on the greatness of the 1925 team. Again, the talent was exceptional as three linemen (Brown, Edwards and Hawkins) were named All-Americans in addition to Benny Freidman and Bennie Oosterbaan.

Game # 21: October 9, 1926 at Ferry Field in Ann Arbor

BACKGROUND INFORMATION:

Once again, the rules makers saw no need to change the game for the 1926 season. Things were going very well for college football. Some minor tweaks were on the horizon, but no changes were made in 1926.

The twenty-first game of the series was played again in Ann Arbor for the sixteenth time. Michigan's Athletic director and Coach Fielding Yost had plans for a bigger and better stadium in 1927. This was the last series game at Ferry Field. Michigan enjoyed a significant advantage in this historic venue. More on that later.) Coach Fielding Yost was back for his twenty-fifth season.

Ralph Young's Spartans began the season with shutout wins over Adrian (16-0) and Kalamazoo (9-0). However, victories over the smaller in-state schools did not always mean that the Aggie/Spartans were ready for Michigan. Unfortunately for the Spartans, this season would be no different. Ralph Young probably did not sleep much the week before the Michigan game. He may have been having nightmares about Friedman and Oosterbaan.

The Wolverines warmed up with an easy win over Oklahoma A & M (42-3) before facing the Spartans. As usual, Coach Yost had a bevy of returning stars (including Friedman and Oosterbaan). Yes, expectations were high for the Wolverines in 1926.

GAME SUMMARY: MSC 3 UM 55

Once again, Michigan played the role of "totally rude" hosts and mauled the Spartans in front of thirty-three thousand fans. The Wolverines scored early and often and probably played every man on the bench. Benny Friedman and Bennie Oosterbaan both played like the All-Americans that they were. The Spartans had no answer for this lethal passing combination. To make matters worse, many other Wolverine stars shined in this one-sided game.

Team	1st	2nd	3rd	4th	Final
MSC	0	3	0	0	3
UM	21	14	6	14	55

The *Detroit Free Press* headline was short and to the point: "Michigan Rolls Over State Eleven. 55-3" (*DFP*, 10/10/1926, Page 19) The only good news for the Spartans was a second quarter drop-kick field goal (35-yards) by MSC 's Paul Smith. The bad news was that Michigan scored a whole lot more. Michigan took charge right from the start and had twenty-one points on the board before the first quarter ended. The Wolverines poured on fourteen more points in the second quarter and led 35-3 at halftime. Yost's footballers added twenty more points in the second half. The avalanche of points ended at 55 for Michigan and 3 for Michigan State.

By the time the game ended, Michigan outgained the Spartans in the air and on the ground. In addition, the Wolverines posted twenty-three first downs to only four for MSC. Seven different Michigan Men scored touchdowns in this game. Fullback Bo Molenda led the way with two scores. Benny Oosterbaan, Benny Friedman, Bill Flora, Harold Greenwald, Sam Babcock, and Bill Puckelwartz all crossed the Spartan goal line. (*DFP*, 10/10/1926, Page 19)

SERIES UPDATE:

Michigan's decisive victory raised their record to 18 wins, 2 losses, and 1 tie. The Spartans left town to ponder another embarrassing defeat at the hands of the hated Wolverines. The Wolverines now had eleven straight series wins! At least the Spartans scored, although it was only a field goal. The sad reality was that unless the MSC footballers could score more points and allow fewer, nothing was going to change.

SERIES MILESTONES:

Once again, series game number twenty-one produced two significant series milestones. The last game at Ferry Field was like most of the others because Michigan won as they usually did. The Wolverines fared very well in the fifteen series games played at Ferry Field. They finished with a final record of 13 wins, 2 losses, and 0 ties.

That type of winning works out to a percentage just below eighty-five percent. (.846). Series game number twenty-one was also the last series game for Coach Fielding Harris Yost. Coach Yost's teams dominated the Aggies/Spartans in the nineteen series games they played. Yost's final record against the East Lansing footballers was a very impressive 16 wins, 2 losses and 1 tie. His final winning percentage was almost eighty-seven percent (.868). It does not get any better than that against a rival!

SEASON SUMMARIES:

After the Michigan loss, the Spartans continued to slide into football oblivion. They lost to Cornell (24-14) and tied Lake Forest (0-0). MSC finished the season with losses against Colgate (38-6) and Haskell Institute (40-7), before winning against Centre College (42-14).

Ralph Young's footballers posted their second straight losing season (3-4-1) and the third in Coach Young's four-year tenure. Lots of questions surrounded the Spartan football program, but the biggest one was, "Would Ralph Young be back to coach the Spartans in 1927?"

The Wolverines hosted Minnesota the next week and beat the Gophers by a score of 20-0. They kept on winning against Illinois (13-0) and then took a one-game break from Big Ten play. The Wolverines traveled to Baltimore to play a strong Navy team. Bad idea! The Midshipmen sunk Michigan's hopes for a perfect season by handing the Wolverines a 10-0 defeat. The Wolverines won their final three games to finish the season with a final record of 7 wins and 1 loss.

It is interesting to note that the final game of the season was also against Minnesota. It was the first and only time in Big Ten conference history that two teams played each other twice during the same season. Michigan finished the season with a perfect conference record (5-0) and won the championship for the second straight year. Benny Friedman and Bennie Oosterbaan were both named All-Americans for the second consecutive season. This was the first time that a passing combination earned such honors.

Fielding Yost probably came within ten points of his seventh national championship. Still, it was an exceptional ending to an extraordinary coaching career. Fielding Yost's Michigan career ended with an overall record of 165 wins, 29 losses, and 10 ties. His teams won 10 Big Ten Titles and 6 national championships. Coach Yost's final winning percentage was just over eighty-three percent (.833). After twenty-five seasons, the Wolverine coaching legend was now focused on two things: 1) Build a magnificent football stadium. 2) Figure out how to fill it for every game!

Game # 22: October 8, 1927 at Michigan Stadium in Ann Arbor

BACKGROUND INFORMATION:

The first adjustments to the rules in five years was enacted in 1927. To increase player safety, the goal posts were moved from the goal line, where players often ran into them, to the back of the end zone. This would, of course, make it harder to kick a field goal since the distance had been increased by ten yards, but there were few complaints.

Player safety trumped scoring and that was the right decision! Another subtle change required any player who shifted to a new spot on the field to come to a stop for at least one second before the snap of the ball. (Herget, Page 167)

The twenty-second game of the in-state series was played in Ann Arbor for the third straight season which was not unusual. What was unusual was the fact that the game was scheduled for a venue called Michigan Stadium. As it turned out, Fieldling Yost decided that the "dedication" game honors for Michigan Stadium would go to the Ohio State Buckeyes, not the Michigan State College Spartans. This gesture was probably interpreted by some Spartan fans as another slap in the face by Michigan since the Aggies had delayed their stadium dedication by one year to include the Wolverines in 1924. Chalk up another reason for Spartans not to like Wolverines! Oh yes, this would be the twentieth series game played in the month of October.

The good news was that Michigan State College began the 1927 season with the same coach for the fifth straight year. The bad news was that Ralph Young had only posted one winning season in his tenure. Worse yet, he was 0-4-0 against the Wolverines. Coach Young was hoping that would change when his Spartans traveled to Ann Arbor for another gridiron battle. With the departure of the legendary Yost, maybe things would change for the better in the one way and one-sided series. The MSC footballers started their season with two wins over Kalamazoo (12-6) and Ohio University (27-0). They were as ready as they were going to be in 1927.

In addition to a new stadium, the Wolverines also had a new coach in 1927. Elton "Tad" Wieman, who captained the 1918 Wolverine football team, was hired to replace Coach Yost in 1927. The Wolverines started fast in their new stadium and chalked up a nice win (33-0) over Ohio Weslayan. The Spartans were the second team to play in Yost's cavernous new creation.

GAME SUMMARY: MSC 0 UM 21

The biggest surprise in this game was not the score, Michigan defeated the Aggies again, but it was not a complete blowout. The Spartans did not embarrass themselves, but they did not win either. No, the real surprise was the sparse attendance.

Although the new stadium seated over eighty-thousand people for the last three home games, the MSC game only attracted about twenty-eight thousand fans. Maybe the previous history between the two schools caused some fans to think it would be another Wolverine blowout, so why bother? Maybe everyone's social schedule was just too busy to get to the game. This would have been a perfect opportunity for Spartans to flood the new stadium in green and white and cheer their Spartans on to victory. It did not happen. Nope, not by a long shot!

The Wolverines played a solid game on offense and dominated the Spartan offense all day. They scored two rushing touchdowns (Louis Gilbert and George Rich) and had a touchdown pass from Leo Hoffman to Bennie Oosterbaan. Once again, the Spartans did not score a point for the eighth time in nine games. It is always impossible to win a game when you do not score. Sadly, this one went down in the defeat column, again, for the Spartans. (*DFP*, 10/9/1927, Page 21)

Team	1st	2nd	3rd	4th	Final
MSC	0	0	0	0	0
UM	7	7	0	7	21

Michigan won easily, but they did not embarrass their guests from East Lansing. The final score was a lot closer than the previous two blowouts. The Aggies/Spartans continued to measure their series progress against Michigan in "baby steps." While wins and ties were harder to achieve, moral victories could be earned by keeping the score close instead of suffering another blowout loss. Maybe the Spartans counted this as a moral victory. What do you think?

SERIES UPDATE:

After twenty-two series games, Michigan owned 19 wins, 2 losses, and 1 tie. The Aggies/Spartans had not won a series game since 1915. The annual football game between Michigan and Michigan State couldn't be called a "rivalry" yet. The Spartans had to start winning a few more games before this "one-way and one-sided" pigskin matchup could officially declared "a rivalry!"

SERIES MILESTONES:

The 1927 game was significant for multiple reasons. First, it was the first series game in Michigan Stadium. Second, it was Michigan's first series win in the new stadium and MSC's first loss. Third, it was the first game for Coach Elton "Tad" Wieman and his first series victory. Fourth, this was the twentieth series game played in the month of October. Finally, it was the last game for Coach Ralph Young. Coach Young loved MSC and he loved his Spartans, but he did not win enough games, especially against Michigan. He did not win any series games. Yes, it was time for another change in East Lansing. The MSC administrators liked the affable Young and elevated him from coach to full-time athletic administrator. He served successfully in this capacity until his retirement in 1954.

SEASON SUMMARIES:

The Spartans lost three straight games after the Michigan game which put them at 2 wins and 4 losses for the season. They won two straight against Albion (20-6) and Butler (25-0) but lost the final game against North Carolina State by a score of 19-0. Coach Ralph Young ended his final season a little better than when he started by finishing with four wins compared to only three in 1923.

Coach Ralph Young's record at MAC/MSC finished at 18 wins, 22 losses, and 1 tie. Unfortunately, he lost all five series games against the Wolverines. Ralph Young's first job as athletic director was to hire his replacement. He was looking for someone special, someone who could get the Spartans to a much better place in their football exploits. No pressure, right?

After their win over MSC, the Wolverines defeated Wisconsin (14-0). Then, it was time to dedicate Michigan Stadium. Michigan defeated Ohio State (21-0) at the "official" stadium dedication game on October 22, 1927. The Wolverines split the last four games with wins over Chicago and Navy and losses to Illinois and Minnesota. Mr. Yost must have been thrilled with the fact that Michigan set two attendance records in Michigan Stadium's first season. A huge throng (84,401) showed up for the Ohio State game and then the same amount plus twenty-three more people showed up for the Homecoming Finale against Minnesota.

Michigan had a winning season under Coach Wieman (6-2-0) and Yost had an impressive attendance record for the first year in his football cathedral. The Wolverines ended with a third-place finish in the Big Ten (3-2-0) which was good for most schools, but not Michigan. I am sure that Athletic Director Yost had an interesting meeting with his rookie football coach at the end of the season. I do not know the exact topics of their conversation, but I am sure that it included things like winning more games, especially Big Ten games. Mr. Yost had a magnificent stadium to fill so things had to improve, or else!

Game # 23: November 17, 1928 at Michigan Stadium in Ann Arbor

BACKGROUND INFORMATION:

The college football rules makers chose not to make any new rules and did not want to tweak anything else for the 1928 season. They were still watching the impact of the goal post shift in 1927. There was no need to change anything else. As always, some minor modifications were being considered, but were not implemented in 1928.

The 1928 Spartan football team had a new leader, a Lansing native and former Michigan All-American, named Harry Kipke. Ralph Young, a former Wolverine himself, thought he had the perfect man at the perfect time. Yost was gone and Tad Wieman was not doing that great. Would this be the start of something big in Spartan football history? The Kipke Era at Michigan State College started off big, really BIG! His Spartans blasted Kalamazoo by a score of 103-0. It was the largest winning margin for a season opener in Aggie/Spartan football history.

Maybe this Kipke guy was just what the Spartans needed. After one game, Harry Kipke probably looked like an incarnation of Fielding Yost himself. Yes, it was only one game, but Athletic Director Ralph Young probably looked like a genius. Not so fast! Kipke's speeding train flew off the tracks the next week against Albion after a 2-0 loss. Harry Kipke's Spartans went into the final two games of the season (Michigan and North Carolina State) with a record of 2 wins, 3 losses, and 1 tie. If the Spartans' won the last two games, they could finish with a winning record (4-3-1) and series bragging rights for one year! Would Kipke have his MSC footballers ready to play?

Michigan began the second season of the Tad Wieman Era in a historic way, but not a good way. First, they lost the home opener to Ohio Weslayan (17-7). It was the first loss in a season opener in the forty-nine-year history of Michigan football. To make matters worse, they loss the next three games which meant that they had lost four consecutive games to start a season.

68

Once again, this had never happened in the forty-nine-year history of Michigan football. The Wolverines were winless in October 1928. It is a miracle that Mr. Yost did not fire his former captain in the middle of the season! Things improved slightly when the calendar moved to November since the Wolverines defeated Illinois (3-0) and tied Navy (6-6). They had a record of 1 win, 4 losses, and 1 tie heading into the MSC game. Would Michigan have enough to defeat MSC?

GAME SUMMARY: MSC 0 MICHIGAN 3

The twenty-third game of the one-way and one-sided series ended like so many of the games in the past. The Wolverines chalked up their twentieth victory against the Aggie/Spartans. Once again, the Spartans played a spirited game. I am sure that the blocking and tackling was ferocious. Michigan found a way to win on a field goal and the Spartans came up empty again.

A *Detroit Free Press* reporter told the game's story in one extended sentence that read: "Through the medium of a placement goal kicked by Maurice Hughes from the 21-yard line early in the second period the eleven representing Michigan qualified to beat Michigan State in the Michigan bowl this afternoon." (*DFP*, 11/18/1928, Page 21)

By all accounts, it was an ugly game. It rained steadily for the entire second half and both teams had more penalties than points. I do not know how many fumbles there were in the game, but I am thinking there were a few, or maybe many! The victorious Wolverines managed to gain a whopping total of 111-yards compared to MSC's 74-yards. The Spartans actually won the first down battle by a margin of 9 to 7.

Unfortunately, it was their only "win" of the day. No doubt, more blood was shed by both teams on that November day and probably some Spartan tears. Once again, the Spartans could claim a small moral victory because of the closeness of the score. Or maybe not. It was simply another bitter disappointment for the East Lansing footballers.

Team	1st	2nd	3rd	4th	Final
MSC	0	0	0	0	0
UM	0	3	0	0	3

SERIES UPDATE:

Michigan's narrow win was their thirteenth consecutive series victory. After twenty-three games, the series remained strongly in favor of Michigan. The Wolverine series record improved to 20 wins, 2 losses, and 1 tie. The frustrated Aggies were now sitting on a disappointing record of 2 wins, 20 losses, and 1 tie. The good news for the Aggies was that things could not get much worse, or could they?

SERIES MILESTONES:

There are many important historical facts that took place in the 1928 Mitten State pigskin matchup. First, it was the first time, and only, time that both schools had former Wolverine captains leading both teams. Second, it was Harry Kipke's first and last game at the helm of Spartan football. Harry Kipke could not beat the Wolverines. Instead, he decided to rejoin them after Mr. Yost asked Tad Wieman to leave. Third, it was Coach Wieman's last game. He finished with a perfect series record (2-0-0), but he did not do as well in the Big Ten. The impatient Yost had seen enough. It was time to find a new leader of the Wolverine football program. Fourth, it was only the third time that the two teams faced off in November. Fifth, Michigan's victory was their twentieth in the series and that accomplishment gave them the distinction of being the first team to win that many series games. Finally, it was also the first time that the rivals finished with the exact same season record (3-4-1).

SEASON SUMMARIES:

Harry Kipke did not stay long enough to do much for Spartan football, but he did accomplish two things. First, he gave the Spartan fans some fun, and probably some "false hope" with a season opening "slaughter" of poor Kalamazoo College (103-0). Unfortunately, he should have told his team to save some of those points for the next week since they lost by a score of 2-0 to Albion. Second, Harry Kipke had his Spartans ready to play against their Wolverine tormentors. The Spartans saved their best effort for Michigan, but it was not enough. Once again, the hated Wolverines found a way to win and the Aggies came up short again. Yes, Harry Kipke was another "one and done" coach in East Lansing. His final Spartan record was 3 wins, 4 losses, and 1 tie. That made it four consecutive losing seasons for the Aggie/Spartans. Worse yet, Ralph Young had to find another new football coach.

The Tad Wieman Era ended with a thud in Ann Arbor on November 24, 1928. Despite going undefeated in his last four games (3-0-1), Wieman's "record setting" start doomed his Wolverine coaching career. Michigan finished with a final record of 3-4-1 in 1928. It was the first losing season in Wolverine football since 1919. Michigan only won two of five games in the Big Ten. A seventh-place conference finish was not good enough for Mr. Yost or anyone else in Ann Arbor! The only good news was that tackle Otto Pommerening earned All-American honors. That made it eight straight seasons with at least one All-American for the Wolverines. Mr. Yost was not a happy man at the end of the 1928 season. Coach Wieman's two seasons had only yielded a record of 9 wins, 6 losses, and 1 tie. Unfortunately, those numbers were not good enough for his former coach. It was time for Tad Wieman to move on.

Fielding Yost had a huge stadium to fill and losing teams would not attract the large followings that he envisioned. The impatient Yost immediately turned to Harry Kipke who was delighted to spurn the Spartans and return to his alma mater. Obviously, Spartan fans felt jilted because of Kipke's abrupt departure, but that is what happened! One more reason for MSC folks not to think too fondly of the fine people in Ann Arbor.

Game # 24: October 5, 1929 at Michigan Stadium in Ann Arbor

BACKGROUND INFORMATION:

Two important rules changes took place in 1929. First, all fumbles were ruled dead at the point of recovery and could not be advanced. Second, in a continuing effort to enhance the passing game, the size of ball was decreased by one-half inch as measured around the middle of the ball. Of course, this made it easier for a man with "average" sized hands to throw the ball more accurately. (Herget, Page 167)

The 1929 football season in Ann Arbor was number fifty for the Wolverines. Maybe the Maize and Blue footballers would do something special in honor of this season. The last game of the decade of the 1920s was the twenty-fourth game of the now annual football series. It was scheduled in Ann Arbor for the fifth straight season. This series tussle would also be the third straight series game at Michigan Stadium.

Both teams were starting new eras as each school had hired new coaches since the last game. Harry "The Traitor" Kipke had jumped ship from East Lansing to his dream job in Ann Arbor. Jim "Sleepy" Crowley, a former Notre Dame standout was brought in to right the listing Spartan football ship!

Mr. Young wanted to set Coach Crowley up for success so the first team on the schedule was Alma College. Crowley's footballers won the game by a score of 59-6. The undefeated Spartans (1-0-0) traveled to Ann Arbor for their second game of the season against Kipke and Michigan. Many of the Spartan players wanted to show their old coach that he should have stayed in East Lansing. They really, really wanted to win this game. Believe it!

The Wolverines got off to a much better start in 1929 than they did in 1928. They began the season with a football "doubleheader" against Albion and Mount Union and won both games on the same day! Fielding Yost borrowed this idea from baseball. He was hoping to create more interest in the early season schedule and, of course, bring more fans to his gigantic stadium. It was great idea, but it did not work that well. Only about sixteen thousand people showed up for this historical event. In fairness to the fans of the era, the nation was in the early stages of the Great Depression. People were thinking carefully about how they spent the money they had, if they had any. Regardless, Coach Kipke's Wolverines appeared to be ready for the Spartans. Of course, Mr. Yost was hoping for a bigger crowd, much bigger.

GAME SUMMARY: MSC 0 UM 17

Michigan defeated the Spartans, but it was another tough game for both teams. Yes, it was another physical battle highlighted by hard tackling and harder feelings! The main story line in the *Battle Creek Enquirer and Evening News* (*BCEEN*) read: "Michigan's game was methodical." The article also reported that the Wolverines did not attempt any sweeps and only threw one pass. (*BCEEN*, 10/6/1929, Page 16) It sounds like Kipke's game plan was simple: Run the ball down their throats and stuff the Spartan offense!

Kipke's plan worked to perfection. His offense rushed for 388-yards compared to only 129-yards for MSC. This approach allowed the Wolverines to control the ball and the clock. Joe Gembis, Michigan's star fullback/kicker, scored all the points that the Wolverines really needed in the first half. Gembis ran for a 1-yard touchdown and kicked a 17-yard field goal and one extra point. Sophomore running back Roy Hudson bolted for an 80-yard touchdown in the fourth quarter to seal Michigan's victory. Joe Gembis kicked the final extra point to finish the scoring at 17 points for Michigan and 0 points for MSC. (*BCEEN,* 10/6/1929, Page 16*)*

The Spartan players gave it everything they had, as did the Wolverines. Once again if you do not score you cannot win. There are no words to express the frustration, disappointment, and disdain that the Spartan players were probably feeling as they walked off the field on October 5, 1929.

Team	1st	2nd	3rd	4th	Final
MSC	0	0	0	0	0
UM	7	3	0	7	17

SERIES UPDATE:

Yes, this game was another step backward in the one-way and one-sided series that could not really be called a rivalry. A true rivalry means that each team gets their fair share of victories and the Spartans just did not have their fair share. Instead, they had their "unfair" share and it was getting old. This was the last series game of a dreadful decade of Aggie/Spartan football games against the hated Wolverines.

Michigan won every game of the decade. The Maize and Blue finished with 10 wins, 0 losses and 0 ties. To say they dominated the decade of the 1920's is an understatement. The Wolverines outscored the Aggies/Spartans by a margin of 307 to 3. At the end of 1929, Michigan now owned a series record of 21 wins, 2 losses, and 1 tie. It does not get any worse than that in football. Absolute rock bottom for the Spartans.

SERIES MILESTONES:

Game number twenty-four of the series marked the first game both Michigan and Michigan State College both had new coaches. It was the first game for Harry Kipke and Jim Crowley. Kipke got his first win and Crowley endured his first defeat. Harry Kipke also became the first, and only, man to coach each team in a series game. As I said earlier, Michigan won their fourteenth straight game which was a new series record. Finally, it was the first time that one team won every series game of a decade. It was the "Roaring Twenties" for Michigan and the "Boring Twenties" for the Aggies/Spartans and their fans. They were sick of losing to Michigan. Time to turn the page and see what the next decade had in store for Michigan and Michigan State.

SEASON SUMMARIES:

Coach Jim Crowley probably had trouble getting his Spartans focused for the next game after losing to Michigan. Unfortunately, MSC had to travel east to play a strong Colgate team. Unfortunately, the Spartans were not ready to play this game. Colgate won by a score of 31-0. Somehow, Coach Crowley got his team on the right track and they won four straight games before losing the finale to Detroit. The good news was that the Spartans finished with a record of 5 wins, and 3 losses. It was their first winning season since 1924. Maybe this Crowley guy could coach. Were things looking up for the East Lansing footballers?

The bad news was that Michigan lost three straight conference games after they defeated MSC. The good news was that they finished with two wins and one tie to end with a winning record of 5-3-1. Their conference record slipped to 1-3-1 which put them in a tie for eighth place. I am sure that the post-season meeting between Mr. Yost and his former All-American was short and to the point. Fortunately, for Coach Kipke, he got the message.

DECADE AND SERIES SUMMARY:

The second decade of the twentieth century was excellent for Michigan, but bad for MAC/MSC. No! It was terrible for the Aggies/Spartans. The Wolverines slipped a little in their overall performance level, but they were perfect against Michigan State. In addition to winning every series game, the Wolverines outscored MAC/MSC by a margin of 307 to 3! This meant that the Spartans had more coaches (5) than points (3) during the decade. There is no way to sugar coat this. It was bad for MSC.

Decade and Series Summary 1898 to 1929

Time Frame	UM Won-Lost-Tied	MSC Won-Lost-Tied
1920-1929	10-0-0	0-10-0
1898-1929	21-2-1	2-21-1

PROGRAM SUMMARIES:

The Aggie/Spartans lost a lot of ground in the series in the 1920s. Michigan now held a decisive edge in the football matchups and there was no end in sight. Things would have to change in the next decade or Michigan State might have to drop the hated Wolverines from their schedule. How much more humiliation could the Spartans and their fans endure at the hands of the hated Wolverines before they just put it in the past and moved on? Although the two teams were located about sixty miles from each other, the distance between the two football programs seemed like a thousand miles, or more! Michigan's overall record from 1920-1929 was better than the previous decade despite some turmoil in their head coaching position.

The Wolverines managed to win six more games in the 1920s and lost two less. They improved their winning percentage by almost fifty points (.724 to .769) and won another national championship to equal the one that they claimed in 1918. Michigan also improved the number of All-American players from nine to eleven in the decade of the twenties.

Program Summaries 1920 to 1929

Statistical Area	UM	MSC
Number of Head Coaches	4	5
Games Played	78	86
Wins	58	36
Losses	16	45
Ties	4	5
Winning Percentage	.769	447
Winning Seasons	9	2
Losing Seasons	1	8
Even Seasons	0	0
National Championships	1	0
All-American Players	11	0

Michigan State's performance declined in too many areas during the 1920s. The program was staggering badly. It was uncertain if they could make things much better in the 1930s. Obviously, the Spartans had to support Jim Crowley in his effort to build a winner in East Lansing. And, of course, Jim Crowley and his footballers had to win more football games, especially against Michigan! Things looked simple at the end of the 1920s: win or else! Any questions?

CHAPTER 6

Finally, A Real Rivalry? 1930 to 1939

Now it's time to take a closer look at the 1930s and see how Michigan and Michigan State did on the college football field. Would they improve on the accomplishments of the previous decade, take a step backward, or just remain the same. It is time to find out!

Coach Jim Crowley made some improvements in his first year and probably won back some wayward Spartan fans in the process. The folks in East Lansing were starving for a winning season in 1929 and he gave it to them. Now, another one was expected. And, of course, a win over Michigan would certainly be on every Spartan fan's mind as October approached. Michigan never measured their progress on the football field by how they did against Michigan State. However, the residents of East Lansing knew that Michigan was always the standard for football excellence in the Great Lakes State. Like it or not, beating Michigan was a BIG, BIG deal. A win against Michigan was something that Coach Crowley had to do if he wanted to keep his job and keep his program moving in the right direction.

Harry Kipke calmed most Michigan football fans down with his winning season in 1929. Of course, a record of 5 wins, 3 losses, and 1 tie did not inspire everyone in Ann Arbor. However, a winning season is always better than a losing one. Coach Kipke had many talented players coming back so he was optimistic about year two of his coaching tenure. Expectations were higher than in 1929, for sure! The fans probably figured they would have a winning season, but they wanted more, a lot more!

Game # 25: October 4, 1930 at Michigan Stadium in Ann Arbor

BACKGROUND INFORMATION:

The rules makers decided to take some air out of the ball for the 1930 season. Literally, that is what they did. In another effort to improve the passing game, the rules makers decided to the decrease the pressure of the ball from 14-15 pounds per square inch to 12.5-13.5 pounds per square inch. Even in those days the "passing pioneers" figured out that it was easier to throw a ball that had some "give." In 1930 the quarterback, or anybody else who was throwing the pigskin, could get a better grip on the ball and that was a good thing for the offense, but not the defense. It is unknown how the rule was enforced and if any "deflate gate" incidents occurred, but it shows you that things change over the years, but not that much! (Herget, Page 116)

Coach Jim Crowley was back for his second year and expectations were higher in East Lansing. Would the Spartans be able to string back-to-back winning seasons together for the first time since 1916? Crowley's footballers had another mismatch on the schedule. They took care of Alma by a score of 28-0. The Spartans would head to Ann Arbor with a modest winning streak of one game. Michigan State was off to a solid start, but they had been down this road before. Game two of the 1930 season was the one that Coach Crowley and his Spartans had been thinking about since the 1929 season. It was time to beat Michigan!

For the second straight year, Harry Kipke's Wolverines began the season with another of Mr. Yost's football doubleheaders. Michigan beat Denison (33-0) and then defeated a feisty Michigan Normal (now Eastern Michigan University) team by the score of 7-0. The Wolverines expected a tough test against the Spartans, or maybe not! Coach Kipke had high expectations for the 1930 season. A defeat at the hands of MSC was not part of the plan.

GAME SUMMARY: MSC 0 UM 0

The twenty-fifth game of the in-state gridiron gathering was another titanic struggle between two exceptional defenses who refused to give in! In typical fashion, the tackling was hard and maybe even vicious at times. I am certain that both teams shed equal shares of blood. The game attracted a smaller crowd (22,571) than Mr. Yost had hoped for. Michigan Stadium must have looked "empty" with such a low turnout, but that was the nature of the times. The scoreless deadlock stopped the Spartan series losing streak at fourteen games.

The game was a good news/bad news scenario for both teams. It was good that they played well-enough not to lose, but it was bad that they did not play well enough to win. Apparently, Michigan had a first- half touchdown nullified by an offside penalty. That's about as close as either team got to scoring. I am certain that Spartan fans "celebrated" the tie more than the Wolverine fans because the scoreless deadlock ended MSC's fourteen game losing streak to Michigan. That is just how it was back then. "Moral" victories were few and far between for the folks in East Lansing.

SERIES UPDATE:

For the first time since 1915, the Wolverine's failed to score in a series game. However, it did not cost them because they kept the Spartans off the scoreboard for the fourth straight year and the twelfth time in thirteen years. The series numbers did not change much. Michigan still had a decisive advantage. The Wolverines now owned a series advantage of 21 wins, 2 losses, and 2 ties which meant that the Spartans now had a series disadvantage of 2 wins, 21 losses, and 2 ties.

Team	1st	2nd	3rd	4th	Final
MSC	0	0	0	0	0
UM	0	0	0	0	0

SERIES MILESTONES:

Once again, the twenty-fifth game in the series became the second tie of the series. Both ties were 0-0 standoffs. It was also the first series game where a team (Michigan) wore uniforms with numbers on the front and back. Finally, it was the first series tie for Coaches Kipke and Crowley.

SEASON SUMMARIES:

The Spartans finished a successful season after their tie with the Wolverines. Michigan State won three straight games after their trip to Ann Arbor. They lost their first ever night game in Washington to Georgetown (14-13) and then defeated North Dakota State by a score of 19-11. Michigan State finished the season with another scoreless tie against the University of Detroit. Coach Crowley finished his second season with a final record of 5 wins, 1 loss, and 2 ties. Spartan quarterback, Roger Grove, became the third player in MSC football history to earn All-American honors in 1930. So, another winning season for the Spartans and a little bit of success against an incredibly good Michigan team. Something for Jim Crowley and Michigan State College to build on!

Even though the Wolverines could not beat Michigan State, they beat everybody else on their schedule. Michigan defeated a strong Harvard squad (15-7) on Homecoming Day. Then, the Wolverines swept their five Big Ten opponents, shutting out three of them. They won the conference title for the first time since 1926. Michigan finished Coach Kipke's second season with an excellent record of 8 wins, 0 losses, and 1 tie. Strangely enough, no Wolverines earned All-Americans honors during this excellent season.

Game # 26: November 14, 1931 at Michigan Stadium in Ann in Arbor

BACKGROUND INFORMATION:

There were no rules changes or "tweaks" for the 1931 season. The rules makers decided not to meddle with anything for this season. Instead, the NCAA rules keepers continued to watch the effect of the ball inflation issue and how it impacted the passing game.

The 1931 season called for the Michigan vs Michigan State game to be played in November for only the fourth time. Coach Crowley's third team began the season with easy wins over Alma (74-0) and Cornell College of Iowa (47-0). They lost to Army the next week but won two more. Syracuse ruined Homecoming Day since they defeated the Spartans 15-10. Maybe MSC was looking too far ahead to the Michigan game which was still two weeks away. It did not really matter because they took their frustrations out on poor Ripon College. Final score: MSC 100 and Ripon 0! Coach Crowley's team had scored in every game and the offense had rolled up some big numbers. Could this be another year when the Spartan offense and defense showed up at the same time in Ann Arbor?

Once again, Michigan started the season with another Yost favorite, the season opening doubleheader. So far, this experiment had been a "failure" from an attendance standpoint. The first set of games drew just over sixteen thousand in 1929, but only about thirteen thousand in 1930. Mr. Yost never scheduled any powerhouse teams for this event. Michigan won the first four games played under this format. The 1931 season would be no different. The Wolverines welcomed Central State Teacher's College and Michigan Normal (EMU) to Michigan Stadium and defeated them both by a combined margin of 61-0 in front of thirteen thousand people. Coach Kipke's team won their next game against Chicago but lost to Ohio State the following week. The Wolverines won three more after the OSU loss and took a record of 6-1-0 into the MSC game.

GAME SUMMARY: MSC 0 UM 0

The twenty-sixth series game ended just like the twenty-fifth game—another 0-0 tie. Michigan scored twenty-two points the week before in a shutout win over Indiana. The Spartans hit the century mark against Ripon. Neither team saved any points for this game. Yes, the Mitten State rivals played to their second straight scoreless deadlock. That made it eight straight series quarters without a point. Certainly, a tribute to the defenses of both teams and a wake-up call for the offensive coaches!

Team	1st	2nd	3rd	4th	Final
MSC	0	0	0	0	0
UM	0	0	0	0	0

SERIES UPDATE:

Once again, the series numbers remained strongly in favor of Michigan. The Wolverines now had an impressive record of 21-2-3. Michigan State's record slipped a little to 2 wins, 21 losses and, 3 ties.

SERIES MILESTONES:

There were four milestones that occurred in game number twenty-six of the UM vs MSC series. First, it was the first time that back-to-back ties happened in the series. Second, it was the only time that back-to-back ties by a 0-0 score ever took place between Michigan and Michigan State. Third, it was the seventh consecutive game played in Ann Arbor, breaking a streak of six games that were played at Ferry Field from 1918 to 1923. Finally, the gathering of 35,844 was a series record for Michigan Stadium although it was still rather small compared to the 42, 000 fans who showed up at Ferry Field in 1922 and 1923.

SEASON SUMMARIES:

Coach Crowley's third team finished flat in 1931. After the tie against Michigan the Spartans lost the final game against Detroit to end the season with a record of 5 wins, 3 losses, and 1 tie. The good news was that it was the third consecutive winning season for Crowley's Spartans. Of course, hitting the century mark against Ripon was another highlight. The bad news was that they failed to score against Michigan for the fifth straight time.

Coach Harry Kipke's Wolverines won their last two games and finished the season at 8 wins, 1 loss, and 1 tie. It was Kipke's third straight winning season. Michigan also earned a share of the Big Ten title with a record of 5-1-0. Center Maynard Morrison earned All-American honors for his stellar play in 1931.

Game # 27: October 1, 1932 at Michigan Stadium in Ann Arbor

BACKGROUND INFORMATION:

The 1932 season saw some important rules changes concerning safe play:

1. The ball would be declared dead and play stopped when any part of a player's body touched the ground except the hands or feet.
2. The use of flying blocks and tackles were prohibited and would result in a five-yard penalty.
3. Defensive players were not allowed to strike members of the offense in the head, neck, or face.
4. All hard, or dangerous, equipment had to be covered with approved padding. (Herget, Page 167)

Mitten State pigskin series game number twenty-seven in the series was played in Ann Arbor for the eighth straight season. Although it did not seem "fair" to Spartan fans, it was a very pragmatic decision by Athletic Director Ralph Young. Now that Michigan was back in the Big Ten, they had less difficulty scheduling games. The simple fact was that Michigan did not need Michigan State as much as Michigan State needed Michigan. If the Wolverines were going to play the Spartans, it would be on Mr. 8Yost's terms or not at all.

Actually, Michigan State did not really have a choice if they wanted to continue the "rivalry." However, there was also a financial advantage here for the Spartans. Even their new stadium was tiny compared to Yost's monstrosity. MSC always received a nice payout for every trip to Ann Arbor. Ralph Young was criticized heavily for this "arrangement," but it allowed him to stay on Michigan's schedule and it gave his athletic department more revenue than if they played a team like Alma, Adrian or Michigan Normal. Yes, Ralph Young sold his Spartan "soul" to the devilish Yost, but he did it for the team and the program.

Once again, Crowley's Spartans had a "warm-up" game under their belt when they faced the Wolverines. Apparently, many of the players from poor little Alma missed the bus or maybe they were just overmatched.

The Spartans came within seven points of reaching the century mark as they dominated from start to finish (93-0). Coach Crowley had nine returning starters on the 1932 team and he felt that this was the year to beat Michigan. Now, it was time to find out if Crowley's Spartans had the fight and the scoring ability to defeat the tormentors from Ann Arbor.

The Wolverines began the 1932 season with lots of question marks. The biggest one was who would replace a pair of star players (Maynard Morrison and Bill Hewitt) who had eligibility remaining but did not return. To make matters worse, they had a difficult schedule that would test them every week. Harry Kipke had his work cut out for him and his Wolverines in 1932. Michigan would open the season against their good friends from East Lansing.

GAME SUMMARY: MSC 0 UM 26

The Wolverines played the 1932 series game as if they were in mid-season form. The Spartans, on the other hand, looked as though they were tired from scoring so many points Alma the week before. Michigan played a strong game on offense, defense, and special teams. The Ann Arbor footballers scored in every quarter and kept the Spartans off the scoreboard for the sixth straight game. Detroit Free Press writer Tod Rockwell summarized the game like this: "Michigan's 1932 football team opened its season here this afternoon by smothering the running attack of Jim Crowley's Michigan State eleven and, unleashing a brilliant mixed running and passing offensive of its own, crushed the Spartans, 26-0." (*DFP*, 10/2/1932, Page 33)

Quarterback Harry Newman used the pass to keep the Spartans off-balance and then sent Michigan's strong runners through gaping holes in the Spartan defense. Four different Wolverines (John Regeczi, Stan Fay, John Heston, and Herman Everhardus) scored rushing touchdowns and Newman kicked two extra points. The game was played in front of another record setting crowd (33,786) for a season opener in Ann Arbor. Considering the hard times that many Americans were still experiencing, this was an impressive gathering!

Team	1st	2nd	3rd	4th	Final
MSC	0	0	0	0	0
UM	7	7	6	6	26

Michigan State went into this game with high hopes and an expectation of another long-awaited victory. Unfortunately, they left Ann Arbor with another disappointing loss. Obviously, the Michigan defense made it hard on the Spartans. Michigan's offense made it look easy and put plenty of points on the scoreboard. Once again, the Spartans did not score so they really did not have a chance in this game either. Yes, it was another big setback for the Spartans, but they still had a season to play. Coach Crowley probably told his men that they would be back next year. In the meantime, they had to get ready for Grinnel College.

SERIES UPDATE:

Michigan's win meant that they had not lost to an East Lansing football team since 1915. Their record over that span was 15 wins, 0 losses, and 2 ties. Yes, the Wolverines continued to hold the upper hand in this one-way and one-sided series. The Maize and Blue footballers record against the Aggies/Spartans now registered 22 wins, 2 losses, and 3 ties. Would MSC ever win another game against the hated Wolverines?

SERIES MILESTONES:

As it turned out, there were quite a few milestones in series game number twenty-seven. First, it was the three-hundredth win in Michigan's football history. Yes, it is always nice to earn historic wins against a rival. Second, although he did not start, end Willis Ward, became the first African American to play for the Wolverines in a series game. Third, Jim Crowley's fourth series game would also be his last. Three weeks after losing to Michigan his Spartans upset a strong Fordham team. At the end of the season, Fordham offered Crowley a job and he was gone. Coach Crowley finished with a series record of 0-2-2.

SEASON SUMMARIES:

The Spartans felt they were a strong team even after losing to Michigan. They went on a six-game winning streak that included two impressive wins over eastern powers Fordham (19-13) and Syracuse (27-13). Coach Crowley's Spartans ended the season with a record of 7 wins, 1 loss, and 0 ties. It was the best Michigan State record in eighteen years and Crowley's fourth straight winning season. The future looked bright in East Lansing. However, the bad news was that someone else would have to lead the East Lansing footballers in 1933. Coach Jim Crowley finished with an overall record of 22 wins, 8 losses, and 3 ties during his four-year tenure in East Lansing. He was moving on to Fordham, but who would keep things going in the right direction for the Spartans?

Harry Kipke's fourth season started with low expectations and much uncertainty. How would he replace two of his star lineman who did not return in 1932? Well, he went to work and found some players who did just fine. After defeating the Spartans in game one, the Wolverines continued to play strong defense and scored enough to win every game on their schedule! They finished the season with a perfect record of 8 wins, 0 losses, and 0 ties.

The Wolverines won the Big Ten title and the national championship to boot. It was an exceptional year in every respect. Quarterback Harry Newman earned All-American honors along with Center Charles Bernard and End Ted Petoskey. Newman was also selected as the Big Ten Player of the year. He also won the Douglas Fairbanks Trophy. This award was the top award that a college player could receive at the time. A few years later this award became the Heisman Trophy. Not a bad season for a team that had some low expectations going into the season. Harry Kipke could do no wrong and his Wolverines were on a roll!

Game # 28: October 7, 1933 at Michigan Stadium in Ann Arbor

BACKGROUND INFORMATION:

The 1933 season was the first season that "hash marks" were used on the field to designate the spot of a ball that was downed within ten yards of the sideline or out of bounds. (Herget, Page 115) As always, the "rules makers" would continue to monitor the changes from 1932 and 1933 and discuss other issues that were being surfaced about the game.

Once again. Michigan State turned to a "Fighting Irishman" to find their next football coach. The administrators liked what Notre Dame alumnus Jim Crowley had accomplished in his four years on the job. They lured a former teammate of Knute Rockne named Charlie Bachman away from Florida. Bachman had been a head football coach since he was a twenty-four-year-old "Boy Coach" at Northwestern. Coach Bachman was a winner with an "attitude." He was welcomed to East Lansing with open arms. This might be the start of something "bigger" in the rivalry. We would find out on October 7, 1933 if that would be the case or not.

Coach Charlie Bachman won his first game against Grinnell College by a score of 14-0. Nothing fancy, nothing overwhelming, but a win is a win. Okay, now that Bachman had a win under his belt, he could focus on another thing that he was hired to do: Beat Michigan! It would be an understatement to say that this was one of the most anticipated series games ever played in the young rivalry between Michigan and the Spartans from East Lansing. The experienced Bachman tried to keep everything in perspective. He wanted his players to regard it as another game against a good opponent. Nothing more, nothing less. Maybe he just told his players to "Keep Calm and Play On!"

The twenty-eighth series game was scheduled, again, for Ann Arbor! This would be the ninth straight game played in the Tree City and the seventh straight game in Michigan Stadium. Harry Kipke would be on the sidelines for his fourth season in Ann Arbor.

Michigan was on a fourteen-game unbeaten streak when the 1933 season began. Mr. Yost did not schedule a warm-up game. The Spartans would be the first test for the highly anticipated season. Expectations were sky-high in Ann Arbor even though the Wolverines had lost their star quarterback, Harry Newman, to graduation. Everyone knew that Coach Kipke had plenty of return-ing "stars" and experienced players. Michigan was going to be a good football team, but would they be good enough to win another national championship? Well, everyone would have to wait for the Wolverines to play their first game before they could really talk about such things. One thing for certain, the Wolverines knew that Michigan State would offer a stiff test. Let the season begin!

GAME SUMMARY: MSC 6   UM 20

As expected, the defending national champions were the team to beat. However, Michigan State made it a hard game for Michigan to win. The physical battles took place in the trenches, as expected. Michigan, however, was a little bit better on both sides of the ball. Both teams played with great passion on a soggy, wet day. The ugly weather probably kept some fair-weather fans at home, but about twenty-two thousand (22,090) die-hard football fans showed up to support their teams.

As expected, the Spartans gave it everything they had. Unfortunately, they did not give enough in the first quarter when the Wolverines scored all their points. History was not on Michigan State's side after spotting Michigan a twenty-point lead. Once again, if you do not score, or score enough, you cannot win. Michigan prevailed for the twenty-third time in the series.

Michigan's offensive line made plenty of holes in the first quarter and the Wolverine runners knew what to do from there. John Heston rushed for one touchdown and Herman Everhardus rushed for two more scores and kicked two extra points. The Spartans scored a fourth quarter touchdown on a 30-yard scoring pass from Charlie Muth to Kurt Warmbein. Detroit Free Press writer Tod Rockwell noted that the MSC touchdown was the first one against Michigan since 1918. Unfortunately, for MSC it was too little, too late! (*DFP*, 10/8/1933, Page 37)

Yes, it was another painful defeat for Sparty and the eighteenth straight time that the Spartans failed to defeat the Wolverines. The good news was that the Spartans were not blown out and they did score a touchdown. Remember, the smallest bit of good that came out of these games was important to the Spartans. Coach Bachman treated it as a loss and that was it! He was a master of the short memory trick that enables coaches to move on after a disappointing loss. Instead, he focused on his next game against Illinois Wesleyan!

Team	1st	2nd	3rd	4th	Final
MSC	0	0	0	6	6
UM	20	0	0	0	20

SERIES UPDATE:

Another game was in the history books and Michigan was still large and in-charge. The Wolverine series advantage now stood at an imposing 23 wins, 2 losses, and 3 ties. The Spartans had not won a series game in eighteen years. Coach Bachman believed he could fix that problem, but he would have to wait until 1934 to try again.

SERIES MILESTONES:

Game number twenty-eight marked the first game for Charlie Bachman and his first loss. Like every Aggie/Spartan coach before him, he lost his first encounter with hated Michigan. The good news was that the Spartans scored a touchdown and that was worth celebrating since it had been an exceedingly long time since the last one. Coach Bachman took the game and the defeat in stride. He was not ready to jump from any bridges after losing to Michigan. He knew the Wolverines were good, but Bachman also knew that his Spartans could play with anybody!

This game also resulted in one of the most interesting facts ever recorded in series history. According to the *Detroit Free Press,* Michigan rushed for 179-yards in this game and had 0-yards passing. Michigan State ran for 93-yards and passed for 86-yards which adds up to, you guessed it, 179-yards. (*DFP*, 10/8/1933, Page 37) As far as I can tell, this is the first time that both teams ended a series game with the same amount of total offense.

SEASON SUMMARIES:

Thanks to Charlie Bachman's leadership, the Spartans were able to put the Wolverine loss in the rearview mirror as soon as they left Ann Arbor. Michigan State still had six games remaining on the schedule. Coach Bachman ensured that his Spartans were focused on winning those games. Coach Bachman's footballers won three straight games after the Michigan loss. Unfortunately, they could not handle Syracuse and lost by a score of 10-0 in New York. They finished the season with a scoreless tie against Carnegie Tech and a loss to Detroit (14-0). Michigan State finished with a record of 4 wins, 2 losses, and 2 ties in the first year of the Charlie Bachman Era.

Harry Kipke's Wolverines started fast with their victory over Michigan State, and they never looked back. Michigan won five straight games by a combined score of 98-12 before battling to a scoreless tie against Minnesota. The Wolverines defeated Northwestern by a score of 13-0 to finish another undefeated season (7-0-1). They won the Big Ten Title for the fourth straight season (5-0-1) and repeated as national champions too! Three Wolverines were named All-American (Charles Bernard, Ted Petoskey, and Francis Wistert) for their excellent play during the 1933 season. All was good in Ann Arbor and Coach Harry Kipke was riding high on the shoulders of his amazing Wolverines. It would be hard to improve on the last two seasons, but Coach Kipke was probably looking for ways to get better the day after his last game in 1933. That is just what coaches do!

Game # 29: October 6, 1934 at Michigan Stadium in Ann Arbor

BACKGROUND INFORMATION:

There was only one small change in the game for the 1934 season. Actually, it was only about one-half an inch of change. For the third time in the history of American college football, the size of the ball was reduced. You may remember that the ball's circumference was 27 inches in 1911. The ball shrunk dramatically in 1912 when it went down to a circumference of 22.5 to 23.0 inches. In 1929 the ball got smaller, but only by one-half inch. The 1934 game ball could be no larger than 22 to 22.5 inches around the middle. (Herget, Page 116) Once again, this small change had more to do with the passing game than anything else. The intent was to continue to improve the passing game which was exactly what happened.

The Spartans started year two of the Charlie Bachman Era with new uniforms. Coach Bachman was trying to build a completely different mindset for his football team. He felt that black and gold uniforms would help. He also added a winged helmet look that was quite distinctive. His new look Spartans began the season with a victory over Grinnell College (33-20). Although he continued to downplay the immensity of the Michigan game, Coach Bachman prepared his team as he did for any other game. At least, that is what he told anybody who would listen. I am certain that he did things a little differently for the Michigan game than he did for Grinnell College. What do you think?

For the third consecutive season, Michigan began the season in Ann Arbor against Michigan State. Harry Kipke's Wolverines had not lost since the fourth game of the 1931 season. Their twenty-two-game unbeaten streak was on the line when they took the field against Michigan State on October 6, 1934. The Wolverine record for the last four years was stunning: 31 wins, 1 loss and 3 ties!

As usual, expectations were high in Ann Arbor which surprised no one. Michigan, the two-time defending national champions lost three All-Americans from the 1933 team, but everyone figured that Coach Kipke had some more waiting in the locker room. As it turned out, that was not the case.

GAME SUMMARY: MSC 16 UM 0

The twenty-ninth game of the series went down in history for Spartan fans everywhere, but not for the Wolverine faithful. The Spartans played the Wolverines to a standstill for the first thirty minutes and the half ended in a scoreless tie. In the third quarter, Michigan State's offensive line took control of the game. Quarterback Kurt Warmbein led the Spartans on a long drive that finally stalled at the Wolverine seven-yard line. Kicker/Halfback Steve Sebo put the Spartans ahead 3-0 with a successful field goal. It was the first time that the Spartans had led the Wolverines since 1915. The Spartans had the lead, but could they keep it? (*DFP*, 10/7/1934, Page 15)

The teams continued to battle, but the Spartans held the edge and spent most of the second half in Michigan's end of the field. In the fourth quarter, Quarterback Warmbein rambled 45-yards to the Michigan 29-yard line. Then, his offensive line opened a big hole in the Michigan line and Warmbein sprinted 29-yards for a touchdown! Although the extra point kick failed, Michigan State had a 9-0 lead and time was on their side. The Wolverines knew they had to take a chance, so they went for a long pass. Unfortunately, for Wolverine fans, Mr. Warmbein intercepted the pass and made it all the way to the Michigan 9-yard line before he was tackled. The Wolverine "killer" scored on a short run which put the last nail in the Wolverine coffin. It was over! Final score: Michigan State College 16 and Michigan 0! (*DFP*, 10/7/1934, Page 15) Michigan State accomplished what few people thought they could do. After nineteen long years, they defeated Michigan. Harry Kipke was probably surprised and extremely disappointed. I doubt that Charlie Bachman was surprised by this victory!

Team	1st	2nd	3rd	4th	Final
MSC	0	0	3	13	16
UM	0	0	0	0	0

The only thing that is sweeter than a "rival" victory is a rival victory in the other guy's stadium. Apparently, some over-exuberant Spartan fans tried to tear down the goal posts which did not go over well with the locals. Some fistfights broke out which probably resulted in some bumps and bruises and maybe some blood! Oh my, not good! Amazingly, the town of East Lansing was still standing the next day. It had survived a night of celebration and hardy-partying that had not taken place since the "Slaughter" of 1915. I could not determine if the Spartan ROTC Cadet Band did their "traditional" march through the streets of Ann Arbor or if they just went home to celebrate with more "friendly" people.

SERIES UPDATE:

Michigan still held a big edge in the series. They now had 23 wins, 3 defeats, and 3 ties. Michigan State was still on the wrong side of the won-lost ledger at 3-23-3, but they had to be feeling great. It is not every day that you can snap a rival's long winning streak and defeat the two-time defending national champions on the same day. Spartan fans did fail to tear down the Michigan Stadium goal posts, but that is the only thing that did not go in favor of the Black and Gold footballers on this day!

SERIES MILESTONES:

There were many significant series milestones in game number twenty-nine. First, it was Coach Bachmans's first series win and Coach Kipke's first series loss. Second, it was the first time that Spartan fans tried to tear down the goal posts in Ann Arbor. Third, it was the first time that the "Spartans" had defeated the Wolverines. (Remember, they were Aggies when they last won in 1915.) Fourth, it was Michigan State's first win in Michigan Stadium. Fifth, this was the first series game that the Spartans played in Bachman's newly designed black and gold uniforms. Finally, it was the first time in a series game that one team (Michigan State) wore a winged helmet. Yes, you heard it right! The Spartans were the first team in the State of Michigan to wear a winged helmet. The helmet was gold, the wing was black and there was a gold "S" in the middle of the wing. Oh, by the way, the Wolverines wore the black helmets they had been wearing for some time, but that would change in due time.

SEASON SUMMARIES:

The Spartans continued to pile up victories and finished the month of October with a record of 4 wins, 0 losses, and 0 ties. They won the first game in November but lost at Syracuse (10-0). MSC finished strong by winning their last three games and ended the season with .

Coach Bachman's team ended the 1934 season with an impressive record of 8 wins and 1 loss. Charlie Bachman's "makeover" idea with the uniforms was a gamble, but it paid off! He wanted to change the football culture in East Lansing. The Black and Gold uniforms made the Spartans look more like Notre Dame and they were starting to play like the Irish too. Coach Bachman had everything going in the right direction, for sure! The second year of the Charlie Bachman Era in East Lansing was definitely one to remember.

The Wolverines were probably stunned that their winning streak had ended at the hands of the Spartans. They did even worse the next week in the Windy City when Chicago blew past them by a score of 27-0. Michigan had not lost two consecutive games since 1928, what was going on? Well, what was going on was the worst season since 1889 when the Wolverines posted a record of 1 win, 2 losses, and 0 ties. Michigan managed to defeat Georgia Tech (9-2) in the infamous "race game." Sadly, African American end Willis Ward was held out of the game so the contest could be played. Otherwise, Georgia Tech would not have played the game with him on the field. Fortunately, that does not happen in football anymore! The Wolverines lost the last five games of the year and finished with a miserable record of 1 win, 7 losses, and 0 ties. Obviously, Coach Kipke went from "hero" in 1933 to "zero" in 1934. What a dramatic turn of events in Ann Arbor!

Game # 30: October 5, 1935 at Michigan Stadium in Ann Arbor

BACKGROUND INFORMATION:

There were no significant rules changes for the 1935 season. It would be another season of monitoring the impact of the change in ball size. The game continued to move forward despite the tough times in the early 1930s.

Charlie Bachman's third year as the Spartans football leader was filled with anticipation. He had the MSC Spartans on a roll and was not about to let it stop. Bachman had some strong players returning to the field and expectations were for more of the same. For the third straight season the Spartans started the season with an easy win over Grinnell (41-0). Now it was time to focus on Michigan!

For the fourth straight year, Michigan began the season with a home opener against Michigan State. The Spartans turned the tables on the Wolverines in 1934 and it still stung. Harry Kipke's sixth season at Michigan was one to forget and that is what he hoped to do. It was time for the Maize and Blue footballers to move on and play better, a lot better in 1935. Unlike 1934, Michigan did not start the season on a long unbeaten streak that spanned three seasons. Instead, they lost the last five games in 1934. It was time to get back on the winning track and start the season the right way! It was time to show the upstart Spartans who was the best team in the State of Michigan!

GAME SUMMARY: MSC 25 UM 6

Game number thirty of the intense in-state football series went down in Spartan history, again, for the Charlie Bachman's fired-up footballers. Not only did the Spartans win the game, but they also won for the second consecutive season! It was a huge series "first" for the hungry footballers from East Lansing. Detroit Free Press writer Tod Rockwell's game summary was short and to the point. He wrote: "Michigan State's resourceful football team took an impressive stride toward National grid honors here today by defeating a greatly improved University of Michigan eleven, 25-6." (*DFP*, 10/6/1935, Page 37)

The Spartans scored first, last and added some more in the middle too! In fact, they scored at least six points in every quarter. MSC Fullback Art Brandstatter scored on the eighth play of the game to set the tone for the Spartans. Michigan quarterback Bill Renner scored on a 35-yard run, but the extra point kick failed. MSC led 7-6 at the end of the first quarter. (*DFP*, 10/6//1935, Page 37) Halfback Dick Colina returned a Michigan punt for sixty yards and another touchdown to give the Spartans a 13-6 lead at halftime. In the second half Quarterback Kurt Warmbein game back to haunt the Wolverines again with a touchdown pass. Michigan State Sophomore running back Al "Agony" Agett broke loose for a forty-seven-yard touchdown run for the final score of the game. (Stabley, Page 91) The Spartans simply dominated the Wolverines on both sides of the ball. Michigan State finished with almost two-hundred-fifty yards of offense and held Michigan to a lot less! MSC fumbled four times in this game. Yes, it could have been a lot worse if they held on to the ball! (*DFP*, 10/6/1935, Page 37)

Team	1st	2nd	3rd	4th	Final
MSC	7	6	6	6	25
UM	6	0	0	0	6

Once again, the only thing that is sweeter than a "rival" victory is a rival victory in the other guy's stadium for consecutive seasons! I am sure that Spartan fans celebrated to the max and enjoyed the "bragging" rights that came with their second straight conquest of not-so-mighty Michigan. Things were starting to get interesting in the rivalry, that is for sure!

SERIES UPDATE:

Michigan still held the edge in the series (23-4-3), but that was not much consolation for the 1935 Wolverine team. They had been beaten by the Spartans again. Now, maybe the Wolverines were starting to grasp the importance of the series and how good a victory over Michigan State really felt. The decade of the 1930s was getting interesting. Michigan and Michigan State were now even for the decade with identical records of 2 wins, 2 losses, and 2 ties. Was this becoming a real rivalry after all?

SERIES MILESTONES:

Yes, the thirtieth game of the series was a milestone. It was also the first time that the Spartans had achieved back-to-back wins in the series and the first time that they won back-to-back games in Ann Arbor. It was also the first time that both teams completed eight passes in this game which had never happened before (Michigan was 8 of 15 for 96-yards and Michigan State was 8 of 16 for 105-yards). Finally, it was the most points ever scored (25) in a series game by a Michigan State team. Were things really starting to change in the series? Although not a series milestone, MSC expanded their stadium (26,000) and "officially" named it Macklin Field after their first great football coach, John Macklin. Maybe Mr. Yost would agree to let the Wolverines play there someday, or maybe not!

SEASON SUMMARIES:

Michigan State rolled over Kansas (42-0) the next week but came up short in week four against Boston College (18-6). The Spartans defeated Washington University of St. Louis (47-13) at the end of October. Coach Bachman's footballers were on a roll (4-1-0) heading into November and a close win over Temple (12-7) gave them their fifth victory. Then, Marquette ruined Michigan State's Homecoming with a 13-7 win over the Spartans. Michigan State finished the season with their first trip to California and returned with a decisive win (27-0).

Michigan State College finished with another winning season for the seventh consecutive year. Their final record was 6 wins and 2 losses. Hard-charging Guard Sid Wagner earned All-American honors—the first Spartan to earn this recognition since 1930. Charlie Bachman's record after three seasons stood at 18 wins, 5 losses, and 2 ties. He had Michigan State football headed in the right direction. Go Black! Go Gold! Go Spartans!

The Wolverines bounced back after the Michigan State loss and defeated Indiana, 7-0. The Wolverines exceeded their victory total of 1934 by winning their next game against Wisconsin (20-12). Okay, maybe they were not as bad as some people thought they were. Michigan took a break from the Big Ten and defeated Columbia (19-7) and Pennsylvania (16-6). They had a record of 4 wins, 1 loss, and 0 ties heading into the final three weeks of the season. Unfortunately, the Wolverines lost their last three games and only the Illinois loss (3-0) was close. The other two defeats were blowout losses to Minnesota (40-0) and Ohio State (38-0). The promising 1935 season started with disappointment and ended with a thud as Kipke's seventh team finished with a final record of 4 wins and 4 losses. Once, again, there were no All-Americans in 1935. Michigan's fifth place finish in the conference was better than dead last in 1934, but not that much better. I am sure that Harry Kipke and Mr. Yost had a focused conversation about Kipke's future and the direction of the Michigan football program. Things had to get better, and soon, or the former Wolverine All-American might not have a job!

Game # 31: October 3, 1936 at Michigan Stadium in Ann Arbor

BACKGROUND INFORMATION:

There were no rules changes or "tweaks" for the 1936 season. The game had evolved nicely over the years and the rules makers decided to let things continue as they were for another season. As always, possible changes were always being discussed, but this would be another season of watching and observing the game.

One additional note was that this was the first season where teams were being ranked, but neither Michigan nor Michigan State was good enough to receive any poll recognition during the season. Of course, that would change in the future!

Coach Bachman's fourth team had a strong core of returning players and everyone in East Lansing was optimistic about the upcoming season. The Spartans were able to get a jump-start on the season with a 27-0 victory over Wayne State. Michigan State was probably feeling confident about their next game against the Wolverines. They had won two games in a row against the hated Wolverines, but the greedy Spartans wanted more. They wanted to make history, again, by defeating Michigan for the third consecutive season.

Michigan was coming off their second straight non-winning season and the natives were getting restless in Ann Arbor. Even former All-American players and national champion coaches can wear out their welcome if they do not keep winning. Winning would have to be the focus for the 1936 Wolverine football season. Once again, Michigan opened the season with a visit from the Spartans. A third straight loss to the MSC footballers was unthinkable. The Wolverines knew what they had to do to get off on the right foot in 1936.

GAME SUMMARY: MSC 21 UM 7

Mitten State series game number thirty-three was another amazing win for the Spartans and another shocking defeat for the Wolverines. Maybe Michigan was starting to understand how MSC was feeling for so many years. The Battle Creek Enquirer and Evening News (*BCEEN*) reported the results as follows: "Michigan State's football Spartans clipped the University of Michigan Wolverine's claws for the third consecutive year Saturday, 21-7, withering Wolverine hopes of a revival of past glories." The teams battled to a 7-7 standoff at halftime, but the Spartans gained the upper hand in the third quarter when John Pingel scored on a twelve-yard run. Al "Agony" Agett dashed for an eighty-two-yard touchdown thanks to some ferocious blocking by his Spartan teammates. (*BCEEN, 10/4/1936, Page 12)* That score sealed the win for the MSC footballers who dominated the Wolverines in the second half. Coach Harry Kipke made no excuses after the game. Michigan State was the better team for the third consecutive season. Hail to the Spartans!

Team	1st	2nd	3rd	4th	Final
MSC	7	0	7	7	21
UM	0	7	0	0	7

SERIES UPDATE:

Michigan State made series history for the third straight year. Yes, they did the "unthinkable" and sent shock waves throughout Ann Arbor and the State of Michigan. This was a BIG DEAL for the Spartans. Although the in-state series numbers still favored Michigan, there was cause for concern. The Wolverine series advantage dropped again and now stood at 23 wins, 5 losses, and 3 ties.

SERIES MILESTONES:

There were four milestones in the thirty-first game of the in-state football series that was starting to look more and more like a rivalry. First, it was the first time that Michigan State defeated Michigan in three straight games. Second, it was also the first time that the Spartans defeated the Wolverines three consecutive times in Michigan Stadium. Third, the Michigan Stadium crowd of 45,656 was a record setter for an Ann Arbor game and a series game. Finally, it was Charlie Bachman's third series win which made him the winningest series coach in Aggie/Spartan history! Apparently, the third time was a charm for the Spartan "Goal Post Assault Team." They tore down the north end goal posts and "…uprights were carried away for souvenirs of the fifth Spartan victory since the rivalry began in 1898." (*BCEEN*, 10/4/1936, Page 12) No injuries were reported, but I know there were bumps, bruises, and hard feelings that resulted from this post-game activity!

SEASON SUMMARIES:

Coach Bachman's fourth team finished with another winning record in 1937. His Spartans won two straight after beating Michigan to push their record to 4-0-0. Unfortunately, MSC lost to Marquette (13-7). They tied the next two games against Boston College (13-13) and Temple (7-7) before finishing strong with two shutout wins over Kansas (41-0) and Arizona (7-0).

The Spartans came within nine points of an undefeated season. Instead, they finished with a final record of 6 wins, 1 loss, and 2 ties. Spartan fullback Art Brandstatter earned All-American honors from the All-American Board. The MSC footballers had now posted eight straight winning seasons. The future looked bright for the Spartan football program. One other item of importance also took place at the end of the season. Michigan State College President Robert S. Shaw proposed to the State Board of Education that MSC be allowed to apply for membership in the Big Ten Conference on November 23, 1936. (Young, Page 267) The Spartans were thinking big, very BIG!

Coach Harry Kipke's Wolverines lost two more games after the Spartan defeat. Michigan was off to another winless start after three games. They finally defeated Columbia (13-0) in week four. With four games remaining they still had a shot at a winning season. Instead, Michigan lost the last four games and finished the season with an "un-Michigan like" record of 1 win and 7 losses. Things had pretty much hit rock bottom in Ann Arbor and the big question surrounding the football program would be the fate of Coach Harry Kipke. Mr. Yost would have a difficult decision to make at the end of the season and the fate of the Michigan football program hung in the balance.

Game # 32: October 2, 1937 at Michigan Stadium in Ann Arbor

BACKGROUND INFORMATION:

There was one small adjustment to the game of American college football for the 1937 season. This would be the first season that numerals were required on the front and back of the player's jerseys. Most teams, including Michigan and Michigan State, had been complying with this rule for years. This rule had no impact on the series game in 1937. Another historical note I would like to share is that the 1937 season was the first season that the National Collegiate Athletic Association (NCAA) began keeping official records for college football. Until this season, records are sketchy at best which is unfortunate for the pioneering players who graduated in 1936 or played before then. Many incredible achievements were not captured for the ages because of the timing of this policy.

Charlie Bachman was now in his fifth season at Michigan State. He raised the bar for Spartan football. Another victory over Michigan was expected since he had won three straight times. Of course, he did not want to get too far ahead of himself since the first game of the 1937 season would be against Wayne State. Coach Bachman continued to downplay the immensity of the Michigan game, but you know that the Wolverines were on his mind before the season started and probably during the 19-0 win over the visitors from Detroit. Once again, I am certain that he did things a little differently for the Michigan game than he did for Wayne State.

Harry Kipke began his ninth season in Ann Arbor in 1937. His coaching career at Michigan was full of "ups and downs," but mostly "downs" since 1933. When you are on top of the mountain, as he was in 1932 and 1933, it can be a long fall when you slip. The Wolverines were in the throes of the "Get Michigan Years" and everybody, except for Maize and Blue fans, seemed to be enjoying it. Many people were surprised that Coach Kipke was back for another year in 1937. Mr. Yost had sent Tad Wieman packing after one losing season and Harry Kipke was sitting on two of Michigan's worst seasons ever. I am certain that Fielding Harris Yost was clear and direct about his expectations for the 1937 season. Once again, Michigan began the season with a home game against the annoying Spartans. A fourth straight loss to the footballers from East Lansing was unthinkable, right?

GAME SUMMARY: MSC 19 UM 14

Game number thirty-two proved to be the beginning of the end of the Harry Kipke Era at Michigan. Both teams played hard and left the field at halftime with zeroes on the scoreboard. Early in the second half, the Spartans took a 6-0 lead on an eighty-nine-yard run by halfback Gene Ciolek. Michigan took their first lead on a 2-yard touchdown pass from Stark Ritchie to Hercules Renda. Fred Trosko kicked the extra point and Michigan led 7-6. The Spartans regained the lead with their second touchdown and their first extra-point. MSC led 13-7 at the end of the third quarter.

With six minutes remaining in the game, the Wolverines regained the lead (14-13) on Trosko's second touchdown and his second extra point. A few minutes later, an angry Spartan named Ole Nelson came to the rescue. Nelson had a reputation as a mild-mannered young man. However, Ole got "fired up" when a disrespectful Wolverine kicked him in the head during a pile-up. The incensed Nelson delivered his own kick to gut of the entire Michigan team when he scored the winning touchdown. (Stabley, Page 98) Yes, Ole's "revenge" clinched the fourth straight win for the Spartans and Michigan State fans probably partied for a week! I do not think that Harry Kipke was partying at the end of the game. He was trying to figure out how to get his team, and his Michigan coaching career, back on track. Things did not look good for the former Michigan All-American and national championship coach. The good news was that there were still seven games to go.

Team	1st	2nd	3rd	4th	Final
MSC	0	0	13	6	19
UM	0	0	7	7	14

Of course, any series win is great. However, it is even sweeter when it is the fourth consecutive win in your rival's own stadium with a series record crowd looking on! The Wolverines could only remember a long winning streak against the Spartans.

SERIES UPDATE:

Michigan still held a sizeable advantage in the series, but now they had an understanding about the pain that goes along four consecutive rival losses. For the record, the Wolverines still held the advantage with 23 wins, 6 losses, and 3 ties. Michigan State was still on the wrong side of the won-lost ledger, but they had to be feeling good. This was not a fun time in Ann Arbor, but the folks in East Lansing were absolutely loving it! The Spartans had their "bragging" rights for another season and Wolverine fans would just have to bite their tongues.

SERIES MILESTONES:

Game number thirty-two of the UM vs MSC series had several interesting milestones. First, it was the first time that the Spartans had won four straight series games. It was also the first time that they had won four consecutive games in Michigan Stadium. It was also Charlie Bachman's fourth straight win over Michigan—a Spartan best! The largest crowd in the history of the series (63,311) attended this game. Finally, it was the thirteenth consecutive game in Ann Arbor.

Interestingly, it was the first time that both series teams scored at least ten points in the in-state rivalry game. The four lead changes also had never happened before in this crazy series. Once again, some over-exuberant Spartan fans tried to tear down the goal posts which resulted in a few post-game fisticuffs and lots of pushing and shoving. Finally, it was the last series game for Coach Harry Kipke who finished with a series record of 3 wins, 4 losses, and 2 ties. He became the first Michigan coach to have a losing record against Michigan State.

SEASON SUMMARIES:

Maybe the Spartans spent too much time celebrating instead of preparing for their next game. It is also possible that a long trip to New York did them in. I am sure that Charlie Bachman went to his grave wondering how his Spartans lost to Manhattan College (3-0). Wow, what could have been a dream season became a nightmarish loss to a team that nobody in East Lansing had ever heard of. That one really hurt, but Coach Bachman had work to do. Bachman got the Spartans out of their hangover, barely, as his footballers beat Missouri in Columbia by a score of 2-0. The Spartans won the last five games of the regular season. They accepted their first ever bowl bid and lost to Auburn in the 1938 Orange Bowl. Michigan State ended another successful season with a final record of 8 wins 2 losses, and 0 ties.

Michigan lost their next two games after the Spartan defeat which extended their winless start to 0-3-0. To their credit, the Wolverines went on a four-game winning streak before losing the last game to Ohio State (21-0). Michigan finished with a record of 4 wins and 4 losses. Harry Kipke ended his Michigan coaching career with an overall record of 46 wins, 26 losses, and 4 ties. His teams won four consecutive Big Ten championships and two straight national championships. His first five years were fabulous and his last four were not fabulous. It was time for a change in Ann Arbor.

Game # 33: October 1, 1938 at Michigan Stadium in Ann Arbor

BACKGROUND INFORMATION:

There was only one minor adjustment to the rules in 1938. The rules makers observed the impact of the "hash marks" and the best place to spot the ball on a play that ended near the sideline or out of bounds. In 1938 the distance from the "hash mark" to the sideline was increased from ten yards to fifteen yards. That was it, no other changes were made for the upcoming season. (Herget, Page 115)

Game number thirty-three of the annual football "blood-letting" between Michigan and Michigan State took place, again, in Ann Arbor. This was the fourteenth consecutive time that the game was played in the Tree City and the twelfth straight game at Michigan Stadium. The Spartans had fared well in Michigan's gigantic football home. Michigan State's record in the Wolverine's new lair was 4 wins, 5 losses and 2 ties. Not bad, not bad at all.

Coach Charlie Bachman had five straight successful seasons under his belt in East Lansing. He also had engineered four consecutive victories over the Wolverines. His five-year coaching record now stood at 32 wins, 8 losses and 4 ties.

Bachman's winning percentage was just over seventy-seven percent (.773). By all measures, the Spartans had earned the title of best football team in the State of Michigan during his tenure. Could he keep up the great work or would things change?

Speaking of change, things changed in Ann Arbor after the 1937 season. Unfortunately, Yost and Michigan had seen enough of Harry Kipke, which meant that his contract was not renewed. Faculty Representative Ralph Aigler, a man who would become a fan "unfavorite" in East Lansing, persuaded Fritz Crisler to come to Michigan. After some negotiating, Crisler agreed to become Head Football Coach and Assistant Athletic Director under Mr. Yost. Crisler had an impressive playing career under Alonzo Stagg at the University of Chicago. He enjoyed successful head coaching stints at Minnesota and Princeton. Michigan believed that Crisler was a perfect fit for the Wolverine football program. Only time would tell if he would be good enough to get Michigan back among the best in the Big Ten Conference and in America.

Although Harry Kipke was gone, he was not totally forgotten or unappreciated. He left several great players (Tom Harmon, Forest Evashevski, and Ralph Fritz to name a few) for Crisler to work with. The Wolverines failed to post a winning season after the National Championship year of 1933. Their record from 1934-1937 was disturbing at 10 wins and 22 losses! Michigan's "winning rate" was only about twenty-four percent (.241). Coach Fritz Crisler had nowhere to go, but up! The question was, "How long would it take to turn things around in Ann Arbor?" The time had passed for empty speculation, let the 1938 season and the Fritz Crisler Era begin!

GAME SUMMARY: MSC 0 UM 14

The Fritz Crisler Era started brilliantly at Michigan with an upset win over the favored Spartans. Crisler threw all kinds of surprises at the Spartans, starting with some crazy looking helmets. They did not look that crazy since the Spartans took the field with their own Black and Gold winged helmets. Michigan, instead of wearing their traditional black helmets, had a blue helmet trimmed with a maize wing and multiple stripes that pushed to the back of the helmet. It was a different look for the Wolverines—a much different look.

Will Perry, author of *The Wolverines: A Story of Michigan Football,* explained that Crisler's plan to beat the Spartans began with stopping their superstar halfback John Pingel. Crisler knew that Pingel led the nation in punting in 1937. Crisler also knew that Pingel completed almost fifty percent of his passes and averaged six yards every time he ran the ball. Oh, yes, he helped beat Michigan with two touchdown passes in the last series game. Pingel, was voted an All-American in 1938, but he was a marked man all day in Ann Arbor. The Wolverines stopped him and, the Spartans, cold! (Perry, Page 163) Michigan's defense, led by Ralph Heikkinen and Fred Janke, forced two fumbles and intercepted four Spartan passes. The Spartans only gained twenty-five yards on the ground and were frustrated all day long by the aggressive Wolverines. Sophomore halfback Paul Kromer scored two touchdowns and a guy named Harmon had three nice runs during limited play.

A record crowd of almost seventy-four thousand (73,589) was on hand to celebrate Fritz Crisler's first win at Michigan and the first series win since 1933. It was the longest ride back to East Lansing for the Spartans in five years. The MSC winning streak ended at four games, but they still had seven games to play. Time to move on!

Team	1st	2nd	3rd	4th	Final
MSC	0	0	0	0	0
UM	0	7	0	7	14

SERIES UPDATE:

Once again, another game was in the history books. Michigan was still large and in-charge, but one game does not a season make. Fritz Crisler's footballers still had a lot of work to do and so did Coach Bachman's Spartans. For the record, the Wolverine series advantage now stood at 24 wins, 6 losses, and 3 ties.

Image 5 The 1938 series game was the first time that both teams wore a winged helmet. (Permission: Bentley Historical Library at The University of Michigan, See Page 369)

SERIES MILESTONES:

Fritz Crisler, like every other previous coach in Michigan football history, won his first series game against Michigan State. As I said earlier, it was also the debut for Michigan's now famous winged helmets. It was also the first time that both teams wore a version of a winged helmet in the game. Thanks to Coach Bachman, Spartan fans had the bragging rights for being the first team in the State of Michigan to wear a winged helmet. Michigan was the second team in the state to wear a winged helmet. Of course, they became the most famous team to wear this distinctive style of headgear. The thirty-third series game also produced the largest crowd (73,859) ever to attend a series game.

SEASON SUMMARIES:

Charlie Bachman's Spartans recovered nicely from the Michigan loss and won three straight games. Then, they lost two straight close games to Santa Clara (7-6) and Missouri (6-0). The MSC footballers finished strong with two solid wins over Marquette (20-14) and Temple (10-0). Michigan State's final record for the 1938 season was 6 wins and 3 losses. It was Coach Bachman's sixth straight winning season.

Coach Fritz Crisler's Wolverines started fast with their victory over Michigan State. They followed the MSC victory with a 45-7 win over Chicago. In week three, they lost a close game to Minnesota (7-6). They did not lose another game that year, although they did tie Northwestern. Michigan ended with an excellent record of 6 wins, 1 loss, and 1 tie. They also finished second in the Big Ten. The Fritz Crisler Era was off to a nice start at Michigan and life was starting to get better again in Ann Arbor.

Game # 34: October 7, 1939 at Michigan Stadium in Ann Arbor

BACKGROUND INFORMATION:

The only rules change in 1939 concerned the wearing of protective headgear. Before this season, helmets were optional. Now, helmets were mandatory! The NCAA determined that some sort of leather, or plastic, helmet must be worn by all field players.

For the eighth straight season, Michigan and Michigan State opened the season in Ann Arbor. The "agreement" between Fielding Yost and Ralph Young was working out nicely for both teams. Michigan no longer had to worry about drawing a small crowd to their season opener. Instead, Yost could count on Spartan fans to show up in large numbers to watch the annual in-state battle. Michigan State returned home, win, or lose, with a nice check that was probably more than the gate receipts they would have received when playing at East Lansing. Yes, MSC fans did not like going to Ann Arbor every year, but that is the only way they could get a shot at the Wolverines.

Coach Charlie Bachman and his Spartans started the season against a "light weight" before their "heavy weight" battle with Michigan in week two. For the fourth consecutive season, Wayne State was the "victim" on Saturday, September 30, 1939. The Spartans sent the Tartars back to Detroit to ponder a 16-0 defeat. Michigan State shifted their entire focus to beating Michigan and getting back on the winning side of the series ledger.

Once again, Michigan opened their season against Michigan State in Ann Arbor. Crisler had a ton of returning players and they were expected to be exceptionally good. They would get their first chance to see how good they were when the Spartans showed up in Ann Arbor on October 7, 1939.

GAME SUMMARY: MSC 13 UM 26

In another classic series battle, the Wolverines prevailed over a determined Spartan team. Michigan was the more talented team in this game. Michigan opened the scoring in the first quarter thanks to a Paul Kroemer touchdown and a Tom Harmon extra point. The Wolverines led 7-0 at the end of the first quarter. Michigan's offense broke the game open in the second quarter. Tom Harmon ran for one touchdown and passed to Forest Evashevski for two more scores. That was all the Wolverines needed to win the game. (*DFP*, 10/8/1939, Page 49)

Michigan team captain Archie Kodros intercepted two Spartan passes and the Michigan defense held MSC to 114-yards of offense. Spartan historian Fred Stabley pointed out two Spartan highlights in his book, *The Spartans, Michigan State Football.* The first was lineman Bill Batchelor's twenty-five-yard interception for a touchdown. The second bright spot for the Spartans was a sixty-five-yard pass and run play from Bill Kennedy to Wyman Davis. (Stabley, Pages 108-109)

Team	1st	2nd	3rd	4th	Final
MSC	0	0	7	6	13
UM	7	19	0	0	26

SERIES UPDATE:

Michigan increased their series advantage again. The Wolverines had now won two straight over the Spartans and the record book now read: Michigan 25 wins, 6 losses, and 3 ties and Michigan State 6 wins, 25 losses, and 3 ties.

SERIES MILESTONES:

Game number thirty-four marked the last game of the decade of the Thirties. It was Michigan's twenty-fifth win in the series, which, of course, was the highest total of either team so far in the annual gridiron grudge matchup. It was also the first decade that every series game was played in Ann Arbor. Finally, it was the first and only time in series history where both teams ended a decade with the same record (4 wins, 4 losses and 2 ties).

SEASON SUMMARIES:

Coach Charlie Bachman's Spartan's lost the next two games after the Michigan loss to put them at 1 win, 4 losses and 0 ties. They closed the season with three wins, a loss, and a tie. MSC's final record for the 1939 season was 4 wins, 4 losses, and 1 tie. This was the first "non-winning" season in Charlie Bachman's seven-year tenure. It was also the first time in eleven years that the Spartans did not record a winning season. Coach Bachman would have to go back to the drawing board and get his Spartans back on track in 1940.

Michigan's season started perfectly with their victory over Michigan State. They used that momentum to win the next three games and finished October 1939 with a perfect record of 4 wins, 0 losses and 0 ties. Unfortunately for Michigan, November was not so kind as they lost two straight games to Illinois (16-7) and Minnesota (20-7). The Wolverines won their last two games to finish with a winning, but disappointing, record of 6 wins and 2 losses. Michigan ended with a Big Ten record of 3 wins, 2 losses and 0 ties which put them at fourth place for the season. It was another solid season for the Wolverines, but Crisler was hoping for more. He knew that he had some great players and would look for more ways to capitalize on the talents of his special athletes.

DECADE AND SERIES SUMMARY:

Decade three of the twentieth century was a mixture of good and bad for both teams. A better description is a "streaky" series decade for both teams. Michigan had a few more streaks such as playing every game of the series in Ann Arbor which was a ten-game streak. The Wolverines also had two two-game winning streaks during the decade along with two straight ties to start the decade. Michigan State had a four-game winning streak in the middle of the decade to go along with two-straight ties at the start of the decade.

Decade and Series Summary 1898 to 1939

Time Frame	UM Won-Lost-Tie	MSC Won-Lost-Tied
1930-1939	4-4-2	4-4-2
1898-1939	25-6-3	6-25-3

As I said earlier, this was the only decade in the history of the series where both teams had the same record. It may never happen again, who knows? From a rivalry standpoint, it cannot get any more "even" than 4-4-2 in ten years. Either Michigan had gotten worse, or Michigan State was getting better. Actually, it looked like a little bit of both.

PROGRAM SUMMARIES:

The first four years of the decade were great ones for Michigan. They won four consecutive Big Ten titles and rolled to back-to-back national championships in 1932 and 1933. Then, the Wolverine train went off the tracks from 1934 to 1937. Harry Kipke was gone. Fritz Crisler came in to get the Michigan football program back on track in 1938 and 1939. The Wolverine "body of work" from 1930 to 1939 was the worst in nearly fifty years. Michigan's winning percentage dropped over 100 points from the Twenties (.769) to the Thirties (.662). They only had six winning seasons in the Thirties compared to nine in the Twenties. The Wolverines declined in every "good" category and increased in some "bad" areas. However, they did win two straight national championships which was great! Overall, it was not up to Michigan standards which is why Fritz Crisler was hired.

Program Summaries 1930 to 1939

Statistical Area	UM	MSC
Number of Head Coaches	2	2
Games Played	83	87
Wins	53	59
Losses	26	20
Ties	4	8
Winning Percentage	.662	.724
Winning Seasons	6	9
Losing Seasons	2	0
Even Seasons	2	1
National Championships	2	0
All-American Players	7	4

Thanks to Jim Crowley and Charlie Bachman, Michigan State made real progress in the Mitten State football rivalry in the 1930s. Crowley led the Spartans to a record of 17 wins, 5 losses and 3 ties before he bolted to Fordham. Charlie Bachman picked up where Crowley left off and posted a record of 42 wins, 15 losses and 5 ties. Of course, he also managed to beat Michigan in four straight series games in Ann Arbor!

For the first time in series history, most of the important numbers on the chart shown above favored MSC. The Spartans had more wins, fewer losses, and a better winning percentage. The Wolverines did manage to win two national championships and MSC won zero. Michigan also had a narrow advantage in All-American players by a margin of 7 to 4. Otherwise, it was Michigan State's decade! Crowley and Bachman brought some football pride back to East Lansing. Of course, this was the first decade in series history where both teams ended with the same record against each other (4 wins, 4 losses, and 2 ties).

Yes, this was starting to look and feel like a "real" rivalry. What would happen in the 1940s?

CHAPTER 7

More Wolverine Perfection 1940 to 1949

The decade of the Forties began like no decade in the history of America. The United States was preparing for war. World events were looking bad for our allies. All free nations were looking for support from the United States. The BIG question was not "Would America be involved in World War II?" It was simply, "When?" And, when America did go to war, would enough young men be available to play football? Yes, there were lots of questions and a world of uncertainty surrounding American life in 1940. Nobody knew what the future would hold, and nobody knew what would happen to the Michigan and Michigan State football programs. It was a very uncertain time in Michigan, America, and the world!

Game # 35: October 5, 1940 at Michigan Stadium in Ann Arbor

BACKGROUND INFORMATION:

There were no rules changes for the 1940 season. It was going to be another season of monitoring the game and looking for ways to upgrade play and make it safer. The game continued to move forward despite the tough times in the early 1930s. The 1940's could be an opportunity to grow the game and get fans back into the stadiums.

Charlie Bachman was now in his eighth season at Michigan State. The energetic coach had enjoyed a remarkably successful run in East Lansing except for the disappointing 1939 season. It was time to reset the course of Spartan football. For the first time since 1908, Michigan State began the season with their hated rivals from Ann Arbor. Coach Bachman would learn a lot from this game since Michigan was expected to be a strong team in 1940.

Fritz Crisler began his third season in Ann Arbor in 1940. His coaching career at Michigan was off to a successful start, but he wanted more. Crisler knew he had the talent to win a Big Ten title and that would be his focus. Crisler and his Wolverines made football history when they became the first college team to fly cross-country to play a football game. The Wolverines flew west to sunny California to play the "Golden Bears" on September 28, 1940. As it turned out, it was a spectacular day for a "birthday boy" named Tom Harmon. Harmon ran over, around and through the California team and scored four touchdowns, passed for another, and kicked five extra points. Final score: Michigan 41 and California 0. It looked like Michigan was ready for the 1940 season. The big question was, "Could the Spartans stop Harmon and the rest of the Michigan football machine?"

GAME SUMMARY: MSC 14 UM 21

The thirty-fifth annual "in-state hate game" was played in Ann Arbor for the sixteenth straight year. The underdog Spartans gave the Wolverines a difficult test, but Michigan prevailed in the end. No one, except Coach Bachman, believed that Michigan State had a chance in this game. Michigan State knew they had to stop Tom Harmon, but they could not do it. The long-striding Harmon scored all twenty-one of Michigan's (three touchdowns and three points after touchdown) points and he helped limit the Spartans to just fourteen. Walt Pawlowski was the star for Michigan State because of his two touchdowns, but in the end MSC ended up on the short end of the score, again. The second largest crowd in series history (69,951) witnessed another fierce football struggle between two teams that, as usual, really did not like each other. (*DFP*, 10/6/1940, Page 31)

In the end, Michigan was the better team and the Spartans had to settle for another "moral" victory in the Tree City. Yes, both teams shed some more blood in this game, but Sparty gave just a little bit more. Another tough loss for the East Lansing footballers and a big sigh of relief for Michigan.

Team	1st	2nd	3rd	4th	Final
MSC	0	7	0	7	14
UM	7	7	7	0	21

SERIES UPDATE:

For the third straight year, Michigan added to their dominant series advantage. For the record, the Wolverines now claimed 26 wins, 6 losses, and 3 ties. Michigan State continued to lose ground. The Spartans could not dwell on it too much because they had to play a tough Purdue team the next week. Time to move on and win as many remaining games as possible.

SERIES MILESTONES:

Oddly enough, game number thirty-five of the annual Mitten State pigskin series did not have any noteworthy milestones. Although it did not happen until the end of the season, Tom Harmon won the Heisman Trophy and was declared the best football player in America. So, it could be said that this was the first series game with a future Heisman Trophy winner on the field. Nothing else to highlight here.

SEASON SUMMARIES:

The Spartans came back after the Michigan loss and defeated Purdue (20-7). Unfortunately, MSC only won two of their final six games and finished with the first losing season in Charlie Bachman's tenure (3-4-1). Michigan State made a lot of progress in the Bachman Era, but the 1939 and 1940 seasons were disappointing. Clearly, this was an important time in Michigan State's football history. Coach Bachman would have to figure out how to get the Spartans back to their winning ways, or else!

After they defeated Michigan State, the Wolverines kept on winning. They finished October 1940 with a perfect record of 5 wins and 0 losses. That streak came to a painful end in Minneapolis when a Harmon missed extra point was the difference. Final score: Minnesota 7 and Michigan 6. That was Michigan's only loss of the season, but it was a big one. It cost the Wolverines an undefeated season and a Big Ten title. Michigan finished another winning season with a final record of 7 wins and 1 painful loss. So far, Fritz Crisler had lost all three games to his former employer in Minnesota. Tom Harmon earned All-American honors and became the first Michigan man to win the Heisman Trophy. Michigan end Ed Frutig also earned All-American honors in 1940.

Game # 36: September 27, 1941 at Michigan Stadium in Ann Arbor

BACKGROUND INFORMATION:

The game of college football just kept "tweaking" along in 1941 as adjustments were made to player substitution rules, the forward pass and handling the ball behind the line of scrimmage. First, to increase participation, coaches could now substitute at any time, but once a player came onto the field or left the field they had to remain on or off the field for at least one play. Second, an incomplete pass into the end zone was changed from a touchback to a simple change of possession at the previous spot of the ball. Finally, it was now legal to hand the ball forward if it was behind the neutral zone. Certainly, no big changes to the game, but some adjustments that streamlined the game and provided opportunities for more players to get on the field. (Herget, Page 167)

One other item of series interest was that Michigan State had a new President. John Hannah became the chief administrator of Michigan State College on July 1, 1941. Mr. Hannah had a BIG vision for his alma mater. He spent one year as an undergraduate student at Michigan before attending Michigan State. That single year had a tremendous impact on his thinking and the role that a major university could play in a state, the nation, and the world. Hannah also saw the importance of a nationally known athletic "brand."

John Hannah made it clear to Athletic Director Ralph Young and all MSC coaches that Michigan State would compete with the best teams in the country in all sports, but especially football! John Hannah's vision also included membership in the Big Ten Conference. Michigan State applied for conference admission in 1937 and was rejected. John Hannah had a habit of not taking "No" for an answer when he wanted something. Mr. Hannah really, really wanted admission into the Big Ten and he would do everything in his power to accomplish this objective.

For the first time in series history, Michigan State and Michigan began a football season against each other. This would not be the typical "practice game" against a weak opponent to get ready for the season. No, there would be no warmup games for either team. This was it! Game number thirty-six was also the first series game ever played in September.

The Spartans started the ninth year of the Charlie Bachman era with many returning lettermen, but nobody expected the Spartans to be a powerhouse team. Coach Bachman always tried to keep the Michigan game in perspective, since it was only one game. He always said that he prepared his team the same way, regardless of who was on the schedule. However, no one really believed him, especially since his teams won four straight rival games in the Thirties. Now that he was on his own three-game losing streak it had to be getting old. This was an important game for the rivalry and for the season. Yes, it was a BIG game!

Michigan lost some serious star-power from the 1940 team as All-Americans Tom Harmon and Ed Frutig graduated. They also lost captain Forest Evashevski and lineman Ralph Fritz. The experts felt that Michigan had lost too much talent to be a good team in 1941. Many believed that they could lose three or four games. (Perry, Page 184) The Wolverines would learn a great deal about their team/season when the Spartans came to town.

GAME SUMMARY: MSC 7 UM 19

Just like thirty-five previous games, series game number thirty-six was another hard-fought battle between two teams who really wanted to beat each other's brains in! Yes, it was getting that bad. Michigan State had the audacity to take the lead on the third play of the game when Jack Fenton ran seventy-four yards for a touchdown. A successful extra point gave MSC a 7-0 lead after fifteen minutes of play. Michigan's Tom Kuzma, Harmon's replacement, scored to even the game in the second quarter. The first half ended in a 7-7 deadlock. (*DFP*, 9/28/1941, Page 41)

Tom Kuzma and fullback Bob Westfall scored touchdowns in the third quarter and Michigan's defense held the Spartans scoreless for the rest of the game. Michigan won the first down battle by a margin of 14-7. The Wolverines controlled the game with 235-yards on the ground compared to only 104-yards for the Spartans. MSC did win the passing game by a margin of 56-yards to 29-yards for the Maize and Blue. Michigan's offensive line punished the Spartans and rushed for over two-hundred-thirty yards on the ground. Meanwhile, the Spartans barely rushed for one hundred yards and probably punted a lot. Yes, Michigan controlled the game, especially in the second half. (*DFP*, 9/28/1941, Page 41)

Team	1st	2nd	3rd	4th	Final
MSC	7	0	0	0	7
UM	0	7	12	0	19

SERIES UPDATE:

Fritz Crisler "officially" re-gained control of the series with his fourth consecutive win over the Spartans. The Wolverines increased their series advantage to 27 wins, 6 losses, and 3 ties. Michigan State was feeling the same way that Michigan felt four years ago. Charlie Bachman and his Spartans must have been wondering when they would beat Michigan again. It would not be until 1942, at the soonest!

SERIES MILESTONES:

As always, the series game produced some interesting firsts and other unique items that added to the colorful history of the rivalry. Jack Fenton's touchdown run in the first two minutes of the game may have been the fastest score in the history of the series. As I mentioned in the beginning of this section, this was the first time in series history that the rivals opened the season against each other. It was also the first game ever between Michigan and Michigan State in the month of September. Finally, it was the fifth consecutive series game that drew at least sixty-thousand fans. Interest in the rivalry was never greater. Fielding Yost must have been smiling because of the "deal" he made with Ralph Young back in the Twenties. Mr. Yost did not have to worry about small crowds showing up for a season opener. No, this was no longer part of the plan unless something drastic happened!

One thing that coach and athletic director Fritz Crisler

had to worry about was halftime crowd control. After the players entered the tunnel for their halftime meetings, hundreds of fans from both schools gathered on the field to share insults. Suddenly, a series of small fist fights and shoving matches took place. Many fans were chasing each other around the field and throwing punches. Wow, you cannot make this stuff up! As far as I know, this was the first "Halftime Brawl: in series history. (For an interesting video of this "event" check out Dr. Sap's You Tube Channel for September 27, 1941)

SEASON SUMMARIES:

Michigan State bounced back from the Michigan loss to defeat a good Marquette team (13-7). Then, the Spartans lost two of the next three games and things looked bad for the MSC footballers. Coach Bachman pushed his team and had them ready for a strong Purdue squad. The Spartans earned a tie (0-0) and finished with three straight wins. Bachman's team posted a final record of 5 wins, 3 losses, and 1 tie. For the first time in three years, Michigan State finished with a winning record and things were looking up again. Charlie Bachman would look to make improvements in the off-season and figure out how to beat Michigan again.

The 1941 Wolverines surprised a lot of experts and maybe some fans too. Michigan finished the season with 6 wins, 1 loss, and 1 tie. Once again, the Gophers from Minnesota ruined things for Crisler and the Wolverines. Fullback Bob Westfall earned All-American honors during the 1941 season. Like everyone in America, Fritz Crisler was paying close attention to world events. The "war years" changed and challenged college football for many years to come. Most people were taking it one day and one week at a time.

Game # 37: October 03, 1942 at Michigan Stadium in Ann Arbor

BACKGROUND INFORMATION:

There were no important changes to the rules prior to the 1942 season. Everyone was thankful to be playing and more concerned with how to find enough players to put a team on the field. Plenty of change was already happening with players leaving school to join the military, wartime travel restrictions and a host of other issues. The rules makers hoped that the war would end sooner than later. However, that did not turn out to be the case. College football continued to be played at schools around the country. However, many institutions lost their football programs for one or more years because they did not have enough players!

Coach Charlie Bachman began his tenth season at the helm of the Michigan State program in 1942. He had several good players returning to the field and was hopeful for another winning season. It would be an understatement to say he was not itching to beat Michigan again. Coach Bachman was even in his last eight games against Michigan. After winning four straight series games from 1934 to 1937, Coach Bachman had had lost the last four to Fritz Crisler's Wolverines. Charlie Bachman had a long off-season to think about Michigan. Once again, the hated Wolverines were the first team on the 1942 Spartan schedule. He knew it was time to get off to a good start and beat Michigan, again, in Ann Arbor.

Michigan had plenty of excellent players returning in 1942. Yes, the Wolverines were expected to win their fair share of games. The Wolverines scheduled a "warm up" game ahead of Michigan State for the first time in a long time. However, it was a difficult game against a service team of former college football players in training for the U. S. Navy. The Great Lakes Naval Training Center game was difficult, but Michigan passed the test with a 9-0 win. Bring on Michigan State!

GAME SUMMARY: MSC 0 UM 20

Series game number thirty-seven was played in Ann Arbor for the eighteenth consecutive season. The impact of the war reduced the crowd to just over forty thousand people which is amazing considering everything that was going on at the time. It was another tough, bruising, bloody football game that pitted two good teams against each other. However, the Wolverines were the better team in this game.

The Wolverines and Spartans played to a scoreless tie for the first half. Then, Michigan asserted itself with two touchdowns in the third quarter and put the game out of reach with another score in the final period. Don Robinson, Frank Wardley, and Warren Yaap scored touchdowns and Jim "Super Toe" Briske kicked two out of three extra points. (*DFP*, 10/4/1942, Page 21)

Once again, some key numbers explained why Michigan won this game so easily. First, they won the first down battle by a margin of 15-3. Second, the Wolverines rolled up 208-yards rushing compared to minus sixteen rushing yards for MSC. Third, Crisler's footballers gained 72-yards in the air compared to only 26-yards for the Spartans. With all the statistics in their favor, the Maize and Blue footballers should have won by a much bigger margin. However, the Black and Gold defenders made enough stops to keep the game close, especially in the first half. (*DFP*, 10/4/1942, Page 21)

106

Team	1st	2nd	3rd	4th	Final
MSC	0	0	0	0	0
UM	0	0	13	7	20

SERIES UPDATE:

Michigan posted another series win and increased their advantage over the feisty Spartans. The Wolverines now had 28 wins, 6 losses, and 3 ties. Both teams moved on to finish their seasons, but the future was uncertain for everyone.

SERIES MILESTONES:

Although it was not known at the time, this was the last series game for two years. The Spartans had a nine-game schedule planned for the 1943 season. However, they had to cancel the season due to a lack of players. A total of 134 Spartans (out of 135 varsity and freshman players) were called to military service before the 1943 season started. (Stabley, Page 111) World War II definitely impacted the Spartan football program. Michigan State did field a team in 1944 but could not arrange a game with Michigan. Series game number thirty-eight did not happen until 1945.

SEASON SUMMARIES:

Michigan State College had an up and down football season in 1942. After losing to Michigan, they defeated Wayne State, but lost the next week to Marquette. The Spartans defeated Great Lakes (14-0) and finished the season with two wins, two ties and another loss. Michigan States posted a final record of 4 wins, 3 losses, and 2 tie games in 1942. It was another winning season, but a disappointment because of the fifth straight loss to Michigan. Charlie Bachman's Spartans were winning their fair share of games against everyone but Michigan. Were the natives starting to get restless in East Lansing?

Michigan's fifth consecutive win over Michigan State kept the season going in the right direction. However, their modest two game winning streak came to an end against another military team called Iowa Pre-Flight. Once again, the roster was loaded with a very impressive list of former college players. They were good enough to defeat the Wolverines by a score of 26-14. The Wolverines won five of their last seven games. on their schedule. Both loses were to old rivals. Minnesota beat them by a score of 16-14 in week five and the Buckeyes beat them in the next to last game of the season by a score of 21-7.

The Wolverines finished with a record of 7 wins and 3 losses in 1942. Guard Julius Franks became the first African American to earn All-American honors at Michigan. Tackle Albert Wistert also earned All-American honors in 1942.

Game # 38: September 29, 1945 at Michigan Stadium in Ann Arbor

BACKGROUND INFORMATION:

There was one small change in the rules for the 1945 season. To encourage the modern "T-Formation," it was now legal to throw a forward pass from anywhere behind the line of scrimmage. That was it, no other changes were adopted for college football in 1943. The primary focus of the season was monitoring the games and getting back to "normal."

One item to note was a new symbol of Spartan pride on the Michigan State campus. A giant statue of a Spartan warrior, created by Professor Leonard Jungwirth of the MSC Art Department, was officially dedicated on June 9, 1945. It was an instant hit with athletes, students, alumni and MSC supporters. Of course, it is affectionately known as "Sparty" to the Michigan State faithful. (Emmerich, Page 96)

Charlie Bachman's twelfth season was an important time at Michigan State College. Once again, Spartan football fortunes appeared to be on the rise. Michigan State posted an excellent record of 6 wins, 1 loss and 0 ties in 1944. Like every coach in America, Coach Bachman did not have an abundance of returning players, but he had enough. His backfield in 1945 consisted of Glenn Johnson, Steve Contos, Jack Breslin and Russ Reader.

Bachman also had some excellent lineman who would help the Spartan backs run to daylight, especially Breslin and Reader. The Spartan schedule did not include Michigan in 1944, but it would be the first game on the schedule for 1945. As usual, the Michigan State vs Michigan game would be an important test for both teams.

Like the Spartans, Michigan had some excellent players returning to the team, but they were young. Many of them started as eighteen-year-old freshmen because of the wartime player shortages. The Wolverines lost captain elect Bruce Hilkene to the Navy. Two excellent freshmen from the 1944 team, Dick Rifenburg and Gene Derricotte joined the military before the season started. Coach Crisler was not sure who would be playing, but he knew that Michigan would have a team in 1945. It was a young team, an incredibly young team. In fact, the team would be so young that the press would simply refer to the Wolverines as "fuzzy-cheeked kids." (Perry, Page 198) Coach Crisler and his "kids" would be ready for the season. However, nobody, including Crisler, knew how good they would be.

GAME SUMMARY: MSC 0 UM 40

For the second time in history and the second time in three-years, the Wolverines and Spartans faced off in September. Game number thirty-eight of the Michigan vs Michigan State football series went to Crisler's "fuzzy-cheeked kids." The Wolverines dominated the Spartans and shut them out for the second consecutive time. Michigan scored in every quarter and made it look easy.

Wally Teninga led the way with two touchdowns for Michigan who also scored on a pass-run play and an interception return. Overall, Michigan rushed for almost three hundred yards (274) and passed for over one-hundred yards (128) as well. The lifeless Spartans were held to eighty-five yards of offense (37-yards rushing and 48-yards passing). (DFP, (9/30/1945, Pages 35-36) Pretty hard to beat anybody with those kinds of numbers!

Team	1st	2nd	3rd	4th	Final
MSC	0	0	0	0	0
UM	7	13	7	13	40

SERIES UPDATE:

Once again, Michigan increased their series advantage at the expense of the frustrated Spartans. Although the war would soon be over and things were promising to return to normal, it was hard to tell when parity would return in the series. The Wolverines "owned" the series again since the arrival of Fritz Crisler and there was no end in sight. Michigan's record against the Spartans now stood at an imposing 29 wins, 6 losses, and 3 ties.

SERIES MILESTONES:

The thirty-eighth game of the series marked the resumption of the annual in-state football blood-letting ritual after a two-year break. Despite the hiatus, both teams moved forward during a difficult time in America's history. Now, maybe the series would continue without interruption for a long, long time. One final item to note was that this was the first time that a series team was ranked in a national poll prior to the game. The Wolverines checked in at number eleven in the Associated Press poll when they resumed their rivalry with the Michigan State Spartans.

SEASON SUMMARIES:

After losing to Michigan, the Spartans defeated an excellent Kentucky team (7-6) coached by Bear Bryant. The next week they won against a strong Pittsburgh team (12-7). Bachman's football team extended their winning streak to three games with a solid win over Wayne State (27-7). They battled to a 13-13 draw against Marquette and defeated Missouri (14-7) on Homecoming Day to push their record to 4 wins, 1 loss, and 1 tie. The Spartans lost two of their next three games and ended with a final record of 5 wins, 3 losses, and 1 tie. Another disappointing winning season is what Spartan fans probably thought about the 1945 season. As usual, a loss to Michigan always left a bad taste in every Spartan's mouth. Once again, Charlie Bachman had to go back to the drawing board and figure out how to win more games and beat Michigan again. Any questions?

Michigan's record was 2 wins and 1 loss after beating Michigan State. Fritz Crisler's "fuzzy-cheeked kids" won five of their last seven games. They defeated five straight Big Ten teams along the way but lost to Army and Navy. Michigan played an amazing game against the defending national champion Army team. Crisler used the 1941 substitution rules to full advantage and allowed his "kids" to compete for three quarters against the heavily favored West Pointers. Michigan eventually lost the game by a score of 28-7.

Crisler's young Wolverines had a slightly worse fate against Navy and lost by a final score of 33-7. Michigan finished with a record of 7 wins and 3 losses. It was another successful season for the Wolverines, but another second-place tie in the Big Ten was disappointing for Crisler and his young team. Michigan would have to find a way to win another conference championship and cut down on their non-conference losses.

Game # 39: November 9, 1946 at Michigan Stadium in Ann Arbor

BACKGROUND INFORMATION:

There were no rule changes or adjustments to the game for the 1946 season. Of course, lots of "adjusting" going on all around the country. The war was finally over. Americans were looking forward to living without the shadow of war darkening their cities and towns. Once again, college football had weathered another crisis. School administrators, coaches and players were hopeful that the game would reach new heights in the last half of the 1940s.

The biggest football news in the state of Michigan came when Fielding H. Yost, one of the legends of college football passed away on August 12, 1946 at the age of seventy-five. The "old man" was a giant of the game and he impacted college football for over fifty years. His loss provided the backdrop for the thirty-ninth series game.

Once again, because of a "deal" that Yost struck with Ralph Young in 1932, the game was played again in Ann Arbor. That made it twenty consecutive games in Ann Arbor and the eighteenth straight game played at Michigan Stadium. The annual grudge match was scheduled for November for the first time in thirteen years. Interestingly, the 1946 season posed the exact opposite problem that challenged Bachman and Crisler during the war years. Instead of scrambling to field a team, both men had an abundance of talent to work with. Now, many excellent players were available at every position. The depth charts were three and four players deep. It was almost a coaches' delight, except that the difficulty of playing all that talent and keeping it "happy" would be the biggest challenge in 1946.

The 1946 season was important in East Lansing because it was the Fiftieth season of SAC/MAC/MSC football. It was also the year that the University of Chicago officially withdrew from the Big Ten, now Big Nine, Conference. Finally, it was the third time that MSC's conference admission request was rejected. Michigan State College's first application was rejected in 1937 and the second one saw the same fate in 1943. According to David J. Young, author of *The Student and His Professor*, john Hannah was undaunted, but the continued rejections were getting old. Hannah's former Michigan law professor, Ralph Aigler, was leading the rejection efforts. As the Big Nine's most senior faculty representative, he wielded enormous power and influence in the conference. Aigler believed that MSC was not adhering to conference standards on athletic subsidies and other important issues. He would not support any Spartan admission efforts until he was assured that Michigan State fully complied with all conference practices. (Young, Page 2) More on that later.

Coach Charlie Bachman entered his thirteenth season as head coach in East Lansing. Bachman's Spartans had lost some of the luster that they had in his early years. Yes, Michigan State was playing a tougher schedule, but that is something that was required if they ever hoped to gain national respect. It was also something that had to be done if Michigan State ever wanted to get in the Big Ten conference. The days of playing Alma, Albion, Adrian, and Grinnell were long gone. The Spartans desperately wanted to join America's football elite. They had to step up their game. The 1946 season was a new opportunity to gain the respect they sought. Of course, there was no better way to get national respect than by beating their football neighbor to the southeast—those hated Wolverines.

Once again, Michigan was expected to field a strong team in 1946. How strong depended upon how well Coach Crisler could mold his returning players and war veterans into a cohesive team. Like Coach Bachman, Fritz Crisler had never coached a team of men, not young men. These were real "men" and these men had given some of the best years of their life in the service of their country. Now, they were home, and they wanted to take advantage of their G.I Bill benefits. Of course, they wanted to get back on the football field and play the game they loved! There was little doubt that Michigan would have an excellent team in 1946. The big question was "How good would they be?"

GAME SUMMARY: MSC 7 UM 55

Once again, the Maize and Blue bullies beat the Spartans up badly on the field. The Wolverines scored twice in every quarter and simply dominated the MSC footballers from start to finish. As usual, the physical battles in the trenches bloodied many of the players. Unfortunately for the Spartans they lost more in this game.

Michigan had plenty of stars on the field in this game. Bob Chappuis scored the first touchdown and passed to Pete Elliott for another. Gene Derricotte also ran for a score and threw one to Paul White. Don Robinson and Jack Weisenbereger also ran for Wolverine scores. Elmar Mader and Tony Momsen each intercepted Spartan passes and returned them for a touchdown. Placekicker Jim Briske converted six of eight extra points. The Spartans scored on a 72-yard pass play from Horace Smith to Frank Waters. (DFP, 11/10/1946, Pages 39 & 41) As usual, some key numbers told the real story of Michigan's big win.

The Wolverines totaled five hundred yards of offense (293-yards rushing and 207-yards passing). Crisler's defenders held the Spartans to 47-yards rushing and 165-yards passing. Yes, it was ugly for Spartan fans, but that is what happened. The game was played in front of a record-breaking crowd and the Wolverine fans must have enjoyed it very much!

Team	1st	2nd	3rd	4th	Final
MSC	0	0	7	0	7
UM	14	14	13	14	55

SERIES UPDATE:

Another Wolverine victory made it seven straight wins against the disheartened Spartans. Yes, it was another painful defeat for Michigan State. There was no good news for MSC in this game except the fact that the Spartans scored. Other than that, it was a total blowout and left Charlie Bachman and his Spartans looking for answers. Michigan's advantage grew to 30 wins, 6 losses, and 3 ties. The distance between the two schools had not changed on the map, but the gap between the two programs was getting bigger and bigger!

SERIES MILESTONES:

First, game number thirty-nine marked the final series game of the Charlie Bachman Era. After thirteen seasons Coach Bachman was ready to hang up his whistle. He finished as the longest tenured and winningest coach in Spartan history with a record of 70 wins, 34 losses and 10 ties. His ten winning seasons in thirteen years produced a winning rate of almost sixty-six percent (.658). Bachman won more games against Michigan than any other man in Spartan football history. Coach Bachman was also the first man to win four straight games against Michigan. He ended his series career with a final record of 4 wins, 8 losses and 0 ties against the Wolverines.

The 1946 game also marked the thirtieth win for the Wolverines which, of course, was a series best. It was also the first game in which one of the teams was ranked going into the contest. The Wolverines were ranked as the eleventh best team in the country when they met the Spartans in Ann Arbor on November 9, 1946. Game number thirty-nine was another series attendance record breaker as a crowd of over seventy-six thousand (76,373) people showed up for the Michigan-Michigan State blood bath. This game was also the first game that saw a team (UM) score at least ten points in every quarter. Finally, this game marked the last series game for the Black and Gold Spartan uniforms. MSC would be going back to the future, almost, with their game attire in 1947.

SEASON SUMMARIES:

Coach Charlie Bachman's final season at MSC was a disappointment. The season began with high expectations and it looked like the combination of returning talent and war-time veterans might be something special. As it turned out, Coach Bachman might have been a little bit uncomfortable working with the "men" that he had to coach in 1946. Author Fred Stabley suggested that Bachman's approach just did not work with the military men that returned from the war to play football at MSC. (Stabley, Page 118)

As it turned out, the Spartans had an "up and down" season and finished with the same number of "ups" as "downs" (5 wins and 5 losses). Bachman had some big losses (Michigan and Kentucky) and had some huge wins against Penn State, Maryland, Marquette, and Washington State. In the end, Charlie Bachman decided to walk away from the Spartans and turn the MSC football program over to someone else. Unfortunately for everyone in East Lansing, the Fiftieth season in MSC football history was nothing to celebrate!

Michigan's football season was successful in 1946, but it was also one that could have been so much better with a little more offense and just a little more defense. The Wolverines won their first two games, lost two, tied one, and ended with four straight victories. If the Wolverines could have scored fourteen more points at the right time, they would have finished with a perfect record of 9 wins, 0 losses, and 0 ties. As it turned out, they finished another successful season (6 wins, 2 losses, and 1 tie). Michigan finished second in the Big Ten for the third straight season. Elmer Madar, who played end, earned All-American honors for his outstanding play. The 1946 season was probably not what Fritz Crisler was hoping for, but it was what it was. Maybe Coach Crisler could put together a magical season in 1947, or maybe not!

Game # 40: September 27, 1947 at Michigan Stadium in Ann Arbor

BACKGROUND INFORMATION:

For the second straight year, the rules makers decided to leave the game alone for another season. The first season after the end of the war years was a success. It was time to enjoy American college football and watch the game grow.

Game number forty of the mostly annual football series was played again in Ann Arbor for the twenty-first straight time. It was also the nineteenth straight series game in Michigan Stadium. Yes, Ann Arbor was MSC's second football "home." It was the season opener for both teams. Spartan fans were probably asking, "Would MSC ever host the Wolverines in East Lansing again?"

Clarence Lester "Biggie" Munn was the next man up in East Lansing in 1947. Coach Biggie Munn was completely familiar with Coach Crisler and Michigan. He played for Crisler at the University of Minnesota. As a matter of fact, Munn played extremely well for Crisler and earned All-American honors in 1930 and 1931. Munn also coached for him at Michigan from 1938 to 1945. Coach Munn probably learned a lot from his former coach and mentor, but it does not appear that they were the best of friends. Apparently, when Crisler met Munn at a pre-season event in 1947, he gruffly asked Munn, "And what are you doing back in the state of Michigan?" (Stabley, Page 121) Not exactly a warm welcome from a former coach and mentor, but it would get worse because Biggie Munn's first game was also his first game against Crisler and Michigan. It was not pretty for MSC!

Michigan entered the 1947 season with another stacked team and Wolverine fans were hoping that Coach Crisler could put together a magical season in Ann Arbor. The Wolverines had a successful seven year run under Fritz Crisler, but they always seemed to come up a little short at the end of the season. Michigan earned one conference title (1943) during Crisler's tenure, but they also had six second place finishes. Michigan fans wanted another Big Ten Championship. Maybe it was time for Michigan to do something special, again!

GAME SUMMARY: MSC 0 UM 55

This series game went down as one of the most one-sided defeats in Spartan football history. To make matters worse, it appeared that Coach Crisler was determined to make Coach Munn look really, bad. It was just awful! Llyal Smith of the *Detroit Free Press* wrote that "Mighty Michigan served notice on the Western Conference that it is ready for whatever the 1947 season has to offer." (*DFP*, 9/27/1947, Page 21)

Michigan scored in every quarter and became the first team in series history to score the same number of points (55) in back-to-back victories. This was the second time in series history that the series game was also the season opener for both teams. As it turned out it was an "eye" opener for Wolverine fans and a "black eye" for the Spartans. Crisler's footballers opened the scoring on a short run by Jack Weisenburger. Then, Bob Chappuis ran for two touchdowns and threw for another. Michigan led by a score of 28-0 at halftime. Bump Elliott, Chappuis and fullback Dick Kempthorn all rushed for touchdowns in the second half. Center Dan Dworsky returned a Spartan fumble for another six points. Michigan kicker Jim "Super Toe" Briske converted seven extra points. (*DFP*, 9/27/1947, Page 21)

The Spartans were battered, bloodied, and bruised when they left Ann Arbor on September 27, 1947. The Wolverines outgained the Spartans by a margin of 504-yards to 56-yards. Yes, you read it right! Only two words come to mind. One is "domination" and the other is "embarrassment." That pretty much summed it up for this game. Yes, it was a long trip back to East Lansing for the Spartans and their fans.

Another thing that just added more insult to the whole affair was a half-time plumbing problem in the Spartan locker room. Apparently, a sewer pipe broke and Michigan State had to walk around in water that was tainted by raw sewage while Biggie tried to get his team ready to play in the second half. Of course, Munn thought that Crisler had arranged this unfortunate event. When he spoke to his players after the game, Coach Munn was enraged! He promised right then and there that he would "Get even with Michigan!" (Stabley, Page 122)

Team	1st	2nd	3rd	4th	Final
MSC	0	0	0	0	0
UM	14	14	20	7	55

SERIES UPDATE:

Yes, the eighth straight Spartan loss was a very bitter pill to swallow, but it was still only one game. Coach Munn would have to worry about Michigan later. Instead, he focused on getting his team ready to play the next game against Mississippi State. It was time to move on. The Wolverines also had bigger fish to fry, Stanford was coming to town and the Wolverines had to get ready for the California boys. For the record, Michigan increased their series advantage to 31 wins, 6 losses, and 3 ties.

SERIES MILESTONES:

The fortieth game in series history was a milestone by itself. Television station WWJ on Detroit televised this UM vs MSC matchup for the first time in series history. This game also marked the first game for Coach Biggie Munn, his first series game and his first series loss. This game was also the final series game for Fritz Crisler. Coach Crisler finished with a perfect record of 8 wins, 0 losses, and 0 ties against the Spartans. No doubt, Michigan State fans were glad to see him go although he would still have plenty to do with the series since he was now the full-time athletic director at Michigan. The 1947 game also saw the return of green and white uniforms for the Spartans. Coach Munn wanted a change in attire for his MSC footballers and going back to the school's original colors seemed like the right thing to do. For the first, and only time, the Spartans wore white helmets with a green wing in a series game.

SEASON SUMMARIES:

Biggie Munn's first game was a disaster, but his first season was not! Coach Munn taught his players to have a short memory after a tough loss. It was time to move on and that is exactly what the Spartans did. Munn decided to break out some new green helmets and home jerseys for the Mississippi State game. The new uniforms worked since Munn's Spartans won 7-0.

Coach Munn's footballers won two more over Washington State (21-7) and Iowa State (20-0) before losing a close one to Bear Bryant and Kentucky (7-6). They won their last four games to finish the season with a record of 7 wins and 2 losses. The Biggie Munn Era had a rocky start, but he turned things around. There is no doubt that he would focus his off-season work on "getting even" with Crisler and Michigan in 1948.

Fritz Crisler did put together a magical season in 1947. You can't get much better than 10 wins and 0 losses. Coach Crisler's veteran team was deep at every position and he became the first coach to embrace the concept of two-platoon football that had specialized players on offense and defense. Only one player, Bump Elliott, played regularly on both sides of the ball. Everybody else was a specialist on the offense and defense. Crisler built a complete team. The offense was so skilled at executing the buck-laterals, spinners, reverses and passes that the press simply called them the "Mad Magicians." (Perry, Page 212) They were magical to watch unless you were the opposing defense. Michigan was also good on defense that year, but there were no fancy nicknames. They did post five shutouts and only allowed fifty-three points in ten games. The Wolverines won two close games against Minnesota (13-6) and Illinois (14-7), but every other win was by twenty-one points or more.

Halfbacks Bob Chappuis and Bump Elliott earned All-American honors in 1947. Michigan's perfect season allowed them to win the "trifecta" which was the Big Nine Championship, the Rose Bowl, and the National Championship. Fritz Crisler decided it was time to stop coaching and become a full-time athletic director. What else was there left to accomplish on the football field? Nothing, absolutely nothing! Fritz Crisler became the first and only Michigan football coach to win a national championship in his final season.

Image 6 Fritz Crisler is the only man in series history to post a perfect record of 8 wins, 0 losses and 0 ties. (Permission: Bentley Historical Library at The University of Michigan, See Page 369)

Game # 41: September 25, 1948 at Macklin Stadium in East Lansing

BACKGROUND INFORMATION:

The 1948 college football season saw two changes to the game. The first one allowed the use of a one-inch kicking tee. Change number two allowed unlimited substitution on a change of possession.

MSC President John Hannah continued his relentless pursuit of Big Nine Conference admission, but the Spartans were rejected for the fifth time in May 1948. (Young, Page 248) In a huge concession to Ralph Aigler and Fritz Crisler, MSC ended their Jenison Awards Program which was a Michigan State subsidy program that raised a lot of eyebrows in the Big Ten. Finally, Hannah's personal lobbying of Big Ten school presidents proved to be successful. MSC was tentatively approved for conference membership on December 14, 1948. (Young, Page 275) But, enough of that, let us talk about the 1948 series game between the Mitten State's hated rivals.

Game number forty-one was one to remember for two important reasons. First, it was another dedication game in East Lansing. The Spartans, in their quest to join the Big Nine conference, invested heavily in the future and expanded College Field. This magnificent new structure was named after one of their greatest coaches, John Macklin. This effort greatly expanded the stadium capacity (51,000) and sent a message to everyone that Michigan State was serious about football and athletics in general. The second reason this game was important was that this would be the first game in East Lansing since 1924. The fine folks in East Lansing wanted to make sure that the wonderful people from Ann Arbor still knew how to get to the home of the Michigan State Spartans!

Michigan was on a fourteen-game unbeaten streak when the 1948 season began. The defending national champions won every game in 1947, but they lost Coach Fritz Crisler to retirement and their entire starting backfield to graduation. There was certainly enough talent for a winning season, but no one was predicting greatness for this bunch, especially with a rookie coach named Bennie Oosterbaan. No one really knew what to expect from the Michigan Wolverines at the start of the 1948 football season. There were just too many questions.

Coach Biggie Munn was back for his second season in 1948. He led his team to an extraordinarily successful season despite being embarrassed by Michigan in his first game as Michigan State's football coach. Fans in East Lansing were optimistic about the season and everyone was looking forward to the Macklin Stadium dedication game. It was a game that Coach Munn had been pointing towards since the 1947 season ended. It was time for his Spartans to shine!

GAME SUMMARY: UM 13 MSC 7

The fired-up Spartans gave the defending national and Big Ten Champions all they could handle in this classic in-state battle. Unfortunately, Michigan State came up short for the ninth straight time. It was another classic gridiron battle. The tackling was hard, the emotions were high, and plenty of blood was spilled to "officially" christen "new" Macklin Stadium for the football ages.

117

Michigan scored early in the first quarter on a 40-yard touchdown pass from Tom Peterson to Dick Rifenburg. When Peterson kicked the extra point, Michigan had a 7-0 first quarter lead which they maintained until halftime. The Spartans evened the game in the third quarter when Lynn Chadnois threw a touchdown pass to Hank Minarik. With a successful point after touchdown kick, the Spartans had evened the score at 7-7. Tom Peterson provided the final margin of victory with a five-yard touchdown run in the fourth quarter, but the kick was missed. The Spartans fought hard until the end and drove the ball to the Michigan two-yard line late in the game. However, an interception by Wally Teninga sealed the win for the Wolverines.

This was the official end to the dedication festivities. Once again, Michigan spoiled another special day in Michigan State football history. Yet, another reason for the folks in East Lansing to really dislike those hated Wolverines! (*DFP*, 9/26/1948, Page 23) The devastated Spartans must have been wondering why Michigan kept winning these series games. The good news was that it was not a "blow out." However, it was still a loss, another tough loss to the disgusting Wolverines! Once again, MSC had too many "moral victories" and not enough wins against Michigan

Team	1st	2nd	3rd	4th	Final
UM	7	0	0	6	13
MSC	0	0	7	0	7

SERIES UPDATE:

The important thing for Oosterbann was that his Wolverines left East Lansing with another victory. Michigan's series road record was still perfect with 5 wins 0 losses and 1 tie. The Wolverines padded their hefty series advantage and extended their winning record to 32 wins, 6 losses, and 3 ties. Biggie Munn had taken two shots at Michigan. Unfortunately, he was 0-2-0. I know this did not set well with him, but he would not have time to worry about it until the off-season. He had a season to finish!

SERIES MILESTONES:

Of course, the dedication of Macklin Stadium was the big news in this game and so was the crowd! A huge gathering (51,526) shattered the old East Lansing series attendance record by about thirty-thousand people. This was the biggest sports crowd ever to witness an event in East Lansing! Another milestone for this game was Bennie Oosterbaan's first series game and his first series win. He became the seventh straight Michigan football coach to defeat Michigan State in his first game. Meanwhile, no Michigan State coach had ever won his first series game against the Wolverines!

SEASON SUMMARIES:

The Wolverines took some heat for not blowing out Michigan State. After allowing seven points in the Michigan State game, they reeled off three straight shutouts against Oregon, Purdue, and Northwestern to push their record to 4-0-0. They won two tough games against Minnesota (27-14) and Illinois (28-20) but allowed thirty-four points over those two games. Were they good enough to win out and claim another perfect season? Yes, they were good enough. Michigan extended their winning streak to twenty-three games with convincing victories over Navy (35-0), Indiana (54-0) and Ohio State (13-3).

Bennie Oosterbaan became the second coach in Michigan football history (joining Fielding Yost) to have a perfect season (9-0-0) and win the national championship and the Big Nine Championship in the process. It was another season to remember for the Wolverines. Three Michigan players (Quarterback Pete Elliott, End Dick Rifenburg and Tackle Alvin Wistert) were all recognized as first team All-Americans in 1948.

Coach Biggie Munn showed everyone that Michigan's narrow victory in game one was not because Michigan did not play well. It was because Michigan State was also a very good football team. The Spartans took their anger from game one and vented it on their guests from Hawaii. Final score: Michigan State 68 and Hawaii 21. Coach Munn's men were thoroughly outplayed in week three at Notre Dame and lost (26-7). Biggie Munn got his team back on track for Homecoming and the Spartans destroyed Arizona by a score of 61-7. A tie (14-14) at Penn State gave the Spartans a record of 2 wins, 2 losses, and 1 tie at the halfway mark of the season. MSC really got their offense rolling and scored over forty-points in four straight games—all wins. They finished the season with another tie (21-21) at Santa Clara. The good news for the Spartans was that they posted a final record of 6 wins, 2 losses, and 2 ties. Yes, it was another winning season for Coach Munn and more progress was made. However, he still needed a win over Michigan to satisfy the fans in East Lansing.

Game # 42: September 24, 1949 at Michigan Stadium in Ann Arbor

BACKGROUND INFORMATION:

There was only one minor adjustment to the rules in 1949. To clean up line-play and give the defense an equal chance, offensive blockers were required to keep their hands against their chest. It was hoped that the rule would reduce the number of holding calls and speed up the game. This rule change was a big adjustment for the offense and the impact on the game would be watched carefully during the 1949 season. (Herget, Page 119)

The big news surrounding the 1949 season occurred in Chicago on May 20, 1949. Big Nine Commissioner Kenneth L. (Tug) Wilson announced that Michigan State College would be the newest member of the Western Conference. Of course, it also meant that the Big Nine Conference was, again, the Big Ten Conference. Yes, Spartans everywhere were elated, but not Wolverine fans. Michigan had opposed Michigan State's efforts to join the conference for over twenty years because of differences in "philosophy" on athletic subsidies and institutional control of intercollegiate athletics. It came as no surprise that Michigan was less than excited about "little brother's" conference admission. Michigan State's official membership would be phased in over the next forty-two months. All sports, except football, began competing for conference championships during the 1950-1951 seasons. However, football would have to wait until the fall of 1953 because of scheduling challenges.

John Hannah, Michigan's States visionary president, was thrilled with the Big Ten admission vote. Steve Grinczel, author of *Michigan State Football: They Are Spartans*, described Hannah's take on this historic achievement. Speaking to a large campus gathering in December 1948 he said, "We are a great university. We needed this to put us over the hump in the minds of a few remaining skeptics (from Ann Arbor?). Now we are over that hump." (Grinczel, Page 46)

The forty-second game of the annual "blood-letting" event between Michigan and Michigan State took place, again, in Ann Arbor. After the 1947 season Michigan Athletic Director Fritz Crisler invested in permanent steel stands around the rim of the stadium which increased capacity to just over ninety-seven thousand people (97,239). Both teams were going to play in front of the largest crowd in series history on September 24, 1949.

Coach Biggie Munn had two winning seasons under his belt and his team appeared to be gaining some momentum. The big question for Biggie was, "Would this be the year that his Spartans would take down the Wolverines?" Coach Munn had many returning starters on both sides of the ball. This might be the year for the Green and White, or maybe not!

Michigan entered the 1949 season on a twenty-three-game winning streak that included two conference championships and two national championships. Coach Fritz Crisler was named Coach of the Year in 1947 and Bennie Oosterbaan received the same honor in 1948. It was the first time that two coaches from the same school had won the award in consecutive seasons. Michigan was definitely on a roll as the 1949 season approached. The only problem with being on top of the mountain is that one slip, one little slip can cause you to fall off your perch. Coach Oosterbaan was cautiously optimistic about his team's chances in 1949.

GAME SUMMARY: MSC 3 UM 7

Series game number forty-two was a punishing defensive struggle with both teams battling hard for every inch of turf. The Spartans scored first. George Smith kicked an eighteen-yard field goal after Michigan State recovered a Michigan fumble deep in Wolverine territory. Unfortunately, for the Spartans they did not get a touchdown which would have been so much better! Later in the first quarter, Coach Ooserbaan's footballers recovered a Spartan fumble at the Michigan State twenty-five-yard line. Quarterback Bill Putich finished the short drive with a nine-yard touchdown pass to Irv Wisniewski to put the Wolverines ahead to stay. A successful extra point made the score 7-3 at the end of the first quarter. That was all the scoring in the game. The rest of the game settled into a back-and-forth struggle to score and hang onto the ball. Both teams fumbled away scoring chances and finished a frustrating day with many failed opportunities. (*DFP*, 9/25/49), Page 21)

For the second straight season, the winner of the rushing battle did not win the game. Michigan State ran the ball for 92-yards which was three yards better than Michigan. However, the Wolverines won the passing game part of the game by a margin of 115-yards to 85-yards. Bennie's footballers also won the first down battle by a margin of 12 to 7. (*DFP*, 9/25/49), Page 21) It was a close one, that is for sure! Thanks to Michigan, Coach Biggie Munn began another season with a bad taste in his mouth. He would have to settle for another moral victory. Time to get ready for Marquette.

Team	1st	2nd	3rd	4th	Final
MSC	3	0	0	0	3
UM	7	0	0	0	7

SERIES UPDATE:

Michigan's win was their tenth straight against Michigan State. For the record, the Wolverine series advantage now stood at 33 wins, 6 losses, and 3 ties. Everyone in Wolverine Nation would enjoy another year of bragging rights against the frustrated Spartans. What else was new?

SERIES MILESTONES:

The forty-second game in series history absolutely shattered the old attendance record. Officially, Michigan stadium was filled to the new capacity of over ninety-seven thousand (97,239) which was twenty-three thousand more than the last record-breaking crowd in 1938. This was the first time in series history where every point was scored in the first quarter. Finally, this was the second time in Michigan vs Michigan State history where the Wolverines won every game, and the Spartans lost every game. After standing nose to nose with the Wolverines in the 1930s, the Spartans slipped badly in the Forties. Now, they had a new battle cry: "Bring on the Fifties!"

SEASON SUMMARIES:

Once again, the Spartans demonstrated the "short memory" that a team must have after a disappointing loss. They reeled off five consecutive wins and outscored their opponents by a margin of 190-41. Two straight losses to Notre Dame (34-21) and Oregon State (25-20) slowed down the Spartans, but they finished strong with a BIG win over Arizona (75-0)! The Spartans finished with a final record of 6 wins and 3 losses. It was another winning season for Biggie Munn, but he wanted more, much more. Despite the words of President Hannah in December 1948, the Spartans still were not over the "hump" on the football field. Coach Munn would spend the off-season fine tuning his "multiple offense" and figuring out how to beat Michigan.

Michigan's win over MSC extended their winning streak to twenty-four games. They pushed that number to twenty-five games with a win over Stanford (27-7). Then, the winning streak ended with a loss to Army (21-7). Northwestern defeated the Wolverines to make it two straight losses. Michigan's record was 2 wins and 2 losses with five games remaining in the 1949 season. Ooosterbaan's footballers won four of the last five games and tied the other. The Wolverines finished with a record of 6 wins, 2 losses, and 1 tie and a share of the conference title. Not a dream season like the last two, but still successful. Tackles Alvin Wistert and Allen "Brick" Wahl earned All American honors in 1949.

DECADE AND SERIES SUMMARY:

The fourth decade of the Twentieth Century was as good as it gets at Michigan and as bad as it can get for the Spartans. For the second time in series history, the Wolverines were perfect (8-0-0) in the decade against Michigan State. Clearly, the Wolverines were the most successful team in the state of Michigan from 1940 to 1949.

Decade and Series Summary 1898 to 1949

Time Frame	UM Won-Lost-Tied	MSC Won-Lost-Tied
1940-1949	8-0-0	0-8-0
1898-1949	33-6-3	6-33-3

The Spartans lost a lot of series ground in the Forties! All the progress they made in the Thirties was part of ancient history in East Lansing. However, it appeared that Biggie Munn was on his way to reducing the gap between the two rivals in 1948 and 1949. Now all he had to do was win a few games against Michigan! With Michigan State entering the Big Ten football battles in 1953, things would change between the two schools. Yes, things were about to get interesting!

PROGRAM SUMMARIES:

Michigan's football program was excellent for the entire decade, but "great" in 1947 and 1948. Their back-to-back national championships were reminiscent of the early Yost years. Crisler's last team and Oosterbaan's first were simply dominant. Michigan was at the top of their game and life was good in Ann Arbor. The numbers on the chart tell the complete story as Michigan increased their winning percentage by almost two hundred percentage points (199) from the Thirties to the Forties. They won twenty-one more games, lost eleven less and produced ten winning seasons in ten years. It does not get much better than that in Ann Arbor, or anywhere else! The decade of the Forties was one of the best in Michigan football history and Wolverine fans were looking for more of the same in the Fifties.

Program Summaries 1940 to 1949

Statistical Area	UM	MSC
Number of Head Coaches	2	2
Games Played	92	80
Wins	74	47
Losses	15	26
Ties	3	7
Winning Percentage	.821	.631
Winning Seasons	10	7
Losing Seasons	0	1
Even Seasons	0	1
National Championships	2	0
All-American Players	14	3

The Spartans had a solid decade of success against everyone but Michigan. Charlie Bachman and Biggie Munn produced consistent winners in East Lansing in all but two seasons. Michigan State's overall winning percentage slipped in the Forties by about ninety points. They won twelve fewer games and lost six more during this period. Biggie Munn finished the decade with three solid seasons and had the Spartans heading in the right direction. The Fifties could be an exceptionally good decade for the young coach and his team if they could keep improving and find a way to beat Michigan!

CHAPTER 8

Spartans Take Charge 1950 to 1959

T he decade of the Fifties began with a lot less national "drama" than the decade of the Forties. America was getting back to normal as the country focused on building the economy instead of winning a global war that threatened the foundations of the free world. Millions of men returned from the war to enter the job market, but millions more went to college to take advantage of the G. I. Bill. The men and women of the now famous "greatest generation" were serious about getting on with their lives and building something special for their families. It promised to be so much better than the 1940s. At least that is what every American was hoping.

Like everyone in America, college administrators were adjusting to "peacetime" living again. College football's popularity was second only to baseball. Fans were coming back to the games in large numbers and everything seemed to be headed in the right direction Well, not everything. The National Collegiate Athletic Association (NCAA) was trying to deal with the issues of "Amatuerism" and recruiting practices. The NCAA wanted to keep everything on a level playing field, but. many southern schools were devising creative ways to attract players and "subsidize" their time on campus. These issues, coupled with the growing popularity of the National Football League, kept college football on edge for the next decade. Oh, by the way, television was becoming a major force in American culture. How would the NCAA deal with this popular media format?

Game # 43: September 30, 1950 at Michigan Stadium in Ann Arbor

BACKGROUND INFORMATION:

Although no new rules were created for the 1950 season that does not mean the administrators in charge of the NCAA were completely happy with everything about college football. In fact, the rules on the playing field were taking a back seat to more important issues about eligibility, scholarships and alumni involvement that had been discussed in smoke-filled rooms for many years. (Watterson, Pages 215-220)

Biggie Munn was off to a great start at Michigan State except for one thing. Yes, he was zero for three against the hated Wolverines. Of course, Coach Munn wanted to win every game he coached, but he desperately wanted a victory over Michigan. After getting embarrassed by Fritz Crisler in 1947, Coach Munn's teams gave the Wolverines all they could handle in 1948 and 1949. Michigan's victory margin was only six points in 1948 and a mere four points in 1949. The Spartans were closing the "scoring gap." Would this be the year that Biggie would get his revenge? To gain an advantage, the Spartans scheduled a game against Oregon State the week before the Michigan game. The Spartans looked strong with a solid win over the Ducks (38-13). Coach Munn was hoping that his team was finally ready to take the next step against the Wolverines.

Bennie Oosterbaan entered his third season at Michigan in 1950. After winning a national championship along with the Big Nine Championship in year one, he slipped a little (6-2-1) in 1949. Wolverine fans had to settle for a conference championship, but no national championship. Oosterbaan also had two straight victories over Biggie Munn and the Spartans. Michigan, for the fourth consecutive year, would start the season with a home game against Michigan State. Coach Oosterbaan had some excellent players returning on offense and defense. Yes. another successful season was predicted for the Wolverines along with a third straight conference title. In fact, Michigan entered the game as the third ranked team in the country and was favored by two touchdowns.

GAME SUMMARY: MSC 14 UM 7

The Spartans accomplished something on September 30, 1950 that they had never achieved in the history of the Michigan State football program. They began a decade with a win over mighty Michigan. It was also Michigan State's first win against the hated Wolverines since 1937. Michigan's tenacious defense slowed down the mighty Spartan offense, but not totally. Michigan State's defense was equally strong. It was another brutal battle in Michigan Stadium. Lots of bumps, bruises, and blood resulted from this gridiron encounter. Finally, Munn's Spartans came away with a hard-fought victory.

A huge crowd (97,239) witnessed one of the biggest upsets in the annual face-off between the Mitten State's football powerhouses. The Spartans drew first blood in the opening quarter on a six-yard scoring pass from Al Dorow to future All-American halfback Sonny Grandelius. The Wolverines tied the game in the third quarter on a touchdown pass from quarterback Don Peterson to end Fred Pickard. The winning touchdown was scored on a controversial play. MSC Fullback Larry Crane was given credit for the deciding score, but newspaper photos indicated that his knee may have been down at the two-yard line. Instead, Crane was credited with a seven-yard touchdown that put the Spartans ahead with eleven minutes remaining in the game. (Grinczel, Page 49)

The Wolverines made a valiant attempt to tie the game, but Michigan State's defense hung on to secure the victory. The Spartans finally got a break against the Wolverines. Green and White fans celebrated another victory over mighty Michigan. Once again, the Spartans ventured to Ann Arbor and left Michigan Stadium with a BIG WIN! I am sure that Coach Munn was happy, but with this game behind him he was probably thinking about his next opponent—the Maryland Terrapins. His team had earned the "bragging rights" and Coach Munn would have all year to celebrate this achievement. It took four attempts, but Biggie finally "got Michigan!"

Team	1st	2nd	3rd	4th	Final
MSC	7	0	0	7	14
UM	0	0	7	0	7

SERIES UPDATE:

Another game was in the history books. Michigan was still large and in-charge, despite this stinging loss. The Wolverine series advantage remained at an imposing 33 wins, 7 losses, and 3 ties. Coach Munn's Spartans were off to a strong in the 1950s. He was intent on building a great team in East Lansing. Now, he had a victory over his arch-enemy—the Michigan Wolverines. Things were looking up for the Spartans and their fans. Maybe Michigan State was finally over the "hump" and ready to become the best football team in the State of Michigan.

SERIES MILESTONES:

Game number forty-three marked the first series win for Biggie Munn and the first series loss for Bennie Oosterbaan. It was also the first time that the two combatants were ranked going into the annual series blood fest. As I said earlier, Michigan was ranked number three going into the game and the Spartans were ranked number nineteen. Again, this was the first time that Michigan State began a decade with a win over Michigan.

SEASON SUMMARIES:

The good news in East Lansing was that Michigan State moved up to #2 (behind Army) after defeating Michigan. The bad news was that the Spartans fell flat on their face in the next game against unranked Maryland. It was not even close. The Terrapins, with a new Split-T offensive system that featured an option play, embarrassed the Spartans as indicated by the final score: Maryland 34 and Michigan State 7. Coach Munn referred to this loss as the "Maryland fiasco" and forgot about it as quickly as possible. (Stabley, Page 135) The Spartans were sitting at 2 wins and 1 loss after three games. Coach Munn fine-tuned his offensive machine and his defense stepped up to dominate every team on the schedule except Notre Dame. Michigan State finished the season with six straight wins and shut out the last three opponents by a combined score of 81-0!

Biggie Munn's fourth team was his best by far. The Spartans ended with a record of 8 wins and 1 loss. Halfback Sonny Grandelius became the first man in Michigan State history to rush for 1,000 yards. His stellar play earned him All-American honors which he shared with end Dorne Dibble. Appropriately, the Spartans finished as the eighth ranked team in the country, just ahead of the ninth ranked Michigan Wolverines.

Coach Oosterbaan's Wolverines did not start the season the way that he wanted. After the MSC loss, a season with so much hope already looked like a disappointment. Things got a little better the next week when nineteenth ranked Michigan defeated Dartmouth by a score of 27-7.

The Wolverines took another gut punch in game three against the number one ranked Army Cadets. The West Pointers proved to be very rude guests as they completely outplayed the Wolverines (27-6). Michigan's record was now 1 win and 2 losses. The only good news was that Michigan was undefeated in Big Nine play since they still had not played a conference game. The Wolverines could still win the conference title and play in the Rose Bowl. Yes, there was plenty to play for. Coach Oosterbaan rallied his team for a run at the conference championship, but after three Big Nine games the Wolverines looked like an average team at 1 win, 1 loss, and 1 tie. Michigan won their final three conference games which included the famous "Snow Bowl" at Ohio State on November 25, 1950. The Wolverines failed to gain a first down in the entire game. Somehow, they left Columbus with a 9-3 victory. Michigan finished at 4 wins, 1 loss, and 1 tie to claim a share of a third straight Big Nine Championship and earned the right to go to the 1951 Rose Bowl. The ninth ranked Wolverines defeated fifth ranked California (14-6) to cap another successful season (6-3-1) for Coach Oosterbaan. Michigan Tackle Allen "Brick" Wahl earned All-American honors for the second straight year. Michigan earned their third straight conference championship and finished as the ninth ranked team in the country.

Game # 44: September 29, 1951 at Michigan Stadium in Ann Arbor

BACKGROUND INFORMATION:

There were important rules changes in the game for the 1951 season. First, freshman were eligible because of player shortages caused by the Korean "conflict." (Perry, Page 264) Second, the rules makers approved the use of face masks for the 1951 season. Once again, this rule change was made to protect players, especially faces, noses, and teeth! Helmets had been the norm since 1939 and now face masks would be legal. The rule was not a mandate, just permission. Many programs chose not to outfit their players with the protective devices in 1951. Fans of Michigan and Michigan State football would not see players wearing face masks for a few more years. (dwilson at cae.wisc.edu, Page 116)

The Spartans began year five of the Biggie Munn Era with high expectations. Coach Munn was on a mission to prove that Michigan State football belonged in the Western Conference and among the best in the country. While he had one eye on the future (1953 specifically—the first year of Big Ten Football competition), Coach Munn also had his eye on the challenging 1951 schedule. The Spartans would play three Big Nine teams (Michigan, Ohio State, and Indiana) as well as some of the nation's top independents (Notre Dame, Penn State, Pittsburgh, and Notre Dame). For the second straight year, Michigan State opened the season against Oregon State. This early game almost backfired as the Spartans only won by a score of 6-0. Despite their poor showing against the Ducks, the Spartans were ranked as the number two team in the country when they traveled to Ann Arbor for series game number forty-four.

Michigan was an outstanding football program for an awfully long time under Fritz Crisler and Bennie Oosterbaan. The 1951 season had lower than normal expectations because of the number of great players the Wolverines lost to graduation. Coach Oosterbaan had some huge holes to fill on both lines and in the backfield. By all appearances, it was going to be a long year for Michigan football. Bennie was hoping that some of his sophomores could step up and be difference makers.

Although freshman would be eligible, Coach Oosterbaan was not expecting much help from his youngest players. As usual, game one against the Spartans would tell him a lot about his team and the upcoming season. Game on!

GAME SUMMARY: MSC 25 UM 0

The forty-fourth game of the series proved to be another highlight game for Spartan fans everywhere, but not for the Wolverine faithful. Spartan quarterback Al Dorow opened the scoring in the second quarter which gave Michigan State a 6-0 lead at halftime. (*DFP*, 9/30/1951, Page 29)

Sophomore defensive back Jimmy Ellis took the second half kickoff back to the Michigan fourteen-yard line before he was knocked out of bounds. Don McAuliffe scored a few plays later on a two-yard run. After the extra point, Michigan State led 13-0. Halfback Leroy Bolden scored on the final play of a 91-yard drive and another extra point made it 19-0 at the end of the third quarter. Halfback Vince Pisano scored the final touchdown of the game to make the final score 25-0 in favor of the Spartans. (*DFP*, 9/30/1951, Page 31)

This series game was simply a dominant effort by second ranked Michigan State. The Spartans finished with just over three-hundred yards of offense (307) compared to Michigan's six. Yes, you read it right, the Michigan was held to minus 23 yards rushing and managed to gain twenty-nine yards through the air. (Perry, Page 264) Michigan State also rolled up twenty-one first downs while the hapless Wolverines only managed four. It was ugly for all Wolverines in the record-tying crowd (97,239) who had to watch Michigan State's fans enjoy their biggest victory ever in the history of the series.

Team	1st	2nd	3rd	4th	Final
MSC	0	6	13	6	25
UM	0	0	0	0	0

Yes, I have said it before, but it is absolutely true. The only thing that is sweeter than a "rival" victory is a rival victory in the other guy's stadium. This day belonged to the Spartans and the ride back to East Lansing was certainly a lot of fun for Biggie Munn, the players, and the fans. Michigan, which had been ranked number seventeen going into the game, dropped out of the ratings. Go Green! Go White!

SERIES UPDATE:

There is no doubt that Spartan fans celebrated into the early morning hours, but amazingly, the town of East Lansing was still standing the next day. It survived a night of celebration and hardy-partying that had not taken place since the "Slaughter" of 1915. Of course, Michigan still held the edge in the series, but Biggie Munn was working hard to close the gap. The Wolverines now had 33 wins, 8 defeats, and 3 ties on the books. Michigan State was still on the wrong side of the won-lost ledger, but they had to be feeling good. The best thing was that MSC was 2-0-0 for the series in the 1950s!

SERIES MILESTONES:

This was only the second time in series history that both teams were ranked going into the game. Michigan State was the higher ranked team (number two) while Michigan, based mostly on history and reputation, was ranked seventeenth. Coach Munn made sure that there would be no upsets in this game. Once again, this was the largest winning margin for any Spartan victory. Of course, this game was also the biggest Wolverine loss in series history. Finally, Michigan State's twenty-five points tied the 1935 game (also a win at 25-6) for the most points scored by a Spartan team in a series game.

SEASON SUMMARIES:

After defeating Michigan, the Spartans traveled to Columbus to face Ohio State and came away with a hard-fought win (24-20). The next week they hosted a feisty team from Marquette but sent them home to ponder a 20-14 loss. Michigan State rolled into Happy Valley to play Penn State and the Spartans were very happy after a 32-21 win. Munn's football team had a perfect record of 5 wins and 0 defeats heading into the last four games of the season. Coach Munn kept his team sharp for the final four games and only one was close (a 30-26 win at Indiana). A blowout victory over Colorado (45-7) gave Biggie Munn and the Spartans a claim to part of the national championship as voted by the Helms Foundation. Tennessee was voted national champions by all the other major polls. It was a great season for Michigan State. Honors poured in as four Spartans earned All-American honors which was the highest single season total in Michigan State football history. Tackle Don Coleman was unanimous selection. End Robert Carey, quarterback Al Dorow and defensive back James Ellis were honored by at least one voting agency. The Spartans were on a sixteen-game winning streak at the end of the 1951 season. I am certain that Biggie Munn spent the off-season finding out how to make it seventeen, and more, in 1952.

The Wolverines made it two straight losses when a rude bunch of visitors from Stanford beat them (23-13). Coach Oosterbaan got his footballers back on track and they won three straight conference games. The Wolverines climbed back into the rankings (fifteen), but a road game against the third ranked Fighting Illini proved to be a turning point. Illinois sent the Wolverines home with their third defeat of the season (7-0). Two more losses against Cornell (20-7) and Northwestern (6-0) ensured that the Wolverines would have their first losing season since 1936. The season did end on a high note as Bennie Oosterbaan and his Wolverines welcomed Woody Hayes to Michigan Stadium for the first time. Final score: Michigan 7 and Ohio State 0! Michigan's final record for the 1951 season ended with 4 wins, 5 losses and 0 ties. End Lowell Perry earned All-American honors and that was about it. Coach Oosterbaan had plenty to think about in the off-season, but the main thing was how to stop the Spartans and their sixteen-game winning streak on September 27, 1952!

Game # 45: September 27, 1952 at Michigan Stadium in Ann Arbor

BACKGROUND INFORMATION:

There were no significant rules changes for the 1952 season. The NCAA and university presidents across the country were trying to figure out how to maintain control over their programs and protect athletes from over-zealous alumni. Well, not all university presidents were interested in doing this. College football was facing challenges everywhere it seemed, except on the football field.

Biggie Munn's sixth year as the Spartans football leader was filled with anticipation. His top ranked Spartans were defending national champions and they were on a fifteen-game winning streak. Life was good in East Lansing! Munn had some strong players returning to the field and expectations were for more winning! The 1952 season was scheduled to begin on September 27th, once again, in Ann Arbor. I am certain that Biggie Munn was thinking about this game as soon as they defeated Colorado on November 24, 1950. The hated Wolverines were never far from his thoughts. Would Biggies Boys be able to make it three straight wins over Michigan?

For the sixth consecutive year, Michigan began the season with a home opener against Michigan State. The high-flying Spartans turned the tables on the Wolverines in 1950 and 1951. It was time to put Michigan State's modest two game winning streak to rest. Michigan was in a "re-building" mode as many good players had graduated. Stopping Michigan State sounded like a good goal, but did the Wolverines have the players to actually do it?

GAME SUMMARY: MSC 27 UM 13

Mitten State series game number forty-five went down in Spartan history again. The #1 Spartans defeated the Wolverines for the third consecutive season! A huge crowd of 96,490 showed up to watch the Spartans run away from the Wolverines. Final score: Michigan State 27 and Michigan 13. Initially, the underdog Wolverines looked like they were poised for a huge upset over the top-ranked Spartans. Michigan scored first and took a 13-0 lead before MSC took control of the game.

After Michigan's second score, Don McAuliffe returned the ensuing kickoff for a seventy-yard touchdown. It was 13-7 at the end of the first quarter. Michigan State really got rolling in the second quarter. Leroy Bolden's 4-yard run tied the game at 13-13. Then, speedster Billy Wells dashed into the end one from the ten yard-line. With the extra point, MSC led 20-13 after thirty minutes of play. Leroy Bolden finished the scoring, and the Wolverines, with a 4-yard touchdown reception from quarterback Tom Yewcic. The final extra point made it 27-13 at the end of the third quarter and that is how the game ended. (*DFP*, 9/28/1952, Page 30) Michigan State's victory extended their winning streak to sixteen games. Again, there is nothing sweeter than beating your biggest rival three straight times in his own stadium!

Team	1st	2nd	3rd	4th	Final
MSC	7	13	7	0	27
UM	13	0	0	0	13

SERIES UPDATE:

Michigan still retained the overall edge in the series (33-9-3), but that was not much consolation for the 1952 Wolverine team. The Maize and Blue lost to the hated Spartans again. In fact, Michigan State was a perfect 3-0-0 against Michigan in the decade of the Fifties. Once again, the Wolverines were starting to grasp the significance of the series and how important a victory over Michigan State really was.

SERIES MILESTONES:

The forty-fifth game of the series was a milestone because it was the last time that Michigan State would play as an "independent" against Michigan. The Spartans were on track to become full-fledged members of the Big Ten Conference in 1953. The stakes were about to get bigger in the bitter in-state rivalry—much bigger! The 1952 game was also the first time that a "rival" team was ranked Number One going into the game. It was also the second three-game win streak for the Spartans. Finally, it was the twenty-fifth series game in Michigan Stadium. Were things really starting to change in the series?

SEASON SUMMARIES:

Michigan State sputtered against Oregon State the next week. Fortunately, they escaped with a 17-14 victory. Then, Biggie Munn's team stepped on the gas! The Spartans racked up three lopsided wins over Texas A&M, Syracuse, and Penn State. In November, Munn's footballers got another stiff test at Purdue. However, they managed to extend their victory streak to twenty-one games with a 14-7 win over the Boilermakers. Michigan State approached the end of the season with strong wins over Indiana (41-14) and Notre Dame (21-3). Now, "the streak" was at twenty-four! The Spartans put an exclamation point on their second straight perfect season by destroying Marquette (62-13). The Spartans finished the season with a perfect record of 9 wins, 0 losses, and 0 ties.

The Spartans earned their second straight national championship trophy and put their Big Ten brothers on notice for the 1953 season. Biggie Munn earned national "Coach of the Year" honors for his splendid season. Six of his players earned some form of All-American honors. Halfback Don McAuliffe earned consensus All-American honors along with linemen Frank Kush and Dick Tamburo. Ellis Duckett, Tom Yewcic and Jimmy Ellis also earned first team All-American honors. (Stabley, Page 155) After winning twenty-four straight games, it appeared that Michigan State was ready for the Big Ten. The big question on everyone's mind was, "Was the Big Ten ready for the Spartans?"

Michigan struggled in week two and lost at Stanford (14-7). Then, the Wolverines bounced back with three straight wins over Indiana, Northwestern, and Minnesota. Michigan finished the season by splitting the last four games. Bennies Wolverines ended the 1952 season with a record of 5 wins and 4 losses. Oddly enough, no Wolverines earned All-American honors for the 1952 season. Bennie Oosterbaan was a three-time All-American and a national championship coach at Michigan. Unfortunately, many folks were wondering if it was time for Bennie to go. Nobody was happy about the football team in Ann Arbor. Nobody! I am sure that Bennie and Athletic Director Fritz Crisler had a very direct conversation about the Michigan football program. Things had to get better, and soon, or Bennie might have to move on to greener pastures!

Game# 46: November 14, 1953 at Macklin Stadium in East Lansing

BACKGROUND INFORMATION:

The 1953 season saw a major change to the game's substitution rules. Michigan Athletic Director Fritz Crisler was also Chairman of the NCAA Football Rules Committee. He knew that many colleges were dropping football because of the costs of maintaining two separate squads (offense and defense). Costs for recruiting and coaching staffs were also becoming prohibitive at some schools. According to the USA Today College Football Encyclopedia (*USA Today CFE*), the "solution" was to make it much more difficult to substitute players in and out of a game, especially in the first and third periods. (*USA Today CFE,* Page 21)

According to Will Perry, "The "effect on college football in 1953 was profound." (Perry, Page 268) The days of the defensive and offensive specialists were on the way out. Now, the "Iron Man" who could play both ways would be the focus of the games. Once again, sixty-minute players became the norm, not the exception in college football.

Game number forty-six was memorable for four important reasons. First, it was the first Big Ten series game. Second, it was the first game in East Lansing since 1948. Third, it would be the first game to be contested for the Paul Bunyan Trophy that Governor G. Mennen Williams created for the rivals. Finally, it would be the first series game in November since 1946.

In 1953, Michigan was coming off another lackluster season. Coach Bennie Oosterbaan had to be feeling some pressure. His Wolverines were winless in three straight series games. Even worse, Michigan State had just won back-to-back national championships. And yes, MSC had a twenty-four-game winning streak in place.

Coach Oosterbaan had a completely new backfield for the 1953 season and new faces just about everywhere. Michigan had some talented players, but nobody was picking them to be in contention for the conference championship. The Wolverines were unranked going into the season. They rose to number five after starting the season with four straight wins. The Maize and Blue footballers lost two of the next three games to drop out of the rankings the week before the Michigan State game. Michigan headed to East Lansing with a record of 5-2-0.

Coach Biggie Munn was riding a tidal wave of success in East Lansing! For six years, he did everything in his power to turn President Hannah's vision into a reality. Now, Michigan State was a full-fledged member of the Big Ten Conference and everybody knew about Michigan State football! Life was good in Spartan Country, but Biggie's Boys could not take any steps backward!

The Spartans started strong with four convincing wins. Purdue's "Spoilermakers" threw them off track with a 6-0 defeat in Lafayette, Indiana. With that, the "streak" which had grown to twenty-eight games—was over! Munn's football men rebounded with wins over Oregon State and Ohio State. Michigan State had a record of 6 wins and 1 loss heading into "Michigan Week." The Spartans were still in contention for the conference title, but they had to win against Michigan to keep that dream alive.

GAME SUMMARY: UM 6 MSC 14:

The largest crowd ever in Macklin Stadium (52,324) showed up to witness history. Michigan State won their first Big Ten "series" game against the hated Wolverines. The Spartans also defeated Michigan for the fourth consecutive year. More importantly, it was the first ever Aggie/Spartan win over Michigan in East Lansing. It was another intense struggle between bitter rivals. However, the fired-up Spartans were just a little bit better than the Wolverines that day.

The Mitten State, and now Big Ten, rivals battled to a scoreless tie after fifteen minutes of play. Earl Morrall threw a touchdown pass to Jimmy Ellis and kicker Evan Slonac booted the extra point to give the Spartans a 7-0 second quarter lead. That is how the first half ended. (*DFP*, 11/15/1953, Page 36)

Halfback Bert Zagers completed his first ever pass for a touchdown to Ellis Duckett and the Spartans led 14-0 in the third quarter. In the fourth quarter, Michigan recovered a Spartan fumble at the four-yard line and quarterback Lou Baldacci scored to put the Wolverines on the board. However, they missed the extra point which made it a 14-6 score late in the game. Michigan had a few more chances later in the game, but the Spartan defense proved too strong. Michigan State prevailed by a final score of 14-6. (*DFP*, 11/15/1953, Page 36)

Team	1st	2nd	3rd	4th	Final
UM	0	0	0	6	6
MSC	0	7	7	0	14

SERIES UPDATE:

There is no doubt that the Spartan players, coaches, and fans thoroughly enjoyed their win over Michigan. There was so much to celebrate! Yes, Michigan still held a big advantage in the series with a record of 33 wins, 10 losses, and 3 ties. However, Sparty had possession of the Paul Bunyan Trophy (officially called "Paul Bunyan-Governor of Michigan Trophy" (1-0-0) and they had a perfect record of 4-0-0 against Michigan in the Fifties. Go Spartans!

SERIES MILESTONES:

There were five important "firsts" in the forty-sixth series game. First, the crowd of 52,324 broke the previous record of 51,526 for an East Lansing series game! Second, it was the first "Big Ten Series Game" game. Third, it was the first trophy game in series history. Fourth, it was the first trophy win for the Spartans. Finally, it was the first trophy series loss for the Wolverines.

There were some other notable milestones that need to be mentioned. First, it was Michigan State's tenth series win. Second, it was the second time that the Spartans had won four consecutive games against the Wolverines. It was also Biggie Munn's last series game since he retired from coaching after Michigan State's Rose Bowl win in January 1954. Biggie started off slowly against Michigan—he lost the first three games. However, he finished strong with four straight wins and became the first coach in Michigan State history to have a winning record (4-3-0) against Michigan.

Image 7 Michigan Governor G. Mennen Williams showed up with the Paul Bunyan Trophy for the first Big Ten game between Michigan and Michigan State in 1953. (Permission: Bentley Historical Library at The University of Michigan, See Page 369)

Yes, Coach Biggie Munn put Michigan State on the map and at the top of the Big Ten Conference. Clarence "Biggie" Munn finished his MSC career with a stellar record of 54 wins, 9 defeats and 2 ties. His teams won almost eighty-five percent of their games (.846).

SEASON SUMMARIES:

The Wolverines bounced back nicely after losing to the Spartans. Bennie's Boys finished strong and defeated Ohio State by a score of 20-0! Michigan finished with a record of 6 wins and 3 losses in 1953. They won 3 and lost 3 in the Big Ten which earned a tie for 5th place. The Wolverines ended the season as the 20th ranked team in the AP Poll and the 19th ranked team in the UPI poll. For the second straight year, no Wolverine football players earned All-American honors.

Michigan State finished the 1953 season with a record of 8 wins and 1 loss. They earned a tie for the Big Ten Championship with Illinois. Thanks to Fritz Crisler, who voted for Sparty, Michigan State won a vote by the conference athletic directors and earned a trip to the 1954 Rose Bowl. The Spartans defeated UCLA (28-20) in an exciting game to finish with a final record of 9 wins and 1 loss. Team Captain Don Dohoney earned consensus All-American honors at the end position. Halfback LeRoy Bolden and tackle Larry Fowler were also named as first team All-Americans.

Like his former coach and mentor Fritz Crisler, Coach Biggie Munn decided to go out while he was at the top of the "football" mountain. He decided it was better to replace Ralph Young as Athletic Director, than try to duplicate his recent success as the Spartan football coach.

Game # 47: November 13, 1954 at Michigan Stadium in Ann Arbor

BACKGROUND INFORMATION:

The NCAA Football Rules Committee followed the dramatic substitution rules changes carefully during the 1953 season. Many coaches voiced their displeasure at every opportunity. The substitution rule was modified slightly for the 1954 season. Players could reenter the game during the last minutes of the second and fourth quarters if they were on the field at the beginning of those quarters. In 1953, players could not reenter until the start of the next quarter. Everything else remained the same for the 1954 college football season. (*USA Today CFE*, Page 35)

The good news for Michigan was that Biggie Munn was gone. In addition to losing Coach Munn, Michigan State lost many great players in 1953. The cupboard was not as full as new Coach Duffy Daugherty would have liked in 1954. Duffy knew he had some BIG shoes to fill and everybody in East Lansing wondered if the likeable Irishman was up to the challenge. Daugherty's footballers lost their first two games by a total of ten points. Then a win was followed by three more losses. Michigan State was having an "up-and-down" season in year one of the Duffy Era. Sadly, it was more "downs" than "ups." The Spartans lost five of their first six games before pounding Washington State (54-6) the week before the Michigan game. Michigan State took their record of 2 wins and 5 losses to Ann Arbor to see if they could defeat the hated Wolverines for a fifth consecutive time.

Michigan was coming off their second straight winning season and several promising soph-omores were looking to make their names know to Wolverine football fans. Guys like Ron Kramer, Tom Maentz, Terry Barr, Charlie Brooks, Jim Maddock, and Dick Hill were ready to show their stuff. Bennie Oosterbaan was also ready to make some changes to his old Single-Wing offense that had produced mixed results since 1950. He jumped on the popular T-Formation bandwagon and installed special plays for the talented Kramer. Despite several key injuries, the Wolverines jumped off to a good start and had a record of 5 wins and 2 losses going into Michigan State Week. More importantly, they were 3-1-0 in the Big Ten. A win against the Spartans would keep them in the hunt for the conference championship. After four consecutive losses to Michigan State, Bennie was hun-gry for a victory!

GAME SUMMARY: MSC 7 UM 33

The forty-seventh game was played in the seventy-fifth season of Michigan football. It turned out to be one to remember for the Wolverines and another one for the Spartans to forget!

Sophomore Ron Kramer played like a future All-American on November 13, 1954. Late in the second quarter, he set up Michigan's first touchdown on an end around play. Lou Baldacci scored on a short run to make it 6-0 in favor of Michigan and that is how the first half ended. Early in the second half, Kramer blocked a Spartan punt, grabbed it out of the air, and bolted to the end zone. With a successful extra point kick, the Wolverines led 13-0. Michigan State came back and scored on a short run by Leroy Bolden to make it 13-7. Michigan took over in the fourth quarter and scored 20 unanswered points. Kramer set up another touchdown with his second blocked kick of the day. (*DFP,* 11/14/1954, Page 43) Finally, after four straight losses, Michigan beat Michigan State. Hail to the Victors!

Team	1st	2nd	3rd	4th	Final
MSU	0	0	0	7	7
UM	0	6	7	20	33

SERIES UPDATE:

Michigan was now even in the Paul Bunyan Trophy series. Each team now had a "Big Ten" series victory. Apparently, Fritz Crisler was not a big fan of the trophy. He made sure it was put in a closet to rest, and collect dust, until 1955. After four long years, Michigan re-gained control over the series and increased their advantage to 34 wins, 10 losses, and 3 ties. MSC was still ahead in the decade of the Fifties with a record of 4-1-0.

SERIES MILESTONES:

There were a few milestones of note in game number forty-seven. First, it was the first series game for Duffy Daugherty and his first loss. Coach Daugherty became the fifteenth straight Aggie/Spartan coach to lose his first game against Michigan. Second, the game tied the all-time series attendance record with a crowd of 97,239. For the first time in four years, neither team was ranked going into the game. Finally, Ron Kramer became the first, and only, player to block two punts in a UM vs MSC series game.

SEASON SUMMARIES:

Duffy Daugherty's first season at Michigan State was nothing to write home about. Biggie Munn had stated that Duffy was like a son to him. Apparently, that relationship changed in season one after the losses started to add up. Apparently, Biggie Munn entered one of Duffy's meetings, uninvited, and started criticizing Daugherty's staff. Duffy basically told his boss to "shut up and get out." (Stabley Page 170) That brief confrontation established Duffy's relationship with his staff, but it also created ill-will between him and Biggie. Not a good way to start your head coaching career, but that is what happened.

For the first time in seven years, Michigan State ended the season with a losing record (3-6-0) and dropped to eighth place in the Big Ten with a record of 1-5-0. Duffy's footballers played hard for their new coach, but not well enough. They were close in just about every game but found a way to lose late in the game. Duffy did not make any excuses even though he had some key injuries that did not help his cause. Coach Daugherty did the only thing he could do and that was focus on getting better in 1955.

Bennie Oosterbaan's Wolverines ended 1954 with a disappointing loss at Ohio State (21-7) and finished with an overall record of 6 wins and 3 losses. A 5-2-0 showing in the conference was good for second place. The Wolverines were an improved team and played well in every game except for a blowout loss to Army (26-7). Michigan's sophomores were solid all season and things were looking good for the 1955 season. Of course, the Wolverines would enjoy "bragging rights" in the State of Michigan for the first time in four long years!

Game # 48: October 1, 1955 at Michigan Stadium in Ann Arbor

BACKGROUND INFORMATION:

The NCAA rules makers carefully monitored the "substitution issue" and came up with another "tweak" for the 1955 season. Now, a player who started any quarter could be withdrawn from the same quarter and allowed to return once during that quarter. New rules were also put in place to prevent "unsportsmanlike" trickery. The "Hideout" or "Sleeper Play" was eliminated when all offensive players were required to be within fifteen yards of the ball when the "ready to play" signal was given by an official. Everything else stayed the same for the 1955 season. (*USA Today CFE*, Page 51)

One "off the field" development at Michigan State caused more "ill will" between the two rivals. In 1954 Michigan State was the only land grant institution that had not achieved "university" status. Michigan State College President, John Hannah, petitioned the legislature to change their name. When the administrators at Michigan heard about Hannah's plan they swung into action and did everything they could to oppose the change. Michigan argued that having two major universities in the great State of Michigan would be confusing. Wolverine supporters argued that it would lead to duplication of programs and wasted tax dollars. (Note-Both of these arguments sound familiar, don't they?) In the end, these arguments fell on deaf ears in Lansing. Well, mostly deaf ears. The legislature's solution was to approve a name change from Michigan State College to Michigan State University of Agriculture and Applied Science (MSU-AAS).

This was not exactly what President Hannah had in mind for the centennial year of his great institution, but that is how it all worked out. According to David Young, author of *The Student and The Professor: John Hannah, Ralph Aigler and the Origin of the Michigan State vs Michigan Rivalry*, the new moniker (MSU-AAS) was official on July 1, 1955. (Young, Page 203)

The affable Duffy Daugherty survived his first year and looked forward to the 1955 football season. He was optimistic about the upcoming season which surprised some of his critics. However, anybody who knew Duffy Daugherty was not taken aback by Duffy's optimism. Daugherty was the classic "eternal optimist." Duffy did not believe that negativity was ever going to help him do anything worthwhile. Instead, he chose to look at the "sunny side." After reflecting on the 1954 season, Duffy knew that his team was in every game. He had some excellent returning players. I am certain that he focused on correcting mistakes and getting better in 1955. Despite Daugherty's optimism, most "experts" figured that Duffy's defense would be a big weakness. The Spartans would win some games, but a second conference championship was probably out of the question!

Michigan State started the 1955 season with a solid road win at Indiana (20-13). For the second week in a row, Duffy hit the road with his football team. Daugherty's team headed to Ann Arbor for the second straight season to face-off against the hated Wolverines. The optimistic Duffy would have a much better idea about how good his team really was on the trip back from Ann Arbor.

Bennie Oosterbaan entered his eighth season as head coach in 1955. His coaching career at Michigan was still going strong although he had not won a Big Ten title since 1950. The 1954 team was in the hunt for a championship until the final game against Ohio State. Bennie had a strong group of returning juniors. He was looking forward to the upcoming season. Once again, Michigan was expected to contend for the conference championship in 1955! However, the biggest question was, "Will Michigan be a as good as everybody says they are?" The Wolverines entered their first game against Missouri as the fourth ranked college football team in America. After pounding of the Tigers (42-7), Michigan hit the polls at number two at the start of Michigan State week.

GAME SUMMARY: MSU-AAS 7 UM 14

Game number forty-eight was another classic. Both teams played hard. It was one of the closest games in series history. The Wolverines scored first after Tony Branoff intercepted an Earl Morrall pass and returned it thirty-six yards to the Spartan twenty-yard line. Branoff scored six plays later. Ron Kramer's extra point put the Wolverines up by a score of 7-0 and that is how the half ended. *(DFP, 10/2/1955, Page 31)*

The Spartans tied the game in the third quarter, but Ron Kramer did what he did best. Michigan's winning touchdown came after Ron Kramer blocked another Spartan punt. His third blocked punt in two games against Michigan State. Halfback Jim Maddock scored on a 1-yard run and Kramer kicked the extra point. Michigan led 14-7 heading into the fourth quarter. The Spartans moved the ball up and down the field in the last quarter but came up short on every drive. Fumbles and two more interceptions really killed the Spartans chances for a win in this game. *(DFP, 10/2/1955, Page 31)*

In an unusual twist, Michigan State won some key statistical battles, but Michigan won the game. Yes, the Spartans out-rushed (177 to 136), out-passed (38 to 15) and had more first downs (14 to 7) than the Wolverines. However, Michigan took great advantage of three interceptions and Kramer's blocked punt. As Hal Middlesworth wrote in *the Detroit Free Press,* "Spartans Do the Work, UM Gets Glory." Michigan's bottom line boiled down to one simple question: "What's on the scoreboard Sparty?" *(DFP*, 10/2/1955, Page 33)

Team	1st	2nd	3rd	4th	Final
MSU	0	0	7	0	7
UM	0	7	7	0	14

Wow, Michigan was off to a perfect start (2-0-0) against Coach Daugherty. I am sure that Duffy was probably scratching his head. However, I doubt that the optimistic Irishman was in a panic because his Spartans had just outplayed the second ranked team in the country.

SERIES UPDATE:

Once again, Michigan increased their series advantage. The Wolverines increased their series record to 35 wins, 10 losses, and 3 ties. Michigan State was still on the wrong side of the won-lost ledger, but they had to focus on the next game against Stanford. Michigan retained "bragging rights" for the second straight year. Time to move on!

SERIES MILESTONES:

The forty-eighth series game had a few notable milestones. First, it was the first time that Michigan played against the team from Michigan State University of Agriculture and Applied Science. Second, it was another record tying crowd as 97,239 people watched the game. Third, this was the last series game played in the original Michigan Stadium. The 1956 season would see a bigger, more modern version of Michigan Stadium. Fourth, Michigan's thirty-fifth series victory was another notable event in the rivalry. Finally, this was the first time that the "loser" of the rival game went on to win a national championship. How did that happen?

SEASON SUMMARIES:

Duffy's optimism started to work after the Michigan game. The Spartans won seven straight games and none of them were even close. Michigan State finished the season with an overall record of 8-1-0. Their record of 5 wins and 1 loss was good enough for second place, just ahead of Michigan. Ohio State won the conference title for the second straight season, but the Big Ten's "no repeat" rule meant that the Buckeyes were staying home on New Year's Day. Michigan State was going to the 1956 Rose Bowl.

Coach Daugherty's footballers had a great time in Pasadena and won a classic game against UCLA (17-14). Michigan State ended the season with a final record of 9 wins and 1 loss and the title of national champions! Go Spartans!

Wow—what a turnaround for the optimistic Daugherty and his Spartans. Duffy was named coach of the year by the American Football Coaches Association. Quarterback Earl Morrall, and linemen Norm Masters and Carl Nystrom were named to multiple All-American teams. In September 1955, Duffy Daugherty was probably the only man in East Lansing who thought that the 1955 team could be special. All that changed on January 1, 1956.

Michigan won four more games and headed into the last three games of the season with a record of 6-0-0. They were on track to win the Big Title, but a stunning loss at Illinois (25-6) threw the train off the tracks. The Wolverines won the next game against Indiana (30-0) but failed to clinch a tie for the title when Ohio State shut them out in Ann Arbor. Final score OSU 17 and Michigan 0!

Bennie's Boys finished with a final record of 7 wins and 2 losses. Their conference record of 5-2-0 was only good enough for third place. What started out as a season of great promise ended with a "thud" in the last game against the Buckeyes! Time to reload and get ready for 1956 and a bigger Michigan Stadium to play in! Superstar end Ron Kramer earned All-American honors for the Wolverines in 1956.

Game # 49: October 6, 1956 at Michigan Stadium Ann Arbor

BACKGROUND INFORMATION:

For the first time in three years, there were no more changes to the "substitution" rules for the 1956 season. The NCAA decided to leave the actual "game" of football alone for a year. However, television continued to be a big topic of conversation in college football. Author John Sayle Watterson (*College Football: History, Spectacle, Controversy*) took a detailed look at the emerging issue of television and the impact (good and bad) that it was having on college football. He pointed out that the NCAA worked to increase the number of regionally televised games and it worked. Everyone was benefitting from increased television exposure, especially the coffers of the NCAA. With additional money coming into the NCAA coffers, more and more "enforcement staff" were being hired. Finally, the NCAA was able to add some "bite" to their "bark!" More tweaks to televising college football games would be made down the road. (Watterson, Page 272)

Once again, the infamous "deal" between Fielding Yost and Ralph Young in 1932 meant that game number forty-nine between Michigan and Michigan State took place, again, in Ann Arbor. It also meant that the annual "blood-letting" between the two rivals took place in a bigger and more modern version of, Michigan Stadium. Fritz Crisler expanded the press box and increased seating capacity from 97, 239 seats to 101,001. Of course, the "001" thing was Athletic Director Crisler's idea, and nobody knew where the seat "001" was located. In fact, nobody ever found out either!

Coach Duffy Daugherty was back for his third season in 1956. Duffy was coming off a national championship season, even though his Spartans finished as the second-best team in the Big Ten. Expectations were much higher than they were in 1955. So far, Daugherty had one losing season and one winning season under his belt. What would 1956 hold for the Spartans?

Michigan State opened the 1956 season on the road in Palo Alto, California. Stanford gave them a good game, but Duffy's Spartans won by a score of 21-7. The Spartans would play a second straight road game in Ann Arbor, but at least it would be a bus ride instead of an airplane flight. Was Michigan State ready to show Michigan what a BIG win looked like in a BIGGER Michigan Stadium?

The 1956 season was Bennie Oosterbaan's ninth year at Michigan. As usual, his goal was another Big Ten Championship—something that had eluded him since 1950. The good news was that All-American end Ron Kramer was back for his senior year. The bad news was that there were many inexperienced players at several key positions. Michigan was expected to have another winning season, but would they be good enough to compete for the conference title? That was the question on everybody's mind in Ann Arbor in August 1956!

Michigan opened the season against UCLA in Michigan Stadium. Wolverine great Tom Harmon was back home in Ann Arbor to see Michigan Stadium's makeover in person. The Wolverines sent the Bruins back to California to ponder a 42-13 loss. Michigan appeared ready to host the defending national champion Spartans on October 6, 1956.

GAME SUMMARY: MSU-AAS 9 UM 0

As expected, a record-setting crowd of 101,001 showed up for the forty-ninth edition of Michigan vs Michigan State pigskin mayhem. It was also the first time that both teams were ranked in the nation's top-five teams in a series game. The Wolverines were ranked number five and the Spartans occupied the second spot in the national rankings. There must have been an incredible amount of anticipation and tension in the stadium. Yes, there was a lot on the line for both teams!

Both teams battled hard in a scoreless first half. Which team would get the first score? Well, as it turned out, Spartan kicker John Matsko put the Spartans on the board in the third quarter with a 30-yard field goal. Michigan could not do much offensively. The biggest play of the game turned out to be a fourth quarter fumble by Wolverine John Herrnstein deep in Michigan territory. The opportunistic Spartans made the most of it when halfback Dennis Mendyk scored on a short run to provide the final points for MSU's 9-0 victory. (*DFP*, 10/7/1956, Page 47)

Team	1st	2nd	3rd	4th	Final
MSU	0	0	3	6	9
UM	0	0	0	0	0

Once again, the team that ran the ball best was the winner of this game. The Spartan offense did not do much in the first half, but really stepped up in the second half. Overall, MSU-AAS runners totaled 143-yards while Michigan's backs only had 80-yards. Michigan won the first down battle (13-9) and the passing part of the contest (79-yards to 0-yards). In the end, the scoreboard told the only story that mattered. MSU-AAS 9 and UM 0. (*DFP*, 10/7/1956, Page 47)

It is often said that the "third time is a charm" and that was certainly true for Duffy Daugherty vs Michigan. After losing his first two series games, he finally had a win against the hated Wolverines. Of course, it was probably a little bit sweeter since it took place in Ann Arbor in front of the largest crowd ever to witness a sporting event in the State of Michigan. Duffy had a great sense of timing, didn't he?

SERIES UPDATE:

Once again, another game was in the history books. Michigan was still large and in-charge, but one game does not a season make. Duffy Daugherty's footballers still had a lot of work to do and so did Coach Oosterbaan's Wolverines. For the record, the Wolverine series advantage now stood at 35 wins, 11 losses, and 3 ties. Both teams now had a record of 2 wins and 2 losses in the Paul Bunyan Trophy game. The Spartans upped their lead to 5 wins and 2 losses in the Fifties.

SERIES MILESTONES:

As always, the annual "bone-rattling and "head-knocking" football ritual between the Wolverines and Spartans produced some more milestones. First, as I pointed out earlier, this was the first time that both teams were ranked in the top ten going into the game. Second, the game was played in front of a record-breaking crowd of 101,001. Third, it was Duffy's first series win and Michigan State is tenth series win in Ann Arbor. Fourth, it was also the first time that both series team ended a season with 7 wins and 2 losses. Finally, it was the first time that the helmets of both teams had numerals on the side. Some players from both teams also sported face masks, but not all of them. Other than that, it was just another memorable battle between two teams who really, really did not like each other!

SEASON SUMMARIES:

Michigan State defeated Indiana and Notre Dame handily, before being upset at Illinois (20-13). The Spartans won two more games over Wisconsin and Purdue before losing a tough game in Minnesota (14-13). Duffy's footballers finished the year with a non-conference win over Kansas State (38-17). Year three of the Daugherty Era ended an overall record of 7 wins and 2 losses. Their conference record (4 wins and 2 losses) was only good enough for a fourth-place tie. Duffy now had two straight winning seasons and he went to work in December 1956 to make it three!

The Wolverines were 1-1-0 after losing to Michigan State. Coach Oosterbaan got his team back on track with two solid wins over Army and Northwestern. Unfortunately, Minnesota ruined homecoming when they upset Michigan (20-7). That one really hurt! The Gopher loss pretty much ended any hope that the Wolverines had for a share of the conference title. It was now a long shot that never happened! The Wolverines finished strong by winning their last four conference games. For the second year in a row, Michigan ended with an overall record of 7-2-0 and 5 wins and 2 losses in the Big Ten. It was good enough for a second-place finish, but that was not the goal! For most teams, it would have been a good season, but it was another disappointing season in Ann Arbor. For the second straight year, end Ron Kramer earned first team All-American honors for Michigan.

Game # 50: October 12, 1957 at Michigan Stadium in Ann Arbor

BACKGROUND INFORMATION:

There were no major rules changes in 1957. The NCAA's rules makers planned to watch the game and listen to the coaches and officials about future changes. While rules seemed to be "okay" in football, recruiting was not. The Big Ten disciplined Michigan State in 1953 and Ohio State in 1955 for recruiting violations. Administrators were trying to figure how to balance the process of taking care of athletes without giving them the world. The Big Ten's answer in 1957 was an allowance of 100 scholarships for all member schools for "all" sports. It was a start, but more work would have to be done in this area.

Coaches Duffy Daugherty and Bennie Oosterbaan shared the same problem in 1957. They were both trying to answer the question, "How do we improve on an overall record of 7 wins and 2 losses?" Unlike Michigan, Duffy had some strong players returning on both sides of the ball. Michigan State's Multiple-Offense appeared to be a strength for the Spartans. It looked like Michigan State would contend for the conference title in year four of the Daugherty Era at Michigan State. The Spartans won their first two games. Duffy's footballers blasted Indiana (54-0) in East Lansihg and then went on the road to defeat California (19-0). Michigan State was 2-0-0 and ranked second in the country. Time to head to Ann Arbor and show the Wolverines who was the "football" boss in the State of Michigan. Game on!

According to Will Perry's book, *The Wolverines: A Story of Michigan Football*, Coach Bennie Oosterbaan mentioned the idea of retiring to Fritz Crisler in early 1957, but Fritz choose to drop the matter. Interestingly, Crisler and Bennie took a big step toward a transition plan with the hiring of Bump Elliott as backfield coach for the 1957 season. (Perry, Page 291) Bennie was trying to figure out a way to improve on two-straight seasons of 7 wins and 2 losses. Certainly, not terrible seasons—just not up to the "Michigan standard."

Two-time All-American Ron Kramer was gone and so were some other talented players. Bennie must have thought it was going to be a rough season when his reserves beat the varsity in a scrimmage. (Perry, Page 293). It appears that expectations for the 1957 edition of the Michigan Wolverine football team were low. Like Michigan State, the Wolverines began the season with solid wins over Southern California and Georgia. Michigan entered Spartan Week as the sixth rated team in the country. A win over second-ranked Michigan State would get the Big Ten season off to a great start! Maybe the Wolverine season would be better than expected.

GAME SUMMARY: MSU-AAS 35 UM 6

The fiftieth game of this hard-fought series was essentially over after the first quarter. The teams traded turnovers (MSU had a pass intercepted and Michigan fumbled the ball in their own territory) before Michigan State opened the scoring. Future All-American fullback Walt Kowalczyk ran for 36 yards on 5 carries—the last one was a one-yard plunge into the Wolverine end zone. The Spartans missed the extra point, so the score remained 6-0. Sam Williams blocked a Wolverine punt that resulted in a safety that pushed the Spartan lead to 8-0 at halftime. (*DFP*, 10/13/1057, Page 51)

144

The Green and White footballers outscored the Maize and Blue by a margin of 13-6 in the third quarter. Michigan State led 21-6 heading into the final stanza. The Spartans added 14 more points before the game ended at 35-6. The last quarter was ugly for Michigan fans, but not for the Spartan faithful. (*DFP*, 10/13/1057, Page 51)

Michigan State's offense gained 326 yards on the ground and another 160 yards in the air. Meanwhile, the Wolverines were only about half as productive. Kowalczyk gained 113 yards on 17 carries which was almost as much as the entire Michigan team. Quarterback Jim Ninowski threw two touchdown passes and Art Johnson scored on a 62-yard touchdown run. Sam Williams, Bob Jewett, and Mike Pantich also scored Spartan touchdowns. Yes, there were many good things for Spartan fans to cheer about, but not so many for the Wolverine followers. (*DFP*, 10/13/1057, Page 51) It was another huge win in Michigan Stadium for the Green and White. Time to party Spartan fans!

Team	1st	2nd	3rd	4th	Final
MSU	6	2	13	14	35
UM	0	0	6	0	6

SERIES UPDATE:

Michigan State chipped away at Michigan's series advantage once again. The annual in-state pigskin slugfest now stood at: Michigan 35 wins, Michigan State 12 wins, and 3 tie games. The Spartans regained the lead at 3 wins and 2 losses for the Paul Bunyan Trophy. MSU-AAS also increased their advantage in the Fifties to 6 wins and 2 losses.

SERIES MILESTONES:

Yes, game number fifty was a BIG series milestone! It was also the biggest Spartan margin of victory (29 points) in a series game. The capacity crowd of 101,001 tied the all-time series attendance record. I wonder how many of those folks were Spartan fans?

SEASON SUMMARIES:

Duffy's footballers came up flat after beating Michigan and lost the next game to Purdue (20-13). Daugherty got his team back on track and the Spartans ran the table with five straight wins. They finished with an overall record of 8-1-0 and ended Big Ten play with a record of 5-1-0. Michigan State finished as the third ranked team in the country behind Auburn and Ohio State. Fullback Walt Kowalczyk and center Dan Currie earned first team All-American honors for the Spartans.

Michigan recovered from the Spartan loss and won two straight games over Northwestern and Minnesota. They tied Iowa in early November. The Wolverines were 2-1-1 heading into the last three games of the season. Technically, they were still in contention for the Big Ten crown, but a lot of things would have to go their way in November. As it turned out, the Wolverines sealed their own Big Ten fate at 3-3-1 when they lost two of the last three games. Michigan ended the 1957 season with a final record of 5-3-1 and finished sixth in the Big Ten. Jim Pace provided Michigan fans with some good news since he was selected as a first team All-American.

Game # 51: October 4, 1958 at Spartan Stadium in East Lansing

BACKGROUND INFORMATION:

The 1958 season saw two important changes to the game. For the first time since 1912, there was a change to the scoring rules thanks to NCAA's Rule Committee Chairman Fritz Crisler. Teams now had the option of earning one point for kicking the ball through the uprights or two points for running or passing the ball across the goal line. The ball would be spotted at the three yard-line and teams could do what they wanted. Coaches now had a choice to make after every touchdown. NCAA rules makers were hoping to make the game more exciting. They also wanted to reduce the number of tie games. It would be interesting to see how it all unfolded during the season. The second change was about player substitutions—again! Now, coaches could have a player enter and leave the game twice in the same quarter. Once again, it was easier for coaches to "platoon" players and allow for more specialization on offense, defense, and special teams. (*USA Today CFE*, Page 87)

Game number fifty-one would be remembered because series game venues were about to change! Athletic Director Biggie Munn never liked the "arrangement" that he inherited from Ralph Young which meant more money for the Spartans, but way too many games in Ann Arbor. He wanted that problem fixed the first day that he took over as Michigan State's AD. The 1958 game was scheduled for East Lansing for the first time since 1953. More importantly, the teams would alternate venues. The days of playing twenty-one straight games in Ann Arbor were over! I am sure that this arrangement made Biggie Munn a happy man. Of course, another win over Michigan would make him even happier!

Bennie Oosterbaan started his eleventh year as Michigan's head football coach in 1958. Michigan was almost unbeatable in his first three years. Big Ten titles rolled in like cars rolled off a Ford assembly line. Then, things slowed down as the Wolverines lost more games each year. The conference championships stopped coming to Ann Arbor after 1950. The 1957 season was one of his worst and the prospects for season number eleven were not much better. The Wolverines had way too many question marks in 1958 for anyone, including Oosterbaan, to consider them a contender for the conference title. Michigan did not have a lot of stars in 1958 and they did not have a lot of depth. If key players could stay healthy, maybe the Wolverines could win their share of games. However, if they had any serious injuries, it could get ugly!

Michigan started the 1958 season in Ann Arbor against Southern California. The Wolverines took advantage of the two-point conversion option and won a close one against the Trojans (20-19). Although they were not ranked going into the USC game, the Wolverines came out as the sixteenth ranked team heading into game number two. That was the good news! The bad news was that number fourteen Michigan State was waiting for the Wolverines in East Lansing.

Duffy Daugherty was back for season number five in 1958. So far, the Smiling Irishman, had plenty to smile about. He had four winning seasons under his belt and a national championship with only one losing campaign. However, the fact that he graduated twenty-seniors in 1957 was nothing to smile about! The Spartans had to replace many outstanding players. It looked like a "rebuilding" year instead of another year to "reload."

Michigan State hosted California on September 27, 1958, but they were not nice to their guests. The Spartans sent the Bears home to ponder a 32-12 defeat. Maybe Duffy had more talent than he thought he had. Or maybe California was just a bad team. MSU-AAS did not have much time to celebrate since Michigan was coming to visit on October 4, 1958. The Spartans would have a better idea of where they stood after the rival game was over, or not!

GAME SUMMARY: UM 12 MSU-AAS 12

If there was ever a tale of two halves of football, this was it! Bottom line, Michigan won the first half of this bloody battle and Michigan State won the second half. However, since both teams scored the same number of points in their "winning" half, the game ended in a draw.

Michigan scored first when MSU quarterback Mike Pantich's pitchout was "intercepted" by Wolverine defensive end Gary Prahst who rambled for a 42-yard touchdown. A few minutes later, the aggressive Prahst caused a Spartan fumble. Wolverine teammate Brad Meyers scooped and scored to make it 12-0 in favor of the Wolverines. After missing the first extra point, Michigan attempted a two-point conversion. The first one in Michigan football history. Unfortunately for Michigan, it failed. The good news for the Wolverines was that they led 12-0 at halftime. The bad news was that they did not lead by 13-0 or 14-0. (*DFP*, 105/1958, Page 43)

I do not know what Duffy said to his team at halftime, but it worked! The Spartans scored quickly on a 90-yard punt return by Dean Look. The extra point kick failed. It was 12-6 in favor of Michigan at the end of the third quarter. Both defenses held their ground for most of the final quarter. It appeared that Michigan would win the game. However, Michigan State intercepted a Wolverine pass late in the game. The Spartans drove the ball 97-yards to the end zone for the tying score. Unfortunately, Spartan standout Sam Williams missed his second extra-point kick and the game ended at 12-12. (*DFP*, 105/1958, Page 43)

There were two things that Fritz Crisler did not like. One was ties, hence, his effort to reduce ties through the two-point play option in 1958. Second, he was not real fond of Michigan State. A tie against Michigan State probably did not set too well with him. However, it was better than a loss to the Spartans. Both teams would have to move on. Plenty more games to play in 1958.

Team	1st	2nd	3rd	4th	Final
UM	0	12	0	0	12
MSU	0	0	6	6	12

SERIES UPDATE:

Interestingly, Michigan was not good enough to beat Michigan State and Michigan State was not good enough to beat Michigan. As it turned out, the Wolverines and Spartans were not good enough to beat a lot of teams in 1958. More about that later. The good news for both teams was that neither team lost the game. The bad news was that they did not win. The series now stood at 35-12-4 in favor of Michigan. Michigan State retained possession of the Paul Bunyan Trophy since they last won it in 1957. Michigan would have to try again in 1959.

SERIES MILESTONES:

There were several milestones in the fifty-first rival game. First, it turned out to be Bennie Oosterbaan's last series game. Coach Oosterbaan finished with a record 4 wins, 6 losses and 1 tie against the Spartans. Second, it was the first time the rivals played a game in Spartan Stadium. The name was changed from Macklin Stadium to Spartan Stadium in 1956, but they had not played in East Lansing since 1953. Third, it was a record setting attendance for an East Lansing game since a crowd of 76,434 crammed into Spartan Stadium. Finally, it was the first series tie that did not end with a score of 0-0.

SEASON SUMMARIES:

Unfortunately, Bennie Oosterbaan saved his worst season for last. After the MSU tie, the Wolverines lost two straight games to Navy and Northwestern. A Homecoming Day win over Minnesota gave Michigan a record of 2-2-1 heading into November. A winning season and a conference title were still possible. Then, the roof fell in on Oosterbaan's Wolverines. Michigan lost the final four games and finished the season with a dismal record of 2 wins, 6 losses, and 1 tie. It was the worst season in Coach Oosterbaan's eleven years at Michigan. He submitted his resignation at the end of the season and Fritz Crisler accepted it. Bump Elliott was named to replace the beleaguered Oosterbaan. Overall, Bennie Oosterbaan had nine winning seasons and two losing seasons at Michigan. He coached 100 games and finished with an overall record of 63 wins, 33 losses, and 4 ties. His winning rate of sixty-five percent was good for a lot of schools, just not Michigan. Things would be different for Michigan in 1959!

Like Michigan, the 1958 edition of the Michigan State Spartans was nothing to write home about. Duffy's footballers were slightly better than the Wolverines. They finished with an overall record of 3 wins, 5 losses, and 1 tie. However, the Spartans ended the Big Ten season with a record of 0-5-1 and had to settle for last place. The only good news for Michigan State was that their talented end, Sam Williams, earned All-American honors. Duffy and Biggie were no longer getting along like "brothers." Duffy had plenty of work to do in the off-season if he wanted to keep his job!

Game # 52: October 3, 1959 at Michigan Stadium in Ann Arbor

BACKGROUND INFORMATION:

The two-point conversion option really spiced up the game in 1958. Coaches chose the two-point option just over fifty percent of the time (51.4). Even more amazing was the fact that 44.7 percent of the two-point attempts succeeded in 1958.

The rules makers decided to add another wrinkle to the post-touchdown strategy. The width of the goal posts was increased from (18 feet six inches to twenty-three feet four inches) which made it much easier to convert after the touchdown and earn another point. Another change called the "Wild-Card" rule led to specialized substitutions that allowed coaches to use one play kickers for field goals and points-after-touchdown. Of course, both changes made it much more likely that coaches would opt for the higher percentage kick after touchdown. (*USA Today CFE*, Page 94)

Coach Duffy Daugherty began his sixth season in 1959. Overall, the first five seasons went well except for the 1954 and 1958 seasons. Duffy was in the midst of a major rebuilding program in East Lansing. Nobody was talking Big Ten Championship, not even the optimistic Duffy! The biggest room in Michigan State's football building was 'the room for improvement." Hopefully, the Spartans would continue to move forward in their quest to become a better football team.

The Spartans opened the season at home against Texas A & M and lost an ugly one (9-7). Not a lot of time to lick any wounds here. The Spartans had to be ready for another game in the Tree City. The good news was that Michigan State had won more games against the hated Wolverines in Ann Arbor than they had won in East Lansing. A tie would not be good enough. For the first time in series history, both teams entered the October 3rd game with a record of 0 wins and 1 loss. Would someone actually win their first game? Or would there be another tie?

The big news surrounding the fifty-second series game was the arrival of Coach Bump Elliott at Michigan. Elliott, another Michigan All-American, was brought on to reverse the direction of Michigan's sagging football fortunes. Chalmers William Elliott was one of the most likeable men to ever play or coach the game. The only question was, "Could this "nice guy" turn things around at Michigan?" The annual fall blood-letting event was scheduled for Michigan Stadium on October 3, 1959. Bump Elliott failed to win all the hearts and minds of Wolverine fans when he told fans that it would take three to five years to re-build Michigan into a Big Ten championship contender. This was the truth, but it was not what Wolverine fans wanted to hear from their new coach.

Michigan began the 1959 season with a home loss to Missouri (20-15). Not a good way to impress Wolverine Nation. The Maize and Blue footballers set their sights on the Michigan State Spartans who were coming to Ann Arbor for game number two of the 1959 season. Hopefully, the Wolverines would play better against Duffy's Spartans.

GAME SUMMARY: MSU-AAS 34 UM 8

Bottom line, the fifty-second series game was a mismatch. Coach Bump Elliott said the turning point in the game was "the opening kickoff." (Perry, Page 299) Michigan State scored early and often in this one-sided contest. It was an embarrassing debut for Coach Elliott against Duffy's Spartans. It was the largest margin of victory (26 points) for Michigan State in an Ann Arbor series game. Michigan State was not a great team in 1959, but they looked like it in Ann Arbor on October 3, 1959!

Team	1st	2nd	3rd	4th	Final
MSU	14	13	7	0	34
UM	0	0	0	8	8

The Spartans jumped out to a 14-0 first quarter lead on short scoring runs by Herb Adderly (2-yards) and Blanche Martin (1-yard). Spartan fullback and kicker Art Brandstatter booted both extra points. Dean Look ran for a 2-yard score and the Spartans lead grew to 20-0. Spartan speedster Bob Suci set a Spartan and series record with a 93-yard pick six. Brandstatter's extra point made it 27-0. That is how the first half ended. (*DFP*, 10/4/1959, Page 55)

149

Series game number fifty-two was pretty much over by the time the third quarter began. Of course, the game was only half over. Of course, the hated rivals kept harming each other's bodies for another thirty minutes. Dean Look connected with Don Stewart for a 25-yard touchdown pass that increased the lead to 33-0. Brandstatter's fourth extra point kick made it 34-0. Late in the game, Stan Noskin finally put Michigan on the scoreboard with a 1-yard run. On the next play, he completed a pass to end Bob Johnson for a 2-point conversion. Unfortunately, it was too little, too late. (*DFP*, 10/4/1959, Page 55) I am certain that the Spartans enjoyed their 34-8 win all the way back to East Lansing.

SERIES UPDATE:

Duffy Daugherty's third series win gave him an overall record of 3 wins, 2 losses and 1 tie against the Wolverines. Even better, the Paul Bunyan Trophy was staying in East Lansing for fourth straight year thanks to the tie in 1958. For the record, the Wolverine series advantage now stood at 35 wins, 13 losses, and 4 ties. However, the Spartans enjoyed another year of bragging rights against the Wolverines. Duffy continued to hold the upper hand in recruiting in the State of Michigan.

SERIES MILESTONES:

The 1959 Michigan vs Michigan State game was significant in series history for many reasons. First, it was the first decade where the Spartans held the advantage (7-2-1) over the Wolverines. This was a really, BIG DEAL for the folks in East Lansing, but not so much for Michigan fans. Second, it was Bump Elliott's first game and his first series loss. Third, it was the first time that a Michigan coach ever lost the first rival game to the Spartans. This would be the start of a disturbing trend that lasts until this day. Another record setting crowd showed up to watch the Spartans toy with the undermanned Wolverines. A total of 103,234 fans showed up to break the old record by over three-thousand people. Yes, this was absolutely the largest crowd to ever witness a sporting event in Michigan. Finally, Michigan States' Bob Suci set a Spartan and series record with a 93-yard pick-six.

SEASON SUMMARIES:

Duffy Daugherty's Spartans failed to capitalize on the momentum of the big win over Michigan. They traveled to Iowa City and lost to the Hawkeyes (37-8). MSU won four of the next five games before ending the season with a loss at Miami of Florida (18-13). Duffy's Spartans finished with a winning season (5 wins and 4 losses), but it was still a disappointment. The Green and White footballers were actually in contention for the conference championship for most of the season. Unfortunately, they finished second with a Big Ten record of 4-2-0. Dean Look earned first team All-American honors.

Bump Elliott's Wolverines played hard, but badly for most of the 1959 season. Michigan finished the season with a final record of 4 wins and 5 losses. They were seventh in the Big Ten with a record of 3 wins and 4 losses. The defense was solid, but the offense was inconsistent. Bump Elliott told everyone that this was going to be hard, but nobody wanted to hear it.

After one season, maybe the reality was starting to sink in. It had been ten seasons (1950) since Michigan won a conference championship and it looked like it was going to be a few more before it happened again. For the second straight season, Michigan failed to have an All-American player on the roster. Time for Bump Elliott to go and find some more star players!

DECADE AND SERIES SUMMARY:

The Spartans, under Biggie Munn and Duffy Daugherty gained a lot of ground in the series during the Fifties. Things were good in East Lansing—that is for sure! Michigan State arrived on the national scene in the Fifties. Of course, they climbed to the top of the college football mountain in 1951, 1952, and 1955. Meanwhile, back in Ann Arbor, things were headed in a different direction. Bump Elliott knew that he had a tough job ahead of him. The only question was, "Would Bump be around long enough to see it through?" Yes, things got interesting in the Fifties. What would the Sixties bring?

Decade and Series Summary 1898 to 1959

Time Frame	UM Won-Lost-Tied	MSU Won-Lost-Tied
1950-1959	2-7-1	7-2-1
1898-1959	35-13-4	13-35-4

PROGRAM SUMMARIES:

Michigan was a consistent winner in the Fifties, but they were not great. The Wolverines began the decade with a Big Ten Championship and that was it! The Wolverines fell off in every measurable category from the 1940s. Wins were down, losses were up, and UM's winning percentage decreased by 233 points (.821 to 588). Maize and Blue fans were still singing "Hail to the Victors," but now it had an empty ring to it. Michigan football was far removed from the prideful claim of "Champions of the West." The Michigan football program took a giant step backward from 1950 to 1959. It was one of the worst periods in the modern era of Michigan football. Wolverine fans were hoping for better results in the Sixties. It was up to Bump Elliott to take Michigan to a more glorious future than the one the Wolverines experienced in the Fifties.

The Spartans had a decade of stunning success against Michigan and everyone else! Biggie Munn and Duffy Daugherty produced consistent winners during the Fifties in all but two seasons. Michigan State's overall winning percentage jumped from sixty-three percent (.631) to almost seventy-seven percent (.766). An impressive increase of 135 "winning" points! They won twenty-three more games and lost five less during this period. Biggie Munn had four impressive seasons in the early part of the decade and Duffy keep the Spartans on the right track for the rest of the decade.

The number that really pointed out the biggest difference between the Mitten State rivals was the "All-American" count. Michigan State only had three outstanding players in the Forties but found twenty-three in the Fifties. Yes, many great players and a lot of good ones helped the Fifties become one of the greatest periods in Spartan football history.

Program Summaries 1950 to 1959

Statistical Area	UM	MSU
Number of Head Coaches	2	2
Games Played	91	92
Wins	52	70
Losses	36	21
Ties	3	1
Winning Percentage	.588	.766
Winning Seasons	7	8
Losing Seasons	3	2
Even Seasons	0	0
National Championships	0	3
All-American Players	6	23

After decades of playing second fiddle to Michigan, the Spartans were the best team in Michigan and one of the best in America. Biggie Munn worked tirelessly to put the Spartans on the nation's football map and Duffy Daugherty kept things going in East Lansing. Now, that both teams were in the Big Ten Conference, every game was doubly important. Fritz Crisler was annoyed with the series trophy that Governor Williams created. However, by the end of the decade, Crisler was hoping to get it back to Ann Arbor sometime during the Sixties. Biggie Munn reduced the gap between the two rivals. Duffy Daugherty was doing his best to keep that trend going. The balance of "football power" in Michigan changed dramatically in the Fifties. What would the Sixties bring to the football wars between Michigan and Michigan State?

CHAPTER 9

Spartans Remain in Charge 1960 to 1969

T he controversial issues of the Sixties landed right in the center of every college campus in America. The students of this decade were vastly different from those who matriculated in the 1950s. Everything was being questioned and nothing was taken for granted by America's youth. Protests became almost as popular as sporting events in some college towns. Meanwhile, college sports administrators were trying to keep up with the popularity of professional football. They were trying to keep amateur sports, well, amateur, but it was getting harder. Television was playing a bigger role in college sports, especially football. Like everything else there was a lot of good with television's influence on sports, but there was some bad too!

Game # 53: October 1, 1960 at Spartan Stadium in East Lansing

BACKGROUND INFORMATION:

There were no significant rules changes prior to the 1960 football season. The NCAA was busy with plenty of "off-field" issues, but the game itself was in a good place. The rules-makers were keeping an eye on the impact of widening the goal posts on field goal scoring. Substitutions were also being monitored, but that was about it.

Michigan fans were hoping that Wolverine football fortunes would improve in 1960. The Wolverine football program had experienced back-to-back losing seasons (1958 and 1959) for the first time since the 1881 and 1883 seasons. Michigan did not have a competitive team in 1882 Technically, 1881 and 1883 were "back-to-back" seasons of competitive play. Bump Elliott did not predict any Big Ten Championships for the 1960 season, but he was hoping for improved play in year two of the Elliott Era at Michigan. Michigan tuned-up for their annual blood-letting event against Michigan State with a 21-0 win over Oregon. Bump would get a better idea about his team after week two in East Lansing.

Spartan coach Duffy Daugherty had seven seasons under his belt in 1960. More importantly, after losing his first two games against Michigan, he was undefeated in the last four (3-0-1). The Spartans were hoping to improve on their disappointing season in 1959 that saw them finish at 5-4-0. Daugherty took his Spartans to Pittsburgh for the first game of the 1960 season and he did not learn much in a 7-7 tie. Was his team good enough to beat Michigan? Were his Spartans good enough to compete for the Big Ten Championship. Game number two against Michigan would provide some answers.

GAME SUMMARY: UM 17 MSU-AAS 24

Game number fifty-three of the annual 'football brawl" between UM & MSU was one of the most keenly contested games in series history. There were five lead changes and two ties during the game. It was not a game for the faint of heart! Michigan scored first on Dave Raimey's 2-yard touchdown run. John Halstead kicked the extra point and Michigan led 7-0. Michigan State responded a few minutes later. Tom Wilson's 6-yard run and Art Brandstatter's PAT made it 7-7 at the end of the first quarter. In the second quarter, Michigan took the lead on Halstead's 35-yard field goal (10-7). The Spartans took their first lead (14-10) on Gary Ballman's 4-yard run and another Brandstatter extra point. Michigan's Dennis Fitzgerald returned the Michigan State kickoff for 99-yards to give the Wolverines a 17-14 lead at halftime. (*DFP*, 10/2/1960, Page 31)

Art Brandstatter's 32-yard field goal was the only score of the third quarter. The game was tied 17-17 heading into the final quarter. Both teams battled hard to score the winning points, but the defenses were too strong. Finally, with just over two minutes remaining the Spartans fullback Carl Charon crashed into the end zone from three yards out. Michigan State took the lead at 24-17 and that is how the game ended. (*DFP*, 10/2/1960, Page 31)

It was a great game to win and a tough one to lose. Both teams had their chances, but the Spartans did just a little bit more. Michigan State ran for 258 yards and passes for 72 more to total 330 yards of offense. Michigan did some good things on offense (192 rushing yards and 112 passing), but not scoring in the second half was the key to their demise. (*DFP*, 10/2/1960, Page 31)

Team	1st	2nd	3rd	4th	Final
UM	7	10	0	0	17
MSU	7	7	3	7	24

SERIES UPDATE:

The hard-fought victory gave Duffy Daugherty his fourth series win. He now had an overall record of 4 wins, 2 losses, and 1 tie against the Wolverines. Even better, the Paul Bunyan Trophy would remain in East Lansing for the fifth straight year thanks to the tie in 1958. Michigan still held the series advantage with a record of 35 wins, 14 losses and 4 ties.

However, Michigan State now owned the "Trophy Series" advantage with a record of 5 wins, 2 losses, and 1 tie. Duffy and his Spartans were already enjoying another year of bragging rights and there was nothing that Michigan could do about it until 1961!

SERIES MILESTONES:

As always, the 1960 edition of Michigan vs Michigan State pigskin madness provided some interesting milestones. First, 76, 490 fans showed up to watch the slugfest which set a new series record for an East Lansing game. Second, Dennis Fitzgerald's first half kickoff return (99-yards) set a Michigan record and a series record. Finally, the game was played in alternating sites (East Lansing 1958, Ann Arbor 1959, and East Lansing 1960) for the first time since 1908-1911.

SEASON SUMMARIES:

Bump Elliott's Wolverines bounced back with two solid wins after losing to the Spartans. Ultimately, it turned out to be an "up and down" season. Michigan played hard in every game. Three of their losses were by 7 points or less. The defense played very well in every game but two (MSU and Wisconsin). Unfortunately, the offense failed to put enough points on the board in too many games. The Wolverines finished the season with a final record of 5 wins and 4 losses. They improved slightly in the Big Ten with a 5th place finish at 3-4-0. Year two of the Elliott Era was in the books. Michigan had a winning season, but Wolverine fans wanted more, much more! They were also getting sick of losing to the farmers from East Lansing. When would things get back to "normal" in Ann Arbor?

Maybe Duffy's Spartans spent too much time patting themselves on the back after their victory over Michigan. Iowa was the better team and left East Lansing with a 27-15 win. Duffy got his team back on track with two nice road wins over Notre Dame (21-0) and Indiana (35-0). They came up short on Homecoming Day and lost to Ohio State (21-10). The Spartans finished the season with three straight wins to end up at 6-2-1 and earned a fourth-place finish (4-2-0) in the Big Ten. Like Michigan, no Spartans earned All-American honors in 1960. Of course, the season was a disappointment. Duffy and his staff would have another year to savor their win over Michigan.

Game # 54: October 14, 1961 at Michigan Stadium in Ann Arbor

BACKGROUND INFORMATION:

The NCAA Football Rules Committee did not have any major changes to the rules of college football in 1961. There was no need to make any big changes. Instead, the rules makers chose to monitor the impact of the wider uprights on field goal scoring and keep an eye on player safety. The NCAA ordered a study of head and neck injuries, but the results were inconclusive. (*USA Today CFE*, Page 126)

The optimistic Duffy Daugherty thought he had a good team heading into 1961. Veteran players, in key positions, were all over his roster. Some promising sophomores only made his smile bigger when he talked about Michigan State's prospects for the upcoming season. The Spartans opened at Wisconsin and came home with a 20-0 victory. They hosted Stanford in week two and sent their guests home to ponder a 31-3 defeat. The Spartans were riding high and looking forward to their trip to Ann Arbor in week three.

Bump Elliott led his team to the first winning season of the Elliott Era in 1960. Michigan was looking to improve again and stay on track for Bump's "Five Year Championship Contender Plan." The Wolverines returned several key players. Some incoming sophomores would help improve the team. If things went right and the team stayed healthy, maybe Bump's footballers could contend for a championship. Yes, it was a lot to ask. Wolverine fans were hopeful.

In the first game of the year, Michigan thrashed ninth ranked UCLA (29-6). The Wolverines destroyed Army (38-8) in week two. Maybe Bump knew something that he had been hiding about his Wolverines before the season started. The good news was that undefeated Michigan (2-0-0) rose to number six at the start of week three. The bad news was that fifth-ranked Michigan State was coming to town on October 14th.

GAME SUMMARY: MSU-AAS 28 UM 0

The fifty-fourth series game was a BIG win for the Spartans and a BIG disappointment for the Wolverines! Michigan State scored first, second, third and fourth, well you get the picture. It was one of the most one-sided games in the history of the series, at least for the Wolverines. Michigan State looked every bit as good as a fifth-ranked team should look. Their offense was balanced and effective. The defense, well, it was about as good as it gets. As usual, feelings were intense on both sidelines and the tackling was hard, almost ferocious at times. The annual blood-letting event between the Spartans and the Wolverines was decided early. Michigan lost more blood this day, no doubt about it!

The Spartans looked like a Fielding Yost team—scoring 14 points in the first twelve minutes of play. They slowed their "Point-a-Minute" pace in the second quarter, but still scored a third touchdown and extra point to make it 21-0 after the first thirty-minutes of play. There were many Spartan Stars on this day, but none for the Wolverines. MSU fullback George Saimes led the team in rushing with 57 yards on 16 carries. He scored one touchdown and Sherman Lewis scored another. Carl Charon, the hero from the 1960 game, also caught a touchdown pass. Michigan State gained more yards in the air (105 to 92) and on the ground (295 to 84). Of course, the Spartans also scored a lot more points than the Wolverines. (DFP, 10/15/1961, Page 49) It turned out to be a great day for everyone wearing Green and White.

Team	1st	2nd	3rd	4th	Final
MSU	14	7	0	7	28
UM	0	0	0	0	0

SERIES UPDATE:

Michigan State extended their advantage in the Paul Bunyan Trophy series to 6-2-1. Michigan still held the overall series advantage at 35 wins, 15 losses, and 4 ties. However, Michigan State was undefeated in the last six games (5-0-1). It was a great time to be a Spartan, but a Wolverine! Michigan State was now ahead by a margin of 2-0-0 in the Sixties. When would this Spartan dominance end?

SERIES MILESTONES:

There was one milestone to mention. Duffy Daugherty became the first Spartan coach to defeat the Wolverines five times. Charlie Bachman and Biggie Munn both won four games against Michigan. Now, Duffy was better with five huge wins over the Wolverines. The crowd was large (103,198). In fact, it was the second largest crowd in the history of the series, but about forty people short of a new record. Bump Elliott remained winless in the series (0-3-0).

SEASON SUMMARIES:

Duffy's Spartans kept on winning after they beat Michigan. They defeated Notre Dame and Indiana to run their winning streak to five games (5-0-0). The Spartans were ambushed in Minneapolis in early November. Final score: Gophers 13 and Spartans 0. The Spartans could not shake that Gopher upset and they lost the next week at Purdue (7-6). Michigan State was out of contention for the Big Ten Championship, but they finished strong with two straight wins against Northwestern and Illinois to end the season with a record of 7 wins, and 2 losses.

The Spartans finished the conference season at 5-2-0 which was good for third place. The bad news for Duffy was that they lost two games and finished in third place in the conference. The good news was that he beat Michigan again. He also had an All-American lineman named Dave Behrman. The Spartans would have another year of bragging rights in the Great Lakes State. Duffy continued to enjoy his recruiting edge in Michigan.

Bump Elliott got his team back on track the next week against Purdue. Michigan defeated Purdue (16-14) which made the Homecoming Day crowd happy. They lost the next week at Minnesota (23-20). Bump's footballers went on a three-game winning streak heading into the final game of the season against Ohio State. The game ended very badly for the Wolverines. Ohio State won 50-20—ouch!

Michigan ended the 1961 season with a final record of 6 wins and 3 losses. The Wolverines finished in 6th place in the conference with a record of 3-3-0. The Wolverines played well for most of the season, but the blowout losses to Michigan State and Ohio State indicated that they still had work to do before they would contend for a conference championship. Bump Elliott went back to the drawing board in December 1961!

Game # 55: October 13, 1962 at Spartan Stadium in East Lansing

BACKGROUND INFORMATION:

The 1962 season saw no major rules changes. It would be "business as usual" in college football for another fall of campus football games. The NCAA people were always looking for ways to improve the game, but it was not the right time.

Michigan was an improved team in 1961 and more progress was expected in 1962. Although the Wolverines played well in most of their games, they were blown out twice (MSU and OSU) in 1961. Bump Elliott was looking for more consistency and probably a little more toughness when playing the "Big Boys" in the Big Ten. Michigan, which had not had an All-American player since 1957, was also looking for some Wolverine footballers to step up and have great seasons.

Bump Elliott's Wolverines started the season at home against Nebraska. It did not go well since the Cornhuskers left Ann Arbor with a 25-13 win over the Maize and Blue footballers. Michigan bounced back the next week with a solid win (17-7) over tenth-ranked Army. The Wolverines were even at 1-1-0 and the Spartans were coming to town. It was time to step up and put an end to the Spartan dominance that had plagued the Wolverines for the last six seasons.

Coach Duffy Daugherty was optimistic, as usual, about Michigan State's prospects for the 1962 season. The Spartans were looking to improve on the 7-2-0 campaign of 1961. The Spartans came within sixteen points of a perfect season and some good players were back to play another year. Michigan State was looking to make another run at the Big Ten Championship.

Unfortunately, Duffy lost some of his optimism when the Spartans came up short in the season opener at Stanford (16-13). His smile returned after the Spartan footballers crushed North Carolina (38-6). Like Michigan, the Spartans would head into the annual gridiron matchup with a record of 1-1-0. It was the Big Ten opener for both teams and "bragging rights" were on the line. The time for talk was almost over. Toe would meet leather in East Lansing in just a few days and the annual blood-letting festivities would begin!

GAME SUMMARY: UM 0 MSU-AAS 28

The largest crowd (77,501) in Spartan Stadium history showed up to witness some series history. Michigan State's second straight win by a score of 28-0 over Michigan was a BIG first in the series. No team had ever won two straight games (or lost two straight games) by the same exact score.

Just like 1961, the Spartans scored early and often. The Michigan State offense rolled up 459-yards (391 rushing and 68 passing). Sherman Lewis rushed for two touchdowns and scored a third on a pass reception. MSU's defense held Michigan's offense to 72-rushing yards and only 40-yards in the air. (*DFP*, 10/14/1962, Page 49) It was a long day for the Wolverine offense.

In addition to winning the game, the Green and White footballers also won the first down battle by a margin of 19 to 9. (*DFP*, 10/14/1962, Page 49) Yes, it was a dominating Spartan victory. There is no doubt that Michigan lost more blood on this day than Michigan State. The Wolverines were embarrassed for the second straight season by Michigan State!

Team	1st	2nd	3rd	4th	Final
UM	0	0	0	0	0
MSU	13	0	8	7	28

SERIES UPDATE:

It was another bad showing for Bump Elliott against Duffy Daugherty's Spartans. Michigan State won their fourth straight series game and remained unbeaten in the last seven! There is no doubt that the Spartan players, coaches, and fans thoroughly enjoyed their decisive win over Michigan. Yes, Michigan still held a healthy advantage in the series with a record of 35 wins, 16 losses, and 4 ties. However, Sparty retained the Paul Bunyan Trophy and increased their advantage over Michigan in the "Big Ten Years" to 7 wins, 2 losses, and 1 tie. Michigan State also remained undefeated in the 1960s against Michigan with a record of 3 wins, 0 losses and 0 ties.

SERIES MILESTONES:

There were five important series milestones for game number fifty-five. First, the crowd of 77,501 fans broke the previous East Lansing record by just over a thousand people (1,011). Second, it was the first time that a series team (Michigan State) won back-to-back games by the same exact score (28-0). Of course, it was also the first time that a team (Michigan) lost back-to-back games by the same exact score (28-0). Third, Michigan coach Bump Elliott remained winless in the series. No Michigan coach ever started off at 0-3-0 against Michigan State until this game! Fourth, it was the tenth game in the Paul Bunyan Trophy series with Michigan State now holding a decisive advantage (7-2-1) Finally, it was the tenth series game ever played in East Lansing and the Spartans made it count!

SEASON SUMMARIES:

The Wolverines could not recover from their blowout loss to Michigan State. In fact, things got worse. Michigan lost the next game Purdue (37-0). The Wolverines continued their scoreless ways with another loss to Minnesota (17-0). The good news for Bump's Wolverines was that they scored twelve points the next week. The bad news was that they still lost to Wisconsin (34-12). The Maize and Blue footballers managed to beat Illinois by a score of 14-10 and then lost the last two games to Iowa and OSU.

Year four of the Bump Elliott Era was a big disappointment for him, his players and everyone in Wolverine Nation! It was a giant step backward. The five-year drive to build a Big Ten championship contender went flying off the road and crashed into a clump of trees just south of Stadium and Main. It was ugly!

Michigan's final record of 2-7-0 was the worst Wolverine showing since the 1937 version of Harry Kipke's Wolverines. Nobody in Ann Arbor was happy about the 1962 football season, NOBODY! To add insult to injury, no Wolverine football player names showed up on any All-American award lists for the fifth straight season!

Michigan State followed up their victory over Michigan with two more wins over Notre Dame and Indiana. The Spartans were undefeated in the conference at 2-0-0 heading into November. Unfortunately, the wheels fell off the bus and Duffy's footballers lost three of four games in November. Michigan State finished the 1962 season with an overall record of 5 wins and 4 losses. They ended at 3-3-0 in the Big Ten which put them in a tie for fifth place.

The bad news for Duffy Daugherty was that his team did not compete for the Big Ten Championship when it counted in November. The good news was that the Spartans finished with a winning record (5-4-0) for the fourth consecutive season. Michigan State remained undefeated against the hated Wolverines for the seventh straight year. Duffy knew he had plenty of work to do to get his team ready to compete for a championship in 1963. However, he was probably smiling because his Spartans still had series "bragging rights" and the Paul Bunyan Trophy. Duffy was also smiling because three of his players (George Saimes, Ed Budde, and David Behrman) earned All-American honors in 1962.

Game # 56: October 12, 1963 at Michigan Stadium in Ann Arbor

BACKGROUND INFORMATION:

Once again, Fritz Crisler and the NCAA Football Rules Committee made some minor changes to the substitution rules, but that was about it. College presidents were starting to get more involved in their "big time" athletic programs thanks to all the television money.

Duffy Daugherty was looking forward to the 1963 season because he was an eternal optimist. He liked his team because it featured some excellent returning players on both sides of the ball. Duffy probably loved the idea that Ohio State was not on the schedule. Hmmm, the Spartans might have a shot at a championship if they played their cards, and their games, right!

Coach Daugherty's footballers started well with a big win over North Carolina (31-0). Things did not go as well the next week in Los Angeles. The Spartans lost a tough one to Southern Cal (13-10). The Spartans had a record of 1-1-0 heading into Michigan Week. The good news for Duffy was that he was undefeated in conference play and he had not lost to Michigan in seven years. Once again, it would be another important conference series game in Ann Arbor.

After showing excellent progress for two straight seasons, Michigan took a giant step backward in 1962. It was just an awful season. Yes, there were some injuries, but every team has injuries. To his credit, Bump Elliott did not make any excuses. Instead, he did all he could do which was stay optimistic and keep things moving forward. Coach Elliott was still looking for an All-American, or two. Nobody in Ann Arbor was talking about a Big Ten Championship in year five of the Elliott Era. It was not going to happen!

The Wolverines opened with a solid win over Southern Methodist (27-16). A guy named Roger Staubach put on quite a show the next week and Navy sailed out of Ann Arbor with a 26-13 victory. Of course, Staubach played well against a lot of teams and won the 1963 Heisman Trophy. Like MSU, Michigan was 1-1-0 heading into Michigan State week. Time for another Mitten State rumble in Michigan Stadium.

GAME SUMMARY: MSU-AAS 7 UM 7

Game number fifty-six in the "nasty" football series was one to remember and one to forget for both teams! The game did not settle anything! Both teams remained undefeated in the conference, but both teams were also winless in Big Ten play. The defenses were outstanding for both teams which made Daugherty and Elliott happy. However, the offenses were quite a different story! Obviously, both teams lost about the same amount of blood in this game since neither team dominated.

The Wolverines opened the scoring in the first quarter on a 15-yard pass from Bob Chandler to John Henderson. Bob Timberlake's extra point made it 7-0 in favor of Michigan and that how the first half ended. Michigan State scored in the third quarter on a Steve Juday scoring pass to Sherman Lewis. Kicker Lou Bobich made the extra point kick, and the game was tied at 7-7 with just over one quarter to play. Both teams had chances to kick winning field goals, but all attempts failed. For the fifth, and final, time in series history, the annual Michigan "Bowl" football game ended in a tie. (*DFP*, 10/13/1963. Page 43)

Team	1st	2nd	3rd	4th	Final
MSU	0	0	7	0	7
UM	7	0	0	0	7

The game ended with some added entertainment. According to Detroit Free Press writer Bob Pille, there was a short boxing match near the end of the game. It seems that the starting fullbacks from each team (Roger Lopes from MSU and Mel Anthony from UM) had some hard feelings toward each other. Pille wrote that "Nobody got hit with anything damaging and both were banished while officials allowed an unused half minute to tick off the clock." (*DFP*, 10/13/1963. Page 43) Like the game, the "fight" also ended in a draw.

SERIES UPDATE:

The "tie" allowed Michigan State to retain possession of the Paul Bunyan Trophy for the eighth straight year. Michigan still had a big edge in the series with 35 wins, 16 losses, and 5 ties. However, the Spartans still held the Big Ten "years" advantage at 7 wins, 2 losses and 2 ties. MSU also remained undefeated in the Sixties with a record of 3 wins, 0 losses, and 1 tie.

SERIES MILESTONES:

There were three milestones that emerged from this game. First, it was the first , and only,7-7 tie in the series and the last! All future games would have an outcome—good or bad, for both teams. No more "kissing your sister" in this rivalry! Second, Bump Elliott remained winless in the series for the fourth straight year, but he was getting closer! Finally, Michigan State extended their unbeaten streak (6-0-2) against Michigan to eight games—their longest ever against the Wolverines!

SEASON SUMMARIES:

Duffy Daugherty's tenth season at Michigan State was another winning campaign, but not completely fulfilling for Spartan fans. The Spartans got rolling after the tie with Michigan and won five consecutive games. Four were Big Ten games and one win was against Notre Dame. Michigan State had a season ending showdown with Illinois that would determine the Big Ten Champion. The game was pushed back one week because of the assassination of President John F. Kennedy.

Illinois came to town on November 28, 1963 and left with a 13-0 victory. The Spartan offense was completely shut down by Dick Butkus and a ferocious Illinois defense. Illinois scored just enough to claim the victory and the conference title. It was a sad time in America, and it got a little sadder in East Lansing with the disappointing loss. The good news for Duffy and MSU was that they had a winning season for the fifth straight year. The bad news was that they lost the conference championship on the last day of the season. Michigan State finished with a record of 6 wins, 2 losses, and 1 tie. They tied for second place in the Big Ten title race. Two Spartan players (halfback Sherman Lewis and guard Earl Lattimer) earned All-American honors in 1963.

Bump's Wolverines suffered a worse fate the next week, losing against Purdue by a score of 23-12. They ended October on a low note with a tough loss at Minnesota (6-0). The Wolverines, with a record of 1-3-1, were not in contention for the Big Ten Title in the final month of the season. Bump's team played well against Northwestern and sent the alumni home with a 27-6 victory to celebrate on Homecoming Day.

Michigan won their second straight game against Illinois (14-8) before tying Iowa 21-21. The disappointing season ended poorly with a loss at Ohio State (14-10). The Wolverines finished year five of the Elliott Era with a record of 3 wins, 4 losses, and 2 ties. This was not what Bump had in mind when he took over in 1959. He genuinely believed that Michigan would be back in contention for a conference title by the 1963 season. The good news was that he did not get fired although some alumni were mumbling to that effect. The personable Elliott would have another off-season to figure out a way to get the Wolverines back on track. A bunch of healthy players would be a big first step! Of course, an All-American or two would certainly help his cause. Of course, it would be nice if he could figure out how to beat MSU too. Bump had never seen the Paul Bunyan Trophy up close so it would be nice to have it in Ann Arbor for a year. Bump Elliott went to work in the off-season—still so much work to do!

162

Game # 57: October 10, 1964 at Spartan Stadium in East Lansing

BACKGROUND INFORMATION:

The NCAA rules makers continued to monitor the "substitution issue" and came up with another change for the 1964 season. Free substitution was going to be the "rule" and player specialization would become the norm in college football. (USA Today CFE, Page 160) That was about it for the rules. As usual, everything else stayed the same for the 1964 season. Fritz Crisler, and his rules committee, would keep a close eye on everything to see when, and if, any changes needed to be made.

One "off the field" development at Michigan State that had rubbed Spartans the wrong way since 1955 was finally resolved. John Hannah, and his administrators, petitioned the legislature to let Michigan State be like all the other Land Grant institutions across the country. The name change that was approved in 1955 "Michigan State University of Agriculture and Applied Science" was incorrect according to Spartan supporters. After much pressure, the legislature recognized that Michigan State University was a full-fledged educational institution that deserved to be titled as such. According to David A. Thomas, author of *Michigan State College: John Hannah and the Creation of a World University, 1926-1969*, the "Agriculture and Applied Science" words were dropped from the school's title—forever! Michigan State University was finally named correctly according to everyone in Green and White Nation! (Thomas, Page xvi)

One final item of interest in 1964 was the death of long-time Michigan law professor and Big Ten "rules" arbiter, Ralph Aigler. Spartan fans did not like Mr. Aigler and that is being kind! As chairman of the Big Ten's Faculty Representative Council, Aigler wielded more power than the Big Ten presidents when it came to athletics. Ralph Aigler used his power to vigorously oppose Michigan State's admission into the Big Ten conference for years. His efforts to keep the Spartans out of the conference until they followed the Big Ten's rules were highly effective. Mr. Aigler had been retired for a few years, but his "evil" memory lived on in East Lansing. I doubt if any Spartan fans attended his funeral.

Bump Elliott began the 1964 football season with cautious optimism. He had a strong returning cast on both sides of the ball. If his team could stay healthy, the Wolverines could be exceptionally good. Coach Elliott knew that he was behind schedule since he told everyone at his first press conference that it would take 3-5 years to re-build the Wolverines into a championship contender. Would this be the year that Bump's Michigan Men put it all together?

Michigan kicked off the 1964 season with a solid 24-7 win over Air Force. The Wolverines jumped to number eight in the country and then they jumped all over a good Navy team! The sixth-ranked midshipmen sailed into Ann Arbor and got towed out by a tugboat (not really) after a 21-0 loss. Heisman quarterback Roger Staubach was nursing an ankle injury. He was not a factor in the game. Michigan was 2-0-0 and people were starting to take notice! Bump Elliot's seventh-ranked football team looked strong after the first two weeks of the season. The burning question was, "Were the Wolverines strong enough to win a game in East Lansing?"

The affable Duffy Daugherty began his eleventh season at Michigan State in 1964. His teams had been good for most of his tenure, but the Spartans had not been a big winner since they won the national championship in 1957. Even more bothersome was the fact that MSU had not won any Big Ten titles with Duffy at the helm. The natives were getting restless in East Lansing. When would Duffy's Spartans win another Big Ten Championship? Well, 1964 might not be the year. Coach Daugherty lost some talented players from the 1963 team that came within one game of winning the Big Ten Championship.

It was looking like a "rebuilding year." Of course, Duffy could not really say that, but not too many people expected Michigan State to be good enough to make another run in 1964. Any Spartan dreams of an undefeated season were shattered in game number one against North Carolina. The Spartans put up a good fight but left Chapel Hill with a 21-15 loss. Things got better the next week when Duffy's footballers beat Southern California (17-7). The bad news was that Michigan State was 1-1-0 after two games. The good news was that they were undefeated in Big Ten play. Once again, everything would be on the line in East Lansing when Michigan came to town. Would Duffy's Spartans be able to send the Wolverines home with another defeat?

GAME SUMMARY: UM 17 MSU 10

The fifty-seventh game between #7 Michigan and #9 Michigan State was another classic. The fireworks began before the warmups were even finished! Author E. Bruce Geelhoed's book, *Bump Elliott, The Michigan Wolverines and Their 1964 Championship Football Season*, provided excellent insight about a memorable pre-game confrontation in Spartan Stadium. Apparently, a burly Spartan defensive lineman named Patrick Gallinagh had a reputation for pre-game intimidation. Michigan's scouting staff noted that he disrupted Southern California's warm-up drills the week before. Maybe his pre-game antics helped MSU win the game.

Michigan's scouts alerted the Wolverines that some MSU "hosts" might try to distract them during their pre-game preparations. Of course, Gallinagh showed up right on time to "welcome" Michigan to Spartan Stadium. A spunky sophomore named Rick Sygar was ready for the loud-mouthed Gallinagh. According to future All-American defensive back Rick Volk "Gallinagh started to come into our drills and Rick Sygar saw him coming and struck him right under his chin [with his helmet] and knocked him right on his back." (Geelhoed, Page 75) Whoa, nobody expected that, especially Gallinagh! Another Spartan restrained #55 which prevented a fight that Sygar was less equipped to win since he was giving up about forty-five pounds to his burly tormentor.

Both teams joined in the fray, but the coaches quickly restored order. It took everything the officials had to keep both teams under control for the remainder of the game. Yes, the pre-game intimidation gesture backfired on MSU and fired-up the Wolverines. Volk went on to say, "I think it proved that we were ready to beat Michigan State that day and we did beat them." (Geelhoed, Page 75) The pre-game festivities raised the intensity level by a factor of ten on both sides of the field. Every block and every tackle was a bone-crunching and teeth rattling event! It was one of the most intense games in series history.

164

The Spartans capitalized on a Michigan fumble and took the lead in the first quarter. Michigan countered with a 29-yard field goal by Bob Timberlake on the last play of the second quarter. It was 7-3 in favor of MSU at halftime. (Geelhoed, Page 75) Michigan State controlled play for the third quarter, but they failed to cash in on more Michigan mistakes. Finally, the Spartans put three more points on the board at the start of the fourth quarter.

Trailing 10-3, Michigan decided to make the last twelve-minutes count! Quarterback Bob Timberlake led Michigan on a twelve play 73-yard drive. Rich Sygar, scored on a short run, but a two-point attempt failed. Michigan State retained a slim 10-9 lead while the clock ticked away on the Wolverines. Michigan State failed to gain a first down on their next drive and Timberlake's offense went back to work. The Wolverines put together a determined drive that ended in a touchdown when Rick Sygar, again, made another big play. He completed a pass to John Henderson for a 31-yard touchdown. The Wolverines went for another two-point conversion and this time it worked. Michigan led for the first time in the game at 17-10. And that is how the game ended. (Geelhoed, Page 75)

Team	1st	2nd	3rd	4th	Final
UM	0	3	0	14	17
MSU	7	0	0	3	10

The Wolverines showed a lot of grit in this game. They proved that they were strong enough to win in East Lansing when it looked like they were going to "give" the game to Michigan State. Michigan was off to a perfect start (3-0-0). More importantly, the Wolverines were 1-0-0 in Big Ten Play. Duffy probably knew that this was a game that got away. Michigan State was the better team for most of the game, but they blew too many scoring chances when they had them.

SERIES UPDATE:

Finally, after eight years, Michigan increased their series advantage. The Wolverines increased their series advantage to 36 wins, 16 losses, and 5 ties. Michigan State was still on the winning side of the Paul Bunyan Trophy ledger with a record of 7-3-2. Michigan players, coaches and fans would enjoy some long-awaited "bragging rights" for the next year, that is for sure! Best of all, Bump Elliott would be able to spend some quality time with Paul Bunyan!

SERIES MILESTONES:

As always, this series game had a few more milestones. First, it was the first time that Michigan played against the team from Michigan State University, not the farmers from Michigan State University of Agriculture and Applied Science. Second, it was another record setting crowd as 78,234 fans showed up for the game. Third, Bump Elliott got a Green and White monkey off his back by notching his first win against the Spartans. It was probably a little sweeter since it came in East Lansing. Finally, it was Michigan's first win of the Sixties. They now had a record of 1-3-1 with half a decade to go.

SEASON SUMMARIES:

Michigan hosted Purdue the next week and lost a heartbreaker to the Boilermakers and a quarterback named Bob Griese. After scoring late in the game, Bump Elliott went for the win instead of a tie and lost the game by a score of 21-20. That one really hurt! Michigan was now 1-1-0 in the conference with five more conference games to play. The Wolverines won them all. They ended the season with another big road win at Ohio State—beating the Buckeyes by a score of 10-0. Michigan finished at 8-1-0 overall and went 6-1-0 in the conference. Bump Elliott claimed his first Big Ten championship one year later than originally predicted.

The Wolverines went on to the Rose Bowl for the first time since January 1, 1951. Michigan made the most of the opportunity by dominating Oregon State 34-7. Bump Elliott's footballers finished the season with an outstanding record of 9 wins and 1 loss. Yes, they came within two points of a perfect season, but there was nothing that could be done about that! The Wolverines finished fourth in both the AP and UPI polls. Quarterback Bob Timberlake and lineman Bill Yearby both earned All-American honors for their stellar play. Everything was good in Wolverine Nation and just about everybody loved Bump Elliott, again!

Duffy's Spartans stumbled the next week at Indiana and came home with a 27-20 loss. Michigan State was sitting at 1-3-0 and things looked bleak for the rest of the season. Somehow, Duffy used some of his motivational "magic" and the Spartans won three straight games. Unfortunately, the Green and White lost to Notre Dame and Illinois to finish with a final record of 4 wins and 5 losses. The Spartans posted a record of 3-3-0 in the conference and finished in sixth place in the Big Ten.

It was a tough season for Duffy and Michigan State. Not too many people expected them to compete for the conference championship, but most expected another winning season from the smiling Irishman. After five straight winning seasons, a losing season will always be a disappointment. Of course, the loss to Michigan and the "kidnapping" of the Paul Bunyan Trophy just added insult to injury. The hated Wolverines had bragging rights for one year and the Spartans did not. Time to move on. For the first time in three years no Spartans earned All-American honors.

Game # 58: October 9, 1965 at Michigan Stadium in Ann Arbor

BACKGROUND INFORMATION:

There were two rule changes for the 1965 season. The first one allowed the use of a two-inch kicking tee on kickoffs and field goals. The second change was about substitutions, one of the big issues in college football for almost twenty years. Unlimited substitutions were allowed after all scoring plays and between periods. Platoon football was back! (*USA Today CFE*, Page 173) Another important change took place in Big Ten Conference in 1965. All teams were going to play a seven-game league schedule. Teams would still be able to play three non-conference games every year. The college football regular season was now a ten-game gauntlet, instead of nine.

Coach Duffy Daugherty was looking to improve on his first losing season in five years. As usual, he was upbeat about Michigan's State's roster for 1965. Duffy tried to stay on the bright side as much as possible. He knew that his Spartans would be good. The big question remained, "How good?" Coach Daugherty got a change to see how good his team was when they opened the season with a nice win over UCLA (13-3). Game number two at Penn State was even better. The Spartans left "Happy Valley," well, happy! A 23-0 road victory will always make you happy. Game number three at home against Illinois also turned out very well. Michigan State defeated the Fighting Illini by a score of 22-12. The Spartans were rolling (3-0-0) and rose to number five in the country heading into Michigan week. Once again, the Michigan game would be the most important game of the young season. Losing again to the hated Wolverines was just not an option. The Spartans headed to Ann Arbor with great resolve. They were on a mission and the Wolverines were the next obstacle to overcome! Game on!

The defending Big Ten Champion Wolverines enjoyed their glory from 1964, but a new season was upon them. Bump Elliott lost some many good football players, but plenty of talent was still on the Michigan roster. Expectations were high for the Wolverines who started the year as the fourth-ranked team in the country.

The Maize and Blue footballers lived up to the expectations in game one against North Carolina. Michigan traveled to Chapel Hill and returned with a hard-fought 31-24 victory. The Wolverines hosted California the next week and won by a score of 10-7. Things did not work out so well the next week as Michigan lost to the Georgia Bulldogs (15-7). Michigan dropped out of the rankings after the Georgia loss, but a win over number five Michigan State would probably get them back in the top ten.

GAME SUMMARY: MSU 24 UM 7

Game number fifty-eight of the "in-state-hate" football series was another titanic struggle with both teams flailing away at each other on every play. The referees made sure that there were no pre-game fisticuffs like the 1964 game. However, there was plenty of "action" on every play. The favored Spartans scored early and often against a valiant, but undermanned Michigan team. Michigan State played a strong game and Michigan was not good enough to compete for four quarters.

Michigan State scored first on a 1-yard dive by Quarterback Steve Juday. A missed extra point kept the Spartan lead at 6-0. Michigan took the lead in the second quarter when Wolverine quarterback Wally Gabler also scored on a one-yard run and the successful extra point made it 7-6. Spartan kicker Dick Kenny made a twenty-yard field goal late in the half and Michigan State led 9-7 at the half. All-American running back Clint Jones put the Spartans ahead for good on a 10-yard run in the third quarter. (*DFP*, 1010/1965, Pages 53 and 57)

Kinney booted another field goal (35-yards) in the fourth quarter to give Michigan State an 18-7 lead with about six minutes to play. Spartan fullback Bob Apisa finished the scoring on the last play of the game when he sprinted into the end zone on a 39-yard run. (*DFP*, 1010/1965, Pages 53 and 57)

Michigan runners had lots of opportunities to meet men like Bubba Smith, Charley Thornhill, Harold Lucas, and George Webster during the game, but the encounters were not pleasant. The rugged Spartan defense held Michigan to a negative thirty-nine yards (-39) rushing. Michigan tried to beat Michigan State through the air when they could not run the ball, but that did not work either. Meanwhile, the Spartans rushed for 210 yards and controlled the ball for long periods of time. (*DFP*, 1010/1965, Pages 53 and 57)

Team	1st	2nd	3rd	4th	Final
MSU	6	3	6	9	24
UM	0	7	0	0	7

It was a closer game than the final score indicated, but there was no doubt which team was better. Michigan State took advantage of Michigan mistakes and scored after two fumbles and one interception. If the Spartan offense were a little sharper, it could have been a real blowout. Bottom line—Michigan State left Ann Arbor with a big win and a perfect record of 4-0-0 which included two straight wins in the Big Ten. The Spartans were in the driver's seat, but would they be able to stay the course?

SERIES UPDATE:

Michigan State's win brought the Paul Bunyan Trophy back to East Lansing. Michigan still held the overall series advantage at 36 wins, 17 losses, and 5 ties. However, the Spartans continued to be the much better team since Michigan State joined the Big Ten. The Spartans now had 8 wins 3 losses and 2 ties after thirteen Paul Bunyan trophy games. Duffy Daugherty and "Spartan Nation" would enjoy another year of bragging rights against the Wolverines. Michigan State increased their advantage in the Sixties to 4 wins, 1 loss, and 1 tie.

SERIES MILESTONES:

The only significant milestone to mention is that Duffy Daugherty became the first Spartan coach to win seven games against the Wolverines. After losing his first two games, Duffy improved his record to 7 wins, 3 losses and 2 ties. Although, a crowd of 103,219 showed up for the annual blood-letting event, it was not a record breaker. The huge gathering was 16 people short of a new record, but that would happen down the road. The annual game between the Wolverines and Spartans was now an excessively BIG game and one to look forward to in the State of Michigan.

SEASON SUMMARIES:

The Spartans just kept winning after they beat Michigan. In fact, they beat everybody they played for the entire regular season. Michigan State finished the 1965 season with a perfect record of 10 wins, 0 losses, and 0 ties. The Spartans gave Duffy Daugherty his first Big Ten Championship with a perfect record of 7 win and 0 losses.

The only downside to the whole season was a Rose Bowl loss to UCLA (14-12), the same team they defeated in the first game of the year. Despite the loss, Michigan State earned a share of the national championship. So, things worked out fine for the Green and White.

Duffy Daugherty's twelfth season at Michigan State produced a memorable season. In addition to all the wins, Michigan State had eight first team All-American players—four on offense (Bob Apisa, Clint Jones, Steve Juday, and Gene Washington) and four on defense (Ron Goovert, Harold Lucas, Charles "Bubba" Smith" and George Webster). The best news for Duffy was that many of the Spartan "stars" were juniors. I am sure that Duffy was eager to get the next season going, but I know that he took some time off to enjoy his best season at Michigan State. Of course, he would get lots of invitations to speak during the off-season and get a chance to enjoy "bragging rights" for another year. It was a great time to be a Spartan!

Bump Elliott saw his Wolverines lose two more games after the loss to the Spartans. Michigan's record was 2 wins and 4 losses with four games to go. If the Wolverines got hot, they could finish strong and end the season with six wins. It looked like that might happen as the Maize and Blue footballers won two straight against Wisconsin and Illinois. Unfortunately, the season ended badly with back-to-back losses to Northwestern and Ohio State. The defending Big Ten Champions ended the season with a final record of 4 wins and 6 losses. They finished with a record of 2-5-0 in the Big Ten which earned them a tie for seventh place.

Michigan was expected to do better in 1965, but things do not always work out as expected. The Wolverines lost three games by a total of five points, but they also had five double digit defeats. It was a disappointment and that is about all you can say. The only good news was that lineman Bill Yearby repeated as an All-American. It was the first time that Michigan had a two-time All-American since 1955-1956 when Ron Kramer accomplished that feat. Bill Yearby was also the first African American Wolverine to earn back-to-back All-American selections. Bump Elliott would have to find and develop more players like Yearby and Kramer to win another championship. It was back to the drawing board in Ann Arbor.

Game # 59: October 8, 1966 at Spartan Stadium in East Lansing

BACKGROUND INFORMATION:

The 1966 season saw something new on the field. Orange pylons had to be placed on the field at the four corners of the end zone to help orient players and officials during the game. It was a subtle change, but important. There was another important rule change regarding uniforms and numbering. The NCAA decided that a position numbering system was needed. All lineman, except ends, would have to wear a number between 50 and 79. No player who wore a number in this range would be eligible to receive a forward pass. (dwilson/rsfc/RuleChanges, 10/16/2020)

Bump Elliott was back for his eighth season at the helm in 1966. So far, he had one great season, a couple good ones and quite a few bad ones. It was time to get Michigan to a level of football play that everyone was accustomed to in Ann Arbor.

Of course, all this was easier said than done. Bump knew exactly what he had to do because he did it in 1964. The really hard thing to do is build a program that wins consistently, year in and year out. That was Bump's goal. The 1966 season would be another attempt to get the Wolverine football train back on a winning track. Michigan was unranked going into the season. After wins over Oregon State and California the Wolverines landed at #8 in the country. Unranked North Carolina came to Ann Arbor in week three and left with an upset win over the Wolverines (21-7). The good news was that Michigan still had a winning record (2-1-0) heading into Michigan State week. The bad news was that MSU was the top ranked team in the country and the game was in East Lansing. Michigan would have to play their best game of the season to compete with the heavily favored Spartans.

After thirteen years on the job, Duffy Daugherty was enjoying the best coaching run in the history of Michigan State football. The irascible Irishman had plenty to smile about in 1966. He had returning All-Americans on both sides of the ball! Duffy also had home games against Michigan and Ohio State. Everyone had the Spartans at the top of the polls at the start of the season. There was no pressure on Duffy and his footballers, no pressure at all! The Spartans started the 1966 season the way everyone expected—three straight blowouts over North Carolina State, Penn State, and Illinois. Duffy's Big Green Machine was rolling over everybody and Michigan was next. Would Michigan pull off the upset of the season? That was the question to be answered on October 8, 1966.

GAME SUMMARY: UM 7 MSU 20

The largest crowd (78, 883) in the history of East Lansing college football jammed into 75,000 seat Spartan Stadium for game number fifty-nine of the storied in-state hate game. Yes, it was packed with thousands of Green and White supporters and some Wolverine fans too.

It was another game where the records really did not matter. Both teams showed up to play "Big Boy" football as they always did in this hotly contested series. The game featured hard-tackling, hard-running and hard feelings on almost every play. Untimely penalties, missed opportunities, and mistakes kept both teams off the scoreboard in the first quarter. The Spartans scored first in the second quarter when quarterback Jimmy Raye ran 5-yards for a touchdown. The extra point was good, and Michigan State led 7-0 at halftime. (*DFP*, 10/9/1966, Page 41)

The Spartan defense forced Michigan to shut down a miserable ground game (47 net yards in 60 minutes) and put the ball in the air. Michigan threw forty-eight passes against the Spartans, but only gained 168-yards on eighteen completions. One of those passes, a fifteen-yard pass from Dave Fisher to Jim Detwiler resulted in Michigan's only touchdown of the game. Unfortunately, that fourth quarter score was too little and too late for the Wolverines. Michigan State countered Michigan's fourth quarter points with thirteen of their own. Fullback Bob Apisa scored on a short run and Gene Washington caught a 28-yard pass for the final six points of the game. (*DFP*, 10/9/1966, Page 41)

Michigan played their best game of the season, but it was not enough. Michigan State controlled the game with a powerful rushing attack (245 yards) and a well-timed passing attack (45 yards) that kept Michigan's defense off-balance. The Spartans were the best team on this day. (*DFP*, 10/9/1966, Page 41)

Team	1st	2nd	3rd	4th	Total
UM	0	0	0	7	7
MSU	0	7	0	13	20

SERIES UPDATE:

The Spartans were back on track against the Wolverines with their second straight win. Yes, Michigan still held a big advantage in the series with a record of 36 wins, 18 losses, and 5 ties. However, the Spartans retained possession of the Paul Bunyan Trophy and they improved their record to 5-1-1 against Michigan in the Sixties!

SERIES MILESTONES:

Of course, the recording setting crowd was the biggest milestone of this game. The throng of 78, 833 was the largest crowd to witness a sporting event in the history of East Lansing. It was the fifth straight record breaker in East Lansing for the series matchup. The only other milestone was the fact that Duffy added to his own record of victories over Michigan which now stood at eight wins.

SEASON SUMMARIES:

The Wolverines played well the next week but came up short against Purdue. The Boilermakers beat them in Ann Arbor by a score of 22-21. Michigan had a record of 2 wins and 3 losses heading into the last half of the season. Bump Elliott kept his team together and the Wolverines won four of the last five games. Although they lost to Illinois, they beat Minnesota, Wisconsin Northwestern, and Ohio State. Michigan finished strong and posted a final record of 6 wins and 4 losses. Their Big Ten record of 4 wins and 3 losses earned them a tie for third place. The outstanding play of Captain Jack Clancy and Rich Volk earned them All-American honors for the 1966 season. Another Wolverine football season was in the record book.

Michigan's two-game losing streak at the start of the Big Ten season really killed their chances for a conference title. There were a lot of positives in 1966, but there was no Big Ten Championship to celebrate. Worse yet, the hated Spartans won the Big Ten and a share of the national championship. Nothing worse than having your rival be the best team in the state, the conference, and the nation! Bump went into the off-season looking for improvements and for ways to beat Duffy and his surging Spartans.

After beating Michigan, Duffy's Spartans rolled into Columbus and returned to East Lansing with a hard-fought win over the Buckeyes. Michigan State dominated the rest of their conference competition—winning every game by twenty or more points. The Spartans won their second consecutive Big Ten title with a perfect record of 7-0-0. The bad news was that Michigan State ended the season with the infamous tie against Notre Dame (10-10). The good news was that they earned a share of the national championship with a record of 9-0-1.

Duffy had six more All-Americans during the 1966 season to cap off a brilliant run for the Class of 1967. Senior tackle Jerry West earned All-American honors for the first time. Bob Apisa, Clinton Jones, Bubba Smith, Gene Washington, and George Webster all earned All-American honors for the second straight season.

The off-season was probably bitter-sweet for Duffy. The good news was that he won his third national championship, his second Big Ten Title, and beat Michigan for the eighth time. The bad news was that six All-Americans would be gone for the 1967 season. Yes, that is always a part of the college football fortunes. The only thing harder than finding six All-Americans is replacing six All-Americans. Daugherty probably enjoyed himself and celebrated his accomplishments. However, he knew 1967 could be a rough season. He had to find some capable replacements and figure out a way to compete in the Big Ten. So much for resting on your laurels!

Game # 60: October 14, 1967 at Michigan Stadium in Ann Arbor

BACKGROUND INFORMATION:

As always, Duffy Daugherty was a popular speaker on the banquet circuit in 1967. He was riding higher than any coach in Spartan Football history, except maybe his boss Biggie Munn. Duffy was enjoying a great run in the Sixties. He had put together six winning seasons in seven years. He "owned" Michigan and his Spartans had just won two straight national championships and two Big Ten Titles.

Life was incredibly good in East Lansing in 1967. The only problem was that Spartan fans expected it all to continue at a high level even though Duffy had lost six of the best players to ever put on a Spartan uniform. Unless Coach Daugherty pulled off a miracle, the 1967 season would be a re-building year for Michigan State. Nobody thought that Michigan State would win the Big Ten Championship in 1967. NOBODY!

The Spartans did something in September 1967 that they had not done since November 1964—they lost two games! Worse yet, they were both home losses as Houston and Southern California totally disrespected the two-time defending national champions. Duffy got things back on track in October as the Spartans blasted Wisconsin by a score of 35-7.

Michigan State had a record of 1 win and 2 losses, but the optimistic Duffy was smiling because his team was undefeated in the conference at 1-0-0. He knew that Michigan was not off to a great start. Coach Daugherty probably felt that another victory over Michigan was a real possibility. There would be plenty on the line when the Spartans traveled to Ann Arbor to face off against the Wolverines. Time to play some Big Boy/Big Ten football!

Bump Elliott was hoping to keep things going in the right direction in 1967. He had not put back-to-back winning seasons together since 1960-1961. It was time for another winning team that could compete for the Big Ten Championship. Coach Elliott had lost his best receiver (Jack Clancy) and his best defensive back (Rich Volk), but he had some young talent waiting in the wings. He knew that he had to develop his new players if he was going to have a winning season.

Expectations for the 1967 edition of the Michigan Wolverine football team were low. Nobody thought that Michigan would compete for the title, but Bump hoped he could prove the doubters wrong! The Wolverines opened the season in Ann Arbor with a close win over Duke (10-7). Michigan traveled to the west coast the next week and returned home with a record of 1-1-0 after losing to California (10-9). Coach Elliott's footballers slipped to 1-2-0 after a tough loss to Navy (26-21). Michigan had to get things heading in the right direction if they were to have a winning season. They could start a winning streak with a win over MSU.

GAME SUMMARY: MSU 34 UM 0

The sixtieth game of this hard-fought series was basically over midway through the second quarter. The Spartans scored early after completing a 90-yard drive in the first quarter. Quarterback Jimmy Raye led Michigan State to three more scores in the first half and it was 27-0 at the half. Raye finished the day with two rushing touchdowns and passed for two more. Receivers Al Brenner and Frank Foremen each caught a Raye touchdown pass. Halfback Dick Berlinski also scored on an 8-yard run for the Spartans. There was plenty to cheer about for Michigan State fans, but not for Wolverine backers. (*DFP*, 10/15/1967, Page 37)

The only good news for the Wolverines was that sophomore running back, Ron Johnson ran for 107 yards on 24 carries. Unfortunately, nobody else on the Wolverine team was able to help him out. Michigan only gained 216 yards all day while the Spartans totaled 424 yards with their balanced attack. (*DFP*, 10/15/1967, Page 37) Michigan State's victory margin of 34 points made this the biggest Spartan victory in the history of the series. No, it wasn't even close to Michigan's 119-point conquest in 1902, but Spartan fans didn't care. It was another sweet victory in Ann Arbor for the Green and White. Of course, it was another bitter pill to swallow for the Wolverines!

Team	1st	2nd	3rd	4th	Final
MSU	7	20	0	7	34
UM	0	0	0	0	0

SERIES UPDATE:

Michigan State continued to chip away at Michigan's series advantage. The Spartans improved their series record to 19 wins, 36 losses, and 5 ties. MSU pushed their advantage in the Paul Bunyan Trophy years to 10 wins, 3 losses, and 2 ties. Michigan State increased their advantage in the Sixties to 6 wins, 1 loss, and 1 tie.

SERIES MILESTONES:

There were five notable milestones in this game. First, game number sixty was a milestone in itself. Second, it was also the biggest Spartan margin of victory (34 points) in a series game. Third, the Spartans became the first series team to win the Paul Bunyan Trophy ten times. Fourth, Duffy became the first coach in Michigan State history to defeat Michigan nine times. Finally, both teams struggled for the rest of the season and did something that they had never done which is tie for fifth place in the Big Ten.

SEASON SUMMARIES:

Duffy did not know it at the time, but the high point of his season was the decisive win over Michigan. His team lost five straight games and only one (Indiana 14-13) was close. The Spartans took their frustrations out on poor Northwestern in the last game of the season. Final score: MSU 41 and Northwestern 27. That was it, the defending champions slipped badly and finished the season with a final record of 3 wins and 7 losses. As I already mentioned, the Spartans tied Michigan for fifth place in the conference at 3-4-0. For the first time since 1964, Michigan State had no All-American players.

Michigan State was a young team in 1967 and they showed it in almost every game, except Michigan and Northwestern. The Spartans also had some key injuries during the season, and they just could not overcome their inexperience and the injuries. Of course, Duffy took some heat from Spartan Nation for such a dismal season, but he had a "respect card" that he could play. Being a three-time national champion will do that for you. University President, John Hannah, was firmly in Duffy's corner, but things had to get better.

Michigan did not exactly recover from the Spartan defeat since they lost the next two games to Indiana and Minnesota. The Wolverines entered November with a record of 1 win and 5 losses. Things were looking bleak in Ann Arbor, but Bump rallied his team. They finished the season with three wins in their last four games. Unfortunately, the season ended on a low note with a home loss to Ohio State (24-14). Bump Elliott's ninth season ended with a record of 4 wins and 6 losses. As I said, their Big Ten record of 3-4-0 earned them a tie with the Spartans for fifth place. Unfortunately, there were no Wolverine All-Americans in 1967.

The likeable Bump Elliott was having a hard time being popular in Ann Arbor. Despite his winning personality and his legendary Michigan resume, he was not winning enough games. Bump knew it, Fritz Crisler knew, and Wolverine Nation knew it. Wins were down, losses were up, and attendance was also down. Not a good combination for a football coach, especially in Ann Arbor. Bump would have another season to get things right at Michigan, but how long would he be able to continue?

Game # 61: October 12, 1968 at Michigan Stadium in Ann Arbor

BACKGROUND INFORMATION:

There were no important changes to the game for the 1968 season. Apparently, the "status quo" in college football was good enough for another season. The NCAA Rules Committee lost their long-time Chairman Fritz Crisler after he retired as Michigan's Athletic Director. Maybe they just wanted to let the new leadership have a year to watch the game and listen for another season.

Duffy Daugherty was back for season number fourteen in 1968. Despite, the dismal 1967 season there was still plenty for Coach "D" to smile about. He had some excellent players returning on both sides of the ball. The optimistic Daugherty thought his team could be good, but he was not sure how good. If they got off to a good start and stayed healthy, the Spartans could have another good season. Of course, the burning question was "How good?"

Michigan State started the 1968 season with a solid home win against Syracuse (14-10). The Spartans showed some improvement in week two and defeated Baylor (28-10). A blow-out victory over Wisconsin in Madison (39-0) pushed the Spartans to 3-0-0 and put them at number twelve in the national rankings. Once again, it appeared that Duffy was working some "magic" with his football team. It was time to show the Wolverines who still owned college football in the great State of Michigan.

In addition to wondering how he was going to win more games in his tenth season at Michigan, Bump Elliott had another thing on his mind in 1968. Fritz Crisler retired after twenty-seven years as Michigan's Athletic Director. Former Michigan Track Coach, Don Canham, was hired to replace Crisler in July 1968. It is never easy having a new boss because you do not know what the "new agenda" might be. I am sure that Don Canham said all the right things to his football coach when they had their first "official" meeting. How do you think that first conversation went?

Michigan started the 1968 season in Ann Arbor against California. The Wolverines were very gracious hosts and sent their guests home with a victory (21-7) which made it two straight losses to the Golden Bears. Bump's footballers woke up and won the next two games over Duke (31-10) and Navy (32-9) which pushed their record to 2-1-0 heading into Michigan State week. Could Michigan finally send the bully Spartans home with a loss? The Wolverines were 0-3-1 in the Sixties at Michigan Stadium against the Spartans. It was time for a series win and it was time to bring Paul Bunyan back to Ann Arbor!

GAME SUMMARY: MSU 14 UM 28

Game number sixty-one was another one for the history books. It was a hard-fought game with every play ending in a thundering cascade of blood, sweat, grunts and groans. This was another game that meant so much to everyone involved.

After a great return of the opening kickoff by George Hoey, Ron Johnson put Michigan up five plays later with a 38-yard touchdown dash. Michigan was up 7-0 after Tim Killian's extra point. The Spartans responded with a touchdown of their own when Charlie Wedemeyer scored on a 37-yard reverse. Michigan retained their narrow lead (7-6) when the Spartans failed to convert the extra point. Michigan came back to score again on a 33-yard pass from Dennis Brown to John Gabler late in the first quarter. Michigan missed the PAT, but still led 13-6 at the end of the first quarter. Both teams had chances in the second quarter, but nobody scored. Michigan still led 13-6 at halftime. (*DFP*, 10/13/1968, Page 37)

The third quarter looked a lot like the second. Michigan State controlled the ball for most of the quarter, but Michigan's defense stiffened when needed and the score remained at 13-6 heading into the fourth quarter. The Spartans, who ran a ton of plays (90 to 55 for UM), finally took the lead early in the fourth quarter. Fullback Earl Anderson scored from 3-yards out to bring MSU within one point of the Wolverines. A two-point conversion pass from Charlie Wedemeyer to Frank Foreman gave the Spartans a 14-13 lead. After the kickoff, Michigan State forced the Wolverines to punt. Things were looking bad for Michigan. Fortunately, the Wolverine defense held and Dennis Brown took over. Michigan drove the ball to their 47-yard line. Brown threw a perfect pass to Jim Mandich and #88 took the ball to the end zone for a 53-yard pass and run play. Michigan took the lead and finished the game a few minutes later with a 25-yard TD run by Garvie Craw. For the second time in Bump's career, the Wolverines had defeated the hated Spartans—28-14. (*DFP*, 10/13/1968, Page 37)

Team	1st	2nd	3rd	4th	Final
MSU	6	0	0	8	14
UM	13	0	0	15	28

SERIES UPDATE:

The good news for Michigan was that they extended their series advantage to 37 wins, 19 losses, and 5 ties after the game ended. The bad news for the Spartans was that they were still on the short end of the sixty-one-year series. Even though Michigan won the trophy game, the Spartans still retained the edge in the Paul Bunyan series at 10 wins, 4 losses, and 2 ties. Michigan State still had a decided advantage in the decade with a record of 6 wins, 2 losses, and 1 tie in the Sixties.

SERIES MILESTONES:

There was only one notable milestone in game number sixty-one of the Mitten State pigskin rivalry. As it turned out, it was Bump Elliott's last game. He went out on a winning note with the big victory over the Spartans. Unfortunately, his body of work against the Green and White was not impressive. Elliott finished with a final record of 2 wins, 7 losses, and 1 tie against the Spartans. Don Canham asked the likeable Elliott to become his Assistant Athletic Director at the end of the season and Bump said "Yes." Michigan State fans were probably sad to see Elliott go since they won a lot of games with Bump at the helm in Ann Arbor.

SEASON SUMMARIES:

Michigan State came out flat against Minnesota after the Michigan loss. They lost their Homecoming game to the Gophers (14-13) but rallied the next week to beat Notre Dame (21-17). The Spartans still had a chance to finish strong in November, but they lost three of four games. The season did end on a high note with a 31-14 win over Northwestern. Obviously, it was too little and too late for Duffy's footballers. Michigan State finished with an overall record of 5 wins and 5 losses. Allen Brenner was the only Spartan to earn All-American honors in 1968.

Duffy Daugherty's fifteenth season in East Lansing was nothing to write home about. It was an up and down season with 5 "ups" and 5 "downs." The good news is that the Spartans did not have a losing season. The bad news was that they did not have a winning season either. Duffy would be back for his sixteenth season in 1969. I am sure that he wondered about what was going on in Ann Arbor. Who would he be coaching against when the Wolverines came to town on October 18, 1969?

Bump's Wolverines kept things going in the right direction the next week in Indiana. They earned a hard-fought win over the Hoosiers (27-22) and put themselves at 2-0-0 in the conference race. Michigan kept on winning and winning BIG. They rolled into Columbus on an eight-game winning streak. Unfortunately, the season ended with a "thud" when Woody's national championship caliber team unloaded on the Wolverines. The Buckeyes prevailed by a score of 50-14. This was the game where the Buckeyes scored late in the game and Woody went for the two-point conversion. Ugh, that was Bump's last game at Michigan. The Wolverines finished with an excellent record of 8 wins and 2 losses. Their record of 6-1-0 in the conference was good enough for second place in 1968. Super running back Ron Johnson was the lone Wolverine to earn All-American honors for Bump's last season.

Overall, Bump Elliott had five winning seasons and five losing seasons at Michigan. He coached 95 games and finished with an overall record of 51 wins, 42 losses and 2 ties. He won the Big Ten Championship in 1964, but he did not win enough for Michigan Nation's liking. His winning record was good compared to a lot of other coaches, but it was not up to the Michigan standard. Unfortunately, Bump's conference record of 33-34-2 was the worst Big Ten record for a Michigan head coach up to that time. There would be a new man on the Michigan sidelines in 1969. The BIG question was, "Who would be the next man to coach Michigan?"

Game # 62: October 18, 1969 at Spartan Stadium in East Lansing

BACKGROUND INFORMATION:

For the second straight season, there were no rules changes for the 1969 season. NCAA administrators liked the place that college football was in. Television ratings continued to rise and so did the money that flowed into the NCAA coffers. Michigan Athletic Director Don Canham took great interest in the "business" of college sports television, especially football. He eventually landed a spot on the NCAA Television Committee.

One other item of note about the 1969 season is that MSU President, John Hannah, retired on July 1, 1969. Mr. Hannah was a Spartan legend who helped the "East Lansing farmers" move forward to build a renowned university. He played a critical role in Michigan State's successful entry into the Big Ten Conference in 1949. John Hannah's vision got the Spartans into the Big Ten Conference and into the national spotlight in football and every other sport on campus. He was a Spartan for life, but his work was done in East Lansing.

The big news surrounding the sixty-second series game was the arrival of a relatively unknown man named Glenn Edward "Bo" Schembechler. "Bo Who" was the first "outsider" to coach a Michigan football team since Fritz Crisler was hired in 1938. Coach Schembechler told reporters at his first press conference that he was hired to change the direction of Michigan's football program and beat Ohio State!

Bo Schembechler did not say much about the Spartans when he arrived in Ann Arbor. However, he learned to pay more attention to the boys from East Lansing in due time. Bo Schembechler inherited some excellent football players from Bump Elliott. He had stars on both sides of the ball. He also had a bunch of players who remembered how the 1968 season had ended in Columbus. Bo set out to get his Wolverines ready for a rematch on November 22, 1969 in Ann Arbor. Of course, he had to play nine games before his Wolverines faced off against the Buckeyes. Michigan started Bo is first season with an impressive 42-14 win over Vanderbilt. The twentieth-ranked Wolverines bounced Washington back to Seattle with a 45-7 win.

The thirteenth ranked Wolverines came back down to earth when ninth-ranked Missouri blasted Bo's Wolverines in Ann Arbor (40-17). Bo won his first Big Ten game against Purdue by a score of 31-20. Bo's thirteenth-ranked Wolverines headed to East Lansing with a record of 3 wins and 1 loss. Would the Wolverines be ready for Duffy and the Spartans and another record crowd?

Coach Duffy Daugherty entered his sixteenth season at Michigan State in 1969. So far, he had produced ten winning seasons, five losing seasons, and one season was even. Duffy also had four national championship trophies and two Big Ten Championships on his resume. All things considered, he was doing an outstanding job, but football coaches know it is always the "What have you done for me lately?" question that gets you in trouble! The 1967 and 1968 seasons were not two of Duffy's best efforts. Now, there was a "new kid' on the block in Ann Arbor. Everyone was wondering how the "old man" would fare against "Bo Who" from Ann Arbor.

The Spartans opened the 1969 season with a nice win over Washington (27-11). They followed up with another win against SMU (23-15) in week two. The Green and White footballers were 2-0-0 heading into October. The Spartans took a trip to South Bend in week three and lost to Notre Dame (42-28). Another difficult road game loomed in Columbus in week four. Ohio State humbled the Spartans with a 54-21 drubbing. Duffy's footballers were now 2-2-0 heading into the Michigan game. Injuries were piling up in Daugherty's backfield and it looked like it would take a miracle to beat Bo's Wolverines. Well, Duffy could do miracles, or so it seemed. Spartan fans should have known that all was not lost. Duffy had a plan to beat Michigan.

GAME SUMMARY: UM 12 MSU 23

The sixty-second series game turned out to be an "upset" as Duffy's Spartans defeated favored, and thirteenth-ranked, Michigan by eleven points. Nobody saw this coming, except maybe Duffy.

Bo Schembechler certainly did not know about the "tricks' that the veteran Spartan coach had up his sleeve. There were no "tricks" because Duffy did not have a lot of options in this game. He really did not have a passing attack because three of his top receivers were injured and could not play. Even if they could play, the winds (30 mph) made it extremely difficult to pass in this game. Besides that, Duffy's passing game was ineffective in the first four games. It was not going to be the key to victory against Michigan.

Actually, Daugherty had a bigger problem than an ineffective passing game. Writer Bob Hoerner described Duffy's dilemma in an excellent publication titled: *Backyard Brawl: The Storied Rivalry of Michigan-Michigan State Football.* According to Hoerner, Don Highsmith was his only healthy running back besides quarterback Bill Triplett. Duffy's "veer offense" required three healthy runners so Duffy got creative. He scrapped his famous offense for a "Power-I" formation. Now he only needed one back and Highsmith was his man! (*Backyard Brawl*, Page 86)

After a scoreless first quarter, Michigan took the lead on a Tim Killian field goal. Michigan State's ground game really got going in the second quarter. The Spartans scored on a short run by Highsmith and a 10-yard run by Triplett. Michigan State also got a safety when Michigan fielded a kickoff improperly. It was 16-3 at halftime. (*Backyard Brawl*, Page 89) The second half was even. Michigan State scored another touchdown when Highsmith scored on a 4-yard run. MSU led 23-3 at the end of the third quarter. Michigan put nine points on the board in the fourth quarter on a 7-yard run by Glenn Doughty. The Wolverines converted the extra point and earned two-points for a safety. Unfortunately, it was not enough to earn a victory over MSU. (*Backyard Brawl*, Page 87)

The Spartans had a simple game plan—run the ball—a lot! It worked to perfection. Michigan State found holes in Michigan's defensive line all day and rolled up 348-yards on the ground. The Wolverines gained plenty of yards (340) in the game but did not get the big plays when they needed them. Michigan State tried to give the game away with three lost fumbles and two missed field goals, but the Wolverines did not make them pay for their mistakes. It was another Spartan victory and Duffy loved it!

Team	1st	2nd	3rd	4th	Final
UM	0	3	0	9	12
MSU	0	16	7	0	23

SERIES UPDATE:

Duffy Daugherty's tenth series win gave him an overall record of 10 wins, 4 losses and 2 ties against the Wolverines. Even better, the Paul Bunyan Trophy would remain in East Lansing for another year and "bragging rights" were claimed again by the Spartan faithful. For the record, the Wolverine series advantage now stood at 37 wins, 20 losses, and 5 ties. However, Michigan State increased their advantage in the Paul Bunyan Trophy series to 11 wins 4 losses, and 2 ties. The Spartans finished the decade of the Sixties with a final record of 7 wins, 2 losses, and 1 tie. Duffy Daugherty was still the "college football king" in the State of Michigan. Would Bo be able to knock Duffy off his throne in the Seventies?

SERIES MILESTONES:

One very BIG milestone marked this game since this game was played in the 100th season of college football. The 1969 series game was also memorable for many reasons. First it was Bo's first game and his first series loss. Second, the Spartans earned their twentieth series victory and Duffy earned his tenth series win. This game was also the first series game to be played on "Tartan Turf." Finally, the crowd of 79,368 was a record for an East Lansing series game. It was also the first time that a Spartan crowd exceeded the 79K mark in a series game. This game was also the first, and only, time that each team scored a safety in the same game. So, the decade of the Sixties ended the way it started with a Spartan victory and Michigan was still trying to figure out how to re-gain control of the "in-state hate" rivalry.

SEASON SUMMARIES:

Bo's Wolverines used the "short memory" trick to put the MSU loss behind them. Michigan still had a goal to win the Big Ten Championship and that, and some Buckeye revenge, was the focus for the rest of the season. The "Maize and Blue Men" went on a five-game winning streak that culminated with their upset victory over top ranked and undefeated Ohio State. Michigan tied for the conference championship with the Buckeyes and earned the right to go to the Rose Bowl game in January 1970. Of course, Bo had a heart-attack on the eve of the big game and Michigan lost to USC (10-3).

Bo Schembechler earned Coach of the Year honors for the American Football Coaches Association for his outstanding season. The Wolverines also celebrated the All-American selections of Captain Jim Mandich and super defensive back Tom Curtis. It certainly looked like Michigan football was back, but only time would tell. Of course, it would only be back if Bo were healthy enough to be on the sidelines in 1970.

Glenn Edward "Bo" Schembechler made it clear when he arrived in Ann Arbor that his primary job was to beat "state," as in Ohio State! He did not talk much about Duffy's Spartans when he first arrived. It was all about "Woody Hayes" in that first season. At least that is the way it was until October 18, 1969. The Wolverine loss to the Spartans gave Bo something to think about on his trip home from East Lansing. Apparently, he told his staff that Michigan now had two rivals to beat—Ohio State and Michigan State. Bo now had Duffy and the Spartans on his radar which would turn out to be a good thing for Wolverine fans, but not for Duffy and the Spartans!

Michigan State remained an un-healthy team that was short on good players for the rest of the 1969 season. The Spartans lost four straight conference games and only Iowa and Minnesota were close. They finished strong with a big win over Northwestern (39-7), but it was a tough year for Sparty! If the Spartan offense were able to score during the season like they did against the Wildcats, things could have been much different. Unfortunately, the Spartans ended the season with a record of 4 wins and 6 losses. They finished in ninth place in the Big Ten with a record of 2 wins and 5 losses. The only good news was that guard Ron Saul earned All-American honors in 1969.

Duffy Daugherty could smile about another victory over Michigan, but that was about it! He now had two losing seasons out of the last three. Spartan fans were starting to grumble and there was not that much to smile about in East Lansing. If he were healthy in 1970, Bo Schembechler would be coming after the Spartans and Duffy knew it. Things were starting to get interesting as the decade of the Seventies approached. Would Duffy continue to dominate Michigan in the future or would things even out? Nobody knew for sure, but everyone knew that the next decade in the series would be interesting.

DECADE AND SERIES SUMMARY:

Duffy's Spartans dominated Bump Elliott and the Wolverines from 1960 to 1969. Michigan State not only gained a lot of ground in the series during the Sixties, but they also stayed on the map as one of the nation's best football programs. Things were good in East Lansing and the Spartans could not play the Wolverines enough on the football field. Bump Elliott's record (2 wins, 7 losses and 1 tie) was the worst in Michigan football history against the Spartans. Don Canham knew that things had to change. He took a BIG gamble on Bo Schembechler to turn things around.

Things were headed in a different direction in early 1970, but it was not clear where they would go. Bo Schembechler did an outstanding job in his first season at Michigan, but his unexpected heart attack raised a lot of doubts about his ability to be effective in the future. The health of Glenn Edward Schembechler was critical to Michigan's success and the Spartans and everyone else in the 1970s. It was also important for the folks in East Lansing. A healthy Bo might be a bad thing for the fine folks at Michigan State.

Decade and Series Summary 1898 to 1969

Time Frame	UM Won-Lost-Tied	MSU Won-Lost-Tied
1960-1969	2-7-1	7-2-1
1898-1969	37-20-5	20-37-5

Image 8 Don Highsmith (#40) helped Duffy Daugherty's "new" offense get the job done in MSU's upset win over Michigan. If you look closely, you can see that the Spartans honored the 100th year of college football with a special helmet decal. Permission: Bentley Historical Library at The University of Michigan, See Page 369)

BIG TEN DECADE SUMMARY:

The Sixties were the first decade that Michigan and Michigan State both played a full conference schedule for all ten years. Now is a good time to start tracking each team's conference success for the remaining decades. I will stick to a similar chart that I used to compare both programs for overall play. Now, we will take a closer look at each team's achievements in the Big Ten Conference—one decade at a time!

Michigan and Michigan State both had "up" and "down" Big Ten stories from 1960 to 1969. Unfortunately, Michigan was a little more "down." Michigan State was a little more "up" during the decade. The Wolverines had four winning seasons, five losing seasons and one season was even.

Michigan State was a little better overall in Big Ten play with five winning seasons, three losing seasons, and two that were even. The Spartans won two conference titles and Michigan earned one. Michigan State had four more wins in conference play and their winning percentage was also better by just over 50 percentage points.

The good news for the Wolverines was that they finished with two straight 6-1-0 seasons at the end of the decade. The bad news for the Spartans was that they ended the decade of the Sixties with three straight losing seasons. Both teams would have to improve if they ever planned on giving Ohio State any kind of competition in the 1970s.

Big Ten Summary 1960 to 1969

Statistical Area	UM	MSU
Number of Head Coaches	2	1
Games Played	69	66
Wins	36	40
Losses	31	25
Ties	2	1
Winning Percentage	.577	.630
Winning Seasons	4	5
Losing Seasons	5	3
Even Seasons	1	2
Big Ten Championships	1	2

PROGRAM SUMMARIES:

Michigan was not a consistent winner in the Sixties—period! Bump Elliott only had two back-to-back winning seasons in the decade (1960 and 1961). He also had two straight losing seasons in 1962 and 1963. Too many times, a winning season was followed by a losing one. Coach Elliott's overall record of 55 wins, 40 losses and 2 ties in the Sixties would be good for a lot of colleges, but not Michigan! The Wolverines had six winning seasons in the Sixties and 4 losing seasons. For the first time in the twentieth century, Michigan did not win a national championship in the decade of the Sixties which ended a five-decade string of some great football. Even worse, the Wolverines only won the Big Ten title once—in 1964. Wins were down in the Sixties and so were the number of All-American players. Oh, by the way, attendance was really starting to slip. It was clear that things had to change in Ann Arbor.

You could also say that Duffy's Spartans had their "ups and downs" in the Sixties. However, the BIG difference was what happened in the "up" years. Duffy Daugherty was able to take Michigan State to the top of the college football mountain for two straight seasons. The 1965 and 1966 Spartan teams were two great teams with tons of All-American players. Interestingly, Michigan State only won four more games than the Wolverines during the Sixties and both teams had six winning seasons.

Program Summaries 1960 to 1969

Statistical Area	UM	MSU
Number of Head Coaches	2	1
Games Played	91	96
Wins	55	59
Losses	40	34
Ties	2	3
Winning Percentage	.577	.630
Winning Seasons	6	6
Losing Seasons	4	3
Even Seasons	0	1
National Championships	0	2
All-American Players	7	16

The biggest difference between Um and MSU in the Sixties was the fact that Michigan State won two national championships. The Spartans also produced sixteen All-Americans while Michigan only had seven. After years of playing second fiddle to Michigan, the Spartans became the best team in the State of Michigan and one of the best in the nation, for nearly twenty years! Biggie Munn and Duffy Daugherty out-recruited, out-coached, and out-played Mighty Michigan on a consistent basis. They worked tirelessly to put the Spartans on the nation's football map. The BIG question was, "What would the Seventies bring to the football wars between Michigan and Michigan State?"

CHAPTER 10

Bo Time-Part One 1970 to 1979

C ollege football continued to captivate America, but the National Football League (NFL) exploded in the late Sixties and into the Seventies. The Super Bowl was now a popular event. Nobody did a BIG GAME like the NFL. Television was really starting to take control of American sports because the money was incredible. Michigan's Don Canham became a member of the NCAA's Television Committee in the Seventies. Canham, the businessman/athletic director, saw the dollars that were coming to help finance athletic departments like his, but there would be a price to pay. Television executives started calling the shots on kickoff times and game days. It started with bowl games and the power, and influence, of television just grew and grew and grew. Nobody, not even the savvy Canham, knew where it would end, but television changed a lot of things about college football and some of those changes were not good.

Game #63: October 17, 1970 at Michigan Stadium in Ann Arbor

BACKGROUND INFORMATION:

The NCAA decided to let schools schedule eleven regular season games if they could make it work in the 1970 schedules. Of course, this option added more money to the athletic department's bottom line and gave teams one more chance to schedule a team that could not make room for in the past. Both Michigan and Michigan State opted to keep their schedules at ten games for the 1970 season. The rule regarding defensive pass interference was also changed. Instead of penalizing the offender 15 yards from the previous spot of the ball, it was stepped off from the spot of the foul. (*USA Today CFE*, Page 233)

Duffy Daugherty took some heat during the off-season, but he was back for his seventeenth season in September 1970. The Smiling Irishman had an impressive record in East Lansing, but the last three years of the Sixties were not his best. Spartan fans were tiring of Duffy's wit and yearning for more wins. The championship years of Bubba Smith, George Webster, and Clinton Jones were a distant memory. Michigan State fans were ready for another big run from Duffy's footballers. The big question was "When will the Spartans challenge for another Big Ten and or national championship?" Duffy was not making a lot of predictions, but, as always, he was optimistic about the 1970 football season. The only problem was that not too many people were excited about the 1970 edition of the Michigan State football team.

The Spartans began the season in Seattle. It did not go well. Washington demolished MSU (42-16). Duffy's footballers returned home to defeat Washington State the next week by a score of 28-14. Two more defeats put the Spartans at 1 win and 3 losses heading into Michigan week. Things did not look good for Duffy and his Spartans. Number six Michigan was waiting for the Green and White in Ann Arbor and Bo was looking to get his first win over the Spartans.

Bo "Who" turned out to be a surprisingly good coach in year one at Michigan. However, his heart attack just before the 1970 Rose Bowl raised a lot of doubts about his health and his ability to carry on at Michigan. When Schembechler's doctor gave him a clean bill of health in early 1970 it was good news for Don Canham and Michigan Nation. Bo Schembechler remained a man on a mission when he resumed his coaching duties. He had a strong cast of returning players on both sides of the ball. The Wolverines and the Buckeyes were the favorites to win the conference title at the start of the 1970 season. Yes, expectations were high for Bo's Wolverines. The only thing that could be better than winning a Big Ten Championship and beating the Buckeyes would be to do it two years in a row!

Eighth-ranked Michigan started the 1970 season just the way the "experts" thought. They defeated Arizona (20-9) in the home opener and then went on the road to beat Washington (17-3) in week two. Bo's Wolverines beat a good Texas A&M team in Ann Arbor by a score of 14-10. Michigan proved that it was ready for the Big Ten season with a 29-0 rout of Purdue in West Lafayette. Michigan owned a record of 4 wins and 0 defeats heading into Michigan State week. Bo would probably be more ready for the Spartans than he was in 1969. He was now aware that Duffy's Green and White footballers had to be considered "rivals" and could not be overlooked! The good news for Bo was that game two against Michigan State would be in Ann Arbor. Bring on the Spartans!

GAME SUMMARY: MSU 20 UM 34

The sixty-third game of the Mitten State gridiron gathering was a departure from recent games. It was still hard-hitting, like always, but the defenses were on their heels most of the afternoon. The offenses were working for both teams although Michigan's was fourteen points better! A record-breaking crowd of 103,580 was treated to non-stop action by both teams. Of course, both teams shed some blood in this game, but the Spartans probably lost more.

Michigan State took the lead in the first quarter on a 42-yard TD run by Eric Allen. Billy Taylor rambled 26-yards for Michigan's first touchdown and the game was tied at 7-7 since both teams made their extra-point kicks. MSU kicker Borys Shlpak made a 26-yard field goal and Sparty led 10-7 after one quarter. Both teams scored in the second quarter. Shlpak kicked his second field goal and Taylor scored his second touchdown on a 2-yard run, but the PAT kick failed. The game was tied at halftime 13-13. (*DFP*, 10/18/1970, Page 39)

Michigan took control of the game in the third quarter. Billy Taylor scored his third touchdown on a 4-yard run and Fritz Seyferth grabbed a short Don Moorhead pass for another touchdown. Glenn Doughty finished the scoring in the fourth quarter for Michigan on a 5-yard run. Eric Allen was the offensive star for the Spartans (23 carries/156-yards), but he did not get much help. Billy Taylor (29 carries/149-yards) and Glenn Doughty (8 carries/85 yards) led a Wolverine offense that rolled up 460-yards of turf. (*DFP*, 10/18/1970, Page 39)

Team	1st	2nd	3rd	4th	Final
MSU	10	3	0	7	20
UM	7	6	14	7	34

SERIES UPDATE:

Michigan's win increased their series advantage. The Wolverines now owned 38 victories, 20 losses, and 5 ties. The Maize and Blue won the first game of the Seventies and went up by a count of 1-0-0. However, the Paul Bunyan Trophy series still favored the Spartans who had a record of 11 wins, 5 losses, and 2 ties since 1953.

SERIES MILESTONES:

Once again, game number sixty-three had the biggest crowd in the history of the series. The Ann Arbor gathering of 103,580 broke the previous high by 326 people. Bo Schembechler earned his first series victory in his second try. Duffy's stellar record against the Wolverines slipped a notch to 10 wins, 5 losses and 2 ties. Finally, it was the first time that both teams scored more than 20 points in a series game.

SEASON SUMMARIES:

The Spartans bounced back after the Michigan loss with three straight wins over Iowa, Indiana, and Purdue. They were even at 4-4-0 heading into the last two games of the season. Unfortunately, Duffy's footballers lost both games to Minnesota and Northwestern. The Spartans finished the season with a record of 4 wins and 6 losses. It was Dufy's second straight losing season and third in the last four years. The trend line for Michigan State football was headed in the wrong direction! To make matters worse, no Spartans earned All-American honors in 1970.

Duffy's seventeenth season in East Lansing did not end well. It was becoming obvious that Michigan was getting much better under Schembechler. Sadly, for Spartan fans, the same could not be said of Duffy's teams. Michigan State had been king of the hill in the State of Michigan since the early 1950s. Was the pendulum was starting to swing back to Ann Arbor. Could Duffy get the Spartans back on track and back to the top of the Big Ten?

Michigan moved to a record of 5-0-0 win their win over Michigan State. They won four more games before Bo's second showdown with Woody in Columbus. Woody Hayes had his fifth-ranked Buckeyes ready for the fourth-ranked Wolverines. This time it was Woody's chance to upset Bo and the Buckeyes prevailed (20-9). Michigan ended the season with a record of 9-1-0. They finished second in the conference with a record of 6 wins and 1 loss. Michigan had three All-Americans in 1970—Dan Dierdorf, Henry Hill, and Marty Huff.

Season number two of the Schembechler Era proved that 1969 was no fluke. It also proved that Bo would not be able to roll over the Buckeyes every year! So far, Bo was 12-2-0 in the Big Ten in two seasons, and he was 1-1-0 against Michigan State and Ohio State. Bo produced back-to-back winning seasons (1969-1970) for the first time since 1960–1961. Attendance was improving and Bo was recruiting the daylights out of Ohio. Woody was livid, but all is fair in love and college football recruiting, right? Don Canham was loving every minute of the Schembechler Era. So far, so good!

Game #64: October 9, 1971 at Spartan Stadium in East Lansing

BACKGROUND INFORMATION:

There were two important rules changes for the 1971 college football season. First, for obvious safety reasons, crack-back blocks and spearing were made illegal. Second, timeouts were reduced from four to three. The rules makers decided not to change anything else for this season. (*USA Today CFE*, Page 272) Of course, NCAA officials would continue to keep an eye on player safety and other issues that coaches and officials were concerned about.

One other item to mention was that Michigan and Michigan State both scheduled eleven regular season games for the 1971 season. Remember, they did not have time to do it, even though it was allowed in 1970. One more home game would be good for the bottom line in both athletic departments! Also, for the first time, both teams would be playing an eight-game conference season in 1971.

Bo Schembechler was back for his third season in 1971. Once again, his Wolverines were co-favorites, along with the Buckeyes, to win the Big Ten Championship. Bo had star players coming back on both sides of the ball. Michigan was expected to have a strong offense and a stingy defense which was bad news for everybody in the Big Ten!

The fourth-ranked Wolverines kicked off the season with a solid win over the twentieth ranked Northwestern Wildcats (21-6). Michigan played their next three games at home and they blew out Virginia (56-0), UCLA (38-0), and Navy (46-0). The Wolverines were 4-0-0 and rose to number two in the national rankings. Michigan had scored 161 points and only allowed 6 so they were playing well!

The Maize and Blue footballers were probably a confident bunch heading into their East Lansing visit. However, Bo knew that the Spartans would be ready. It promised to be another backyard brawl. Bo was hoping that his team would be declared the "winner" when it was over!

Duffy Daugherty entered his eighteenth season in 1971. By now, fans and sportswriters were less trustful of the optimistic Duffy. His recent pre-season assessments of Spartan football fortunes had been way off the mark. Michigan State was becoming an average football program. They were slipping in the conference and Michigan had earned victories over the Spartans in two of the last three games. It was time for Duffy's Spartans to "put up or shut up."

The 1971 model of the Michigan State football team rolled off the assembly line and won a hard-fought game against Illinois (10-0). It was a good start for the Duffy's footballers. The Spartans journeyed to Atlanta the next week to play Georgia Tech. Interestingly, Duffy's team lost by the same score (10-0) that they had won by in week one! After two games the Spartans had a record of 1-1-0 and they had scored ten points and allowed ten points. I am sure that Duffy was liking his defense, but the offense was another story! The Spartans bounced back the next week and put some points on the board. They defeated Oregon State by a score of 31-14. A loss to Notre Dame (14-2) the next week gave the Spartans a record of 2-2-0 heading into Michigan week. Once again, Duffy's defense was not the problem, it was the offense that was inconsistent. Duffy had to find a way to score more points if MSU expected to defeat the Wolverines. Would Coach Daugherty be able to surprise Bo and his Wolverines like he did in 1969?

GAME SUMMARY: UM 24 MSU 13

The sixty-fourth game in series history was another classic "in-state hate" battle. A record-breaking East Lansing crowd (80,093) showed up to cheer their Spartans to victory over the "enemy" from Ann Arbor. Both coaches had a surprise for the other man that made the game interesting. Bo Schembechler started Sophomore Tom Slade at quarterback, and it proved to be a good decision. Slade guided the option attack skillfully and played error-free football in his first game. Duffy, desperate for offense, switched offenses again. He installed a "Wishbone Offense" in the week leading up to the game. Unfortunately, it did not work this time. The Spartans only gained 59 yards rushing against the stout Michigan defense. (*DFP*, 10/10/1971, Page 39)

Billy Taylor silenced the crowd and gave Michigan a first-quarter lead with a 38-yard touchdown run. A Dana Coin field goal with just over two-minutes remaining in the half gave the Wolverines a 10-0 lead. The Spartans finally scored with one-second on the clock on a 1-yard plunge from Quarterback Frank Kolch. Michigan held a narrow 10-7 lead at halftime. Both teams continued to battle hard, but no points were scored in the third quarter. Michigan put the game out of reach with two scores midway through the final stanza. Billy Taylor scored on a 3-yard touchdown run and Tom Slade ran 9-yards for another. Michigan State's Eric Allen scored on a 1-yard run with just over four minutes remaining in the game, but it was too little and too late for the Spartans. Michigan State gave Michigan all they could handle for most of the game, but Bo's machine kept on rolling back to Ann Arbor. (*DFP*, 10/10/1971, Page 39)

Team	1st	2nd	3rd	4th	Final
UM	7	3	0	14	24
MSU	0	7	0	6	13

SERIES UPDATE:

The Wolverines increased their series advantage for the second straight season. Michigan now owned a series record of 39 wins, 20 losses, and 5 ties. Bo's footballers now had a perfect record for the Seventies (2-0-0). The only good news for the Spartans was that they still owned the best record in the Paul Bunyan Trophy series at 11 wins, 6 losses, and 2 ties. Unfortunately for Sparty, the Wolverines had "bragging rights" for the second straight year—ouch! A loss to a rival is always harder to take!

SERIES MILESTONES:

There was only one milestone that emerged from game number sixty-four and that was the crowd. For the sixth consecutive time, Michigan State set a series attendance record in East Lansing against the Wolverines. The crowd of 80, 093 was the first East Lansing series crowd to exceed the 80K threshold. Another in-state classic was in the books. There were no other milestones to mention.

SEASON SUMMARIES:

Bo Schembechler's Wolverines kept rolling after the victory in East Lansing. Michigan won four-straight blowouts over Illinois (35-6), Minnesota (35-7), Indiana (61-7), and Iowa (63-7) before escaping Purdue's upset attempt (20-17). Interestingly, the Wolverines slipped to number three in the nation after their win in East Lansing and did not rise in the standings for the rest of the year. Michigan finished off a perfect regular season with a close win over Ohio State. Unfortunately for Bo, Stanford upset his Wolverines (13-12) and millions of UM fans too in the 1972 Rose Bowl. Michigan ended the season with a final record of 11 wins and 1 loss. They finished as Big Ten Champions with a record of 8-0-0. Four Michigan players earned All-American honors for the Wolverines in 1971—Thom Darden, Reggie McKenzie, Mike Taylor, and Billy Taylor.

Coach Daugherty's eighteenth team was nothing special, but MSU did have a winning season. After losing to Michigan, the Spartans went to Wisconsin and lost to the Badgers by a score of 28-31. Things were looking bad in East Lansing, but Duffy's offense started working and the Spartans won four consecutive games over Iowa (34-3), Purdue (43-10), Ohio State (17-10), and Minnesota (40-25). The Spartans had a chance to win seven games, but they lost the season finale to Northwestern (28-7). Duffy's footballers finished the season with a record of 6 wins and 5 losses. They ended the Big Ten season in a tie for third place with a record of 5-3-0. Unfortunately, the Spartan offense was the major culprit in the 1971 season. The backs/ends fumbled 46 times during the season which proved to be their "Achilles Heel" in 1971. (Stabley, Page 252) It is hard to beat the best teams when you put the ball on the ground an average of four-times every week. The good news was that Erick Allen, Brad Van Pelt, and Run Curl earned All-American honors in 1971.

Game # 65: October 14, 1972 at Michigan Stadium in Ann Arbor

BACKGROUND INFORMATION:

The 1972 season saw three important rules changes to the game:

1. Freshman eligibility was restored for the first time since the war years in the early 1940s.
2. Mouthpieces were mandated for all players on the field starting with the 1973 season.
3. Officials could now call "time-out" for players who were "obviously" injured and the stop in play would not be charged to that player's team. (*USA Today CFE*, Page 254)

Series game number sixty-five would be played in Ann Arbor for the fifty-second time compared to only thirteen games in East Lansing. Fortunately, things were on a more even plane since MSU entered the Big Ten. Both teams had alternated venues since 1958. Also, the Big Ten had rescinded their outdated "no-repeat" rule to send the best team to Pasadena. Michigan was hoping to be the first team to play in back-to-back Rose Bowls in January 1973!

The good news for Duffy Daugherty was that he was back for his nineteenth season in 1972. The bad news for Spartan fans was that Duffy Daugherty was back for his nineteenth season in 1972. The last five seasons had been disappointing for Spartan fans since Duffy took them to the top of the mountain in 1965 and 1966. It was getting harder to laugh at his quips and smile about his one-liners. As always, Coach Daugherty was optimistic about the 1972 season, but that was nothing new. He had fifteen starters back on his roster. Duffy's Wishbone offense would have to deliver more production than it did in 1971. Would this be the year that Duffy's footballers returned to glory, or would they stay on the road to mediocrity that they had been traveling on since 1967? Oh, by the way, would Duffy ever be able to beat Bo Schembechler again?

Game one of the 1972 Spartan football season started strong with a 24-0 win at Illinois. Michigan State was 1-0-0 in the conference and could really set themselves up for a BIG season with some non-conference victories. Unfortunately, it did not work out that way for Duffy's footballers.

Michigan State lost three straight games to Georgia Tech (21-16), Southern California (51-6) and Notre Dame (16-0). It was a rough stretch and now the Spartans were sitting on a record of 1 win and 3 losses heading into Michigan week. Maybe MSU could start a winning streak to save the season against the hated Wolverines, or maybe not!

The Wolverines began the 1972 season with lots of question marks about who was going to replace some of the stars who graduated in the Spring of 1972. Bo Schembechler only had nine returning starters, but he had some promising sophomores who were eager to earn starting spots. Tom Slade returned at quarterback along with Kevin Casey. A kid named Dennis Franklin looked good in fall practice.

If Bo knew who his starting quarterback was, he was not telling anybody else. Bo was not counting on any freshman to contribute, even though the new rules allowed it. Once again, the Buckeyes were the favorite to win the conference title. Michigan was expected to have a winning season, but that was about it!

Eleventh ranked Michigan started with a win over Northwestern, but it was not pretty. The Wolverines almost let this one slip away before beating the Wildcats by a score of 7-0. After one game, the Michigan offense needed more work and more points! The Maize and Blue footballers won three straight non-conference games over UCLA (26-9), Tulane (41-7), and Navy (35-7). Michigan State week was on the horizon and the Wolverines were looking good at 4-0-0. Would fifth-ranked Michigan be ready for those pesky Spartans on October 14, 1972?

GAME SUMMARY: MSU 0 UM 10

The underdog Spartans gave the favored Wolverines all they could handle in this game. Michigan was favored by two touchdowns in this game, but Duffy's football team did not think it would happen that way. As it turned out, they were right! Most of the Detroit area newspaper writers criticized Michigan for failing to blow out the Spartans. Schembechler responded, "To hell with those guys who make spots. They don't know anything about Michigan-Michigan State football." (*DFP*, 10/15/1972, Page 41) Yes, this game was a classic example of why you ignore the "experts" and why you must play your opponent on the field, not in the paper.

Michigan had the best of the play for most of the game, but the MSU defense kept them out of the end zone until the fourth quarter. Mike Lantry put Michigan on the board in the second quarter with a 22-yard field goal. It remained 3-0 until speedy Gil Chapman dashed for a 58-yard touchdown on an end-around play. Lantry kicked the only PAT of the game and Michigan led 10-0 with less than seven minutes remaining. Michigan's defense held their ground. The Wolverines earned another hard-fought victory over the Spartans. (*DFP*, 10/15/1972, Page 41)

This game was not for the faint of heart. It was hard-hitting from the first play until the last. Michigan's offense rolled up 355-yards (323 rushing and 32 yards passing) and earned 19 first downs. However, points were much tougher to come by against the fired-up Spartan defenders. Duffy's "Wishbone Offense" was worse than awful. The Spartans only posted 176-yards and 9 first downs. The best that Duffy could have hoped for was a tie thanks to his lackluster offense. (*DFP*, 10/15/1972, Page 41)

Team	1st	2nd	3rd	4th	Final
MSU	0	0	0	0	0
UM	0	3	0	7	10

SERIES UPDATE:

The Spartans, as they had done so many times, went into this game with high hopes and an expectation of another long-awaited victory. They left Ann Arbor with another disappointing loss. The hated Wolverines increased their series advantage to 40 wins, 20 losses, and 5 ties. Michigan also remained "perfect" in the 1970s with a record of 3-0-0. The Spartans still retained the advantage in the Paul Bunyan Trophy series with a record of 11 wins, 7 losses, and 2 ties. However, they were losing ground quickly to Bo and his Wolverines. The Spartans had only seen the trophy from a distance for the last three years and that is the way it would stay until 1973.

SERIES MILESTONES:

As it turned out, there were quite a few milestones in series game number sixty-five. First, it was the last series game for the smiling Irishman. Duffy Daugherty called it quits after nineteen years at the helm in East Lansing. He finished as the winningest coach in Spartan football history. Duffy's record (109 wins, 69 losses and 5 ties) was the best for a Spartan head coach for many years. He also retired with the best record ever (10-7-2) against the hated Wolverines. Second, it was another record-breaking series crowd as 103,735 jammed into the Big House to watch the blood-letting festivities. Third, it was Bo's first shutout win in the series and Michigan's first shutout against the Spartans since 1947 (55-0). Fourth, the Wolverines became the first team to win forty games in the series. Finally, it was the twentieth game of the Paul Bunyan Series.

SEASON SUMMARIES:

Duffy's Spartans bounced back from the disappointing loss to the Wolverines with a big Homecoming Day victory over the Badgers (31-0). The next week, MSU played to a 6-6 tie with the Iowa Hawkeyes. Michigan State ended the month of October with a record of 2-4-1. Four games remained and a winning season was still possible. The Spartans played well in the last four games and kept Duffy smiling. They beat Purdue (22-12) and Ohio State (19-12) before losing a tough one at Minnesota (14-10). Duffy's Spartans won the last game of Duffy's career against Northwestern (24-14). Michigan State finished the 1972 season with a record of 5 wins, 5 losses, and 1 tie. Three Spartans (Brad Van Pelt, Joe DeLamielluere, and Billy Joe Dupree) earned All-American honors in 1973.

Unfortunately, the 1973 Spartan football season was not up to Duffy's normally high standards. Daugherty knew it was time to go. The longest coaching tenure in Spartan football history was over. Duffy left as Michigan States best coach ever. The big question was, "Who would try to fill Duffy's very, very, very BIG shoes?"

Bo Schembechler's Wolverines kept on winning after the Michigan State game and winning BIG. Michigan won four-straight Big Ten blow-outs over Illinois (31-7), Minnesota (42-0), Indiana (21-7), and Iowa (31-0) before getting a wake-up call against Purdue. The Spoilermakers came to Ann Arbor and almost upset the third-ranked Wolverines. Fortunately, Bo's Boys won the game 9-6 to set up his fourth straight showdown with his "Football Father" Woody Hayes.

The ninth-ranked Buckeyes defended their home turf and beat Michigan by a score of 14-11. Michigan finished with a final record of 10 wins and 1 loss in 1972. They settled for second place in the conference with a record of 6-1-0. Randy Logan and Paul Seymour earned All-American honors for the Wolverines at the end of the season.

Game # 66: October 13, 1973 at Spartan Stadium in East Lansing

BACKGROUND INFORMATION:

The 1973 season was the first season in college football where every player was required to wear a mouthpiece when playing in the game. The rules makers also decided that teams could use the ball of their choice when they were on offense. (*USA Today CFE*, Page 265) As always, the NCAA would continue to monitor the changes from recent years and discuss other issues that were being surfaced about the game.

Bo Schembechler entered the 1973 season with high expectations and a national ranking to match those expectations. Michigan began the season with a new "Option Offense" that was ideally suited to the skills of Quarterback Dennis Franklin. The fifth-ranked Wolverines went to Iowa for game one and came back winners by a score of 31-7. Michigan won their next three non-conference games against Stanford, Navy and Oregon by a combined score of 85-10. The Wolverines were on a roll heading into Michigan State week. Michigan was undefeated at 4-0-0 and still the fifth best team in the country.

Schembechler would face see a new man at Michigan State since Duffy retired in 1972. Denny Stolz, who had great success at Alma College and as a Defensive Coordinator for Duffy, was hired to fill the shoes of a Spartan coaching legend. Like Schembechler, Stolz was young and energetic. Would he be able to get the Spartans back on track and win one, or two, or three against the hated Wolverines?

Oops, things did not start off that well for Coach Stolz and his team since MSU lost the season opener at Northwestern (14-10). In week two, the Spartans beat the Syracuse Orangemen (14-8) in New York. UCLA came to East Lansing in week three and left with a 34-21 victory. Notre Dame added to MSU's misery with a narrow 14-10 victory over the Spartans. So, Michigan State had a record of 1 win and 3 losses heading into their annual match-up against Michigan. Worse yet, the Spartans were averaging just under fourteen points a game on offense. The defense was playing well except for the UCLA game. Michigan would offer a stiff test for the Spartans. Game on!

GAME SUMMARY: UM 31 MSU 0

Game number sixty-six in the Mitten State pigskin series was a mauling! The game was played on a very rainy day in East Lansing. Only 78,263 fans showed up to watch the slip-sliding game. Both teams had trouble hanging onto the ball and keeping drives alive. The Spartans fumbled nine times and lost six of them. Michigan was not perfect since they fumbled four times and lost one to the Spartans.

The Wolverines opened the scoring on a 53-yard punt return by Dave Brown with about three minutes remaining in the first quarter. Mike Lantry kicked the extra point and added a 35-yard field goal a few minutes later to give Michigan a 10-0 lead after one quarter. In the second quarter, Gil Chapman scampered 53-yards for Michigan's second touchdown and Lantry added the extra point. Michigan led 17-0 at halftime. (*DFP*, 10/14/1973, Page 67)

Neither team scored in the third quarter and Michigan retained their 17-0 lead heading into the final stanza. Quarterback Dennis Franklin hit Paul Seal for a 6-yard touchdown pass and Lantry's extra point made it 24-0 with about fourteen minutes to play. Fullback Ed Shuttlesworth rammed into the end zone from 2-yards out for Michigan's final touchdown. Mike Lantry kicked the final point of the game. Bo's Wolverines defeated Denny Stolz and his Spartans by a final score of 31-0. (*DFP*, 10/14/1973, Page 67) Yes, it was another painful defeat for Michigan State and their rookie coach. The good news for Coach Stolz was that his defense played well enough to keep MSU in the game. However, the offense (46 plays for 142 yards) made it hard to win with all the fumbles and a pass interception. The Wolverine offense played better (66 plays for 250 yards), and their turnovers (1 fumble and 1 interception) were not costly. (*DFP*, 10/14/1973, Page 67)

Team	1st	2nd	3rd	4th	Final
UM	10	7	0	14	31
MSU	0	0	0	0	0

SERIES UPDATE:

Series game number sixty-six was in the history books. Michigan was still large and in-charge, despite the presence of a new coach at Michigan State. The Wolverine series advantage now stood at an imposing 41 wins, 20 losses, and 5 ties. Schembechler and his Wolverines remained "perfect" in the Seventies with 4 wins, 0 losses, and 0 ties. The only good news for the Spartans was that they still had the advantage in the Paul Bunyan Trophy series with a record of 11 wins 8 losses, and 2 ties. Unfortunately, that advantage was rapidly slipping away since Bo had defeated the Spartans four straight times! Michigan kept the "bragging rights" and the recruiting advantage for another year. Oh boy, all the Wolverine "winning" was already getting old again in East Lansing.

SERIES MILESTONES:

The 1973 "Michigan Bowl," as one newspaper writer called it, marked the first game for Denny Stolz and his first loss. Yes, like every Aggie/Spartan coach before him, he lost his first encounter with hated Michigan. Michigan's second straight series victory was their first back-to-back shutouts since the 1942 and 1945 seasons. (Remember the teams did not play in the "War Years" from 1943 to 1944).

SEASON SUMMARIES:

Michigan kept right on rolling after their win over MSU. The Wolverines returned home and won a Homecoming Day blowout over Wisconsin (35-6). Bo's footballers won four more conference games (Minnesota, Indiana, Illinois, and Purdue) and none of them were close. Once again, Michigan and Ohio State would play for the Big Ten Championship for the fifth straight season.

Michigan battled the top-ranked Buckeyes to a 10-10 tie and would have been the Big Ten's representative to the Rose Bowl if traditional conference policy were followed. However, Commissioner Wayne Duke, who was looking for a way to win a Rose Bowl game, got approval to let the athletic directors vote on the Big Ten representative in case of a tie for the championship. As it turned out, it was the perfect time for some "Spartan Revenge."

All the years of hating Michigan were avenged by Athletic Director Burt Smith who, apparently, cast the deciding vote to send Ohio State to the 1974 Rose Bowl. Bo was livid about the whole affair. He did not like the change in Big Ten policy in case there was a tie. He did not like, what he thought was Wayne Duke's undue influence regarding the health of Quarterback Dennis Franklins injured shoulder. Of course, he did not like the fact that a Michigan graduate named Burt Smith, voted against his Alma Mater in this most unusual situation.

Michigan finished the season with a final record of 10 wins, 0 losses and 1 tie and a tie for first in the conference. The only good news out of the whole mess was that Dave Gallagher and Dave Brown both earned All-American honors for their outstanding play in 1973.

Coach Denny Stolz saw his Struggling Spartans play hard, again, against Illinois, but it was not good enough. The Spartans lost by a score of 6-3 and their record slipped to 1 win and 5 losses. Things improved and the Spartans won four of their last five games. The bad news was that they finished with an overall record of 5 wins and 6 losses. The good news was that their late-season surge lifted them to a record of 4-4-0 in the conference which was good for fourth place. The best news for Spartan fans was that defensive back William Simpson earned All-American honors in 1973. Unfortunately, the Denny Stolz Era at Michigan State was off to a rocky start, but he knew what he had to do. Win more games, beat Michigan, and get a team ready to compete for the Big Ten title. Sounds simple enough, right?

Game # 67: October 12, 1974 at Michigan Stadium in Ann Arbor

BACKGROUND INFORMATION:

The 1974 season saw four important rules changes in college football:

1. Substitutions were further modified so that the new player had to be on the field for at least one play and the outgoing player had to be off the field for at least one play.
2. In the interest of player safety, blocking below the waist was no longer allowed except within three yards of the line of scrimmage.

3. Again, in the interest of player safety, goalposts could be offset behind the end-line if they arched over the end-line.
4. All players, even kickers, were required to wear shoulder pads. (*USA Today CFE*, Page 275)

The Spartans began year two of the Denny Stolz Era with a big conference win over Northwestern (41-7). Syracuse came to town in week two and the Spartans sent them home to ponder a 19-0 defeat. Things were looking good for the Spartans until UCLA came to town the next week. The Bruins blasted the Spartans (56-14) and sent Denny Stolz back to the drawing board to figure out what was wrong with his offense and his defense. Things improved on defense in week four against Notre Dame, but the Spartans still lost (19-14). The Spartans were even at 2-2-0 and it did not look like it would be a fun trip to Ann Arbor for their BIG game against the Wolverines. Denny Stolz would need some Duffy "magic" to steal another win.

Michigan was picked to compete, again, with Ohio State for the Big Ten Championship in 1974. College football writers were now calling the Big Ten the "Big Two" (Michigan and Ohio State) and the "Little Eight" (Michigan State plus the other seven conference teams) because the Wolverines and Buckeyes had either tied or won the Big Ten Title every year since 1968. Michigan had plenty of starters returning for Bo's sixth season and one of them was talented quarterback, Dennis Franklin.

Bo's Wolverines started the season as the sixth best team in the country and they looked the part with a solid win over Iowa (24-7). Michigan rolled through three straight non-conference games by defeating Colorado (31-0), Navy (52-0), and Stanford (27-16). Bo's footballers were 4-0-0 for the fifth consecutive season heading into Michigan State week.

This game probably had a little more "meaning" for Bo since MSU Athletic Director Burt Smith had bragged about voting for Ohio State in the infamous Rose Bowl vote of 1973. If Schembechler's team could score 120 points against the Spartans, he would let them do it. Hell, he might even go for two late in the game with a big lead! Bring on the Spartans!

GAME SUMMARY: MSU 7 UM 21

The sixty-seventh game of the series was like so many of the previous rivalry games. It was hard-hitting and both teams were not nice to each other. The record gathering of 104,682 watched both offenses struggle in the light rain. Michigan fumbled four times and lost two of them. The Spartans did even worse with six fumbles (four lost) and two interceptions.

Michigan opened the scoring midway through the first quarter on a 13-yard run by Gordon Bell. Mike Lantry kicked the PAT and it was 7-0. In the second quarter, defensive end Dan Jilek recovered a Spartan fumble in the end zone and Michigan had another touchdown. Lantry's second extra point gave the Wolverines a 14-0 lead.

Dennis Franklin connected on a 44-yard touchdown pass to Jim Smith with five-seconds to play in the half to make it 20-0. The half ended on Lantry's third extra point and Michigan went to the locker room leading 21-0. It looked like Bo's team had plenty of points, but I am certain that he wanted more in the second half—a lot more! (*DFP*, 10/13/1974, Page 67) Fortunately, the Spartans defense settled down and played well for the rest of the game. MSU finally scored in the final quarter, but they could not overcome the 21-point hole that they dug for themselves. Michigan won, for the fifth-straight year, by a final score of 21-7.

Team	1st	2nd	3rd	4th	Final
MSU	0	0	0	7	7
UM	7	14	0	0	21

SERIES UPDATE:

Once again, Michigan increased their Mitten State series advantage to 42 wins, 20 losses, and 5 ties. Michigan State still held the advantage in the Bunyan Trophy series at 11 wins, 9 losses, and 2 ties. The Wolverines remained undefeated in the Seventies at 5-0-0. It is hard to know what Denny Stolz was thinking, but it probably was not good. Michigan had "bragging rights" for another year.

SERIES MILESTONES:

The only milestone to speak of was the crowd. It was a record-breaker, even with the lousy weather conditions. This game was becoming too important to miss which is why 847 more people showed up than the last Ann Arbor gathering in 1972! Don Canham had a new number to shoot for in 1976 when the Spartans returned to Ann Arbor for another earth-shaking battle with the Wolverines. Of course, Denny Stolz was still looking for his first series win since he slipped to 0-2-0 against hated Michigan.

SEASON SUMMARIES:

Coach Denny Stolz took his team on another tough road trip in week six. The Spartans journeyed to Champaign and matched the Fighting Illini point for point. The game ended in a 21-21 tie. Michigan State had a record of 2 wins, 3 losses, and 1 tie after six games. Stolz had to get his team ready for homecoming and that is exactly what he did! The Spartans won BIG over Purdue (31-7) and sent the alumni home smiling. Amazingly, the Green and White just kept on winning. They beat Wisconsin (28-21), Ohio State (16-13), Indiana (19-10) and Iowa (60-21) to finish the season with a five-game winning streak.

Michigan State was in the Big Ten Title race for most of the season. They finished with an overall record of 7 wins, 3 losses, and 1 tie. Their conference record of 6-1-1 earned them third place for 1974. The energetic Stolz kept his team on track for the entire season and gave Spartan fans their first winning season since 1971. It was big step in the right direction in year two of the Stolz Era at Michigan State. For the first time since 1970, no Spartans earned All-American honors in 1974. However, Coach Stolz was named "Big Ten Coach of the Year" for his outstanding work in the conference in 1974.

The Wolverines kept right on winning after their conquest of the Spartans. They had a tough time with Wisconsin at Camp Randall Stadium but came home with a hard-earned win (24-20). Bo's footballers demolished Minnesota (49-0) on homecoming to push their record to a perfect 7-0-0. Indiana and Illinois provided tough back-to-back road tests, but Michigan passed both exams. They beat the Hoosiers by a score of 21-7 and escaped Champaign with a 14-6 win. Purdue was the final home opponent for the 1974 season and the seniors led a 51-0 rout of the Boilermakers. For the seventh straight year, it came down to Michigan vs Ohio State for the Big Ten Championship. It was another close game, but the Buckeyes prevailed (12-10). Michigan finished the season with an overall record of 10 wins and 1 loss. They tied Ohio State for the conference title with a record of 7-1-0, but the conference athletic directors voted Ohio State to represent the conference in the 1975 Rose Bowl. Defensive back Dave Brown earned All-American honors for the second time in 1974.

Game # 68: October 11, 1975 at Spartan Stadium in East Lansing

BACKGROUND INFORMATION:

Subtle rules changes continued to be made as the 1975 season saw three more adjustments to the game. Robert Ours, author of the *College Football Encyclopedia: The Authoritative Guide to 124 Years of College Football,* provided a nice summary of these changes:

1. The game ball composition and appearance were standardized and striped footballs showed up for the first time in the Big Ten and other conferences.
2. Referees were given the authority (without asking coaches for support) to suspend games due to severe weather and other emergencies.
3. The mouthpiece rule that was put into effect in 1973 needed some teeth (pun-intended) since there were many violators and officials could only give warnings. Now, a player without a mouthpiece would earn a charged time-out for his team. If the team were out of time-outs, each infraction would result in a five-yard penalty. (Ours, Page 4)

Michigan State fans, and college football fans in general, mourned the loss of Biggie Munn who passed away on March 18, 1975. Biggie put the Spartan football program on his back in 1947 and personally raised it to the highest level before retiring from coaching in 1953. His legacy lives on at Michigan State. Every year the "Biggie Munn Award" is presented to the most motivational Spartan(s) at the end of the season.

One other interesting development took place in Chicago where the Big Ten voted to allow teams (other than the league champion) to accept post-season bowl invitations. It also changed the policy of resolving championship ties since the 1973 fiasco. All the points that Bo Schembechler made about the unfairness of the process were pretty much fixed. A complicated "tie-breaker" system was implemented which took it out of the hands of the athletic directors. Bo was okay with the changes, but as he always said, "It was a helluva price to pay" for his players who missed out on the opportunity to play in a bowl game for three straight years.

Bo Schembechler was back for season number seven in 1975 which was great news for Michigan fans, but not much for the Spartans and the rest of the league. Once again, the Wolverines were expected to battle the Buckeyes for conference supremacy. Michigan had lots of returning starters, but the quarterback situation was unsettled. Senior Mark Elzinga had the most experience, but a freshman phenome named Rick Leach was turning heads in fall drills. As it turned out, Bo decided to "bet the farm" on young Leach. Rick Leach would start against Wisconsin and become the first freshman to ever start at quarterback for Michigan. Rick Leach was up to the challenge because he could run and pass, just like Dennis Franklin before him.

The pollsters believed in Bo's team and the second-ranked Wolverines went to Wisconsin and took care of business (23-6). Leach was solid in his first game but was pressed hard in the next two games by Stanford and Baylor. Both games ended as ties. Michigan slipped to number twelve but put it all together in a win over fifth-ranked Missouri (31-7). Once again, the Wolverines were undefeated (2-0-2) heading into the Michigan State game in week five.

You better believe that Bo was going to get his freshman ready for an onslaught by the Spartans. He probably started by teaching his young quarterback how to tighten up his helmet chin-strap—real tight! The Spartans were going to hit Leach harder than he had ever been hit before. Game on!

Denny Stolz was back for his third year as the Spartans football leader in 1975. So far, he had produced one losing season and one winning season. His overall record after two years was 12 wins, 9 losses and 2 ties. Not a terrible body of work for the young coach. However, it was obvious that more progress was required if he were to compete with the "Big Two" for a conference championship. Like Michigan, Stolz had plenty of returning talent (39 letterman) for the 1975 season. Many people thought that it was time for the Spartans to make a run for another conference title.

Denny Stolz was probably eager to get started in season number three, but not too eager. The first game of the season was against Ohio State! The Buckeyes looked like "contenders" that day and the Spartans looked like "pretenders." Woody's boys won the game by a score of 21-0 over Michigan State. The Spartans won three straight non-conference games against Miami of Ohio (14-13), N.C. State (37-15) and Notre Dame (10-3) to push their record to 3-1-0 heading into Michigan Week. You know that Stolz, Duffy's former Defensive Coordinator, was going to have a stop-Leach game plan in place that would force the freshman into mistakes. This game had all the makings of another bitter backyard brawl in East Lansing.

GAME SUMMARY: UM 16 MSU 6

For the first time since 1964, both Michigan (#8) and Michigan State (#15) were ranked at the start of a series game. Mitten State pigskin scuffle number sixty-eight lived up to expectations. It was another typical edition of the intense in-state football series. There were bone-crunching blocks and teeth-rattling tackles on every play. The mothers of the players feared for the lives of their offspring. Yes, it was another intense and nasty football game!

It turned out to be a big win for Michigan. Not only did the Maize and Blue footballers win the game—they won for the sixth-straight season. It was another precious series win for the Wolverines and another disappointing loss for the Spartans. The Spartans kicked off the scoring with a 46-yard field goal by Hans Nielson. The first quarter ended with MSU holding a 3-0 lead. Bob Wood of Michigan matched the Nielson's field goal early in the second quarter and added another one before the end of the first half. After thirty minutes of play, Wood led Nielson by a score of 6-3. Michigan State's Nielson tied the game at 6-6 midway through the third quarter and it remained that way into the fourth quarter. Finally, Bo's high-powered offense put together a drive and Gordon Bell dashed into the end zone from 18-yards out to put Michigan ahead 12-6. Wood's PAT kick made it 13-6 in favor of Michigan. Bob Wood finished the scoring with his third field goal and Michigan had a 16-6 lead that made them a winner. (*DFP*, 10/12/1975, Page 33)

Team	1st	2nd	3rd	4th	Final
UM	0	6	0	10	16
MSU	3	0	3	0	6

Michigan outrushed the Spartans 258 yards to 117 yards. Leach directed the offense effectively but did have some trouble with the intense Spartan pressure. He only competed 2 of 6 passes for 38-yards and threw one interception. Michigan also lost three fumbles which did not help their cause. The Spartans fared better in the air with Charley Baggett competing 10 of 16 passes for 162 yards. However, the Spartan quarterback could not get the Spartans into the end zone. Rick Leach did make one HUGE play that kept Michigan's only touchdown drive alive. It turned out to be the biggest play of the game. Once again, the only thing that is sweeter than a rival victory is a rival victory in the other guy's stadium. I am sure that Wolverine fans sang "Hail to the Victors" more times than necessary. That is just how winning rival fans handle things after a big series win.

Image 9 Michigan center Jim Czirr is about to snap a striped football to quarterback Rick Leach in the 1975 series game in East Lansing. (Permission: Bentley Historical Library at The University of Michigan, See Page 369)

SERIES UPDATE:

Michigan's advantage over Michigan State grew again. The Wolverines now owned 43 wins, 20 losses, and 5 ties in the in-state hate football series. Bo's footballers remained undefeated in the Seventies at 6-0-0. The Spartan advantage in the trophy series had decreased to 11 wins, 10 losses, and 2 ties. The Spartans were probably wondering if they would ever see Paul Bunyan back in their trophy room. Obviously, it would not be until 1976, at the soonest!

SERIES MILESTONES:

Sixty-eight series games were in the history books. The big item of note was the abrupt departure of Coach Denny Stolz. In January 1976, he was forced to resign. The NCAA put Michigan State on a three-year probation for recruiting violations and other issues. Stolz finished his career at Michigan State with an overall record of 19 wins, 13 losses, and 1 tie. Unfortunately, he went 0-3-0 against the Wolverines. According to author Fred Stabley, Woody Hayes turned Stolz in for crossing the line with Ohio recruits. The only other small milestone to mention was that Michigan achieved their tenth win in the Paul Bunyan Trophy series. (Stabley, Pages 282-283)

SEASON SUMMARIES:

After the close win in East Lansing, Michigan put their offense into high-gear and ran off huge wins over Northwestern (69-0) and Indiana (55-7). They also posted convincing wins over Minnesota, Purdue, and Illinois. Once again, one obstacle remained—the Ohio State Buckeyes! Things did not go well since Woody's footballers gave Bo his first home loss in 41 games with a 21-14 victory over Michigan. The bad news was that the Wolverines finished second in the Big Ten with a record of 7-1-0.

The good news was they were the first team other than a conference champion to accept a bowl bid. Unfortunately, this came along with some more bad news since the game was against third-ranked Oklahoma. The Sooners beat the Wolverines in the Orange Bowl (14-6). Bo's bad bowl luck continued. The Wolverines ended the 1975 season with a final record of 8 wins, 2 losses, and 2 ties. Interestingly, the Sooners were named national champions after Ohio State and Texas A & M lost their bowl games. Defensive back Don Dufek was the only Wolverine to earn All-American honors in 1975.

After losing to the Wolverines, Michigan State bounced back nicely to win easily over Minnesota (38-15). Illinois ruined Homecoming the next week by defeating the Spartans 21-19. Purdue also handled the Spartans by a score of 20-10. Things looked bad for the Stolz and his footballers, but they woke up and played well in the last three games of the season. Michigan State beat Indiana, Northwestern, and Iowa to finish the regular season with a record of 7 wins and 4 losses.

The Spartans broke even in the Big Ten at 4-4-0 and ended up in a tie for third place. Michigan State was just a few points away from an excellent season, but they just could not score enough in the close games. The Michigan State program was still competitive in year three of the Stolz Era. Unfortunately, the methods that Denny Stolz used eventually cost him his job. He was three and out in East Lansing. The next guy would have to take the hits for the probation penalties. Bo probably did not shed any tears when he heard that Athletic Director Burt Smith was fired in the aftermath of the NCAA findings. Unfortunately, it was a sad time in Michigan State football history.

Game # 69: October 9, 1976 at Michigan Stadium in Ann Arbor

BACKGROUND INFORMATION:

There were two more important rules changes for the 1976 season. First, to increase the impact of the passing game, blockers could now partially extend their arms during pass protection. Second, the scores in a forfeited game would be changed to the actual score of the game at the time of the forfeit if the offended team were ahead. Otherwise, it would be 1-0 as in previous years. (*USA Today CFE*, Page 296)

One other item of note was that Michigan Stadium, the site of the 1976 Michigan vs Michigan State football game was expanded. The capacity at the "bigger" Big House grew to 103,159.

Darryl Rogers came from San Jose State to clean up the mess in East Lansing, but he knew it was going to be a tough job. Spartan football fortunes were not looking too bright with all the NCAA penalties in place. Coach Rogers did not know much about the Big Ten because he was a California guy. I think that he probably knew that Michigan and Ohio State were quite good. Of course, he knew that Woody turned the Spartans in for the Stolz recruiting violations which turned out to be good thing for Rogers since he got a good job out of it. Rogers was successful in three years at San Jose State, posting a record of 22 wins, 9 losses, and 3 ties. He favored the pass over the run. Rogers would have to adjust to Big Ten football. Or, maybe the Big Ten would have to adjust to his wide-open style of play!

Darryl Rogers got a chance to meet Woody Hayes in person on September 11, 1976. Woody brought his Buckeyes to town and left with a 49-21 win. "Woody's parting shot was probably something like "Nice to meet you Rogers and good luck in your new job!" The Spartans bounced back the next week and beat Wyoming (21-10). They tied North Carolina State the next week in Raleigh (31-31). A loss to Notre Dame (24-6) put the Spartans at 1-2-1 heading into Michigan week. Darryl Rogers knew that a trip to Ann Arbor to play number one Michigan probably would not be much fun, unless his Spartans could pull off a huge upset!

Michigan was coming off another successful, but disappointing season in 1975. The good news was that they won eight games. The bad news was that they lost the last two games of the season to Ohio State (21-14) and national champion Oklahoma (14-6). Bo was almost never satisfied because he usually lost that last game of the year to the Buckeyes or to some PAC Ten bowl team. Michigan had a ton of lettermen returning for the 1976 campaign, but the best news was that Rick Leach was back for his Sophomore year.

Once again, Michigan and Ohio State were expected to battle it out at the end of the season for the Big Ten Championship. Bo's Wolverines began the season as the second-best team in the country. They played well in game number one against Wisconsin and beat the Badgers by a score of 40-27. The Wolverines jumped to the top spot and promptly routed Stanford by a score of 51-0! Navy (70-14) and Wake Forest (31-0) also went down hard, and Michigan was 4-0-0. The Spartans were coming to town looking for another upset in Michigan Stadium. Bo had other plans!

GAME SUMMARY: MSU 10 UM 42

The sixty-ninth series game was one to remember for the Wolverine faithful and another one for Spartan fans to forget! Michigan State came out swinging and landed the first punch of the "football fight" when Hans Nielsen kicked a 24-yard field goal. The Spartans led 3-0. That would be their last lead of the game. (*DFP*, 10/10/1976, Page 76)

A few minutes later, Rob Lytle scored on a seventy-five-yard run and Harlan Huckleby sprinted 38-yards for another score. Bob Wood kicked both extra points and Michigan led 14-3 with six minutes remaining in the first quarter. To their credit, the pesky Spartans came right back to score their first touchdown on a 10-yards pass form Eddie Smith to Mark Brammer. Hans Nielsen kicked the extra point, and the Spartans were only down 14-10 at the end of the first quarter. Michigan's defense stiffened and the offense went back to work with two more scores in the second quarter. Quarterback Rick Leach scored from 3-yards out and Harlan Huckleby got his second touchdown on a 1-yard plunge. Two more Bob Wood extra points gave Michigan a 28-14 advantage at halftime. (*DFP*, 10/10/1976, Page 76)

Michigan's defense forced the Spartans into a passing attack for the rest of the game, but it did not produce any more points. Meanwhile, Harlan Huckleby scored his third touchdown on a 2-yard dive at the end of the third quarter and Michigan pushed their lead to 35-10. Jerry Zuver intercepted a Smith pass early in the fourth quarter and returned it 60-yards for the final touchdown. Bob Wood kicked his sixth, and final, extra point to increase the score to 42-10. That's how the game ended. (*DFP*, 10/10/1976, Page 76)

Team	1st	2nd	3rd	4th	Final
MSU	10	0	0	0	10
UM	14	14	7	7	42

Rick Leach ran Bo's option offense almost to perfection as the Wolverines pounded out 442 rushing yards and Leach added 93-yards in the air. The only down-side to the day was that the Maize and Blue lost three fumbles. Unfortunately, the Spartans did not fare as well on offense. They only rushed for 98-yards but gained 251-yards in the air. The Wolverine defense did some bending, but it did not break, especially in the last three quarters of the game when they held the Green and White to zero points. (*DFP*, 10/10/197, Page 76)

SERIES UPDATE:

Yes, Michigan won for the seventh consecutive season. The Wolverine series advantage grew to 44 wins, 20 losses, and 5 ties. Bo upped his perfect record in the Seventies to 7-0-0. Finally, the Paul Bunyan Trophy series was even at 11-11-2. Wow, things changed fast for the Spartans who had been riding high in the Sixties. Michigan had bragging rights again and it was really getting old in East Lansing!

SERIES MILESTONES:

There were a couple milestones in the sixty-ninth game of the in-state football series. First, it was the first series game for Darryl Rogers and his first loss. It was also the first time that the series had been tied since 1956. The crowd of 104, 211 was another huge gathering, but it was not a record-setter.

SEASON SUMMARIES:

The Darryl Rogers Era did not start as well as hoped, but probably as well as could be expected under the circumstances. After losing to Michigan, the Spartans lost on Home-coming Day to Minnesota (14-10). Then, the Green and White went on a three-game winning streak and defeated Illinois (31-23), Purdue (45-13), and Indiana (23-0). Unfortunately, MSU lost the last two games to Northwestern and Iowa to finish the season with a record of 4 wins, 6 losses, and 1 tie. MSU's record of 3 wins and 4 losses in the Big Ten was only good enough for a seventh-place tie. In retrospect, it could have been worse! No Spartans earned All-American honors in 1976. Darryl Rogers survived his first year under difficult circumstances. There was plenty of work to do in East Lansing—for sure!

Bo's Wolverines continued to win and win big. After defeating the Spartans, Michigan defeated Northwestern, Indiana, and Minnesota before going on the road to face Purdue. The "Spoilermakers" did what they have done so many times in the past. They pulled off another huge upset and beat top-ranked Michigan (16-14). One of Bo's friends, Alex Agase, masterminded the big win, and sent him home in a bad mood! The Wolverines bounced back in the final two games with wins over Illinois (38-7) and Ohio State (22-0) to claim a share of the Big Ten title along with Ohio State! Michigan finished the season with an overall record of 10-2-0 after losing the Rose Bowl to Southern California. Michigan had five All-American players on the 1976 team—Bill Dufek, Rob Lytle, Calvin O'Neal, Jim Smith, and Mark Donahue.

Game # 70: October 8, 1977 at Spartan Stadium in East Lansing

BACKGROUND INFORMATION:

There was only one important adjustment to the game of American college football for the 1977 season. Offensive lineman would now be able to block downfield when a receiver caught the ball behind the neutral zone. That was it, the NCAA rules makers would keep an eye on the game and see what changes might be needed in the future. (*USA Today CFE*, Page 306)

Coach Bo Schembechler was back for his ninth season at Michigan in 1977. So far, Bo's coaching career at Michigan was a series of winning seasons, Big Ten Championships, and some lousy bowl games. In a big surprise, the Wolverines were expected to compete with the Buckeyes for Big Ten "bragging rights" again. The Big Two were making life tough for the rest of the conference teams.

Bo and Woody were in the ninth year of the "Ten-Year War." Their epic clashes were always high drama for college football. Bo had plenty of good players coming back and one of them was Rick Leach. Coach Schembechler was confident about his team in 1977. The second-ranked Wolverines won their season and conference opener at Illinois by a score of 37-9. They won three straight non-conference games against Duke (21-9), Navy (14-7) and fifth-ranked Texas A & M (41-3). Once again, Michigan (which slipped to #3) was 4-0-0 heading into Michigan State Week. Could Bo's footballers make it eight straight wins over the Spartans?

Year two of Rogers Era in East Lansing promised to be better than his first year. His wide-open offense was working and his players loved it! Nobody who favored Michigan State knew what to expect from the 1977 Spartans. All they could do was support them and hope for the best. Things started well in the season opener as the Spartans defeated Purdue by a score of 19-14. Michigan State was undefeated in the conference at 1-0-0. The Spartans may have been looking ahead to Notre Dame or Michigan because Washington State came to town and left with a 23-12 win. The Green and White footballers bounced back with a solid win over Wyoming to push their record to 2-1-0. However, a loss to Notre Dame (16-6) pushed them back to 2-2-0 heading into Michigan Week. The good news was that the Spartans would host the Wolverines for series game number seventy. The bad news was that Michigan was ranked third in the country and playing well. Oh well, there is never a bad time for an upset over Michigan. Spartan fans were hopeful.

GAME SUMMARY: UM 24 MSU 14

Game number seventy was another series classic. Every play featured hard-hitting on both sides of the ball. Early in the game, the Spartans put together a drive, but it stalled. Hans Nielsen missed a 57-yard field goal which was the only real scoring attempt in the first quarter. MSU scored first when Kirk Gibson caught a 19-yard scoring pass from Eddie Smith. Nielsen kicked the PAT for a 7-0 lead. Michigan came back a few minutes later a pass from Rick Leach to Richard White for 12-yards and a touchdown. Michigan's Greg Willner kicked the extra point. The game was tied at 7-7. Five minutes later, Willner kicked a 50-yard field goal that gave Michigan a 10-7 halftime lead. Michigan dominated play in the third quarter. The Wolverines scored two touchdowns (Russell Davis and Rick Leach both ran for 3-yard scores) and two more extra points to take a commanding lead (24-7) at the end of the third quarter. The Spartan offense moved the ball on the Wolverines, but they fumbled five times and lost four of them. Jim Early finally scored MSU's second touchdown, but it was too little and too late. Michigan had won again by a score of 24-14. (*DFP*, 10/9/1977, Page 76)

Yes, it was another painful defeat for Michigan State and their second-year coach. The Spartans were an improved team and were in this game all the way. The good news for Coach Rogers was that his offense gained 254-yards and earned 13 first downs against Michigan's stubborn defense. The bad news was that they made too many mistakes (1 interception and 4 lost fumbles) to win. In the end, the Wolverine offense played better (79 plays for 413 yards) and made fewer mistakes (2 fumbles and 1 interception). Michigan's series win streak grew to eight games and everyone in Spartan Nation was sick of it. (*DFP*, 10/9/1977, Page 76)

Team	1st	2nd	3rd	4th	Final
UM	0	10	14	0	24
MSU	0	7	0	7	14

SERIES UPDATE:

Michigan remained "large" and "in-charge" of the Mitten" State's annual "blood-letting" contest. For the record, the Wolverine series advantage grew to 45 wins, 20 losses, and 5 ties. Of course, the Wolverines were now 8-0-0 in the Seventies. To make matters even worse for Spartan fans, Michigan took the lead in the Paul Bunyan Trophy series at 12 wins, 11 losses, and 2 ties. Things were about as bad as they could be in East Lansing. The Spartans would have to listen to more "crap" from the fine folks in Ann Arbor and wait until 1978 for another rematch. Ugh!

SERIES MILESTONES:

The seventieth edition of the Michigan vs Michigan State pigskin series had four milestones to mention. First, game number seventy was a milestone, right? Second, it was the first time that Michigan ever held the lead in the trophy series. Third, it was also the twenty-fifth trophy game of the series. Finally, it was the first series home game for Darryl Rogers and his first home loss.

SEASON SUMMARIES:

Michigan rose to the number one ranking for the second year in a row after their win over the Spartans. The Wolverines looked like the nation's best team when they blasted fourteenth ranked Wisconsin (56-0). The Minnesota Gophers were waiting for the Wolverines the next week in Minneapolis. They stopped Rick Leach and the vaunted Michigan "Option Offense" on a slippery field and won the game 16-0. That would be the last loss of the regular season as Michigan rolled to four straight wins over Iowa (23-6), Northwestern (63-20), Purdue (40-7) and Ohio State (14-6). Michigan and Ohio State tied for the conference title, again, and Michigan lost the Rose Bowl, again. Yes, the 1977 Michigan football season was a lot like the rest of them in the 1970s. The Wolverines finished with an excellent record of 10 wins and 2 losses. Bo's team shared another Big Ten Championship with OSU and they lost another bowl game. Three more Michigan Men (Mark Donahue, John Anderson, and Walt Downing) earned All-American honors for the season.

The Spartans came out flat against Indiana the next week, but left Bloomington with a 13-13 tie. Of course, a loss would have been worse. At this point, Michigan State, and a record of 2 wins, 3 losses, and 1 tie. Darryl Rogers was able to keep his team together and the Green and White footballers won five-straight games! After a close win over Wisconsin (9-7), the Spartans rolled to three straight blow-out wins over Illinois (49-20), Minnesota (29-10) and Northwestern (44-3). Iowa provided a little stiffer test, but the Hawkeyes still lost to MSU (22-16). Michigan State finished STRONG in year two of the Darryl Rogers Era.

208

The Spartans finished the 1977 season with a record of 7-3-1. More importantly, the Green and White finished third in Big Ten play with a record of 6-1-1. Darryl Rogers had an excellent season in East Lansing in 1977! Now, if he could just figure out a way to beat Michigan, things would really be good again in East Lansing!

Game # 71: October 14, 1978 at Michigan Stadium in Ann Arbor

BACKGROUND INFORMATION:

The NCAA Rules Committee studied the games in 1977 and listened to the concerns of coaches and officials. As a result, several important changes were made to the rules in 1978. Here are the ones that had the most impact on the game:

1. All unsuccessful field goal attempts would now be returned to the previous line of scrimmage. This change made coaches think twice about attempting long field goals. It also encouraged the use of the "pooch" kick to pin an opposing team deep in their own territory.
2. Pass receivers who were knocked out of bounds by a defender were eligible to return to the playing field and catch passes.
3. Intentional grounding was more closely defined and roughing the passer rules were tightened. *(USA Today CFE, Page 316)*

The 1978 football season marked Bo Schembechler's tenth season at Michigan. His first nine years had been phenomenally successful, but his habit of losing bowl games was a sore spot with Wolverine fans. The man had won seven Big Ten Titles in nine years, but it was not good enough for some of the folks in Ann Arbor. Are you kidding? Bo did not like losing to anybody. He had the same goals that he always had: beat the rivals, win the Big Ten Championship, and win the Rose Bowl. Maybe this would be the season where Bo could accomplish all three objectives! Expectations were high, as usual, in Ann Arbor.

Bo's footballers began the season as the fourth-ranked team in the nation when they hosted Illinois for the first game of the 1978 season. Michigan took the fight out of the "Fighting Illinois" and sent them home with a 31-0 loss. Fourteenth-ranked Notre Dame was finally back on the schedule and the Wolverines beat them by a score of 28-14. So far, so good. Michigan defeated Duke the next week (52-0) and finished off their non-conference schedule with a 21-17 win over Arizona. Everything was going according to plan. Michigan was 4-0-0 heading into Michigan State Week. Would "Bo's Boy's" be able to make it nine in a row over MSU?

The Michigan State Spartans showed much improvement in season two of the Darryl Rogers Era. His wide-open attack was perfect for the athletes he had on his offense. His defense was still a work in progress, but it was playing well by the end of the 1977 season. It looked like his team could compete for a Big Ten Title. Yes, it sounded like a big order, but he had some really good players coming back.

Unfortunately, all optimism and lofty predictions get tested when a team loses the season opener (at Purdue 16-14) to a lesser team. It must have been an aberration since the Green and White footballers pounded Syracuse (49-21). It was time for the Spartans to really get going in their last two non-conference games. Unfortunately, South California and Notre Dame did not buy into the Spartan "game plan." The Trojans trounced Michigan State (30-9) and Notre Dame did not treat them much better in a 29-25 victory over the Spartans. Coach Rogers must have been pulling his hair out! Instead of going to Ann Arbor with a record of 4-0-0, the Spartans limped in with 1 win and 3 losses. It looked like it was time to call Duffy Daugherty and see if he had some "magical advice" for Coach Rogers. It did not look like the Spartans would have a chance against fifth-ranked Michigan. Poor Michigan State!

GAME SUMMARY: MSU 24 UM 15

I do not know if Darry Rogers called Duffy or not. Maybe Coach Daugherty showed up at a practice. All I know is that "something" happened to the sagging Spartans and they came out ready to play against Michigan.

The visiting Spartans scored all the first half points. Morten Andersen opened the scoring with a 38-yard field goal near the end of the first quarter. Eddie Smith threw a 10-yard scoring pass to Alonzo Middleton and with Anderson's extra-point it was 10-0 Spartans early in the second quarter. Middleton ran for another 1-yard score with five minutes to play in the half. Andersen kicked the extra point, and it was 17-0 at halftime. (DFP, 10/15/1978, Page 65)

Both teams traded touchdowns and extra points in the third quarter. Rick Leach ran for a 3-yard score and Greg Willner kicked the extra-point. It was now 17-7 in favor of MSU with nine minutes remaining in the third quarter. The Spartans came back on an 11-yard scoring pass from Smith to Mark Brammer. Anderson's extra point gave the Spartans a 24-7 lead at the end of the third quarter. Michigan scored late on a 3-yard run by Russell Davis, but Michigan State held on for a 24-15 victory. Of course, it was even sweeter since it was in the Big House! (DFP, 10/15/1978, Page 71)

The Spartans had as much balance as a team could have in a football game! They ran for 248-yards and passed for 248-yards! Wow, almost 500 yards (496) on a Bo Schembechler defense, are you kidding? The Spartan defense really stepped up in this game. Yes, Michigan ran for 233-yards, but three Rick Leach interceptions really killed some great scoring chances. Michigan State's offense clicked for the entire game. Michigan State was the better team on this day. They out-blocked, out-tackled, out-passed, out-ran, and out-scored the hated Wolverines. Time to party Sparty! Go Green! Go White! (DFP, 10/15/1978, Page 71)

Team	1st	2nd	3rd	4th	Final
MSU	3	14	7	0	24
UM	0	0	7	8	15

SERIES UPDATE:

Once again, another game was in the Mitten State football series history book. Michigan was still large and in-charge, but one game can make a BIG difference when you have not beaten your rival in eight years. Michigan still had a dominating series margin (45-21-5), but Spartan victory #21 was sweet! The Wolverines were no longer undefeated in the Seventies, but still had a record of 8-1-0 for the decade. Interestingly, the trophy series was even again at 12-12-2. Both teams had a season to finish, so, it was time to move on. However, the Spartans would really, really enjoy their bragging rights and a long visit with Paul Bunyan in the next twelve months!

SERIES MILESTONES:

As always, there were some interesting milestones that emerged from series game number seventy-one. First, the crowd of 105,132 was a record-breaker (by 450 people) and Don Canham probably loved it! I mean, if you are going to lose to a rival, it might as well be in front of a record crowd, right? Second, as I mentioned earlier, the trophy series was tied again at 12-12-2. Third, the Spartans and Wolverines finished their seasons in a tie for the Big Ten Championship for the first time in history. Finally, it was series victory number one for Darryl Rogers in his third attempt.

SEASON SUMMARIES:

The Spartans just kept on winning after they defeated Michigan. Darryl Rogers and his high-flying offense won every remaining game by at least twenty-four points and many were by more than thirty! The Spartan defense went into "lock-down" mode for the rest of the season. I cannot imagine a team that was playing any better than Michigan State at the end of the 1978 season. It would have been interesting to see how they would have fared in a re-match against Southern California in the Rose Bowl. Of course, we will never know, will we?

Year three of the Darryl Rogers Era was a Spartan success story. Michigan State finished with a record of 8 wins and 3 losses and went 7-1-0 in the conference. The Spartans did three things that a Michigan State team had not accomplished in one season since 1966. They beat Michigan, won seven straight games, and they won the Big Ten Championship (share). Mark Brammer and Kirk Gibson earned All-American honors for the Spartans in 1978. Darryl Rogers earned Big Ten Coach of the Year honors for MSU's brilliant season.

Bo's Wolverines picked themselves off the mat after losing to MSU and took it out on the Badgers in Wisconsin (42-0). Michigan had to finish strong, if they were to have a shot at the Big Ten championship. However, knowing what you must do and doing it are two vastly different things.

Fortunately, Michigan did what they had to do and won five more games to clinch a tie with the Spartans for the conference title. Because Michigan State was still on probation, the Wolverines got the Rose Bowl bid. And, true to form, the Wolverines lost to Southern California (17-10) to end the season with a record of 10 wins and 2 losses. Quarterback Rick Leach earned All-American honors in 1978.

There is one more thing to mention about the 1978 season. Coach Darryl Rogers attended a "Spartan Bust" event in Detroit, Michigan in December 1978. It was the first of five or six post-season events around the State of Michigan that honored Spartan football. These venues gave Michigan State coaches a chance to recognize Spartan players from various regions of the state. It was also a chance to and build MSU good-will. Darryl Rogers built a lot of good will and endeared himself to Spartan fans forever with a comment that he made at that gathering.

Dr. David J. Young, author of *Arrogance and Scheming in the Big Ten*, wrote an excellent summary about one of the most memorable phrases ever uttered by a MSU football coach. According to Young, Rogers told the Spartan gathering, "And despite beating' em on their own turf, those arrogant asses in Ann Arbor are taking our spot in Pasadena." (Young Page 71) It was the shot heard "round the State of Michigan" and halfway around the country. Of course, Coach Rogers said nothing about the NCAA probation that was the real reason for Michigan State losing the Rose Bowl spot to the Wolverines. Anyway, it was one more bit of fuel that added to the already intense flames that burned between the rival schools. Now, there was one more way for the East Lansing "farmers" fans to irritate and disrespect the fine folks from Ann Arbor! Yes, the ill-feelings between these two fine institutions of higher learning continued to intensify! Is that even possible?

Game # 72: October 6, 1979 at Spartan Stadium in East Lansing

BACKGROUND INFORMATION:

The major rules changes in 1979 centered on "rough play" and stiffer penalties for players who crossed the line of fair play. The new rules called for adding an automatic first down to defensive penalties for kicking an opponent. Spearing and blows to the head or helmet would also warrant a yardage penalty and an automatic first down. Some other rules concerned penalties on punts and kickoffs. Once the ball crossed the line of scrimmage, penalties on the receiving team would be from the spot of the foul. (*USA Today CFE*, Page 327)

Once again, Michigan began the year highly ranked and expected to battle for another Big Ten championship. Bo's outstanding work in the previous ten years required nothing less. He would continue his relentless pursuit of excellence and a bowl game victory. Of course, a national championship would also be nice, but Schembechler rarely talked about such things. Bo never bet the farm on the "mythical" national championship process. He was quite content to beat his rivals, win the Big Ten championship and beat somebody, anybody, in a bowl game.

Michigan opened at number seven in the country when they hosted Northwestern in the season opener. Bo sent his former employer home to ponder a 49-7 defeat. Week two was the second game in the renewed series with Notre Dame. The Irish, who lost to Michigan at South Bend in 1978, returned the favor by defeating Michigan (12-10) in Ann Arbor. Michigan recovered and proceeded to beat Kansas (28-7) and California (14-10) in the next two games. The Wolverines were ranked as the nation's eleventh best team heading into their game in East Lansing. Michigan was 3-1-0 and looking for some revenge against the Spartans.

Coach Darryl Rogers probably had an outstanding off-season from December 1978 to August 1979. The Spartan football program was finally off probation. Yes, life was incredibly good for Rogers and Spartan fans in 1979. The first three years of the Rogers Era at MSU were successful. Everyone in East Lansing was hoping for more of the same in 1979. Unfortunately, hoping for a good season and having one depends on a lot of factors. Michigan State graduated some all-star star players like Eddie Smith and Kirk Gibson. There was some good talent returning, but the success of the 1979 Spartan football team was anybody's guess.

The 1979 Spartan football season began with a Big Ten win over Illinois (33-16). Non-conference wins over Oregon (41-17) and Miami of Ohio (24-21) had MSU fans thinking about a Rose Bowl date in 1980. Unfortunately, the Spartans went to South Bend for game number four and the Irish sent them home with a heavy dose of "reality." The final score was not even close. Notre Dame pounded the Spartans by a score of 27-3. The sixteenth-ranked Spartans had the exact same record as Michigan at 3 wins and 1 loss. Could Darryl Rogers get his first home win against the "Arrogant Asses" and make it two in a row?

GAME SUMMARY: UM 21 MSU 7

In one of the more evenly matched games of the series, Michigan prevailed over a determined Spartan team. Both teams battled hard, but Michigan eventually wore down the Spartans to post another series victory. MSU's mauling defense slowed down the Wolverine running attack for most of the first half. Late in the second quarter, Butch Woolfolk scored on a 2-yard plunge and the extra point gave Michigan a 7-0 at halftime. (*DFP*, 10/7/1979, Page 78)

In the third quarter, MSU's Derek Hughes pounded in from 6-yards out to even the score at 7-7 when the Spartans converted the PAT. A few minutes later, Michigan quarterback, B. J. Dickey put the Wolverines back in front when he connected on a 66-yard scoring pass to Ralph Clayton. It was 14-7 in favor of Michigan heading into the final quarter. Michigan State had their chances, but Michigan stopped them at every turn. Dickey put the final nail in the Spartan coffin when he hit Anthony Carter for a 6-yard touchdown pass. Michigan's lead grew to 21-7 and that is how the game ended. (*DFP*, 10/7/1979, Page 81)

As usual, game number seventy-two was hard-hitting all the way. Michigan State got after the favored Wolverines and the game was really in doubt until the final minutes. Michigan had the edge in total offense by a margin of 366 yards to 242 yards. Interestingly, Michigan's State's passing attack only netted 186-yards as two Spartan quarterbacks combined for 6 completions in 18 pass attempts. Michigan's air attack (8 of 13 passes for 147-yards) was the reason why the Wolverines won the game. I am sure that there was plenty of blood left behind, but Michigan State probably lost a little bit more on this day! (*DFP*, 10/7/1979, Page 87)

Team	1st	2nd	3rd	4th	Final
UM	7	0	7	7	21
MSU	0	0	7	0	7

SERIES UPDATE:

The Wolverines increased their series advantage once again. Michigan's series lead now stood at 46 wins, 21 losses, and 5 ties. Once again, the Wolverines regained the trophy series lead at 13 wins, 12 losses and 2 ties. Michigan finished the decade of the Seventies with an overall record of 9 wins and 1 loss. Michigan had bragging rights for another year and there was nothing that Sparty could do about it!

SERIES MILESTONES:

Game number seventy-two marked the last game of the decade of the Seventies. It was Michigan's first "winning decade" since the 1940s. As usual, the game was played in front of a capacity crowd (79, 311) at Spartan Stadium, but it was not a record-breaker. As it turned out, this was the last game that Darryl Rogers ever coached against the "AAs" from Michigan. He finished with a series record of 1 win and 3 losses. Finally, the win was Bo Schembechler's 100th win at Michigan. Yes, a milestone win is always fun, but when it is against a rival, in his own stadium, it is even sweeter!

SEASON SUMMARIES:

Michigan kept right on rolling after their win over the Spartans. They won four more conference games and were on track for another conference championship pending the outcome against Ohio State. Unfortunately, the "Spoilermakers" did it again and Michigan left Lafayette, Indiana with a 24-21 loss. Even worse, they lost at home to Ohio State (18-15) the following week to finish the regular season at 8-3-0.

Another disappointing loss to North Carolina in the 1980 Gator Bowl put Michigan's final record at 8 wins and 4 losses for 1979. They finished in 3rd place in the Big Ten at 6 wins and 2 losses. In a bit of good news, Curtis Greer and "tackling machine" Ron Simpkins earned All-American honors in 1979.

The wheels of the MSU football bus pretty much fell off after the disappointing loss to Michigan. Apparently, the Spartans were not as good as they looked in the first three games. Several key injuries did not help either. Michigan State lost to Wisconsin, Purdue, and Ohio State before winning again. As November approached, the Spartans had a record of 3 wins and 5 losses. With three games remaining, they could still have a winning season. It looked that would happen when the Green and White footballers defeated Northwestern and Minnesota. Unfortunately, a season ending loss at Iowa (33-23) gave MSU a final record of 5 wins and 6 losses for the 1979 season. Punter Ray Stachowicz was the only Spartan to earn All-American honors in 1979.

In one of the most unusual scenarios in college football history, MSU's Athletic Director Joe Kearney resigned to take the same spot at Arizona State. Two days later, on January 18, 1980, he announced that he had "hired" Darryl Rogers to be the next coach at ASU. Just like that, Rogers was gone, and new Athletic Director Doug Weaver was looking for MSU's next football coach.

DECADE AND SERIES SUMMARY:

The decade of the Seventies brought BIG changes for both Michigan and Michigan State. In Ann Arbor, the changes were exceptionally good thanks to Bo Schembechler. The Wolverines dominated the series from 1970 to 1979. Michigan won 9 games and only lost 1 which was much better than what they did in the Fifties and Sixties. In East Lansing, the series changes were bad. Duffy lost the first three series games of the decade to Schembechler. Then, Denny Stolz lost three more. Finally, Darryl Rogers took his best shots, but only posted one win in four series games. Michigan's return to dominance was good for Michigan and bad for Michigan State.

Decade and Series Summary 1898 to 1979

Time Frame	UM Won-Lost-Tied	MSU Won-Lost-Tied
1970-1979	9-1-0	1-9-0
1898-1979	46-21-5	21-46-5

BIG TEN SUMMARY:

Now, we will a quick look at how the Wolverines and Spartans fared in Big Ten play from 1970 to 1979. The first full decade of the Bo Schembechler Era at Michigan was much better than the two previous decades in Ann Arbor. In fact, the Wolverines were greatly improved in the Seventies. Michigan more than doubled the number of conference wins from the Sixties (36) to the Seventies (79). Losses and ties were down, and the Wolverines won, or shared, seven conference titles in ten years. Michigan did not have one losing season in the Seventies compared to five in the 1960s. Even more impressive was the fact that UM's winning percentage had a three-hundred and two-point improvement under Schembechler in the 1970s (.577 to .879). It is no exaggeration to say that Michigan Athletic Director Don Canham was probably feeling good about his decision to hire "Bo Who" back in December 1968.

Big Ten Summary 1970 to 1979

Statistical Area	UM	MSU
Number of Head Coaches	1	3
Games Played	79	79
Wins	69	46
Losses	9	30
Ties	1	3
Winning Percentage	.879	.601
Winning Seasons	10	4
Losing Seasons	0	5
Even Seasons	0	1
Big Ten Championships	7	1

Duffy Daugherty's stellar career ended on a low note in 1972. Michigan State had to hire two coaches in the 1970s and neither one worked out in East Lansing. Both Denny Stolz and Darryl Rogers had short tenures which is never good for any college football program. The good news is that the Spartans had four winning conference seasons. The bad news is that they had five losing seasons. Their winning percentage dropped slightly from sixty-three percent to just over sixty percent. The East Lansing footballers did manage to share one conference championship (1978) with the hated Wolverines.

The numbers show that Michigan was the best Big Ten team in the State of Michigan in the Seventies. All the progress that the Spartans made in the Fifties and the Sixties was now overshadowed by recent history. New Athletic Director Doug Weaver had to find somebody like Don Canham did in 1969. He had to find a man who could beat Bo at the recruiting game and win against him on the field. If he did not find such a man, it would be another tough decade in East Lansing.

PROGRAM SUMMARIES:

Michigan was a consistent winner in the Seventies. In fact, Bo's regular season record in the Seventies was the best in college football. Yes, nobody did the 1970s better than Glenn Edward "Bo" Schembechler. His record of 96 wins, 10 losses, and 3 ties produced a winning percentage of almost ninety percent (.894). It is no wonder that his team finished in the top ten every year and won, or shared, seven Big Ten Championships. The only thing that kept him humble during the decade was a record of 0 wins and 6 losses in bowl games.

Meanwhile, things were not going as well in East Lansing. Duffy Daugherty's great run ended badly and neither Denny Stolz nor Darryl Rogers could match Duffy's penchant for winning. The Spartans lost ground in every positive category in the Seventies. Wins were down, even though they played thirteen more games from 1960 to 1970. The Spartans did have five winning seasons, but they also had four losing seasons. The NCAA probation kept them out of the 1979 Rose Bowl which rubbed all Spartan fans the wrong way!

After two decades of Spartan dominance, Bo Schembechler turned things back to the way they were supposed to be for the "arrogant asses" in Ann Arbor. Bo returned Michigan to the glory years of past times although he did not quite reach the heights that Duffy took the Spartans in 1965 and 1966. Bo did produce consistent winners, that is for sure. He also learned how to beat the Spartans at their own game and was able to keep Paul Bunyan in Ann Arbor for nine of the ten years of the decade.

Michigan State was making good progress under Darryl Rogers before he bolted to ASU. It was back to the drawing board for the Spartans. The next coach would have to take on Bo and Michigan if Michigan State wanted to get back to some winning ways. Everybody in East Lansing knew that the balance of power had shifted back to Ann Arbor. Would the Spartans be able to find a man who could bring the Spartan football program back to a prominent position in Eighties?

216

Program Summaries 1970 to 1979

Statistical Area	UM	MSU
Number of Head Coaches	1	3
Games Played	115	109
Wins	96	58
Losses	16	47
Ties	3	4
Winning Percentage	.847	.550
Winning Seasons	10	5
Losing Seasons	0	4
Even Seasons	0	1
National Championships	0	0
All-American Players	24	10

CHAPTER 11

Bo Time Part Two 1980 to 1989

America's colleges were enjoying some relatively "calm" years towards the end of the Seventies. Campus demonstrations, protest and riots were down. School enrollments and degrees awarded were on the rise. College football continued to grow in popularity because of the way the players were playing the game, but also because of the way television was broadcasting them. Thanks to television, coaching salaries continued to grow to the point where many of the top coaches in America were making more than the college presidents that they worked for! College football still had plenty of challenges as the Eighties approached, but nothing that was holding the game back.

Game #73: October 11, 1980 at Michigan Stadium in Ann Arbor

BACKGROUND INFORMATION:

The NCAA Rules Committee made a few changes in 1980, but nothing earth shaking. First, they expanded the definition of "chop blocks" to clarify what coaches should teach and what officials should penalize. Second, offensive players could fully extend their arms during "retreat blocking" to allow lineman to better protect their quarterbacks and improve the passing game. Third, a "facemask" penalty could also be called on the defense for grabbing a player's helmet or facemask. (*USA Today CFE*, Page 337)

Michigan and Michigan State started the decade of the Eighties in vastly different ways. Bo Schembechler was back on the sidelines for his twelfth season in 1980. Muddy Waters was hired to replace Darryl Rogers who left abruptly for Arizona State in January 1980. The likeable Waters was the fourth man to lead Spartan football fortunes in nine seasons which is never good! Would Muddy Waters be able to stay awhile and build something special again in East Lansing?

Frank "Muddy" Waters was the next man up for the Spartans in 1980. He played full-back for Michigan State from 1946 to 1949. He became a coaching legend at Hillsdale College where he won almost seventy-four percent (.739) of his games from 1954 to 1974. He was in the fifth year of building a successful program at Saginaw Valley State College when the Spartans came calling for his coaching services. Muddy Waters had a job that was simple, just not easy. First, he had to play by the rules. Second, he had to build a winning Big Ten program. Third, he had to beat Bo Schembechler and his hated Wolverines frequently. Of course, one win over UM would be a good start.

The Waters Era began in Champaign, Illinois when the Spartans faced off against Illinois. It did not start well since MSU lost to the Fighting Illini (20-17). Game two, at Oregon, was even worse. The Ducks pounded the Spartans by a score of 35-7 and MSU was 0-2-0 in the early weeks of the Muddy's tenure. Coach Waters earned his first win against Western Michigan University with a 33-7 victory in his first game at Spartan Stadium. A tough home loss to Notre Dame (26-21) put the Spartans at 1-3-0 heading into Michigan Week. Things did not look good for Muddy and his Spartans for game number five in Ann Arbor.

Michigan was expected to field another outstanding football team in year twelve of the Schembechler Era. Bo had plenty of returning talent, but questions still lingered about the way the 1979 season ended. The Wolverines lost three straight games to end that regrettable season. The 1979 campaign was Bo's "worst" at Michigan. His team ended the season at 8 wins and 4 losses and lost another bowl game to an un-ranked North Carolina team. Some people were already questioning if it might be time for Bo to hang up his whistle.

The eleventh-ranked Wolverines hosted Northwestern in the season opener and won by a score of 17-10. Yes, it was not pretty, but it was still a win, and a conference win at that! However, a heartbreaking loss to Notre Dame (29-27) in week two got Bo's attention! Michigan had lost four of the last five games going back to the 1979 season. Schembechler had seen enough. Bo took a page out of Duffy's "playbook" and decided to scrap the option offense that had served him so well since the early Seventies.

Instead, he committed to a more balance attack that would showcase the skills of a quarterback named John Wangler and a receiver named Anthony Carter. Oh yes, he had a running back named Butch Woolfolk who was pretty good. Bo's "experiment" resulted in a home loss at the hands of South Carolina (17-14). Michigan was 1-2-0 after 3 games which is something that had never happened in the Bo Era! The new Wolverine offense "woke up" in week four against California and Bo's Boys won easily by a score of 38-13. Unranked Michigan was 2-2-0 heading into Michigan State Week. Would Bo Schembechler's new offense produce enough points to whip the Spartans?

GAME SUMMARY: MSU 23 UM 27

Game number seventy-three was played in front of a record-breaking series crowd (by 131 people) in Ann Arbor. It was Michigan's tenth win in the last eleven games against the Spartans. It was another classic "blood battle" between two intense rivals.

Michigan kicker Ali Haji-Sheikh opened the scoring in the first quarter with a 25-yard field goal. A few minutes later, MSU tied the game (3-3) on Morten Anderson's 49-yard field goal. Lawrence Ricks gave Michigan another lead with a 1-yard touchdown run and Haji-Sheikh's extra point made it 10-3. MSU quarterback John Leister scored on a 7-yard run in the second quarter. Andersen's extra point tied the game at 10-10. Later in the quarter, Andersen and Haji-Sheikh traded field goals. The first half ended at 13-13. (*DFP*, 10/12/1980, Page 58)

A big third quarter mistake by the Spartans changed the momentum of this close game. With the game tied at 13-13 in the third quarter, the MSU defense drew a roughing penalty (15-yards) on a successful field goal by Haji-Sheikh. Bo took the three points off the scoreboard and let his offense go for more. John Wangler made Schembechler look like a genius when he threw a touchdown pass to Anthony Carter later in the series. Wangler also tossed another scoring strike to Craig Dunaway in the fourth quarter. The Spartans scored a late touchdown, but Michigan's defense closed out the game. In one of the more exciting games in series history, Michigan won by a final score of 27-23. (*DFP*, 10/12/1980, Page 58)

Team	1st	2nd	3rd	4th	Final
MSU	3	10	7	7	23
UM	10	3	7	7	27

SERIES UPDATE:

Seventy-three games were now in the books and Michigan remained in complete control of the series. The Wolverines lopsided advantage grew to 47 wins, 21 losses, and 5 ties. Michigan jumped ahead in the Eighties with a record of 1-0-0. The Maize and Blue footballers also increased their advantage in the Paul Bunyan Trophy series to 14 wins, 12 losses, and 2 ties. The Spartans could not dwell too much on the disappointing loss because they had to get ready to make a better showing against Wisconsin on Homecoming Day.

SERIES MILESTONES:

Game number seventy-three produced many new milestones. This was the first series game for Coach Waters and his first loss. Yes, like every other Aggie/Spartan coach before him, he lost his first series game. Of course, the large crowd (105,263) broke the old series record of 105,132 that was set in 1978. Muddy Waters "struck out" in his first "at-bat" against Bo and Michigan. The good news was that his Spartans made life difficult for the favored Wolverines. This game marked the first time that both teams scored in every quarter. Coach Waters had some work to do against Michigan, but it would have to wait until next year. Morten Andersen's 57-yard field goal was also a series record.

SEASON SUMMARIES:

The Spartans played hard the following week against the Badgers, but the 1980 Homecoming Day crowd did not go home happy since the Spartans lost (17-7). Michigan State could not get untracked and lost two more games to Purdue (36-25) and Ohio State (48-16).

221

MSU finally got a short streak going—winning two straight over Northwestern (42-10) and Minnesota (30-12). The 1980 season ended with a "thud" at Spartan Stadium after Iowa shut out the Spartans (41-0). It was ugly. The Spartans ended the first season of the Muddy Waters Era with a record of 3 wins and 8 losses. They won two of eight games in conference play and finished in ninth place. As it turned out the most important man on the MSU team in 1980 was the doctor. Unfortunately, he could not "heal" the nineteen Spartans who lost playing time during the season. It is hard enough to win when everybody is healthy. It is even harder when everybody is not healthy. Muddy Waters did not make any excuses, but his first season at the Spartan helm was bad. The good news was that he would be back again to get things going in the right direction. Spartan punter Ray Stachowicz earned All-American honors for the second straight season

Michigan's offense continued to score points and the defense did not allow more than fourteen points in any game for the rest of the season. In fact, they shut out three straight teams at one point and did not allow a touchdown in the final twenty-two quarters of the season! After the close win against MSU, the Wolverines won five straight blowouts. The Wolverines finished the 1980 season with a win at Ohio State to post a perfect record of 8-0-0 in the conference. Better yet, Michigan defeated Washington in the 1981 Rose Bowl to give Bo his first bowl win. After twelve years, it was the first time that Bo ended a Michigan football season with a victory. The Wolverines ended the 1980 season with an overall record of 10 wins and 2 losses. Michigan's outstanding center, George Lilja, and receiver Anthony Carter both earned All-American honors for the 1980 football season.

Game # 74: October 10, 1981 at Spartan Stadium in East Lansing

BACKGROUND INFORMATION:

The NCAA rules committee made two important changes to college football in 1981. First, the penalty for "holding" was reduced from fifteen-yards to ten-yards. Players were not allowed to step on another player or receive assistance to elevate high enough to block a field goal or point after touchdown kick. Otherwise, the game was doing fine. *(USA Today CFE*, Page 348)

One big change that took place in the Big Ten Conference was the addition of another conference game. All teams would now play nine games during the conference season. Things just got tougher in the Big Ten!

Once again, expectations were high for Bo's Wolverines in 1981. In fact, the pollsters did not think any team was better than Michigan. The Wolverines started the season as the top-ranked team in the nation when they went to Wisconsin. When they returned from a 21-14 defeat, the Wolverines were in a free-fall that took them down to number eleven in the country.

The eleventh-ranked Wolverines hosted the top-ranked Irish in week two. Michigan turned the tables on Notre Dame and won a big game (25-7). Bo's Wolverines won two more games against Navy and Indiana to push their record to 3 wins and 1 loss. The sixth-ranked Wolverines looked good heading into MSU Week. Could they make it four straight wins over the Spartans?

Frank Waters played fullback at Michigan State. Yes, he was a tough guy. If he were not so tough, Muddy would not have made it through his first season in 1980. Nobody in East Lansing was happy about Muddy's first season as head coach. Mr. Waters knew how to coach. He was still confident that he could turn things around at Michigan State. Unfortunately, the Spartan faithful were already losing faith. Yes, the 1981 season was critically important for Frank Waters and his MSU Spartans.

Michigan State did not start well in 1981. They lost their first two games to Illinois (27-17) and Ohio State (27-13). They barely defeated a Bowling Green (10-7) team coached by former Spartan leader, Denny Stolz. The victory over the Falcons did not give the fans much hope for the rest of the season. Notre Dame beat the Spartans in week four by a score of 20-7. For the second year in a row, the Spartans entered Michigan Week with a record of 1 win and 3 losses. Oh boy, things did not look good for the Green and White footballers.

GAME SUMMARY: UM 38 MSU 20

The sixth-ranked Wolverines prevailed again in series game number seventy-four and it was not that close. Michigan scored first, last and added some more points in the middle. The Spartans opened the scoring midway through the first quarter on a 5-yard pass from Bryan Clark to Otis Grant. Super kicker Morten Andersen made the extra point to give the Spartans a 7-0 lead. Michigan got a" two-point gift" from their gracious hosts when a bad snap resulted in a safety. The first quarter ended with MSU leading 7-2. (*DFP*, 10/11/1981, Page 85)

Both teams picked up the pace in the second quarter. Anthony Carter scored on a 23-yard run and quarterback Steve Smith rushed for a 1-yard score. Ali Haji-Sheikh kicked both extra points. Meanwhile, the Spartan offense was also busy scoring ten points of their own. Andersen kicked a 26-yard field goal and Clark threw his second touchdown pass (28-yards) to Ted Jones. With Anderson's extra point, MSU led 17-16 at halftime. (*DFP*, 10/11/1981, Page 85)

Michigan's Lawrence Ricks rushed for a 3-yard score in the third quarter and the Wolverines made a 2-point conversion to take a 24-17 lead. Andersen kicked a field goal to narrow UM's advantage to 24-20 at the end of the third quarter. The Wolverines did all the scoring in the final quarter thanks to Steve Smith, Lawrence Ricks, and Ali Haji-Sheikh. Michigan left East Lansing with a big 38-20 victory. Go Blue! (*DFP*, 10/11/1981, Page 85)

Technically, the Wolverines ran the ball down the Spartan's throats. Butch Woolfolk had 39 carries for 253-yards to set a series rushing record. The Wolverines racked up a total of 423-yards on the ground and had five rushing touchdowns. Michigan State could not run effectively against the Michigan. The Spartans tried to pass their way to victory. That did not work out too well either as the Wolverines picked off four MSU passes. It was one of those games where Michigan had a good day of football and the Spartans did not. Simple as that! (*DFP*, 10/11/1981, Page 85)

Team	1st	2nd	3rd	4th	Final
UM	2	14	8	14	38
MSU	7	10	3	0	20

SERIES UPDATE:

Once again, the Spartans went to their locker room with a big frown on their faces. They lost another home game to the hated Wolverines. All the losing to Michigan was getting really, really old—again! Michigan added one more victory to their win total. The Wolverine series advantage grew to 48 wins, 21 losses, and 5 ties. Bo's footballers were undefeated in the Eighties against the Spartans (2-0-0). Michigan increased their advantage in the trophy series to 15 wins, 12 losses, and 2 ties. The hated Wolverines retained "bragging rights" and recruiting advantages for another year. Hail to the Victors!

SERIES MILESTONES:

Game number seventy-four was the second series game for Coach Muddy Waters who was now 0-2-0 against Michigan. He had been to bat twice against the Maize and Blue and he struck out again. Would Muddy get a chance to bat a third time? Michigan's win at East Lansing was their tenth series "road" win.

SEASON SUMMARIES:

The Wolverines rose one spot in the rankings after defeating the Spartans. Bo's fifth-ranked Maize and Blue footballers hosted an Iowa team coached by the new guy on the Big Ten block. Hayden Fry's twelfth-ranked Hawkeyes made a big impression on everyone in Ann Arbor after he left town with a 9-7 win. Michigan recovered from that shocking loss to win four straight games. Unfortunately, the Wolverines lost to OSU to end the regular season at 8 wins and 3 losses. The good news was that the Wolverines played UCLA in the Bluebonnet Bowl and won by a score of 33-14. After seven straight bowl losses, Bo won two bowl games in the same calendar year! Michigan ended the 1981 season with a final record of 9-3-0. They finished with a conference record of 6 wins and 3 ties which earned them a third-place tie. Five of Bo's Michigan Men (Kurt Becker, Ed Muransky, Bubba Paris, Butch Woolfolk, and Anthony Carter) earned All-American honors in 1981. Interestingly, Iowa shared the conference title with Ohio State and lost the Rose Bowl to Washington in January 1982.

Michigan State went through a "tale-of-two-seasons" in 1981. After losing to the Wolverines, again, the Spartans had a record of 1 win and 4 losses. With the brutal part of their schedule behind them, the MSU footballers won four of six games to finish the season with a record of 5 wins and 6 losses. Of course, this was an improvement from year one of the Waters Era, but it was nothing to brag about. Spartan fans were still grumbling after another disappointing football season. After two seasons, Muddy Waters was sitting on an overall record of 8 wins and 14 losses. His Big Ten record was slightly better at 6-11-0. It was getting harder to come to a Spartan football game without a bag over your head. Michigan State fans wanted things to get turned around—yesterday! There was no pressure on the former Spartan football star to turn Spartan football fortunes around, absolutely no pressure at all!

Game # 75: October 9, 1982 at Michigan Stadium in Ann Arbor

BACKGROUND INFORMATION:

The NCAA implemented thirty-two (yes, 32) rules changes in 1982! It was the biggest rules "make-over" in the history of college football. Some of the biggest changes included further clarification of the facemask rules. Game officials could now distinguish between an 'incidental" face mask (5-yard penalty) and a "deliberate" face mask (15-yard penalty). Also, pass interference could only occur on catchable throws. Players would no longer be able to use adhesive material, like "stickum" on their hands, or body, to catch, or hold the football. Finally, teams could ground the ball "intentionally" to stop the clock. (*USA Today CFE*, Page 357)

Frank "Muddy" Waters was back again in 1982. A lot of the fine folks in East Lansing were not happy with the lack of progress in his first two years at MSU. He was entering the third year of a five-year contract with Michigan State. Maybe Waters thought he had time to turn things around. About half of the Spartan team was made up of players that Waters and his staff had recruited. It was time for them to step up and play for Muddy and MSU!

Michigan State began the season at Illinois for the second time in Muddy's three-year tenure and it was not good. Illinois defeated the Spartans (23-16). Things did not get any easier, or better, in week two since Ohio State came to town and left with a 31-10 victory. The Spartans played well against a good Miami of Florida team, but still lost by a score of 25-22. Maybe the MSU footballers could get a win against Notre Dame and get some momentum for a conference win over the Wolverines. Or maybe not! The Irish came to East Lansing and left with a close win (21-13) over the Spartans. For the first time since 1917, the East Lansing footballers lost their first four games of the season. Michigan State was 0-4-0 heading into their annual battle with the Wolverines. Nobody favoring the Green and White was looking forward to this game.

The main topic of conversation in Ann Arbor in early January 1982 was whether Bo would leave Michigan for bucket-loads of money at Texas A & M. As it turned out, loyalty trumped money and Schembechler decided to stay at Michigan. He was ready to show everyone that his Wolverines were good enough to compete for a Big Ten Championship again after falling to a third-place tie in 1981.

Bo Schembechler had some talented players returning on both sides of the ball. Most "experts" figured that Michigan could compete for another championship. Ohio State and Iowa figured to be in the mix as well. The "Big Two" were starting to get more competition so it made things more interesting for everyone. Bo was not really worried about anybody else, just Michigan. He knew if his Wolverines played "their game" they could beat anybody.

Twelfth-ranked Michigan started the 1982 season with a solid win over Wisconsin by a score of 20-9. The Wolverines jumped up two spots in the rankings before they went to South Bend to play Notre Dame. The twentieth-ranked Irish were the better team on September 18, 1982 and tenth-ranked Michigan went home with a 23-17 loss. UCLA (ranked #12) came to Ann Arbor the following week to face Michigan (#20) and the Bruins went home with a 31-17 win. Bo got his football team back on track with a win over Indiana (24-10) to put the Wolverines at 2-2-0 heading into the annual "blood-bath" with MSU.

GAME SUMMARY: MSU 17 UM 31

Once again, Michigan defeated Michigan State and it was not pretty! The Wolverines built a 21-3 lead at halftime and coasted for the rest of the game. Michigan quarterback Steve Smith opened the scoring with a 2-yard touchdown run. Ali Haji-Sheikh's extra point kick made it 7-0 and that is how the first quarter ended. Spartan kicker Ralf Mojsiejenko's made a 31-yard field goal early in the second quarter to reduce the score to 7-3. Michigan scored two touchdowns to push their halftime advantage to 21-3. Lawrence Ricks ran for a 7-yard touchdown and Smith tossed a 7-yard scoring pass to tight end Craig Dunaway. Haji-Sheikh added two more extra points. (*DFP,* 10/10/1982, Page 43)

The Wolverines increased their lead by ten more points in the third quarter on another Haji-Sheikh field goal (27-yards) and Smith is third touchdown pass to Anthony Carter (14-yards). Haji-Sheik's fourth PAT kick made it 31-3 at the end of the third quarter. Michigan State posted two touchdowns thanks to senior running back Darrin McClelland in the final quarter, but it was not enough. (*DFP,* 10/12/1980, Page 58)

This game was clearly a case of two football teams going in completely different directions. Michigan was still on the road to a conference championship and Michigan State was sitting at 0 wins and 5 losses. Clearly, MSU was a team, a program, in disarray. MSU was a football entity that was spinning out of control. Where would the Spartans land in 1982?

Team	1st	2nd	3rd	4th	Final
MSU	0	3	0	14	17
UM	7	14	10	0	31

SERIES UPDATE:

The 1982 version of the Mitten State "bowl" game was another huge setback for the Spartan football program. They probably lost a lot of hope after this game as well as some more blood. The hated Wolverines had won four straight games against the farmers and twelve of the last thirteen games. Michigan's hefty advantage grew again. It was now 49 wins for the Wolverines against 21 victories for the Spartans. Five games out of seventy-five had been ties. Michigan's series game record remained perfect in the Eighties at 3-0-0. Once again, Paul Bunyan remained in Ann Arbor. Rumor had it that Paul hired a real estate agent to find him a permanent residence in the Tree City—yikes! Michigan's trophy series lead grew to 16 wins, 12 losses, and 2 ties.

SERIES MILESTONES:

The seventy-fifth series game was a milestone all by itself! It was also the thirtieth game of the Paul Bunyan Trophy series. The Ann Arbor throng of 106,113 was another record-breaker! It marked the first "blood-fest" gathering to exceed the 106K mark. Game number three of the Muddy Waters Era also proved to be his last. Frank Waters was inducted into the College Football Hall of Fame for his work in "small-college" football at Hillsdale and Saginaw Valley.

Unfortunately, Muddy's work at Michigan State was not a bright part of his football legacy. Coach Waters went to bat three times against the hated Wolverines. He went to bat three times against Michigan and struck out every time. In baseball, three strikes always make an OUT! This time, in football, three strikeouts meant that Frank "Muddy" Waters was "out" at Michigan State University.

SEASON SUMMARIES:

Michigan State's football season continued to get worse after losing to Michigan. The Spartans lost two more games to Wisconsin (24-23) and Purdue (24-21) and pushed their winless streak to seven games (0-7-0). The long-awaited win finally came at Indiana. MSU defeated the Hoosiers 22-14 which removed the threat of a winless season. The Spartans split their last two games—winning against Minnesota (26-7) but losing the last game of the Waters Era to Iowa (24-18). Yes, Muddy Waters saved his worst season (2-9-0) for his last. The former Spartan player loved his university, but he finished with an overall record of 10 wins and 23 losses. His Big Ten record ended at 8 wins and 18 losses. Worse yet, he was 0-3-0 against Michigan. Even though he had a five-year contract, Doug Weaver had no choice but to pay Muddy and send him into retirement. Another disappointing chapter in MSU football history had been written. It was time to find a new leader. The Spartan football train had rolled off the tracks again. It was time to find a man who would get the train re-positioned and moving in the right direction again. Where would Doug Weaver find such a man?

The Wolverines remained undefeated in the Big Ten Conference after their win over the Spartans. Bo's Michigan Men kept on winning and posted five more conference wins to push their Big Ten record to 8-0-0 heading into the Ohio State game. The Buckeyes had already lost two games. Michigan would win the conference title even if they lost to OSU. That is exactly what happened as Ohio State beat Michigan (24-14).

Michigan went to the Rose Bowl and lost another game to UCLA (24-14). It was the first time that Bo ever lost twice to the same team (UCLA) in the same season. The Maize and Blue footballers finished the 1982 season with a final record of 8 wins and 4 losses. Anthony Carter, Michigan's super-receiver, earned All-American honors for the third straight season. He joined Bennie Oosterbaan as the only two Wolverines to accomplish this amazing feat!

Game # 76: October 8, 1983 at Spartan Stadium in East Lansing

BACKGROUND INFORMATION:

The 1983 season was also the birth of Proposition 48 legislation that was designed to establish minimum floors for high school grades and standardized test scores for student-athletes who wanted to compete at the college level. To be eligible for college athletics, athletes had to have a minimum high school Grade point average (GPA) and achieve a minimum score on the Scholastic Aptitude Test (SAT) or the American College Test (ACT). The minimum goals would not affect prospective athletes until 1986. (*USA Today CFE*, Page 369)

In one final development, the Big Ten Conference become the first conference in NCAA football to expand their officiating crews from six members to seven. Hopefully, it would lead to better officiating and fewer "missed" calls, or maybe not!

Bo Schembechler's fifteenth season unfolded the way they usually did during his coaching tenure. Expectations were high because Bo continued to attract outstanding players from Michigan, Ohio, Florida, and other places as well. Bo's track record at Michigan made him extremely hard to beat on the recruiting trails, especially in Michigan. The Wolverines were expected to be strong on offense, defense, and special teams, No surprises in Ann Arbor!

Bo's sixth-ranked Wolverines opened the 1983 season with a 20-17 victory over Washington State. It was not very pretty and it was not dominating. The pollsters dropped Michigan to a number eight ranking the next week. Things got worse the next week when the Wolverines traveled to Seattle to play sixteenth-ranked Washington and lost (25-24). Coach Schembechler was not a happy man on the long plane ride home. Michigan played better at Wisconsin. Bo's mood improved after a 38-21 win over the Badgers. After a 43-18 drubbing of Indiana, Michigan was ranked fourteenth and sitting on a record of 3 wins and 1 loss. It was time to focus on Michigan State and their new coach!

It took MSU Athletic Director Doug Weaver about three weeks to find his next coach. George Perles, another former Spartan football player, made quite a name for himself in the National Football League. He also coached for Duffy during some of Daugherty's best years. George Perles was a "defensive genius" who built the Pittsburgh Steeler defense into multiple Super Bowl Champions. He loved his alma mater. Perles embraced the challenge of re-building the Spartan football program. Coach Perles knew what he was up against and he was in it for the long haul. Since he was hired in early December 1982, he still had time to recruit. Coach Perles, with his NFL pedigree, put together a talented class of 32 recruits. (Stabley, Page 304)

The George Perles Era started well with a 23-17 win over Colorado. Week two was even better after the Spartans defeated Notre Dame (28-23) in South Bend! Whoa, talk about making a good impression on Spartan fans! Game three turned out to be his first loss. Illinois played well in Spartan Stadium and went home with a 20-10 win. Coach Perles was still wondering how good his team really was. A 29-29 tie against Purdue in week four did not teach him much. The Spartans had 2 wins, 1 loss and 1 tie heading into Michigan Week. Time to teach the boys how to button their chin straps a little tighter. This one would be a real head-knocker!

GAME SUMMARY: UM 42 MSU 0

The first series game of the George Perles Era ended a lot like Biggie Munn's first game against Michigan. It was bad, but not as bad as the 55-0 pounding that Fritz Crisler gave Coach Munn in 1947. The Wolverines did just about everything right in this game and the Spartans did just about everything wrong. Yes, it was ugly. Michigan scored on their first four possessions and had a 25-0 lead before the Green and White footballers knew what hit them. Michigan State played without starting quarterback Dave Yarema.

Bob Bergeron kicked two first half field goals (38 yards and 41-yards) along with one extra point. Tight end Milt Carthens grabbed a 23-yard scoring pass from Steve Smith. Dan Rice (1-yard) and Rick Rogers (8-yards) ran for two more scores. The second half was a little better for the MSU defense, but not by much. Bergeron kicked his third field goal (23-yards) and two more extra points after touchdown runs by Smith (3-yards) and Ben Logue (2-yards). It was an awfully long day for George Perles and his defense. (*DFP*, 10/11/1983, Page 91)

The Spartans only managed 111-yards of offense. Michigan quarterback Steve Smith outgained the Spartans all by himself with 149-yards in the air on 11 pass completions in 16 attempts. He ran for a touchdown and threw for another. The Wolverines rolled up 292-yards on the ground and controlled the game for all four periods. Both teams lost one fumble, but MSU shot themselves in both feet with two interceptions. (*DFP*, 10/11/1983, Page 91)

George Perles knew that things had not gone well against Michigan recently and now he knew why! Michigan ran better, passed better, blocked better, and tackled better. Well, you get the picture! Perles would use this game as a benchmark to measure his future progress. He had a good memory. Coach Perles would make sure that he remembered being embarrassed in East Lansing by Bo Schembechler and his Wolverines. Yes, there was lots of work to do for George Perles and his Spartans.

Team	1st	2nd	3rd	4th	Final
UM	9	16	3	14	42
MSU	0	0	0	0	0

SERIES UPDATE:

After seventy-six games, Michigan and Michigan State were headed in different directions. Michigan was marching for another Big Ten Championship and the Spartans were heading down the road to the bottom third of the conference. The Wolverines now had an outstanding record of 50 wins, 21 losses, and 5 ties. The overmatched Spartans had now lost five straight games to Michigan. Rumor had it that Paul Bunyan had no idea where East Lansing was since he had not been back to stay since 1978. Michigan remained undefeated in the Eighties at 4-0-0. The Maize and Blue footballers increased their trophy series advantage to 17 wins, 12 losses, and 2 ties. George Perles, and company, would have to wait another year before they could earn series "bragging rights" again.

SERIES MILESTONES:

The seventy-sixth game of the series produced a few more milestones that need to be mentioned. First, Michigan became the first series team to win fifty games. Second, it was the first series game for George Perles and, of course, his first series loss. Third, Michigan's shutout win was their twenty-fifth series whitewash which was a series record. Although it was not a series milestone, Michigan coach Bo Schembechler won his 100th Big Ten game with the decisive win.

SEASON SUMMARIES:

Bo Schembechler's football machine gathered more momentum after their big win over MSU. The Wolverines rolled through Northwestern (35-0) and beat Iowa on Homecoming Day (16-13). Bo got a big shocker the next week when the eight-ranked Wolverines traveled to Champaign to play the ninth-ranked Fighting Illini. Coach Mike White, who had replaced Gary Moeller, made sure his team was ready. Illinois shut down Michigan and sent Bo home to ponder a 16-6 defeat! Schembechler helped his Wolverines return to their winning ways with victories over Purdue (42-10), Minnesota (58-10) and Ohio State (24-21). Michigan finished the regular season with a record of 9 wins and 2 losses. Unfortunately, their conference record of 8 wins and 1 loss was only good for second place. Mike White's Illinois football team posted a perfect record of 9-0-0 to claim the Big Ten Championship and the Rose Bowl bid. Michigan lost their first Sugar Bowl game to Bo Jackson and Auburn (9-7). Tom Dixon and Stefan Humphries earned All-American honors for the 1983 season.

Michigan State played a little better after losing to the Wolverines, but not well enough to win the next two games. MSU lost to Indiana (24-12) and Ohio State (21-11) to push their record to 2 wins, 4 losses and 1 tie heading into Homecoming Week. George Perles made sure his footballers were ready for Minnesota. He earned his first Homecoming Day victory over the Gophers (34-10). The Spartans beat Northwestern the next week by a score of 9-3. Things were looking better for the Green and White, but the season ended badly with two more losses to Iowa (12-6) and Wisconsin (32-0).

Year one of the George Perles Era at Michigan State ended with a record of 4 wins, 6 losses and 1 tie. The Spartans completed Big Ten play with a record of 2 wins, 6 losses, and 1 tie. (MSU finished in seventh place) Yes, the 1983 season was a slight improvement over 1982, but it was not a winning season. The only good news in 1983 was the All-American selections of linebacker Carl Banks and punter Ralf Mojsiejenko. George Perles probably learned a lot during the 1983 season. Yes, the biggest room in the Spartan football building was the room for improvement. George Perles knew what he had to do. He just had to figure out how to do it.

Game # 77: October 6, 1984 at Michigan Stadium in Ann Arbor

BACKGROUND INFORMATION:

The NCAA only made one important change to the rules in 1984. Any kickoff that went out of the end zone would be spotted at the thirty-yard line instead of the twenty-yard line. Yes, kicking teams were going to be "penalized" ten yards for having a powerful kicker. An interesting rule change, don't you think? (*USA Today CFE*, Page 382)

George Perles promised that things would be better in 1984, but he did not really say how much better. He did not predict a conference championship for his young football team which was a good idea. He just knew that more improvements were on the way in East Lansing. Michigan State started year two of the Perles Era with a win at Colorado (24-21). Unfortunately, they lost the next game to Notre Dame (24-20).

Week three was even worse as Illinois hammered the Spartans by a score of 40-7! Michigan State played hard in week four but lost a close one to Purdue (13-10). The Spartans had a record of 1 win and 3 losses heading into Michigan Week. Things did not look good for the Green and White.

The Wolverines entered Bo's sixteenth season with a lot of question marks. Of course, everyone knew what to expect from a Schembechler team—good defense, strong running game, and good special teams. However, there was a big question about the quarterback position. Michigan began the season as the fourteenth-ranked team in the country, but they would have earned a higher ranking if the quarterback position were not so unsettled. Schembechler thought he had a promising quarterback in a guy named Jim Harbaugh.

All Jim Harbaugh did in his first game was lead the Wolverines to a 22-14 upset of the top-ranked Miami Hurricanes. Wow! Michigan jumped to number three when they hosted sixteenth-ranked Washington in week two. The Husky defense caused all kinds of problems for young Harbaugh and the defense was not as sharp as expected. The result was a 20-11 loss to the Huskies. Michigan was even at 1-1-0 to start the season. Then, they won two close games against Wisconsin (20-14) and Indiana (14-6) to push their record to 3 wins and 1 loss. Michigan was now the thirteenth-ranked team in the country. Time to get ready for another visit by the Green and White footballers from East Lansing.

GAME SUMMARY: MSU 19 UM 7

As always, the fired-up Spartans gave the Wolverines all they could handle in this classic in-state battle. Game number seventy-seven was played in front of another huge crowd (105,612), but it was not a record-breaker.

The Spartans jumped out to a 13-0 lead after a Carl Butler touchdown run (1-yard) and an 87-yard punt return by Bobby Morse. Fullback Eddie Garrett put Michigan on the board in the second period and Bob Bergeron's extra point made it 13-7 at halftime. (*DFP*, 10/7/1984, Page 53) Michigan State's defense played well for the entire game. Of course, things got a lot easier in the third quarter after Jim Harbaugh left the game with an injury. He was trying to lead his team to the tying touchdown in a 13-7 game. As it turned out, he tried to recover a teammates fumble and broke his left arm in the process. Michigan's back-up quarterbacks (Chris Zurbrugg and Russ Rein) were constantly harassed and pressured by the aggressive Perles defense. Spartan kicker Ralf Mojsiejenko kicked two second half field goals to seal MSU's upset victory. (*DFP*, 10/7/1984, Page 53)

Michigan State quarterback Dave Yarema (who missed the 1983 game due to injury) was one of the Spartans to star on this day. He completed 18 of 27 passes for 180-yards. His crisp passing opened things up for the running game. Michigan State rolled up 303-yards of offense and controlled the ball for 34-minutes of the game. Michigan's vaunted running game was held to a mere 119-yards. The Wolverines averaged just 3.2 yards per play which usually does not lead to victory. The biggest difference in the game turned out to be special teams play. Spartan special teams scored 12 of the 19 points in the game which proved to be the margin of victory. Bottom line—the stingy Spartan defense did not allow many yards and they picked off three Michigan passes.

The Wolverine offense only earned one (1) first down in the final twenty-two minutes of the game. Bottom line—Michigan State was the better team on this day in all three phases of the game. (*DFP*, 10/7/1984, Page 53)

Team	1st	2nd	3rd	4th	Final
MSU	7	6	3	3	19
UM	0	7	0	0	7

SERIES UPDATE:

For the first time since 1978, the Spartans left Ann Arbor with a victory. The MSU footballers savored the opportunity to rescue Paul Bunyan Trophy from those hated Wolverines. Although Michigan still held a big series advantage at 50 wins, 22 losses, and 5 ties, it did not matter. Michigan's record for the Eighties slipped to 4 wins and 1 loss. Michigan State climbed back in the trophy series which now stood at 17-13-2 in favor of the Wolverines. Michigan State's players, coaches, and fans started enjoying their hard earned "bragging rights" as soon as the game was over. It would not stop until October 12, 1985! Go Green! Go White!

SERIES MILESTONES:

There were a few milestones to mention about game number seventy-seven, First, Coach George Perles got his first series win over the hated Wolverines. Second, it was the first, and only, time that a series coach (Bo Schembechler) lost seven times on the same day. Yes, he lost the game to MSU, it was a Big Ten game which counts as another loss. Schembechler also lost a rival game, he lost "bragging rights," he lost his recruiting advantage for a year and he lost his quarterback for the rest of the 1984 season. Finally, he lost possession of the Paul Bunyan Trophy for the first time since 1978. Other than those seven losses, it was a great day for Coach Schembehler. One more note to mention was how the seasons ended for both teams. For the first time in their history, both Michigan and Michigan State finished a football season with the exact same records in the same way. Michigan ended with a record of 6 wins and 6 losses and ended at 5-4-0 in the Big Ten just like Michigan State. Another similarity was that both teams lost their bowl game to end the season on a bad note in 1984. Finally, Bobby Morse's 87-yard punt return was a series record.

SEASON SUMMARIES:

Coach George Perles did not have a lot of time gloat over his "upset" win over Michigan. He enjoyed the win, I will promise you that, but he had work to do. The Spartans made it two wins in a row with a 13-6 decision over Indiana. MSU's short winning streak came to an end with a tough loss to Ohio State (23-20). Michigan State won their next three games over Minnesota (20-13), Northwestern (27-10), and Iowa (17-16). Unfortunately, they ran out of magic in Madison and lost to the Badgers (20-10). The good news was that they had a winning regular season record of 6 wins and 5 losses. The bad news was that they finished at 6-6-0 after losing the Cherry Bowl to Army (10-6). No Spartans earned first-team All-American honors in 1984.

Bo Schembechler had a BIG problem after losing to MSU. He had to find a quarterback to replace Jim Harbaugh—and fast! It looked like the season might turn out okay after Michigan defeated Northwestern (31-0) on Homecoming Day. Hayden Fry, and his Hawkeyes, were ready for Michigan's inexperienced quarterbacks the next week. Michigan left Iowa City on the short end of a 26-0 drubbing. It was only the second time that the Wolverines had been shut out in Bo's tenure. Russ Rein and Chris Zurbrugg did their best, but lady luck was not on Michigan's side in 1984. After losing to Iowa, Michigan beat Illinois by a score of 26-18, but lost a close one at Purdue (31-29). The Michigan seniors won their last game at Michigan Stadium with a 31-7 victory over Minnesota. General Bo's troops played hard but lost at Ohio State (24-17). The good news was that the 6-5-0 Wolverines were invited to play in the Holiday Bowl The bad news was that they lost another heartbreaker to eventual national champion Brigham Young University (24-17). Michigan's final record of 6 wins and 6 losses also meant that no Wolverines earned any All-American honors for the first time since 1967!

Game # 78: October 12, 1985 at Spartan Stadium in Ann Arbor

BACKGROUND INFORMATION:

Bo smiled a lot in 1985 because he had a healthy Jim Harbaugh running his offense. Bo also had some other "star" type players coming back on both sides of the ball. Schembechler thought that his Wolverines would be good enough to compete for another Big Ten Championship in 1985. However, the pollsters did not agree. Bo's Boys would have to prove their worth before anybody put them in the rankings.

A season opening win over thirteenth-ranked Notre Dame was a good start. Eleventh-ranked South Carolina hosted the Wolverines in week two and the nineteenth-ranked Wolverines beat them up by a score of 34-3. In week three, Michigan hosted their third straight ranked opponent. Maryland (#17) came to Ann Arbor to upset #12 Michigan, but it did not happen. Michigan beat the Terrapins (20-0). Wow, Bo's football team looked good heading into their Big Ten opener against Wisconsin. Michigan had risen to number five in the rankings, and they looked the part as they destroyed the Badgers (33-6). For the first time since 1978, Michigan was undefeated (4-0-0) heading into MSU Week. The Wolverines were looking to avenge their loss to the Spartans in 1984. Game on!

George Perles was back for his third season in 1985. His first two teams showed improvements each year. The good news was that his offense, defense, and special teams were getting better. Hopefully, the Spartans would continue their progress and have a winning season. Perles was not predicting any Big Ten championships just yet, but he was recruiting plenty of players who he hoped would get him a conference title—sooner than later!

For the third straight season, the Spartans began a Perles season with a win. This time MSU defeated Arizona State (12-3). Week two did not work out as well as Notre Dame beat the Green and White footballers 27-10. Michigan State barely beat Western Michigan University (7-3) but lost the next week to Iowa (35-31). George Perles probably did not know what to think about his Spartans after four games. Their record was even at 2 wins and 2 losses.

The defense had played two good games and two bad games. On offense, the Spartans only had one game over thirty points. He was hoping that he could get better play on both sides of the ball. Otherwise, it was going to be long day when Michigan came to town!

GAME SUMMARY: UM 31 MSU 0

Series game number seventy-eight went into the history books as a Mitten State mauling. The annual in-state battle drew another capacity crowd (78,235) in East Lansing. Once again, interest throughout the state drew the large crowd and the Spartans in attendance were hoping to be "dancing" in the streets after another upset victory. The Wolverines took advantage of two MSU mistakes (fumble and blocked punt) to take a 14-0 lead in the first four minutes of the game. Although no one knew at the time, the game was basically over at that point. It was another one of those games where just about everything went right for Michigan and just about everything that could go wrong, did go wrong for MSU.

Michigan's first touchdown came after a Bobby McAllister fumble. Jim Harbaugh threw a 9-yard touchdown pass to tight end Eric Kattus and the PAT kick made it 7-0. Dieter Heren blocked a punt on the next MSU series and Ed Hood recovered it in the end zone for another score. Mike Gillette's second PAT kick made it 14-0. Gillette kicked a 29-yard field goal and UM led 17-0 at halftime. (*DFP*, 10/13/1985, Page 92)

Both defenses played well in the third quarter and the score stayed at 17-0 heading into the final quarter. Early in the fourth quarter, Harbaugh connected with Kattus again for a 14-yard touchdown and Gillette's kick made it 24-0 in favor of the Wolverines. Michigan's Phil Webb scored the final touchdown of the game on a 4-yard run. Mike Gillette's seventh point of the game made it 31-0 and that is how the game ended. (*DFP*, 10/13/1985, Page 92)

Michigan posted 336-yards of offense and totaled 20-first downs. The Spartans offense was not particularly good, mostly because of Michigan's defense. McAllister, and his teammates, only gained a total of 139-yards. MSU's Lorenzo White, the Spartan "Rushing Machine" was held to 47-yards by the Maize and Blue defenders. Unfortunately, Michigan State could not take advantage of three pass interceptions. The Spartans went back to their locker room with another humbling loss in front of the home fans! (*DFP*, 10/13/1985, Page 92)

Team	1st	2nd	3rd	4th	Final
UM	14	3	0	14	31
MSU	0	0	0	0	0

SERIES UPDATE:

For the second time in three games, Michigan shut out the Spartans in East Lansing. George Perles was probably wondering if his team would ever score against Michigan in Spartan Stadium! The third-ranked Wolverines increased their series advantage to 51 wins, 22 losses, and 5 ties. They pushed their "decade" record to 5 wins and 1 loss. Finally, the Maize and Blue bumped their Trophy series advantage up to 18 wins, 13 losses, and 2 ties.

SERIES MILESTONES:

Believe it or not! The 1985 version of the in-state series game produced zero milestones. Really! I mean there were none, nada, zip. I looked as hard as I could, but there was nothing noteworthy about this series game. Maybe the next game would create some more interesting facts and events about the annual "In-State-Hate" game.

SEASON SUMMARIES:

The good news was that the Wolverines rose to the second spot in the national rankings after their big win over MSU. The bad news was that they were headed to Iowa City to play number one Iowa next week.

Hayden Fry's defense shut down the Michigan offense for most of the game. Both teams battled hard. Iowa won on a last-second field goal (12-10). The Wolverines bounced back the next week and blasted Indiana (42-15) on Homecoming Day. Fourth-ranked Michigan traveled to Illinois to play the unranked Fighting Illini and were lucky to return with a 3-3 tie. After eight games, the Wolverines had 6 wins, 1 loss, and 1 tie. As it turned out, they would not lose, or tie, a game for the rest of the season. Michigan blew out Purdue (47-0) and Minnesota (48-7) and handled Ohio State (27-17). Fifth ranked Michigan faced off against eighth-ranked Nebraska in the Fiesta Bowl and the Wolverines won a close one—27-23.

The Wolverines finished with a record of 10 wins, 1 loss, and 1 tie. They ended up in second place in the Big Ten. The Wolverines also finished as the second ranked team in the nation—the highest ranking that a Schembechler coached team ever achieved in the end of season rankings! It was an interesting year for sure. Two stellar Michigan defenders, Brad Cochran and Mike Hammerstein, earned All-American honors in 1985.

George Perles never dwelled on losses for too long. He watched the film, looked for improvements and focused on getting ready for the next game. After losing to Michigan, Coach Perles, had to figure out what went wrong at Illinois. The Spartans lost to the Fighting Illini (30-17) on Homecoming Day! Magically, the Spartans played better the next week at Purdue and returned to East Lansing with a 28-24 win. The offense suddenly came to life and the defense kept improving. Michigan State won their last four games over Minnesota (31-26), Indiana (35-16), Northwestern (32-0) and Wisconsin (41-7).

Coach Perles had his Spartans playing very well at the end of the 1985 season. Unfortunately, the campaign ended badly when MSU lost the All-American Bowl to Georgia Tech (17-14). Michigan State finished the season with a final record of 7 wins and 5 losses. They tied for fourth place in the Big Ten with a record of 5 wins and 3 losses. There was a lot of good news for Spartan Nation in 1985. However, there was still more work to be done. Lorenzo White earned All-American honors for his workhorse season!

Game # 79: October 11, 1986 at Michigan Stadium in Ann Arbor

BACKGROUND INFORMATION:

The NCAA decided to deal with the kickoff issue again in 1986. This time, instead of penalizing kickers, they challenged them by moving the kickoff position back five-yards from the kicking team's 40-yard line to the 35-yard line. (*USA Today CFE*, Page 405)

George Perles was back for his fourth season at Michigan State in 1986. Many of the players that he recruited in his first year were juniors and a few were seniors. The 1986 Spartans were "his" players. He had been building this team and this program for four years. The fine folks in East Lansing thought it was time to compete for a Big Ten Championship.

Not so fast Spartan fans! Michigan State lost their 1986 season opener at Arizona State (20-17). Ugh! Nothing deflates a team with high hopes more than a season-opening loss. Coach Perles his team back on track with a solid win over Notre Dame (20-15). Week three was even better since the Spartans blasted Western Michigan (45-10). Iowa halted MSU's modest two-game winning streak with a 24-21 win over the Green and White footballers. After four games, Michigan State had 2 wins and 2 losses heading into the annual showdown with Michigan. Could George Perles get the Spartans ready to play to the level of the fourth-ranked Wolverines?

Unlike 1985, everybody was on Michigan's bandwagon for the 1986 season. Bo's Wolverine team was loaded with talent and ready to compete for a conference championship that had eluded them since 1982. Technically, Bo had not lived up to his "promise" that "Those Who Stay Will Be Champions" to the Class of 1987. Every player who had played for Bo since 1969 left Michigan as a Big Ten Champion, or Co-champion. There was no pressure here, but it was time to win a title or change the sign that hung over his office door! (Those Who Stay Will Be Champions)

The 1986 Michigan football team was on a mission! Bo's third-ranked Wolverines journeyed to South Bend for the season opener and escaped with a 24-23 win. The Maize and Blue footballers beat Oregon State in week two by a score of 31-12. Bobby Bowden brought his twentieth-ranked Florida State team for Homecoming Day and left town with 20-18 loss. The fourth-ranked Wolverines traveled to Madison and came home with a 34-17 victory over the Badgers. Once again, Michigan was 4-0-0 heading into Michigan State Week. Time for the trainers to order extra band aids and other first aid items. The Spartans were coming to town for another Mitten State pigskin blood-letting event!

GAME SUMMARY: MSU 6 UM 27

Once again, Michigan played the role of "totally rude" hosts and beat up the Spartans in front of 106,141 spectators. The Wolverines scored early and often. It was another easy win for the Wolverines. Things started slowly for the Wolverines. All they could manage was a 34-yard Pat Moons field goal which put them in the lead at 3-0 after one quarter of play. Early in the second quarter, Jim Harbaugh ran for a 1-yard score to increase Michigan's advantage to 9-0. Pat Moons made the PAT kick and the Wolverines led 10-0.

Chris Caudell got the Spartans on the board with a 28-yard field goal that closed the gap to 10-3. Pat Moons kicked his second field goal of the game (19-yards) to put Michigan up by a score of 13-3 at the end of the first half. (*DFP*, 10/12/1986, Page 54)

Both teams scored in the third quarter, but Michigan scored more. John Kolesar caught a 43-yard touchdown pass from Harbaugh and Moons made the extra point. Michigan was now up 20-3. MSU's Caudell kicked his second field-goal (37-yards) to make the score 20-6 at the end of the third quarter. Harbaugh threw his second scoring pass to tight end Jeff Brown and Pat Moons finished the scoring with his final extra point kick. Michigan led 27-6 late in the fourth quarter and that is how the game ended. (*DFP*, 10/12/1986, Page 54)

Team	1st	2nd	3rd	4th	Final
MSU	0	3	3	0	6
UM	3	10	7	7	27

Bo's offense controlled the ball and the game with almost 400-yards of offense (161 rushing and 219 passing) and made 22-first downs. The Spartans were only about half as productive with 13 first downs and only 193 total yards (54 yards rushing and 139 passing). Michigan's defense sacked Spartan quarterbacks six times which made it hard for the Spartan offense. Both teams had three turnovers, but the Spartans did not make theirs count. Once again, Michigan was the better team. The Spartans would have to wait another year for their next shot at the hated Wolverines.

SERIES UPDATE:

The Wolverines added another win to their series advantage. Michigan's rivalry record grew to 52 wins, 22 losses, and 5 ties. Bo's series record in the Eighties grew to 6 wins and 1 loss. Michigan pushed their advantage in the Paul Bunyan Trophy series to 19 wins, 13 losses, and 2 ties. The Wolverines welcomed Paul Bunyan back to Ann Arbor with open arms. They liked having the 'big guy" hanging around the trophy room. Michigan regained the in-state "bragging rights" and started reminding Spartan fans of the final score as soon as the game was over. Hail to the Victors!

SERIES MILESTONES:

Series game number seventy-nine produced one BIG milestone. The gigantic crowd of 106,141 broke the series attendance record by 28 people! It was the second largest crowd in Michigan football history which was very impressive. Jim Harbaugh set a Michigan series record for most passing yards. He became the first Wolverine quarterback to throw for over 200-yards against the Spartans (219).

SEASON SUMMARIES:

After the Michigan loss, the Spartans had to pick themselves up off the mat and try to start a winning streak. Fortunately, that is exactly what happened. The Green and White footballers beat Illinois (29-21), Purdue (37-3), and Minnesota (52-23) to push their record to 5-3-0 with three games remaining. Unfortunately, MSU lost to Indiana and Northwestern before beating Wisconsin (23-13). The fourth season of the George Perles Era ended at 6 wins and 5 losses. The Spartans broke even in the conference with a record of 4 wins and 4 losses which earned them a tie for fifth place.

The good news was that MSU owned two consecutive winning seasons. The bad news was that they were in the middle of the pack in the Big Ten and way, way behind Michigan in conference competitiveness! Spartan punter, Greg Montgomery, was the only MSU player to earn All-American honors in 1986. Coach Perles had to find some All-Americans that could play guard, tackle, end, running back and linebacker if he expected to compete for a Big Ten championship. There was more work to do in East Lansing—much more work to do!

The Wolverines continued their winning ways after defeating the Spartans. They hosted eighth-ranked Iowa and sent Hayden Fry home to dwell on a 20-17 loss. Michigan rolled over Indiana (38-14), Illinois (69-13) and Purdue (31-7) to run their record to 9-0-0 and their ranking to number two in the nation. However, Minnesota was not impressed with Michigan's lofty status and escaped Ann Arbor with a huge win (20-17). With the Big Ten title on the line, Jim Harbaugh guaranteed a win in the final game at Ohio State. Michigan won the game and a share of the conference title with a 26-24 win in the Horseshoe. The Wolverines went to Hawaii for a "bowl like" game and beat the Rainbow Warriors (27-10). Unfortunately, Michigan ended the season with another Rose Bowl loss to Arizona State (22-15). Michigan finished the 1986 season with a final record of 11 wins and 2 losses. The Big Ten Co-Champions finished with a record of 7-1-0. Three Wolverines (Jim Harbaugh, John Elliott, and Garland Rivers) earned All-American honors at the end of the season.

Game # 80: October 10, 1987 at Spartan Stadium in East Lansing

BACKGROUND INFORMATION:

The 1987 season was Bo Schembechler's nineteenth as Michigan's Head Coach. His Ann Arbor track record was impressive. All-American quarterback Jim Harbaugh was gone and so were some other outstanding players. However, with strong players returning on offense and defense, it appeared that the Schembechler "Football Machine" would keep on rolling. To no one's surprise, Michigan was expected to compete again for another conference championship.

The pollsters placed Michigan in the number nine slot for the season opener against sixteenth-ranked Notre Dame. The Irish thought they were better than the Wolverines and they proved it with a 26-7 victory! This time, Michigan had to get up off the mat and win their first game of the season. So, that is what they did. In fact, they won three straight games against Washington State (44-18), Long Beach State (49-0), and Wisconsin (49-0) to push their record to 3 wins and 1 loss heading into MSU Week.

238

The fifth year of the Perles Era was critical for him and for MSU. On paper, this was the best team that Coach Perles had built in East Lansing. Strong players were returning on offense, defense, and special teams. It was hard not to feel good about the Spartans, but they had a tough non-conference schedule to add to the difficulty of the 1987 season. Perles figured that his team would be good. "How good?" was the BIG question.

Michigan State began the 1987 season with a big win over Southern California (27-13) in the first night game in the history of Spartan Stadium. It was a great start, but things really changed in the next two weeks. Notre Dame came to town and left with a 31-8 victory over the Green and White. A rising Florida State team did the same thing and left town with a 31-3 win over the Spartans. A season that started with so much hype and hope, was starting to unravel. The bad news was that MSU was 1-2-0 in the first three games. The good news was that they were undefeated in the Big Ten Conference. The Spartans went to Iowa city to battle Hayden Fry's Hawkeyes and came home a winner (19-14). Michigan State's record was now 2-2-0 and they were getting ready for Michigan Week with some confidence. You can bet that George Perles and his defensive coaches were putting a plan together to shut down the Michigan offense that had scored over 40-points in the last three games. If the MSU could not slow down the Wolverines, it would be another long day in East Lansing.

GAME SUMMARY: UM 11 MSU 17

The eightieth game of the in-state series was a titanic struggle between two determined, football teams. As usual, the hitting was hard, even thunderous at times. This was a "Big Boy" football game. Nobody backed down at any point in the contest—nobody!

Michigan drew first blood on a 31-yard field goal by kicker Mike Gillette. Lorenzo White scored on a 6-yard run and a successful PAT kick made it 7-3 Spartans at the end of one quarter. Following an interception of a Michigan pass, the powerful running of Lorenzo White put MSU in position for another score in the second quarter. When White pounded across the goal line on a 2-yard run, the Spartans led 13-3. Kicker John Langeloh booted the extra point to give MSU a 14-3 halftime lead. (*DFP*, 10/11/1987, Page 90)

Both teams had plenty of chances in the third quarter but did not capitalize. The score remained at 14-3 heading into the final fifteen minutes of play. Michigan quarterback Demetrius Brown hit Jamie Morris for a 17-yard touchdown pass to make it 14-9. Brown then converted a two-point conversion pass to John Kolesar. It was 14-11 in favor of MSU with twelve minutes to go. Spartan fans were now biting their nails as there was plenty of time for another Michigan score. (*DFP*, 10/11/1987, Page 90)

However, the Spartan defense, which had effectively shut down the Wolverine running game, dared Brown to pass. It turned out to be a good strategy as Brown threw two big interceptions in the fourth quarter. John Langeloh gave MSU some breathing room with a 42-yard field goal to push the Spartan lead to 17-11 and that is how the game ended. (*DFP*, 10/11/1987, Page 90)

Normally, the number "7" is a lucky number, but it is not lucky when that number is attached to the number of interceptions thrown by your quarterback! The Perles Plan for this game was to shut down the Michigan running game and force the inexperienced Demetrious Brown to throw into multiple-coverage schemes. It worked to perfection as Brown threw "7" interceptions. Four of the picks went to MSU's John Miller who caught more of Brown's passes than any Michigan receiver except John Kolesar, who also caught four Brown passes.

The Wolverines had 93 net rushing yards compared to MSU's 193 (185 by Lorenzo White). Brown had 158 passing yards compared to 68-yards for Michigan State. Unfortunately, the biggest difference in the game was the seven interceptions. Actually, Michigan was in the game until the final minute, but their last scoring chance ended with, you guessed it, an interception. Final Score: MSU 17 Michigan 11. (*DFP*, 10/11/1987, Page 90)

Once again, this was a tough, hard-hitting game. Nothing was easy for either team. The game went right down to the wire. The Spartans made fewer mistakes and that was the difference. Michigan State had not beaten the Wolverines since Bo's first season (1969). Yes, this was a sweet win! It turned out to be a record-setting day in many ways. No Michigan quarterback had ever thrown seven interceptions in a single game so that was a record setter. Of course, the Spartans had never intercepted seven passes in one game.

Team	1st	2nd	3rd	4th	Final
UM	3	0	0	8	11
MSU	7	7	0	3	17

SERIES UPDATE:

Michigan still led the series by a very wide margin, but that did not devalue this Spartan victory in any way. Yes, the Spartans were still on the short end of a record of 23 wins, 52 losses, and 5 ties, but one game better than the year before! Michigan State reduced the Maize and Blue advantage in the Eighties to 6-2-0. Finally, MSU inched back a little closer in the trophy series which now stood at 18-14-2 in favor of the Wolverines.

SERIES MILESTONES:

The 1987 game was significant for three reasons. First, it was the eightieth game in the series. Second, it was the thirty-fifth game in the Paul Bunyan part of the series. Third, it was a record-setting day for pass interceptions for both teams. Finally, John Miller became the first man to tan to pick off four enemy passes in one game.

SEASON SUMMARIES:

The Wolverines bounced back with a big win over Iowa (37-10). In a BIG surprise, Indiana played a great game in Bloomington and sent the Wolverines back to Ann Arbor with a 14-10 defeat. Michigan posted three straight wins over Northwestern (29-6), Minnesota (30-20), and Illinois (17-14) before losing to Ohio State.

The Wolverines finished in fourth place in the Big Ten with a record of 5-3-0. They ended the season on a high note with a win over Alabama (28-24) in the Hall of Fame Bowl. Michigan finished with a final record of 8 wins and 4 losses. John Elliott and Mark Messner earned All-American honors in 1987.

Michigan State got things going on offense and defense the next week against Northwestern. Final Score: Spartans 38 Wildcats 0! Illinois stopped MSU's three game winning streak, but they did not defeat the Spartans. Instead, they both struggled to a 14-14 tie. In week eight, the first-place Spartans traveled to Columbus, Ohio to take on the Buckeyes. It was a "championship" type game and the MSU footballers prevailed by a score of 13-7.

None of the last three games were even close as MSU rolled over Purdue (45-3), Indiana (27-3) and Wisconsin (30-9). Michigan State finished with a regular season record of 8 wins, 2 losses and 1 tie. They were undefeated in conference play at 7-0-1 which earned them a trip to the 1988 Rose Bowl. Interestingly, the Spartans beat Southern California (20-17) in the Rose Bowl to finish the 1987 season with a final record of 9-2-1. It was the first, and only, time that MSU defeated the same team in the first and last game of the season. Three Spartans (Tony Mandarich, Greg Montgomery, and Lorenzo White) were named to at least one All-American team in 1987.

Game # 81: October 8, 1988 at Michigan Stadium in Ann Arbor

BACKGROUND INFORMATION:

There was a change in college football scoring in 1988 concerning two-point conversions. Now, if a defensive team intercepted a pass or recovered a fumble on a two-point conversion play, the defense could score two points if they returned the ball to the other team's end zone. (*Wikipedia*, 1988 NCAA Division I-A Football, Rules Changes)

George Perles was the most popular man in East Lansing after defeating Southern California in the 1988 Rose Bowl. However, coaching success can bring distractions and that is what happened in late January 1988. The "rumor mill" had Coach Perles going to the Green Bay Packers for a very large amount of money. Finally, on January 28th, Perles held a press conference to announce that he was staying at Michigan State. Like Bo, who turned down big money from Texas A & M in 1982, Perles cited his "loyalty" to Michigan State as his primary reason for staying in East Lansing. No doubt, the money was attractive, but Perles decided to remain at his beloved alma mater. Michigan State officials rewarded George's loyalty with a five-year extension to his current five-year contract which meant that he would be at MSU for a long time. With the off season "drama" behind him, George Perles went back to work to defend the Big Ten Championship that his players won in 1987.

The Spartan's lost some outstanding players from that stellar team, but there was sufficient talent returning on both sides of the ball. Perles would have another tough defense and hopefully he would find a running back to fill the void left by All-American Lorenzo White.

Season number six of the George Perles Era did not start out as expected. Unranked Rutgers came to East Lansing and left town with a 17-13 upset over MSU. Notre Dame came to Spartan Stadium in week two and left happy with a 20-3 victory. Things got worse in week three when the Spartans lost at Florida State (30-7) September was finally over and MSU's record was 0-3-0. Maybe October would be better, or not! The good news was that Iowa came to town on October 1, 1988 and the Spartans did not lose to the Hawkeyes. Unfortunately, they did not beat the visitors either since the game ended in a 10-10 tie. Michigan State had a record of 0 wins, 3 losses. and 1 tie heading into Michigan Week. The only good news was that the Spartans had not lost in the conference, but they were still winless at 0-0-1. The Michigan game was their best chance to prove that they belonged in the conference race, despite their shaky start.

Bo Schembechler was back for his twentieth season in 1988, but football was no longer the only thing on his mind. Effective July 1, 1988, Glenn Edward Schembechler was serving as Michigan's head football coach and athletic director. Bo was going to be a terribly busy man starting in August 1988. Many people wondered how he would be able to do it all because of his health history. Apparently, his doctors said he was healthy enough to wear two hats. Bo knew he could do it all, or he would not have taken the AD job. Football would remain his top priority in the Fall of 1988, and, hopefully, into the new year! Michigan started the season as one of the favorites in the Big Ten race. Ohio State, Iowa and maybe the Spartans were all expected to fight for the championship. Like every year before, Schembechler was on a "championship" mission. Time to play some football men!

Ninth-ranked Michigan started the season in South Bend, Indiana. It did not go well! Lou Holtz's thirteenth-ranked Irish beat Bo's Wolverines in another close one by a score of 19-17. Things did not get any better the next week since Michigan lost to top ranked Miami of Florida (31-30). Bo's Wolverines were sitting on a "perfect" record of 0-2-0 to start the season. The Wolverines slipped to #19 in the country, but they did not slip any more thanks to a 19-9 victory over Wake Forest. Despite their record of 1-2-0 Michigan was still undefeated in the Big Ten and they stayed that way with a 62-14 pounding of Wisconsin. Bo was 2-2-0 heading into Michigan State Week. He knew that the annual bloodbath with MSU would be another tough game. It was time for the Wolverines to button up their chinstraps just a little tighter for some "Big Boy" football in The Big House!

GAME SUMMARY: MSU 3 UM 17

The eighty-first series battle ended like so many of the games in the past. The Wolverines chalked up another victory against the Spartans. However, this one was not easy. As usual, it was hard-hitting, even violent at times. Both teams spilled some more blood in this contest, but the Spartans lost the most.

The Wolverines took the lead in the first quarter on a 30-yard Mike Gillette field goal. Michigan's Tony Boles scored on a 5-yard run in the second quarter. Gillette's PAT kick gave Michigan a 10-0 lead and that is how the half ended. In the third quarter, Michigan State's John Miller returned a Michigan interception forty-seven yards to the UM five-yard line. It was Miller's fifth pick in the last two games against Michigan, but all the Spartans could muster was an 18-yard field goal from John Langeloh which made it a 10-3 game. (*DFP*, 10/9/1988, Page 89)

As it turned out, the biggest play of the game came from kicker Mike Gillette. Bo called for a fake-punt and it worked to perfection. Gillette caught the Spartans by surprise and went 40-yards, untouched, into the end zone. Gillette was still breathing heavily after his run, but he nailed the extra-point kick to give Michigan a 17-3 lead and that is how the game ended. (*DFP*, 10/9/1988, Page 89)

Team	1st	2nd	3rd	4th	Final
MSU	0	0	3	0	3
UM	3	7	7	0	17

The Wolverines won the statistical battles and the game. Michigan rushed for 249-yards and passed for 94-yards. Quarterback Michael Taylor helped the offense total 364-yards. More importantly, Taylor only threw one interception which is six less than the Wolverines threw to MSU in 1987. Bo's defense held the Spartans to a total of 151-yards of offense. (*DFP*, 10/9/1988, Page 89)

SERIES UPDATE:

Michigan's victory pushed their series record to 53 wins, 23 losses, and 5 ties. It also increased their advantage in the Eighties to 7 wins, 2 losses, and 0 ties. Michigan became the first series team to win twenty games in the Paul Bunyan Trophy games. The Wolverines increased their trophy advantage to 20 wins, 14 losses, and 2 ties. Everyone in Ann Arbor was glad to see Paul Bunyan again and "bragging rights' would be enjoyed by the "arrogant ones" for another year. Go Blue!

SERIES MILESTONES:

Once again, the colossal football battle between Michigan's two Big Ten teams generated some interesting milestones. First, it was another record-setting crowd in the Big House. The huge throng of 106,208 broke the previous record by sixty-seven people. Second, as I already mentioned, it was Michigan's twentieth win in the trophy series so that was a big first for the Wolverines. Finally, Michigan's win gave Bo Schembechler his sixteenth series victory which tied him with Fielding Yost for the most wins in series history.

SEASON SUMMARIES:

Michigan State's 1988 football season was in dire straits after five games. The Green and White footballers had a record of 0 wins, 4 losses and 1 tie. It appeared that they may not score a touchdown for weeks which meant it would be extremely hard to win one football game, let alone more! Amazingly, George Perles got his team refocused and they defeated Northwestern on Homecoming Day (36-3). At least it would not be a winless season in 1988. Then MSU traveled to Champaign, Illinois the next week and came home with a 28-2 win over the Fighting Illini.

MSU's win-streak grew to three games when the Spartans defeated Ohio State (20-10). Michigan State finished strong in the final two games with wins over Indiana (38-12) and Wisconsin (36-0). The Spartans were almost given up for dead. Yet, they bounced back to win six straight games, and none were close! Coach Perles had his team playing as well as anybody in the conference, including Michigan.

MSU finished the regular season with a winning record of 6 wins, 4 losses, and 1 tie. Even more impressive, they earned a second-place finish in the Big Ten with their record of 6-1-1. The first five games of the season may have been the worst five games of the Perles tenure. However, the last six games were probably his best. Unfortunately, the 1988 season ended on a losing note with a Gator Bowl loss to Georgia (34-27). Three Spartans earned first team All-American honors for the 1988 season (Tony Mandarich, Andre Rison, and Percy Snow).

Michigan was looking good at 2-0-0 in the Big Ten after beating the Spartans. Iowa was the next team on the schedule and the Hawkeyes did the same thing to Michigan that they did to MSU. The Iowa vs Michigan game ended in a 17-17 tie! Amazing! Michigan got serious in the next game in front of another large Homecoming Day gathering. Bo's Wolverines defeated the Hoosiers (31-6). Then, Michigan blasted Northwestern in Evanston (52-7). Minnesota put up a surprisingly good fight, but eventually lost (22-7) to the streaking Wolverines. The Maize and Blue finished strong with two more wins over Illinois (38-9) and Ohio State (34-31) to end the regular season at 8 wins, 2 losses, and 1 tie. More importantly, they won the Big Ten Championship with a record of 7 wins, 0 losses and 1 tie. Michigan ended the season on a high note with a 22-14 win over Southern California in the Rose Bowl. Mark Messner, John Vitale, and Tripp Wellborne earned All-American honors in 1988.

Game # 82: October 14, 1989 at Spartan Stadium in East Lansing

BACKGROUND INFORMATION:

Bo Schembechler's twenty-first season at Michigan began in August 1989. After Michigan won the 1989 Rose Bowl, Bo had little time to celebrate. His athletic director duties crushed his off-season time schedule. In mid-March of 1989, Schembechler got right in the middle of the Wolverine basketball season when he declared that a "Michigan Man" would coach the Wolverines in the NCAA tourney, not Bill Frieder, the ASU turncoat! Miraculously, interim coach Steve Fischer led Michigan to six-consecutive wins and the NCAA basketball championship.

Bo went to every game while Gary Moeller and the assistant coaches ran Michigan's Spring Football practice. It was just a crazy time for Bo. He was probably happy to see another football season roll around in August 1989. Once again, his Wolverines were expected to be a formidable team.

Schembechler's second-ranked Wolverines started the season against top-ranked Notre Dame. It ended badly for Bo and his team as the Irish won by a score of 24-19. Michigan slipped to number five when they went to California to play UCLA. This time Michigan won a close game against the Bruins 24-23. Game number three against Maryland was a big 41-21 win for Michigan.

Schembechler's footballers continued their winning ways in the Big Ten opener against Wisconsin. The Wolverines shut out the Badgers by a score of 24-0 to push their record to 3 wins and 1 loss. MSU Week was here again! Time to get ready for the Spartans!

The 1989 season was the seventh of the George Perles Era at Michigan State. Would it be lucky a lucky season for Coach Perles and his Spartans? Michigan State had plenty of excellent players returning on both sides of the ball. Michigan State was one of the favorites to win another Big Ten championship.

The Spartans started well with a 49-0 victory over Miami of Ohio. A trip to Notre Dame did not go as well as MSU came home to ponder a 21-13 loss. MSU played another team from Miami in week three. The Hurricanes, from Miami of Florida bested the Spartans (26-20). With the non-conference season behind them, the Spartans focused on Big Ten play. They journeyed to Iowa and beat the Hawkeyes by a score of 17-14. After four games, Michigan State had a record of 2 wins and 2 losses. Fifth-ranked Michigan was coming to town and Coach Perles was getting his team ready for another upset of the highly rated and much hated Wolverines! The pollsters showed their respect for MSU's difficult schedule and rated them at #21 in the country heading into the Michigan game.

GAME SUMMARY: UM 10 MSU 7

Series game number eighty-two lived up to the billing of two Big Ten heavy weights slugging it out for a chance to win the championship. Yes, ever since 1953, this rivalry game had even more at stake than just "bragging rights." Every series game was a chance to earn what amounted to two wins or two losses depending upon where you ended up on the scoreboard. Michigan was the higher ranked team (UM #5 and MSU #21), but you could not tell from watching the game. The blocks and tackles were registering high numbers on the Richter Earthquake Scale! Yes, it was another very, very intense football game between two intrastate rivals.

Michigan drew first blood in this game when Leroy Hoard scored on 1-yard run. Kicker J. D. Carlson kicked the extra point and Michigan had a 7-0 lead at the end of the first quarter. Carlson added to the Wolverine lead with a 35-yard field goal and Michigan went into the visitor's locker room with a 10-0 lead. (*DFP*, 10/15/1989, Page 62)

Although Michigan was moving the ball, the Spartans stopped several good chances. Michigan's defense was also incredibly good. Both teams held each other scoreless in the third quarter. Michigan still led by a score of 10-0 in the fourth quarter when the Spartans tipped a Michigan punt that only traveled 12-yards. The MSU offense was in business and quarterback Dan Enos finally got the Spartans into the end zone on a 4-yard touchdown pass to Courtney Hawkins. John Langeloh's extra point cut Michigan's lead to 10-7 with just over 5-minutes to play. The Spartans had one more chance in the final minutes, but Michigan intercepted an Enos pass with six seconds remaining in the game. Wow, what a game! (*DFP*, 10/15/1989, Page 62)

Michigan State's offense was a little bit better in this game, but not by much. They fought hard to post 291-yards of offense (77-yards rushing and 214 passing). Unfortunately, MSU failed to take advantage of many good scoring chances. The Spartans missed two field goals, had another one blocked, and failed to score on a fourth downplay from the 1-yard line at the beginning of the fourth quarter. The Wolverines totaled 245-yards of offense (169-yards rushing and 76 passing), but they made their yards count when they had to. It was another frustrating defeat for Michigan State. They were in the game right until the end, but the missed opportunities haunted them for the rest of the season! (*DFP*, 10/15/1989, Page 62)

Team	1st	2nd	3rd	4th	Final
UM	7	3	0	0	10
MSU	0	0	0	7	7

SERIES UPDATE:

This game was another step backward for Michigan State. Despite having played an excellent game, their effort still resulted in a loss to the hated Wolverines. This was the last series game of a dreadful decade of UM vs MSU football games. Michigan increased their advantage to 54 wins, 23 losses, and 5 ties. The Wolverines finished the decade with an advantage of 8 wins to only 2 wins for MSU. Finally, Bo's footballers added to their trophy series lead with a record of 21-14-2. Of course, Paul Bunyan did not have to "move" back to East Lansing since he would remain in the Tree city for another year!

SERIES MILESTONES:

Mitten State series game number eighty-two marked the last game for Glenn Edward Schembechler. His final win over the Spartans gave him a final record of 17 wins and 4 losses in the series. He was now the winningest coach in the history of the UM vs MSU football rivalry. The Wolverines were way down in the Paul Bunyan Trophy series when Bo arrived. However, they were large and in charge when he left! Bo Schembechler retired from the Michigan coaching job with a record of 194 wins, 48 losses and 5 ties. He won, or shared, thirteen Big Ten Championships which tied him with Woody Hayes for the most titles in conference history. I am sure that Spartan fans were hopeful in January 1990 when Bo retired. It was hard to imagine another Michigan football coach beating up on the Spartans as much as he did! Maybe things would get better again against the hated Wolverines, or not!

SEASON SUMMARIES:

Bo Schembechler probably felt good about escaping with his narrow win over the Spartans. However, he did not' have a lot of time to rest on his laurels, since Hayden Fry's Hawkeyes were waiting in Iowa City. The fifth-ranked Wolverines traveled well and returned with a 26-12 win over the Hawkeyes. Michigan won another Homecoming Game over Indiana (38-10) and pushed their conference record to 4-0-0.

Schembechler's footballers finished strong and ran the table with four more wins over Purdue, Illinois, Minnesota, and Ohio State. Every victory was by at least ten points. Michigan ended the regular season with a record of 10 wins and 1 loss. They won Bo's 13th and final Big Ten Championship with a perfect record of 8 wins, 0 losses and 0 ties. Unfortunately, Bo finished his final season the same way that he finished so many others. He lost the Rose Bowl to USC by a score of 17-10. That was it. After twenty-one years at the helm, Glenn Edward Schembechler turned his beloved football team over to Gary Moeller in January 1990. Now, Bo could focus on his duties as athletic director. Finally, Safety Tripp Wellborne earned All-American honors in 1989.

It is possible that the 1989 Spartans took the Michigan loss a little harder than other years. They came out flat against Illinois and lost their Homecoming Game to the Illini (14-10). Once again, George Perles helped his footballers get off the mat and got them focused on a strong finish. They went to Purdue and beat the Boilermakers (28-21). Indiana was next and it was not even close as MSU blew out the Hoosiers (51-20). Minnesota was next and MSU won by a score of 21-7. Northwestern was the next victim. The Spartans scored the most points in the Perles Era and blasted the Wildcats (76-14)! Michigan State ran their winning streak to five straight games with a season ending victory over Wisconsin (31-3). Once again, Michigan State was playing as well as anybody in the Big Ten and maybe anybody in the country.

The Spartans earned an invitation to the Aloha Bowl and they defeated Hawaii by a score of 31-3. Michigan State ended the 1989 regular season with a final record of 7 wins and 4 losses. They finished third in the Big Ten with a final mark of 6 wins and 2 losses. It was another successful season in East Lansing. The Spartans earned an invitation to the Aloha Bowl where they defeated Hawaii (31-3). Michigan State ended the 1989 season with a final record of 8 wins and 4 losses. Harlan Barnett, Bob Kula, and Percy Snow earned All-American honors in 1989.

DECADE AND SERIES SUMMARIES:

The Eighties turned out to be another winning decade for Michigan and Michigan State. However, the Wolverines won a lot more than the Spartans did. The Wolverines slipped a little in their overall performance level compared to the decade of the Seventies, but they were still excellent in Bo's last decade. The Spartans survived the Muddy Waters years and George Perles stabilized things after a couple of losing seasons. The last five years were better as Coach Perles put MSU football back on track.

Decade and Series Summary 1898 to 1989

Time Frame	UM Won-Lost-Tied	MSC Won-Lost-Tied
1980-1989	8-2-0	2-8-0
1898-1989	54-23-5	23-54-5

Image 10 Bo Schembechler (far right) finished his career with seventeen wins against Michigan State. This number equaled the total achieved by four of his predecessors shown from left to right: Harry Kipke (3), Fritz Crisler (8), Bennie Oosterbaan (4) and Bump Elliott (2). (Permission: Bentley Historical Library at The University of Michigan, Page 369)

BIG TEN SUMMARY:

Once again, let us look at some numbers and reflect on how the Wolverines and Spartans compared in Big Ten play from 1980 to 1989. First, the final ten years of the Schembechler Era at Michigan were outstanding. Although Bo's Big Ten record in the Eighties slipped little, it was still better than what happened in East Lansing. Michigan still won a lot of games and plenty of championships. It was another strong run for the Wolverines. Yes, "Bo Time" was over in Ann Arbor and the fine folks in East Lansing were happy about that.

Michigan had the edge in all the "good" categories in the chart below. The Wolverines earned twenty-five more wins in the Eighties than the Spartans. MSU had a "winning" decade, but it wasn't what Spartan fans had hoped for. Paul Bunyan spent way too much time in Ann Arbor in the 1980s. Two wins out of ten games against Michigan was not good enough.

Unfortunately, Michigan State had twenty-four more losses during this time. Schembechler's footballers posted ten winning conference seasons compared to five for the Green and White. Finally, Michigan won five conference championships during this decade and the Spartans earned one.

The good news for Spartan fans was that George Perles won almost sixty-three percent (.629) of his games during the last seven years of the Eighties. He was building a winning program and making progress!

Big Ten Summary 1980 to 1989

Statistical Area	UM	MSU
Number of Head Coaches	1	2
Games Played	84	84
Wins	68	43
Losses	14	38
Ties	2	3
Winning Percentage	.821	.530
Winning Seasons	10	5
Losing Seasons	0	4
Even Seasons	0	1
Big Ten Championships	5	1

For the second straight decade, Michigan was clearly the best Big Ten team in the State of Michigan. The years of Spartan dominance were "long gone." Once again, it was "Wolverine Time" in the Mitten State. George Perles was making progress, but he had a long way to go. Michigan State fans were hoping that the changing of the guard in Ann Arbor would yield better results in East Lansing. The Wolverines were winning way too many of the recruiting wars and the football battles in Michigan. Maybe the Nineties would see the Spartans return to dominance in the State of Michigan and in the Big Ten Conference.

PROGRAM SUMMARIES:

The 1980s continued to be exceptional for Michigan and not as good for Michigan State. Bo's teams slipped a little in the Eighties, but they still achieved at a high level. Coach Schembechler's teams still won 90 games in the decade and lost 29 to go along with 2 ties. Michigan's winning percentage of seventy-five percent was not as good as the Seventies when the Wolverines won almost ninety percent (.894) of their games. Overall, it was another excellent body of work that kept Michigan at the top of the conference and among the best teams in the country.

It did not take MSU Athletic Director, Dough Weaver to figure out that Muddy Waters was not the answer for Michigan State football. However, many Spartan fans thought that one year of Coach Waters was plenty. Muddy Waters had a chance to make a difference in East Lansing, but it just did not work out. George Perles turned things around quickly and moved the program forward. Winning the Big Ten Championship in 1987 was a huge step for Coach Perles and his football program. Now that Bo Schembechler was gone, things might turn in MSU's favor again.

Program Summaries 1980 to 1989

Statistical Area	UM	MSU
Number of Head Coaches	1	3
Games Played	121	115
Wins	90	56
Losses	29	56
Ties	2	3
Winning Percentage	.752	.500
Winning Seasons	9	5
Losing Seasons	0	4
Even Seasons	1	1
National Championships	0	0
All-American Selections	20	16

In the meantime, Michigan State had to deal with the reality that the Wolverines had the best football program in the State of Michigan. It was a hard pill to swallow, but the numbers did not lie. George Perles knew that there was still plenty of work to do in East Lansing. Unfortunately, it would have to be done in the shadow of the "arrogant ones" in Ann Arbor until he had the best numbers! That was his challenge for the Nineties: keep building his MSU football program, beat Michigan and win more games against everyone else!

Bo Schembechler finished strong in his final decade in Ann Arbor. He got the Wolverines back to being the best team in the Mitten State in the Seventies and he kept them there in the Eighties. Bo returned Michigan to the glory years of past times although he did not quite reach the heights that Duffy took the Spartans in 1965 and 1966. Glenn Edward Schembechler produced consistent winners for twenty-one straight years.

After losing his first game to Duffy's Spartans, he learned how to beat the Spartans at their own game. Bo won seventeen of his last twenty-games against Michigan State and still holds the record for most series wins at seventeen. I am sure that the fine folks in East Lansing had a party when he announced his retirement from coaching. The Spartans had their fill of "Bo Time"—it was time to move on.

Michigan State football took a giant step backward from 1980 to 1982. George Perles came in to fix a big mess in East Lansing. It was amazing that he turned things around as quickly as he did. No, he did not build a program that equaled Michigan in his first seven years, but he got MSU on a winning track and he restored some Spartan football pride. With Schembechler gone in early 1990, George Perles had a chance to fill the void left by the Michigan legend. Maybe Coach Perles could get more kids to come to play for him in East Lansing. One thing for sure was that George Perles would be coaching against a different man in Ann Arbor in 1990.

CHAPTER 12

Mo and Lloyd Carry On 1990 to 1999

T
he Nineties brought a whole new set of challenges to America's citizens starting on January 1, 1990. Technology continued to be one of the major themes of the final decade in the 20th Century. The World Wide Web and the increasing availability of the Internet continued to change communication around the world. Snail mail was taking a back seat, in many ways, and instantaneous messages grew in favor with hundreds of millions of people around the world. Technology industries exploded which helped create high-tech and high-paying jobs. America saw an unprecedented period of economic growth starting in 1991 under the Clinton Administration. Cable television continued to grow and the major American television networks were starting to scramble for viewers. The world of television would undergo major transformations in the Nineties. The Gulf War came and went in less than four days! Everything seemed to be happening faster and faster. Terrorist attacks were broadcast into our homes on a regular basis. The world seemed to be getting less safe by the day.

Game #83: October 13, 1990 at Michigan Stadium in Ann Arbor

BACKGROUND INFORMATION:

College administrators, and athletic directors continued to grapple with the role of television in the sport of college football. Other issues like player safety, scholarships, and the delicate balance between academics and athletics continued to occupy the time of "the folks in charge" also known as the NCAA. Of course, none of these issues were new. Some of the discussions about the best way to handle them went back to the early decades of the twentieth century. One thing that did change was that "testing for anabolic steroids and related masking agents became mandatory in 1990." (*USA Today CFE*, Page 448) Any player who violated these rules would lose one year of eligibility. The NCAA did not plan to mess around with this issue, they were serious!

George Perles knew what Gary Moeller would bring to Michigan football and it was not going to be a ton of losses! Interestingly, the eighth season of the Perles Era almost did not happen. The New York Jets came calling in January 1990 and, once again, George Perles listened to another NFL team. Remember, he turned down the Green Bay Packer job a few years earlier. As it turned out, his loyalty to MSU was still stronger than "Big Bucks." Once again, he stayed on and added the title of Athletic Director to his job description. Coach Perles knew that his eighth season would be especially important to his program. George Perles had to send a message to Spartan Nation and to the fine folks in Ann Arbor that MSU football was still on the rise. The pollsters did not show the Spartans any respect since they were not ranked going into the season. MSU would have to play their way into the 1990 polls with some early season wins.

The Spartans began the 1990 season with an uninspiring tie at Syracuse (23-23). Of course, the good news was that MSU did not lose. The bad news was that the Spartans did not win either. They played well against top ranked Notre Dame in week two but lost (20-19). That one hurt! The Spartans finished the non-conference season with a win over Rutgers (34-10) which put them at 1 win, 1 loss and 1 tie heading into the conference season. The Green and White footballers started the Big Ten season with a disappointing home loss to Iowa (12-7). They could not afford to lose a second conference game to Michigan if they wanted to stay in the Big Ten Title chase. Once again, there would be a lot riding on the trip to Ann Arbor for MSU!

In January 1990, Bo Schembechler announced that he was retiring from coaching. He handed the job to Gary Moeller and became Michigan's full-time athletic director. Unlike Schembechler, Coach "Mo" was a known quantity at Michigan and throughout college football. There would be no "Mo Who" questions about Michigan's newest football coach. It was expected that Gary Moeller's first team would look a lot like Bo's team in 1989 since Schembechler recruited most of the players on the roster. Gary Moeller knew about the importance of good defense. He might spice up the offense a little and throw a few more passes, but his teams would be able to run the ball as well. For Michigan fans, it looked like business as usual in Ann Arbor.

The pollsters thought that things would be good under Gary Moeller since Michigan was rated at number four to start the 1990 season. However, the Gary Moeller Era did not start as well as Wolverine fans hoped. Michigan lost Mo's first game at #1 Notre Dame (28-24). Mo's footballers bounced back with two straight wins over UCLA (38-15) and Maryland (45-17) to finish the non-conference portion of the season at 2 wins and 1 loss. Gary Moeller won his first conference game against Wisconsin by a score of 41-3. Michigan's record jumped to 3-1-0. And, with a Notre Dame loss, the Wolverines jumped to number one heading into MSU Week. Interestingly, Michigan fans were looking for a BIG win over the Spartans in Gary Moeller's first series game. Michigan students began boasting that this game was "No. 1 vs No One." Tee shirts displaying this slogan were selling like hotcakes in Ann Arbor the week before the big game. Of course, this did not sit well with George Perles and his Spartans. Oh boy, this was going to be some game!

GAME SUMMARY: MSU 28 UM 27

Game number eighty-three in the annual 'football brawl'' between the Maize and Blue & the Green and White was a "nail biter" all the way. As usual, it was a hard-hitting game full of intense effort on every play.

Michigan scored first and took an early first quarter lead on a 16-yard touchdown pass from Elvis Grbac to Derrick Alexander. Kicker J.D. Carlson's extra point made it 7-0. Michigan State came back to even the score at 7-7 on an 8-yard run by quarterback Dan Enos and the PAT by John Langeloh. Michigan failed to score on a fourth down and 1-yard line play at the end of the first quarter. This turned out to be the second most important play of the game. Both defenses stiffened in the second quarter and it was still 7-7 at half time. (*Battle Creek Enquirer (BCE)*, 10/14/1990, Page 18)

In the second half, Michigan's defense stopped MSU on their first possession and began to move the ball. Twelve plays and 81-yards later Jarod Bunch crashed into the end zone on a 1-yard dive. Carlson kicked the extra point and Michigan led again at 14-7. Michigan State got the ball with just over 7-minutes remaining in the third quarter. Dan Enos took the Spartans on a long drive of their own. It ended after 15 plays and 80-yards with a 4-yard pass from Enos to tailback Hyland Hickson. MSU kicked the point and the game was tied at 14-14 heading into the fourth period. (*BCE*, 10/14/1990, Page 18)

In the last quarter, the intensity level inched higher and higher as both teams struggled to defeat the other. Both teams had fought too hard in this game to let the other team win. It looked like the game might go right down to the last play! Midway through the final stanza, the Spartans picked off a Grbac pass and made the Wolverines pay for this mistake. MSU drove 60-yards in 8 plays. Hickson scored his second touchdown. After the extra-point, the Spartans had a 21-14 lead. Desmond Howard fielded the MSU kick-off at the UM five-yard line and roared down the sidelines before cutting back over the middle and heading to the end zone. Michigan's successful PAT kick tied the score again at 21-21 with just over 5 minutes to play. The determined Spartans took the kickoff and headed to the Michigan end zone. They drove 70-yards in 9 plays. Tico Duckett went off left tackle from 9-yards out and MSU had the lead, again! Langeloh's kick made it 28-21 MSU with just under two minutes remaining in the game. (*BCE*, 10/14/1990, Page 18)

The Wolverines went into their "two-minute" offense and headed towards the Spartan end zone. Elvis Grbac led Michigan on a 71-yard drive that took 13 plays. The next to last play of the game was a 7-yard pass from Grbac to Derrick Alexander. The scoreboard now read: Visitor 28 Home 27. It was decision time for Gary Moeller. "Should I kick and go for the sure tie with 22-seconds on the clock?" Or "Should I go for the win and remain #1?" As it turned out, Mo went for two-points, but it did not work out so well. Desmond Howard was isolated on MSU defensive back Eddie Brown. Howard made his move, but his legs got tangled up with Brown's legs. As he was falling, Howard got his hands on the ball, but could not catch it. Wow—the Michigan sidelines went crazy! Everyone was screaming "Interference," "Interference," "Interference," but there was no call. (*BCE*, 10/14/1990, Page 18)

The game ended with MSU celebrating, again, in Michigan Stadium. Of course, everyone on the Spartan sideline thought it was a good "no call." All is fair in love, war, and football, right? Michigan fans claimed that they were "robbed" and that Sparty got away with one, which turned out to be true. Michigan State fans argued that Michigan always finds a reason to explain away a Spartan victory. Interestingly, the Big Ten Conference reviewed the controversial play the next day and Dave Parry, the Director of Officiating, issued an apology to Gary Moeller. (*LA Times,* Bill Dwyre, 10/16/1990) Oh boy, what a way to get knocked out of the top ranking in college football! Obviously, this game went down in series history as the most controversial ending in the history of the Mitten State pigskin battles, so far!

As it turned out, Gary Moeller's first quarter decision to go for a touchdown instead of kicking a short field goal turned out to be the critical call of the game. The Spartan defense made one of the great goal-line stands in series history and it proved to be the difference of the game! Bottom line, it was a great game to win and a tough one to lose. Michigan State ran for 222-yards and passed for 143 more to total 365-yards of offense. Michigan did some good things on offense (176 net rushing yards and 213 passing) but failing to win on the final gamble was the difference. Since, you cannot assume that the Wolverines would have scored on another play, there is no "asterisk" in the final score. As my third son would say, "It is what it is!"

Team	1st	2nd	3rd	4th	Final
MSU	7	0	7	14	28
UM	7	0	7	13	27

SERIES UPDATE:

The hard-fought game gave George Perles his third series win. He improved his overall record to 3 wins, 5 losses and 0 ties against the Wolverines. Even better, the Paul Bunyan Trophy returned to East Lansing after the Wolverines kidnapped it for two years. If you are keeping score at home, Michigan still held the series advantage with a record of 54 wins, 24 losses and 5 ties. However, Michigan State closed the gap in the "Trophy Series," but still trailed with a record of 15 wins, 21 losses, and 2 ties. George Perles and his team of "No One's" would enjoy another year of bragging rights and there was nothing that Michigan could do about for another year. I wonder if Coach Perles sent a "Thank You' note to Dave Parry at the Big Ten offices in Chicago?

SERIES MILESTONES:

The 1990 edition of Michigan vs Michigan State provided some interesting milestones. First, the crowd of 106,188 was huge, but it was 21 people short of a new record. Nonetheless, it was another amazing crowd for another "bitter Big Ten battle" between UM and MSU. Second, it was Gary Moeller's first series game and his first loss. It was also the third straight time that a Michigan Football Coach lost his series opener to the Spartans (Bump Elliott in 1959 and Bo Schembechler in 1969). Third, this was easily the closest, and most controversial, game in the history of the eighty-three-game series. The closest previous wins were both 3-0 which Michigan accomplished twice (1914 & 1928).

Fourth, this game also marked the first time that an opposing coach received an "apology" from the Big Ten for the way that a series game ended. It is no wonder that this series is so heated and so controversial. One final note about how the season eventually ended for both teams. For the second time, Michigan and Michigan State shared the Big Ten Championship along with Iowa and Illinois. Yes, this was the first time that four conference teams shared the title. If this game/season were any indication of how things would go for the rest of the decade, it was going to be a wild ride in the last nine years of the Twentieth Century!

SEASON SUMMARIES:

George Perles probably did not send a "Thank You" note to the Big Ten because he was too busy getting his Spartans ready for their next game at Illinois. The Spartan offense was ineffective against the Illini and they lost in Champaign (15-13). MSU was now 1-2-0 in the conference and it did not appear that they had a chance for the championship unless they got some help and won the rest of their games. Well, that is exactly what happened! Michigan State's offense woke up and their defense played very well. The Spartans beat Purdue (55-33), Indiana (45-20), Minnesota (28-16), and Northwestern 29-22). Wisconsin came to town and shut down the Spartan offense, but still left East Lansing with a 14-9 loss. The Spartans beat Southern California in the John Hancock Bowl to finish with a final record of 8 wins, 3 losses, and 1 tie. It was quite a turn-around for the Green and White and another excellent coaching job by George Perles. Interestingly, no Spartans earned any first team All-American honors for the 1990 season.

Gary Moeller's team took the loss very hard. They dropped to tenth in the rankings and then proceeded to drop their second straight home game to Iowa (24-23). Yes, another one-point loss! Gary Moeller was halfway through his first season and he was probably wondering if he was ever going to get a break! He had three wins and three losses. Yes, the difference between being 3-3-0 and 6-0-0 was nine-points. Moeller could not really feel sorry for himself because he had another game to play in week seven. Besides that, there is no feeling sorry for yourself in football! The good news was that the next game was against Indiana. The Wolverines traveled to Bloomington and returned home with a satisfying win (45-19). Suddenly, things started going Michigan's way. The Wolverines won the next four games to push their record to 8 wins and 3 losses. As I already mentioned, they finished in a four-way tie for the Big Ten Title with a record of 6-2-0. Michigan blew out Mississippi in the Gator Bowl (35-3) and finished with an overall record of 9 wins and 3 losses. Safety Tripp Wellborne earned All-American honors for the second straight season and lineman Dean Dingman was named an All-American for the first time in his career.

Game #84: October 12, 1991 at Spartan Stadium in East Lansing

BACKGROUND INFORMATION:

Gary Moeller was back for his second season in August 1991. He had to be wondering how it could top season one. His team survived some disappointing losses and still bounced back to earn a share of the Big Ten Championship. That made it three in a row for Michigan going back to 1988 and 1989 when Bo won his last two titles.

Things started much better in 1991 as the second ranked Wolverines defeated Boston College (35-13) and Notre Dame (24-14) to start fast at 2-0-0. Speaking of fast, the third-ranked Wolverines hosted #1 Florida State on September 28, 1991 and the game looked like a track meet! The game was played at hyper-speed especially when FSU had the ball. Michigan tried to stay with the Seminoles, but they blazed out of town with a 51-31 win over the Wolverines. Moeller's footballers went to Iowa the next week. This time, Michigan was the faster, and better, team. The Maize and Blue defeated the Black and Gold by a score of 43-24. The fifth ranked Wolverines were 3-1-0 and looking forward to some revenge in East Lansing in week five!

George Perles entered his ninth season at the Spartan helm in 1991 which was good news for MSU fans. In his first eight years, he built a winning football program in East Lansing. Coach Perles was proud of what his team had accomplished, especially in the last six years. As always, he lost some excellent players to graduation, but he had some returning letterman that he knew he could rely on. Coach Perles thought his team would be pretty darn good. He did not promise another championship, but if things worked out, it could happen again!

The Spartans began the 1991 season with a game against Central Michigan and it turned out to be a shocker! The Chips acted like they owned Spartan Stadium and they left with a 20-3 win over the dazed and confused MSU footballers. Game two was even worse. Notre Dame sent the visiting Spartans back to East Lansing with a 49-10 defeat. Lowly Rutgers added insult to injury by beating the Spartans in Spartan Stadium (14-7). The Big Ten season started with MSU's fourth consecutive loss. Indiana beat the Spartans in Bloomington, Indiana (31-0). Wow! Michigan State lost four straight games at the start of a season for the first time since 1982. At 0-4-0, the Spartans did not appear to be ready to face fifth-ranked Michigan, but that is what makes rivalry games so great! MSU could really get back on track with another series upset win at home!

GAME SUMMARY: UM 45 MS 28

The eighty-fourth game Mitten State series game was another one to remember for the Wolverines and another one for the Spartans to forget! Michigan scored early and often . Yes, they controlled the game right from the start. Michigan jumped out to a 14-0 first quarter lead thanks to two Desmond Howard touchdowns on pass receptions (7 and 12-yards) and two J.D. Carlson extra points. Elvis Grbac threw his third touchdown pass of the first quarter to Dave Diebolt (1-yard) and Carlson's PAT made it 21-0. Late in the second quarter, Jim Miller finally got MSU on the board with a 7-yard scoring pass to Courtney Hawkins. Jim Del Verne's extra point closed the gap to 21-7 at halftime. (*Detroit News,* 10/13/1991, Page 46)

Michigan scored two more touchdowns in the third quarter on two scoring runs from tailback Jesse Johnson (17 and 29-yards). MSU scored on a 10-yard pass from Jim Miller to Courtney Hawkins to make the score 35-14 after forty-five minutes of playing time. Michigan State outscored the Wolverines in the final quarter by a margin of 14-10, but it did not really matter. Michigan celebrated another big victory in East Lansing and Sparty lost more ground in the series race. (*Detroit News,* 10/13/1991, Page 46)

The eighty-fourth edition of the annual blood-letting event between the Spartans and the Wolverines was decided early. Michigan lost some blood this day, but MSU footballers lost more. Both offenses rolled up and down the field. Michigan earned 31 first downs and gained 501 net yards (325 rushing plus 175 passing). The Wolverines lost two fumbles, but it didn't matter. Elvis Grbac was sharp with his three touchdown passes. MSU's Jim Miller had a big day. He completed 31 of 40 passes for 323-yards. He matched Grbac's three TD passes, but also threw two interceptions. Michigan State's running game was held to only 84-net yards which forced Miller into predictable passing situations which resulted in three key sacks. Overall, it was another hard-fought series game, but Michigan was the better team on this day. (*Detroit News,* 10/13/1991, Page 46)

Team	1st	2nd	3rd	4th	Final
UM	14	7	14	10	45
MSU	0	7	7	14	28

SERIES UPDATE:

Michigan pushed their series advantage to 55 victories, 24 defeats, and 5 ties. The Wolverines increased their Paul Bunyan Trophy series lead to 22-15-2. Michigan and Michigan State were even at 1-1-0 in the decade of the Nineties. Once again, it was a great time to be a Wolverine, but not so much for Spartan fans.

SERIES MILESTONES:

There were many series milestones to mention from game number eighty-four. First, the Spartan Stadium crowd of 80,157 broke the old record of 80, 093. Second, Gary Moeller earned his first series win on his second try. Moeller also earned his first series road win. One other item of note was that Desmond Howard added to the impressive resume that he was building for the 1991 Heisman Trophy. He caught 8 passes for 101-yards and 2 touchdowns. Howard also gained 4-yards on an end around play. Desmond returned two punts and two kickoffs for a total of 33-yards. Finally, Michigan's forty-five points set their series record for most points scored in East Lansing.

SEASON SUMMARIES:

Gary Moeller's team kept the pedal to the metal in week six and defeated Indiana by a score of 24-16. The high-powered Wolverine offense went into high gear and finished the season with five straight wins and none of them were closer than twenty-points. Michigan won the Big Ten Championship with a perfect record of 8-0-0 and earned the Rose Bowl game for their reward. The Washington Huskies (1991 National Champions) figured out a way to slow down the high-scoring Wolverines which helped them defeat Michigan (34-14). Michigan ended the 1991 season with a final record of 10 wins and 2 defeats. The offense, led by Elvis Grbac and Desmond Howard, scored 420 points which was the first time that a Michigan team scored that many points since 1976 (432).

Michigan's outstanding season helped Erick Anderson, Matt Elliott, Greg Skrepenak, and Desmond Howard earn All-American honors in 1991. Of course, Howard also became Michigan's second Heisman Trophy winner too!

After losing to Michigan, George Perles did the only thing he could do and that was keep on keeping on! He must have said and done all the right things because the Spartans defeated Minnesota on Homecoming Day (20-12)! Thankfully, the losing streak was over. Now it was time for the MSU footballers to go on one of their famous season-ending win streaks. Unfortunately, Spartan fans saw the Green and White "gridders" lose the next two games to Ohio State (27-17) and Northwestern (23-16) to lower their record to 1 win and 7 losses with three games to go. Michigan State was able to defeat Wisconsin (20-7), but they lost to Purdue in Lafayette (27-17). The dismal 1991 season ended on a high note when the Spartans beat Illinois (27-24). Finally, the agony was over! MSU finished the season with an overall record of 3 wins and 8 losses. They went 3-5-0 in the Big Ten which put them in sixth place. Once again, no MSU Spartans earned All-American honors in 1991.

Wow, what started out as a promising season ended up being the worst campaign of the George Perles Era. Unfortunately, the Spartan football program took a giant step backward in the ninth year of the George Perles Era. Everyone had their work cut out for them in the off-season. Things had to get better in 1992, or else!

Game #85: October 10, 1992 at Michigan Stadium in Ann Arbor

BACKGROUND INFORMATION:

There was only one rule change in 1992 and it favored the defense. Now, a defender could advance a fumble from any spot on the field. (*USA Today CFE*, Page 473).

Coach George Perles was not the most popular man in East Lansing after the awful 1991 season. He did not spend a lot of time listening to the critics, he just focused on how he could improve his football team. Fortunately, there were no expectations, or pressure, for a Big Ten Championship in 1992. Everyone in East Lansing just wanted to see MSU get back to playing winning football again.

Michigan State invited Central Michigan to open the season in East Lansing for the second straight season. Unfortunately for Spartans fans, the rude guests from Mount Pleasant left with another win (24-20) over MSU.

That made it two wins in a row for the Chips and the folks in East Lansing were not happy! In week two, visiting Notre Dame left with a 52-31 win over Sparty. Oh boy, everyone was thinking "Here we go again!" The Spartans flew to Boston to face the BC Eagles and that did not work out too well either. Final score Boston College 14 & MSU 0. Wow, MSU was off to another 0-3-0 start heading into their first Big Ten game against Indiana. Finally, the Spartans played some good football on Homecoming Day and sent their fans home to celebrate a 42-31 win. Once again, it was time for Michigan Week, but nobody in East Lansing was looking forward to the trip to Ann Arbor. This one could get ugly, real fast!

The Gary Moeller Era entered year three in 1992 and things had gone well, so far. The Wolverines posted a record of 19 wins and 5 losses over that period and won two conference championships. As expected, Michigan had plenty of talent coming back for the 1992 season, but not Desmond Howard. Michigan's second Heisman Trophy winner left early for the NFL. Still, everyone expected the talented Wolverines to compete for their fifth consecutive Big Ten Title. The pollsters ranked Michigan as the sixth-best team in the country when the Wolverines left for South Bend, Indiana for game number one.

Notre Dame was ranked #3 when they kicked off against Michigan. For the first time in series history, Michigan and Notre Dame tied 17-17. Michigan got into the win column with a 35-3 win over Oklahoma State. The Wolverines finished the non-conference portion of their schedule with a 61-7 blowout over Houston. Another big win (52-28) over Iowa gave the Michigan an overall record of 3-0-1 heading into MSU Week. Time to get ready for another Spartan invasion in Ann Arbor.

GAME SUMMARY: MSU 10 UM 35

The largest crowd in series history (106, 788) filled Michigan Stadium to watch the 85th edition of the "Bitter Football Battle" between Michigan and Michigan State. Once again, Michigan was the better team and nobody in East Lansing was happy about it! The Wolverines ran better, passed better, and defended better. That sums it up for this game!

Just like 1991, the Wolverines scored early and often. Tyron Wheatley opened the scoring midway through the first quarter on a 10-yard run. Peter Elezovic kicked the extra point and Michigan led 7-0. Mo's footballers poured it on in the second quarter with three touchdowns (Jesse Johnson's 3-yard run, Derrick Alexander's 80-yard punt return, and Bernie Leggett's 1-yard run), and three more Elezovic extra points. Michigan led 28-0! MSU kicker Bill Stoyanovich put the Spartans on the board with a last-minute field goal (21-yards). The Wolverines went to the locker with a 28-3 halftime lead. (*Lansing State Journal*, (*LSJ*), 10/11/1992, Page 69).

Both defenses played well in the third quarter which slowed the game down. However, the Spartans closed the gap when Jim Miller threw a 27-yard scoring pass to Mill Coleman. The extra point cut the Michigan lead to 28-10. As it turned out, the Spartans did not score again, but the Wolverines did. Ty Wheatley scored his second touchdown of the game in the final minute. Peter Elezovic ended the scoring with his fifth extra point. Michigan won by a final score of 35-10. (*LSJ*, 10/11/1992, Page 69)

There is no doubt that the Spartans "donated" more blood on this day. It was another bad showing for George Perles and his Michigan State football team. MSU had come so far in recent years, but the trend line was heading in the wrong direction, again! Once again, it is nice to win a home game, but at Michigan, it is always better against a rival!

Team	1st	2nd	3rd	4th	Final
MSU	0	3	7	0	10
UM	7	21	0	7	35

SERIES UPDATE:

Yes, Michigan players, coaches, and fans thoroughly enjoyed their decisive win over the Spartans. There was so much to celebrate! The Wolverines increased their series advantage to 56 wins, 24 losses, and 5 ties. They retained possession of the Paul Bunyan Trophy for the second straight year and increased their advantage over Michigan State in the "Big Ten Years" to 23 wins, 15 losses, and 2 ties. Michigan took the lead in the decade with 2 wins and 1 loss.

SERIES MILESTONES:

There were two more important series milestones for game number eighty-five. First, the crowd of 106,788 fans broke the previous series record by almost six-hundred people (580). Second, it was the fortieth game of the Paul Bunyan Trophy series with Michigan in front with 23 wins, 15 losses and 2 ties.

SEASON SUMMARIES:

Michigan State followed up their loss to Michigan with a road win over Minnesota (20-15). Maybe things would turn around for the Green and White, or maybe not since the next game was against Ohio State! The Buckeyes came to East Lansing and left with a 27-17 win over the Spartans.

Finally, in week eight, the Spartans began playing some good football. They barely beat Northwestern (27-26) but rolled over Wisconsin (26-10) and Purdue (35-13) to chalk up three straight wins. The season ended with a disappointing loss at Illinois (14-10). Tenth year of the George Perles Era ended on another sour note. Although improved, the Spartans still posted their second straight losing season at 5 wins and 6 losses. They played better in the Big Ten and finished with a winning record of 5-3-0 which was good enough for third place. Not a good year, but they did win four of the last six games. For the third straight year, MSU was shut out in the All-American honors program. Once again, Coach Perles would spend the off-season looking for answers and as many good recruits as he could find. The natives in East Lansing were starting to get restless, which is never good for the job security of a football coach!

The Wolverines continued to play well after their victory over Michigan State. Indiana went down the next week by a score of 31-3. A Homecoming blowout over Minnesota (63-13) gave Michigan a record of 7-0-1 with four games to go. The red-hot Wolverines beat a scrappy Purdue team (24-17) and hammered Northwestern (40-7) in game nine. Interestingly, the next two weeks ended in consecutive ties against Illinois (22-22) and Ohio State (13-13) for the first time in Michigan football history.

Michigan finished the regular season as an unbeaten team with a record of 8-0-3. The back-to-back ties dropped them to #6 in the country. Michigan's Big Ten record of 6-0-2 gave them another championship and another shot at Washington in the Rose Bowl. This time, the Wolverines beat the Huskies (38-31). Gary Moeller's third season ended with 9 wins, 0 losses, and 3 ties. As Frank Sinatra would say, "It was a very good year!" Derrick Alexander, Joe Cocozzo and Chris Hutchinson earned All-American honors for their stellar play in 1992.

260

Game #86: October 9, 1993 at Spartan Stadium in East Lansing

BACKGROUND INFORMATION:

Once again, it was time to fine tune college football. The "hash marks" were moved toward the center of the field to give the offenses more room on the "short side" of the field. The "fumblerooski" play was outlawed because it was "too difficult to officiate." (*USA Today CFE*, Page 486)

There was BIG news in the Big Ten since Penn State was welcomed into the conference for the 1993-1994 academic year. Of course, the addition of Penn State expanded the number of conference schools to eleven, but the name was not changed to the Big Eleven.

Gary Moeller's best season would have turned out even better if his high-scoring offense could have mustered three more points in their three tie games. Wow, they were so remarkably close to a perfect 12-0-0 campaign. Everybody thought Michigan would be strong again in 1993. The Wolverines had plenty of talent on offense, defense, and special teams. Michigan started the season as the third-ranked team in the country. Would the Maize and Blue footballers make a run for the National Championship? Could Michigan win a sixth-straight Big Ten Title? Those were the BIG questions surrounding year four of the Gary Moeller Era.

The Wolverines began the 1993 season with a solid 41-14 win over Washington State. Week two did not go as well against, you guessed it, Notre Dame. The rude Irish had the audacity to beat the Wolverines, again, in the Big House (27-23). Mo's team bounced back with a nice win over Houston (42-21) to end the non-conference season at 2-1-0. The Big Ten season started better as Michigan beat the Hawkeyes by a score of 24-7. The win pushed Michigan's conference winning streak to twenty-two straight games dating back to 1990. Ninth-ranked Michigan was now focused on another series game against those pesky Spartans. Time for some "Big Boy" football in East Lansing!

After six-straight winning seasons, the Michigan State football program went back to their losing ways. Back-to-back losing seasons did not sit well with the Spartan faithful. Coach Perles was trying to figure out how to get MSU back on the winning side of the "won-lost" column. There was no pressure, but this could not continue. Actually, there was a lot of pressure on George Perles to get the Spartan football train back on the "winning" tracks again.

The MSU footballers started well with a big 31-14 win over Kansas. Once again, Notre Dame messed up a good thing and sent the visiting Spartans home to ponder a 36-14 defeat. Central Michigan came to town in week three and the East Lansing faithful were probably nervous since CMU had won the last two games against the Spartans. Finally, MSU beat the Chips by a score of 48-34. The good news was that Michigan State had a record of 2-1-0 in their noncomference games. The bad news was that ninth-ranked Michigan was coming to town to start MSU's Big Ten season. This would be another critically important series game for both teams. Big Ten superiority, "bragging rights" and the Paul Bunyan Trophy would be on the line. Game on!

GAME SUMMARY: UM 7 MSU 17

Game number eighty-six in the "blood" series was a lot of fun for the Michigan State faithful, but not for Wolverine fans! The underdog Spartans came out swinging hard! Their offense took command with 17-first half points and then the defense really went to work.

Michigan won the toss and chose to give the Spartans the ball to start the game. That proved to be a bad call! MSU quarterback, Jim Miller, was very sharp on the opening drive. He led the Green and White offense on an eleven-play drive that covered sixty-five yards. Fullback Brice Adams scored on a 3-yard run and the extra-point made it 7-0. MSU forced a fumble on the ensuing kickoff. Michigan's defense held, but Spartan kicker Bill Stoyanovich nailed a 47-yard field goal that increased the Spartan lead to 10-0. The Spartans scored their second touchdown on a 3-yard scoring pass from Miller to backup fullback Scott Green. The Stoyanovich PAT kick made it 17-0 Spartans and that is how the first half ended. (*DFP*, 10/10/1993, Page 56)

Michigan's State's defense continued to play well in the third quarter, but they did allow a Michigan touchdown. The score was 17-7 at the end of the 45-minutes of play and that is how the game ended! Michigan State's defense played their best game of the year against one of the best offenses in the country. Michigan entered the game averaging over 32-points (32.5) per game and over 400 yards of offense (436) per contest. At the end of the day, they only mustered 245-total yards (212 passing and 33 rushing). The Spartan defense forced a fumble and had three quarterback sacks. (*Lansing State Journal*, (*LSJ*), 10/11/1992, Page 69)

MSU's offense totaled just over three hundred yards which was good enough to score their seventeen points. More importantly, the Spartans did not self-destruct and hurt themselves with costly turnovers. (*DFP*, 10/10/1993, Page 56) In the end, Michigan State was the lower ranking team on this day, but they clearly out-played the ninth-ranked Wolverines. Obviously, both teams lost some blood in this game but Michigan lost more!

Team	1st	2nd	3rd	4th	Final
UM	0	0	7	0	7
MSU	10	7	0	0	17

SERIES UPDATE:

Michigan State regained possession of the Paul Bunyan Trophy. Michigan still held their big advantage in the series with 56 wins, 25 losses, and 5 ties. Michigan State closed the gap in the trophy series tally with 16 wins, 23 losses, and 2 ties. The Spartans pulled even with the Wolverines in the Nineties with a record of 2 wins and 2 losses.

SERIES MILESTONES:

There were two milestones that emerged from this game. First, it was the first time that both teams were even in a decade (2-2-0) after the first four games of a decade. Usually, one team was already leading by a good margin of the season in other years. Second, the Spartans won their 25th series game which was a good thing for MSU.

SEASON SUMMARIES:

Gary Moeller admitted that MSU outplayed his Wolverines after the disappointing loss in East Lansing. However, at 1-1-0, his team was still in the conference race. Instead of ruminating about the loss, he focused on getting his 18th ranked Wolverines ready for 7th ranked Penn State. It must have been a good week of practice since Michigan beat PSU 21-13 in Happy Valley. Unfortunately, Michigan's title chances ended with two-straight losses to Illinois and Wisconsin. Moeller got his team refocused and the Wolverines finished with four straight wins that included a 42-7 win over North Carolina State in the Hall of Fame Bowl. The Wolverines ended the season with a record of 8 wins and 4 losses. They finished in a fourth-place tie in the Big Ten with a record of 5-3-0. No Michigan players earned All-American honors in 1993.

The Spartans faced Ohio State the week after beating Michigan, but the results were not good. Michigan State traveled to Columbus and lost to the Buckeyes (28-21). The rest of the season continued to be an "up-and-down" pattern of one win and one loss or two wins and then two straight losses. The last regular season game against Wisconsin was played in Tokyo, Japan. The Spartans must have had a bad case of "jet lag" since the Badgers pounded them by a score of 41-20. The good news was that MSU was invited to play in the Liberty Bowl in December. However, the bad news was that the Green and White footballers ended the season with a 28-7 loss to Louisville.

Michigan State finished the eleventh season of the Perles Era with a record of 6 wins and 6 losses. They were also even in the Big Ten with a record of 4-4-0. The only thing to celebrate was another win over Michigan. Paul Bunyan was back home where Green and White fans felt he belonged. In the end, it was not a winning season. And it was not a losing season. However, it was not good enough for most of the fine football folks in East Lansing. The Michigan victory probably saved George's job, but how long could this go on?

Game #87: October 8, 1994 at Michigan Stadium in Ann Arbor

BACKGROUND INFORMATION:

There were no significant changes to mention for the 125th season of college football. The NCAA was enjoying great success and football (college and professional) was the only game "in town" since Major League Baseball, the NBA and the NHL all had labor problems that disrupted their seasons. Yes, it was a great time to be a football fan! (*USA Today CFE*, Page 498)

The twelfth season of the George Perles Era began with pressure, a lot of pressure. Many people in East Lansing, including university president M. Peter McPherson, were tired of watching losing football. In fact, McPherson commented before the season that he was expecting an "outstanding" season in 1994, but never clarified what that meant in term of Spartan victories. George Perles still loved Michigan State University, but that love was not being returned for the beleaguered football coach. The only way for George Perles to survive in 1994 was to win more games and lose less. Pretty simple to talk about, but not easy to do!

Unfortunately for Coach Perles, the 1994 season did not begin with a win. In fact, the Spartans lost the first two games of the season to Kansas (17-10) and Notre Dame (21-20). Then, they won two straight games against Miami of Ohio (45-10), and Wisconsin (29-10). Michigan State's record was 2 wins and 2 losses heading into Michigan Week. Would MSU be able to win another tough game in Ann Arbor?

Gary Moeller began the 1994 football season with cautious optimism. He had a strong returning cast coming back on offense and defense. If his team could stay healthy, they could be exceptionally good. Like everyone else in Ann Arbor, Moeller was not happy with Michigan's 1993 season. He was totally focused on getting the Wolverines back to the top of the Big Ten. The pollsters thought that he had a good team and listed Michigan as the fifth best team in the country at kickoff time.

Moeller's Wolverines began the season with an unimpressive win (34-26) over Boston College. Even though they beat the Eagles, they dropped to number six before heading to Notre Dame in week two. The Wolverines escaped South Bend with a 26-24 win over the Irish to run their record to 2-0-0. Game number three was the "Hail Mary" loss to Colorado (27-26). A ticked off Michigan team kicked off the Big Ten season with a 29-14 win over Iowa. Once again, it was time for 3-1-0 Michigan to get ready for MSU and avenge their loss in 1993!

GAME SUMMARY: MSU 20 UM 40

Game #87 between Michigan and Michigan State was another Michigan blowout. The Wolverines played the role of very rude hosts as they doubled-up on their guests by a final score of 40-20. Moeller's footballers did a lot of things right, but George's boys did not do enough to win. In fact, the Spartans were only half as good as they needed to be on this day.

For one of the few times in series history, both Michigan and Michigan State scored in every quarter. However, the Wolverines scored twice as much as Sparty. Michigan scored first on a 38-yard field goal by Remy Hamilton. Five minutes later Spartan kicker Chris Gardner tied the game at 3-3 with a 28-yard field goal. Early in the second quarter, Michigan State took a 6-3 the lead on another Gardner field goal (39-yards). The lead change seemed to fire up the Wolverines since they scored seventeen points in the last twelve minutes of the second quarter. (*DFP*, 10/9/1994, Page 45)

Ty Wheatley caught a 5-yard scoring pass from Todd Collins, Hamilton kicked another field goal (26-yards), and Wheatley ran 2-yards for another score. Michigan led 20-6 at halftime. The Wolverines added seventeen more points to their total in the third period of play. Meanwhile, the Spartans only scored seven points. Hamilton booted his third field goal (33-yards), Wheatly ran for his third score (11-yards) and Tim Biakabutuka dashed for another score (26-yards). Michigan State countered with an 18-yard touchdown pass from Tony Banks to Scott Greene. Both kickers made their extra points. Michigan led 37-13 at the end of forty-five minutes of Mitten State football mayhem. (*DFP*, 10/9/1994, Page 45)

Remy Hamilton's fourth field goal (21-yards) pushed the Wolverine advantage to 40-13 with ten minutes to play in the game. The Spartans responded with their final points on a 9-yard pass play from Banks to Nigea Carter. Chris Gardner's final extra point made it 40-20. It was another embarrassing loss for MSU. Now, with a bad finish, George Perles might be gone since he did not have a victory over Michigan to hang his hat on. (*DFP*, 10/9/1994, Page 45)

Team	1st	2nd	3rd	4th	Final
MSU	3	3	7	7	20
UM	3	17	17	3	40

SERIES UPDATE:

The Wolverine series advantage grew again. Michigan increased their record to 57 wins, 25 losses, and 5 ties. Michigan also remained on the winning side of the Paul Bunyan Trophy ledger with a record of 24-16-2. The Wolverines also took the lead in the Nineties with a record of 3-2-0. Michigan players, coaches and fans were already enjoying "bragging rights" at the end of the game. Of course, they welcomed Paul Bunyan home with open arms.

SERIES MILESTONES:

Although no one knew it at the time, this was the last series game for George Perles and Gary Moeller. The tenures of both men ended abruptly, for different reasons, and not for wins and losses! I will explain more of the "details" later in this chapter, but here is how the series resumes for George Perles and Gary Moeller ended. Coach Perles finished his career with a final record of 4 wins and 8 losses against Michigan. Gary Moeller posted an overall series record of 3 wins and 2 losses against Michigan State. Michigan kicker Remy Hamilton became the first man to kick a field goal in every quarter of a series game. Finally, it was the first trophy game where both teams scored in every quarter!

SEASON SUMMARIES:

Michigan State's season did not get any easier after losing to Michigan. Ohio State came to town on October 15th and left with a 23-7 win. The Spartans went to Iowa and lost a close one to the Hawkeyes (19-14). A winning season was still possible, especially since MSU won two straight games against Indiana (27-21) and Northwestern (35-17).

Unfortunately, the roof blew off the football building when President Mc Pherson fired George Perles after an investigation revealed that MSU had "lost institutional control" of the football program. Coach Perles stayed until the end of the season and the Spartans beat Purdue (42-30) and lost to Penn State (59-31). It did not matter since all five wins in 1994 were forfeited which gave Michigan State their second winless season in program history at 0 wins, 11 losses, and 0 ties. It was an ugly time at MSU because George Perles always bragged about running his program the right way. An extensive investigation revealed that some MSU football "insiders" were providing illegal payments to players and fixing grades to keep players eligible. Technically, George Perles was not found responsible for the infractions, but he was the man in charge, so he had to go.

Fifth-ranked Michigan hosted Penn State the next week and lost a tough one to Joe Paterno's Nittany Lions. Michigan followed up with a 19-14 win over Illinois to stay in the conference race at 3-1-0. A conference championship appeared unlikely after an upset loss to Wisconsin (31-19). Maybe the Wolverines could do it if they won every remaining game and got some help. As it turned out, they won two straight over Purdue (45-23) and Minnesota (38-22). Unfortunately, they ran out of magic and lost the season finale to Ohio State (22-6). The season did end in a good way with a 24-14 win over Colorado State in the Holiday Bowl. Michigan finished the 1994 season with another record of 8 wins and 4 losses. They landed in third place in the Big Ten with a record of 5 wins and 3 losses. Kicker Remy Hamilton and cornerback Ty Law earned All-American honors for the Wolverines in 1994.

Game #88: November 4, 1995 at Spartan Stadium in East Lansing

BACKGROUND INFORMATION:

Things really fell apart for the Spartan football program in November 1994. Meanwhile, things in Ann Arbor were not running smoothly either. Nobody in Wolverine Nation was happy about back-to-back seasons of 8-4-0, especially Gary Moeller. Some of the natives were getting restless, but it did not matter since it appeared that Gary Moeller would be back for his sixth season in August 1995. All that changed in late April 1995 when Gary Moeller and some friends went out for dinner at a restaurant in Southfield, Michigan. Apparently, Moeller had too much to drink and made a big scene. A few days later, he resigned from one of the best coaching jobs in America.

Early May is generally not a good time to go looking for a new football coach. Michigan Athletic Director Joe Roberson had to make the biggest decision of his tenure at a less than ideal time. Because of the timing, looking outside the program was not possible. All the best coaches were in place evaluating their spring football programs and planning fall camps. Mr. Roberson had a short list to work from—a really short list! He turned to a man named Lloyd Carr who was Moeller's Assistant Head Coach in 1994. Carr was a solid football coach and a loyal Michigan Man (15 years for Bo and Mo). He also knew the Michigan system. There were lots of plusses here, but Carr had only been a head coach in high school and that was over twenty years ago. It is a big jump from John Glenn High School to the Big House, but that is what happened. Lloyd Carr was named as the "interim" Head Coach at Michigan. He would have a chance to prove that he was the right guy, but nobody knew how long his "head coaching tryout" would be.

Lloyd Carr's Michigan coaching career began with a last second 18-17 win over Virginia on a sweltering day in Michigan Stadium. Things got better the next week with a more convincing win over Illinois (38-14). Carr's footballers won three more games over Memphis (24-7), Boston College (23-13), and Miami of Ohio (38-19). The Carr Era was off to a perfect start at 5 wins and 0 losses. His team was ranked sixth best in the country and Northwestern was coming to town. Unfortunately, the underdog Wildcats were ranked (#25) and they had something to prove. Northwestern left town with a big upset over the Wolverines (19-13). Michigan bounced back to stay in the conference race with wins over Indiana (34-17) and Minnesota (52-17). It was time for Lloyd Carr to get his Maize and Blue footballers ready for the annual blood-letting contest in East Lansing. Hopefully, he could reverse the trend of losing a first series game to the Spartans that began with Bump Elliott.

Nick Saban was one of the "hot" head coaching hires of the 1995 season. Saban punched his coaching "ticket" at many good places at the college level and in the National Football League. Maybe he would be the guy to rebuild the Spartan football program. Coach Saban knew that his first year would be better than the way the 1994 season ended. Even if he only won a single game, it would be better than 0-11-0!

GAME SUMMARY: UM 25 MSU 28

The eighty-eighth game of the "in-state-hate" football series was another titanic struggle with both teams battling hard on every play. Two new coaches were facing off in the same series game for the first time in sixty-eight years. Both men knew about the importance of this game, believe me they knew!

Seventh-ranked Michigan scored first on a 35-yard field goal by Remy Hamilton which put the Wolverines up 3-0 after fifteen minutes of play. Early in the second quarter, the Spartans struck like lightening with a 70-yard punt return by Derick Mason and the kick made it 7-3. The MSU footballers increased their lead near the end of the first half on a 7-yard run by fullback Scott Green. The first half ended with Michigan State leading 14-3. (*DFP*, 11/5/1995, Page 41)

Michigan dominated the third quarter, but only had a touchdown and a 2-point conversion to show for their efforts. The Wolverine touchdown came on Will Carr's 3-yard touchdown run. The third quarter ended with Michigan State still leading 14-11. In the early minutes of the final quarter, Michigan took the lead on a 5-yard run by Tim Biakabutuka. After the extra point, it was 18-14 in favor of the Wolverines. Quarterback Tony Banks led the Spartans on a scoring drive that ended with a 42-yard touchdown pass to Muhsin Muhammad. After the extra point kick, MSU was back in front 21-18 with just over six minutes to play. (*DFP*, 10/9/1994, Page 45)

Michigan quarterback Brian Griese answered the Banks play with a 22-yard scoring pass to Mercury Hayes and Michigan kicked the extra point for a 25-21 lead. Three minutes remained in the game and the Spartan faithful urged their heroes on to another score. Tony Banks, again, led MSU on a long drive that ate up just over two minutes of precious time. He threw a 25-yard scoring pass to Nigea Carter for the winning touchdown. The extra-point made it 28-25 in favor of the Spartans and that is how the game ended. (*DFP*, 11/5/1995, Page 41)

It was an exhausting game from start to finish, but the second half was completely full of intense drama. Michigan outscored the Spartans in the second half by a score of 22-14, but MSU won the game. Both offenses played at a high level and many key players made some big plays. In the end, Tony Banks and Nigea Carter made the game's BIGGEST play and that was the game!

Team	1st	2nd	3rd	4th	Final
UM	3	0	8	14	25
MSU	0	14	0	14	28

SERIES UPDATE:

Michigan State's win kept the Paul Bunyan Trophy in East Lansing. Michigan still held the overall series advantage at 57 wins, 26 losses, and 5 ties. The Spartans closed the gap in the trophy series with their 17th win against 24 losses, and 2 ties. Things were even in the Nineties again at 3 wins and 3 losses for each team. Everyone in Spartan Nation would enjoy another year of bragging rights. Of course, the Wolverines would not! Paul Bunyan was home when MSU fans thought he belonged. Yes, life was good again in East Lansing, Michigan.

SERIES MILESTONES:

This was the first time since 1929 that both teams faced off with first year coaches on the sidelines. Nick Saban became the first coach in MSU history to win his first series game. Wow, it took a long time for that to happen, but it was good for the Spartans! Unfortunately, Lloyd Carr became the fourth straight Michigan coach to lose his first game to the Spartans. Even though Carr called Paul Bunyan the "ugliest trophy in college football" he also said you still wanted it in your locker room after the game. Coach Carr would have to wait until 1996 to have Mr. Bunyan in his locker room after the MSU game. Finally, this was the first time that the series game was played so late in the season. It was the ninth game for both teams in 1995. There were no turnovers in this game which may have been a series first, but I am not certain because of the incomplete game records in the early years.

SEASON SUMMARIES:

Interim Coach Lloyd Carr's record dropped to 7-2-0 with the loss at East Lansing. However, things got better the next week in a wet, rainy, slippery game against Purdue in the Big House. Michigan won the strange game by a score of 5-0. Athletic Director Joe Roberson had seen enough. He removed the "interim" tag on Carr's title. Lloyd Henry Carr was now the head coach at The University of Michigan. With his increased job security, Carr proceeded to get his team ready for a big game against eleventh-ranked Penn State. Unfortunately for Coach Carr, the visitors from "Happy Valley" went home happy with a 29-17 victory over the Wolverines. Carr's eighteenth-ranked footballers ended the regular season on a high note with a huge upset over second-ranked OSU (31-23). Michigan earned a spot in the Alamo Bowl against Texas A & M but lost (22-20). The Wolverines finished with a final record of 9 wins and 4 losses. Coach Carr's first team went 5-3-0 in the Big Ten and tied for third place. Jason Horn and Joe Runyan earned All-American honors for the Wolverines in 1995.

Image 11 Nick Saban became the first coach in Aggie/Spartan history to defeat Michigan in his first series game in 1995. (Permission: Bentley Historical Library at The University of Michigan, See Page 369)

Nick Saban's Spartans went on the road after beating Michigan and they defeated Indiana by a score of 31-13. Penn State proved to be a tougher test that the MSU footballers could not pass. The Nittany Lions beat the Spartans by a score of 24-20. The Spartans finished Nick Saban's first regular season with a record of 6 wins, 4 losses, and 1 tie. They earned a trip to the Independence Bowl. Unfortunately, they ended with a disappointing 45-26 loss to Louisiana State University. The good news was that the Green and White still finished with a record of 6-5-1 which gave them their first winning season since 1990. They also ended the Big Ten campaign with a winning record of 4-3-1 which was good for 5th place. The first season of the Nick Saban Era in East Lansing was in the books and the future looked bright for Spartan Nation.

Game #89: November 2, 1996 at Michigan Stadium in Ann Arbor

BACKGROUND INFORMATION:

The 1996 season saw a big change to the rules with the provision that there would be no more tie games in college football. The NCAA had instituted the "no tie" rule in the 1995 bowl season. Now, the no tie rule would apply to all college football games. The Michigan vs Michigan State series had not seen a tie game since 1963 and there would never another! (*USA Today CFE*, Page 524)

The hundredth year of Aggie/Spartan football was the second year of the Nick Saban Era. Coach Saban's first season was a success in East Lansing. He had a winning record in the regular season and in the Big Ten. Of course, one of his victories was over the hated Wolverines so that counted for a lot! Coach Saban also had some excellent players returning on both sides of the ball. Everyone in East Lansing expected Nick Saban to improve on the results of year one. No one, not even the university president, was talking Big Ten Championship just yet, but more wins would be an improvement. Another win over Michigan would also be nice in year two of Coach Saban's tenure.

The Spartans began the 1996 season with a big win over Purdue (52-14). Unfortunately, a road trip to Nebraska was a big wake up call for Saban's Spartans! Nebraska won by a score of 55-14. Louisville came to East Lansing and beat the Green and White by a score of 30-20. The Spartans showed no mercy to Eastern Michigan and blew out the Eagles 47-0. Iowa proved to be a much tougher opponent in week five. The Hawkeyes sent the Spartans back to East Lansing to think about a 37-30 loss. Coach Saban was probably frustrated by the Spartan's inconsistent play in the first five games of the season. MSU was sitting on a record of 2 wins and 3 losses, but all that changed in weeks six, seven and eight.

Saban's offense finally got going and his defense started to get very stingy. This resulted in three straight wins over Illinois (42-14), Minnesota (27-9), and Wisconsin (30-13). Saban's footballers were 5-3-0 heading into Michigan Week. They had some momentum going and a visit to Ann Arbor was not an intimidating prospect. Michigan State had plenty of wins in Michigan Stadium over the years. Why not get another one in 1996?

By all measures, Lloyd Carr's first season at Michigan was a success. His job performance in season one clearly indicated that he had what it took to lead the Michigan Football program. Carr's first team won nine games and finished in the top twenty in both polls (AP=17 and CNN/USA=19). He had some excellent players coming back and everyone expected that it would be another good season for Michigan. Many thought that his team could compete for the conference championship. After all, this was still Michigan, right?

The Wolverines began the season as the twelfth ranked team, but rose to number seven after starting the season with wins over Illinois (20-8), Colorado (20-13), and Boston College (20-14). They easily defeated a good UCLA team (38-9). The sixth-ranked Wolverines headed to Evanston in week five to face off against #22 Northwestern. For the second season in a row, the Wildcats won a close game (17-16) and sent Michigan home to ponder their first loss of the season.

The Wolverines bounced back with wins over Indiana (27-20) and Minnesota (44-10) to stay in the Big Ten race. Now, it was time to get ready for another visit from the MSU Spartans. Would the ninth-ranked Wolverines be ready for MSU this year?

GAME SUMMARY: UM 45 MSU 29

The second largest crowd (106,381) in the history of the series was on hand for series game number eighty-nine. Yes, it was packed with thousands of Maize and Blue fans and a fair representation of Spartan faithful. Once again, it was another game where the records really did not matter. Both teams showed up to play "Big Boy" football as they always did in this hotly contested series. However, it was clear, that Michigan was intent on gaining revenge for the "upset loss" they suffered at the hands of the Spartans in 1995. It was also clear that Sparty would fight for every inch of turf for all sixty minutes!

Michigan scored first on a 28-yard pass from Scott Dreisbach to Jerame Tuman. Remy Hamilton's extra point kick gave the Wolverines a 7-0 lead. Michigan State responded with a 37-yard field goal by Chris Gardner. Michigan led 7-3 at the end of the first quarter. The Spartans took a 10-7 lead on a 7-yard touchdown pass from Todd Schultz to Derrick Mason and Gardner's second extra point. (*Detroit News,* 11/3/1996, Page 40)

Then, Michigan went on a scoring blitz that pretty much put the game away. Scott Dreisbach threw an eight-yard touchdown pass to Russell Shaw with just over two-minutes to play in the half. With the Hamilton extra point, Michigan regained the lead at 14-10. The Wolverine defense picked off a Spartan pass a few plays later and Dreisbach tossed a 15-yards scoring pass to Jerame Tuman. Remy Hamilton kicked the point and Michigan led 21-10 with 15 seconds to play in the half. Amazingly, MSU fumbled the ensuing kickoff and the Wolverines recovered. Dreisbach threw a perfect 26-yard pass to Charles Woodson who scampered into the end zone as time expired. Wow—Michigan led 28-10 at halftime. (*Detroit News,* 11/3/1996, Page 40)

The Wolverines scored first in the third quarter on a 13-yard run by Chris Howard. Hamilton's fifth extra point pushed the Wolverine advantage to 35-10. The Spartans responded with a touchdown of their own on a 4-yard run by Sedric Irvin. The score was 35-17 after Gardner nailed the extra point and that is how the third quarter ended. The Spartans outscored Michigan (12-10) in the final quarter, but it was too little and too late.

Michigan's defense played a little bit better than the Spartan defenders. In one of the highest scoring games of the series, Michigan earned a 45-29 victory. Todd Schultz threw for over 260-yards. He also threw four interceptions that killed MSU's chances for the upset win. Michigan's Scott Dreisbach only threw for 203-yards, but his four touchdown passes were the big difference in the game. The game was closer than the score indicated. Michigan's 21-point outburst in the final two minutes of the half proved to be the turning point of the contest. (*Detroit News,* 11/3/1996, Page 40)

271

Team	1st	2nd	3rd	4th	Final
MSU	3	7	7	12	29
UM	7	21	7	10	45

SERIES UPDATE:

Yes, the Wolverines got their revenge against the Spartans. It was a good win for Michigan and another tough loss for MSU. Michigan increased their series lead to 58 wins, 26 losses, and 5 ties. The Wolverines regained possession of the Paul Bunyan Trophy and improved their record to 25-17-2 since Big Ten play began in 1953. Michigan also regained the lead in the Nineties with a record of 4 wins and 3 losses.

SERIES MILESTONES:

The first milestone in game number eighty-nine was that Michigan became the first team to win the Paul Bunyan Trophy twenty-five times. It was also Lloyd Carr's first series win on his second attempt. Yes, the "ugliest trophy in college football" was back for a long winter and summer's stay in Ann Arbor! This game was also the first time that the teams played two consecutive series games in November.

SEASON SUMMARIES:

After losing to Michigan, the Spartans entertained Indiana. MSU sent the Hoosiers home with a 38-15 loss. The Green and White footballers finished their season with a loss at Penn State (32-29). Michigan State's regular season record of 6-5-0 earned them a spot in the Sun Bowl. Unfortunately, the Spartans got burned by Stanford 38-0! Michigan State finished with a final record of 6 wins and 6 losses in Nick Saban's second season. MSU's record of 5 wins and 3 losses tied them with Michigan for fifth place. Once again, no MSU players earned All-American honors in 1996. Bottom line—the one hundredth year of Aggie/Spartan football was nothing special in East Lansing!

Apparently, the Michigan offense forgot to get on the bus for their next game at Purdue. Michigan lost to the Boilermakers (9-3). It was Michigan's first game without a touchdown since 1994. The good news was that the offense scored seventeen points the next week against Penn State. The bad news was that PSU scored twenty-nine points and Michigan was on a two-game losing streak. The Wolverines finished strong with a 13-9 win over Ohio State.

Michigan earned a spot in the 1997 Outback Bowl but lost to Alabama (17-14). Season two of the Lloyd Carr Era ended with a record of 8 wins and 4 losses. For the fourth straight year, Michigan finished with a record of 5 wins and 3 losses in the Big Ten. Four Wolverines earned All-American honors in 1996 (William Carr, Jarrett Irons, Charles Woodson, and Rod Payne).

Game #90: October 25, 1997 at Spartan Stadium in East Lansing

BACKGROUND INFORMATION:

The NCAA decided to tweak the overtime rule for the 1997 season. If the game was still tied after two overtime periods, both teams had to attempt a two-point conversion after a touchdown. The "rules committee also toughened crackback block and punt returner protection penalties." (*USA Today CFE*, Page 537)

Lloyd Carr spent the off-season looking for ways to improve Michigan football, especially in Big Ten play. Michigan's head coach was painfully aware that the Wolverines had not won a Big Ten Championship since 1992. Carr wanted to get his team to top in 1997. Coach Carr did a lot of things the same in 1997, but one thing he did differently was declare a "theme" for the season. He read a book about the difficulties of climbing the world's tallest mountains. He decided to use "mountain climbing" as a metaphor for the upcoming season. Carr taught his players the importance of concentrating on every step of the journey and embracing the moment. He gave every player a small "pickax" like the ones used by mountain climbers to get player "buy-in." Yes, Michigan was on a mountain climbing mission in 1997. They planned to take season one step and one game at a time!

The fourteenth-ranked Wolverines opened the season in Ann Arbor with a nice win over Colorado (27-3). Baylor came to town in week two and eighth-ranked Michigan pounded them by a score of 38-3. Carr's footballers continued their climb with victories over Notre Dame (21-14), Indiana (37-0), Northwestern (23-6) and Iowa (28-24). By the time they got to MSU week, the fifth-ranked Wolverines had a record of 6-0-0. They were halfway up the mountain and getting more focused and more confident each week. However, a journey to East Lansing awaited. Could the Wolverines take the next step up the mountain, or would the hated Spartans knock them from the ranks of the unbeaten?

Nick Saban also spent the off-season looking for ways to improve his program and his players. Although he did not declare a theme like Carr, he made changes that could result in better play by his football team. No one was predicting any conference championships for the Spartans in 1997. However, it appeared they would be in the upper third of the Big Ten's best teams. Of course, only time would tell.

Michigan State kicked off their 1997 season with a non-conference win over Western Michigan (42-10). Week two went even better as MSU pounded Memphis (51-21). The Spartans continued to roll on their trip to South Bend. Saban's footballers beat the Irish (23-7) to push their season record to 3-0-0. Michigan State stayed focused and won two more games against Minnesota (31-10) and Indiana (38-6).

A trip to Northwestern brought the five-game winning streak to a halt. The Wildcats won a close one (19-17). The Spartans entered Michigan Week as the fifteenth best team in the country with a record of 5-1-0. It was time to end Michigan's stupid mountain climbing adventure and bring them back to earth! The Wolverines were going down in East Lansing!

GAME SUMMARY: UM 23 MSU 7

Game number ninety of this hard-fought series was in doubt for most of the game. As expected, this contest resembled an old-fashioned fist fight. Oh yes, the gloves were off for this Mitten State blood donating event.

Michigan took the lead midway through the first quarter on a 30-yard field goal by Craig Baker. The Spartans scored five minutes later on a "trick play" when Bill Burke threw out of a field goal formation. Running back Sedric Irvin was wide-open for a 22-yard touchdown and a 7-3 Spartan lead. (*Detroit News*, 10/26/1997, Page 42)

That play served two purposes. First it gave the fired up MSU footballers the lead. Second, it woke up a "sleeping Blue Giant!" Michigan regained the lead when quarterback Brian Griese finished a 95-yard drive with a 1-yard scoring run. Michigan kicked the point and Michigan went to the locker room with a 10-7 lead. (*Detroit News*, 10/26/1997, Page 42) Both defenses continued to play well in the third quarter, but Michigan moved the ball enough to get another 30-yard field goal from Baker. Michigan led 13-7 at the end of the third quarter. Chris Howard gave Michigan some breathing room with a 2-yard touchdown run and Baker's kick made it 20-7 with twelve minutes to play. Michigan's defense continued to stop the Spartans at every turn. Kraig Baker finished the scoring with a 27-yard field goal to give the Wolverines a 23-7 lead and that is how the game ended! (*Detroit News*, 10/26/1997, Page 42)

Michigan's defense was the difference in the game. The Wolverine defenders held the high-flying Spartan offense (averaging 34-points a game) to just one touchdown and one extra point! The MSU offense could only generate 272 total yards and only 95-yards came on the ground. Worse yet, Todd Schultz threw six interceptions which killed many promising Spartan drives. The Wolverine offense was efficient, but still had to fight for every yard they gained on the rugged MSU defense. Michigan's backs, led by Chris Howard (21 carries for 110 yards), ran for a total of 173-yards. Brian Griese hit ten of seventeen passes for 102 yards. (*Detroit News*, 10/26/1997, Page 42) More importantly, the Wolverines played errorless football with no turnovers. It was another sweet series road win for Michigan. Of course, it was another bitter pill to swallow for the Spartans!

Team	1st	2nd	3rd	4th	Final
UM	3	7	3	10	23
MSU	7	0	0	0	7

SERIES UPDATE:

Michigan added another victory to their sizeable series advantage. The Wolverines now had 59 wins, 26 losses, and 5 ties in the annual in-state pigskin slugfest. The Maize and Blue footballers increased their trophy series lead to 26 wins, 17 losses, and 2 ties. Michigan pushed their lead in the Nineties to 5-3-0. Paul Bunyan went back to Ann Arbor for another long visit. Wolverine fans started enjoying another season of "bragging rights" as soon as the game ended! Go Blue!

SERIES MILESTONES:

There were four notable milestones in this game. First, series game number ninety was a BIG milestone in history of UM vs MSU football. Second, it was the first time since 1989 that both teams were ranked. Third, it was the first time that a Spartan quarterback threw six interceptions in a series game. Fourth, it was the forty-fifth trophy game in series history.

SEASON SUMMARIES:

Michigan continued to climb higher and higher after their hard-fought victory in East Lansing. The Wolverines sent a Homecoming Day crowd home happy with a win over Minnesota (24-3). Carr's football team went on the road and secured convincing road victories at Penn State (34-8) and Wisconsin (26-16). The only team that stood between the top-ranked Wolverines and a perfect regular season was Ohio State. The Buckeyes (#4) came to Ann Arbor on November 22, 1997 with one purpose—BEAT MICHIGAN! Fortunately, the Wolverines landed on top of the Big Ten football mountain after they defeated the Buckeyes (20-14).

Lloyd Carr's "mountain climbers" had one more peak to conquer and that was at the 1998 Rose Bowl. Michigan defeated eight-ranked Washington State to cap a perfect season at 12-0-0. The Wolverines were named national champions by the Associated Press and their mission was complete! Now, they were sitting on top of college football's highest mountain, although they had to share some of the space with Nebraska! Three Wolverines earned All-American honors in 1997 (Glenn Steele, Jerame Tuman, and Charles Woodson). Yes, Lloyd Carr, the former "interim" coach at Michigan, did something that had not been done at Michigan in fifty years. He took a Wolverine football team to the national championship—one step at a time!

The Spartan loss to Michigan really took a toll on them. They lost the next two games to Ohio State (37-13) and Purdue (22-21) before they got back on track. Of course, they were now out of the Big Ten title chase, but Coach Saban was hoping for a strong finish. MSU did play much better in the final two games of the year. They defeated Illinois (27-17) and Penn State (49-14) to end the regular season with a record of 7-4-0. MSU finished the Big Ten season with a record of 4 wins and 4 losses which tied them for sixth place. Things ended badly at the Aloha Bowl since the Spartans lost big to Washington (51-23)! Season number three of the Nick Saban Era was his second winning season in three years. Unfortunately, Saban and his players had bigger plans for 1997.

Yes, it was another winning, but disappointing season for Spartan Nation! Coach Saban had more work to do in East Lansing, Flozell Adams and Scott Shaw earned All-American honors for MSU in 1997.

Game #91: September 26, 1998 at Michigan Stadium in Ann Arbor

BACKGROUND INFORMATION:

Only one rule change took place in 1998. Now, errant lateral passes could be advanced by the defense as if they were fumbles. (*USA Today CFE*, Page 548)

Nick Saban was back for his fourth season in 1998. His first three seasons were not terrible, but they were not that great either. Spartan fans were getting restless. It was time for Coach Nick Saban to show Spartan Nation that he was the right man for MSU football. He had some excellent players returning on both sides of the ball. Nick Saban thought his team could be good, but he was not sure how good.

Michigan State began the 1998 season with a home loss to Colorado State (23-16). It got worse in week two when MSU was embarrassed by Oregon (48-14). Coach Saban had plenty to worry about since he was having problems with his offense and his defense. Fortunately, miracles do happen! The Spartans put it all together with a convincing win over Notre Dame (45-23). Wow, what a turn-around. It certainly could not have happened at a better time since the next game was at Michigan. The Spartans had some momentum. They beat Notre Dame while Michigan lost to the Irish. I am sure that the Spartans were thinking they could win in Ann Arbor on September 26, 1998. Oh yes, they were thinking that the Wolverines were going down!

After two frustrating seasons in 1995 and 1996, Lloyd Carr's Wolverines won it all in 1997. Okay, he won half of "it all" since Michigan won the Associated Press National Championship Trophy, but not the championship trophy from ESPN/USA Today. Anyway, now Coach Carr had a different kind of a problem. What would he and his Michigan Men do for an encore? Would they be able to repeat like the Wolverines did in 1947 and 1948? Or could they duplicate what Duffy did at MSU in 1965 and 1966? Lloyd Carr knew that the 1997 team was special. He lost many talented players including Heisman Trophy winner Charles Woodson who left a year early for the NFL. It appeared that Michigan would be coming down from the top of the mountain. The only question was, "How low would they go?"

The pollsters thought Michigan might land in a good place. The Wolverines were ranked as the fifth-best team in the country at the start of the 1998 season. The co-defending national champions started the season at Notre Dame. It did not go well. The Irish "whupped up" on Michigan and sent them home with a 36-20 loss. Syracuse came to Ann Arbor in week two and left town with a convincing win (38-28). After two games, the Maize and Blue footballers were sitting on a record of 0 wins and 2 losses. The bad news was that they dropped completely out of the rankings. Michigan won big in their final non-conference game against Eastern Michigan (59-20). Now, Michigan could focus on the Big Ten season since the next game was against Michigan State. Even though his team had one win out of three games, Coach Carr liked what he saw in his hungry Wolverines. Bring on the Spartans!

GAME SUMMARY: MSU 17 UM 29

Game number ninety-one was another Mitten State pigskin classic. It was a hard-fought game with every play ending in a cascade of blood and sweat. The crashing of pads, helmets and exceptionally large human bodies was thunderous at times. Once again, mothers feared for the lives of their offspring playing on the field. The stakes were high for both coaches and both teams. Yes, this was a game that meant so much to everyone involved.

Michigan State drew first blood in this one when they converted a pass interception into 3-points on a Paul Edinger field goal (43-yards). The Wolverines responded with three points of their own on a 51-yard field goal by Jay Feely and the game was tied 3-3 at the end of the first quarter. (*Detroit News*, 9/27/1998, Page 46)

Early in the second quarter, the Spartans took the lead on a 12-yard touchdown pass from Bill Burke to Plaxico Burress. Edinger's PAT kick made it 10-3 in favor or MSU. Michigan State got another break when Michigan fumbled on the next series, but MSU could not score. A few minutes later, Anthony Thomas broke away on a 69-yard run and Feely's extra point tied the game (10-10). A few minutes later, the Wolverines took the lead when Tom Brady threw a 5-yard scoring pass to Tai Streets. Feely kicked the extra point and Michigan led 17-10. The Wolverines took advantage of a Plaxico Burress fumble when Jay Feely kicked his second field goal. The Wolverines had a 20-10 lead late in the second quarter. Bill Burke led the Spartans on a nice drive that he ended successfully with a 1-yard run. Paul Edinger's extra point-kick made it 20-17 in favor of Michigan and that is how the first half ended. (*Detroit News*, 9/27/1998, Page 46)

Both teams made some needed adjustments on defense and the only scoring of the third quarter was a 38-yard field goal by Feely of Michigan. The Wolverines led 23-17 at the end of forty-five minutes of play. Tom Brady did his best impersonation of Bill Burke in the fourth quarter when he led Michigan on an 80-yard drive that he ended with a 1-yard scoring run to make it 29-17. The Maize and Blue went for a two-point conversion, but it failed. MSU missed a field goal later in the game and that was as close as they could come to scoring on Michigan's stingy defense. Once again, hated Michigan sent the Spartans back to East Lansing with another tough loss. (*Detroit News*, 9/27/1998, Page 46)

Paul Bunyan was staying in Ann Arbor for the third consecutive year and nobody wearing Green and White was happy about it. Of course, the Maize and Blue faithful were thrilled! Michigan State was in this game right from the start, but they came up short. It would be another year before the Spartans had another shot at the Wolverines.

Team	1st	2nd	3rd	4th	Final
MSU	3	14	0	0	17
UM	3	17	3	6	29

SERIES UPDATE:

The good news for Michigan was that they extended their series advantage to 60 wins, 26 losses, and 5 ties with their hard-fought victory. The bad news for the Spartans was that they lost more ground in every measurable area of the 91-year football series. Michigan's trophy game victory gave them a 27-17-2 record when Paul Bunyan was on the line. Finally, the Wolverines increased their margin in the Nineties to a record of 6 wins and 3 losses.

SERIES MILESTONES:

There were three notable milestones in game number ninety-one of the Mitten State pigskin rivalry. First, Michigan became the first series team to win sixty games with their victory. Second, it was the fiftieth series game played in Michigan Stadium. Finally, the monster crowd of 111,238 absolutely destroyed the old record of 106, 788 that was set in 1992. Wow— that is a lot of people!

SEASON SUMMARIES:

Michigan State played well in the next two games against Central Michigan and Indiana and the Spartans won them both. Their modest two-game win streak ended with a loss at Minnesota (19-18). Saban's footballers went on another two-game winning surge and defeated Northwestern (29-5) and Ohio State (28-24).

The Spartans could finish a nice season with three more wins. However, it was not meant to be since they lost two of the last three games to end the season at 6 wins and 6 losses. Once again, Saban's team finished even in the Big Ten with a record of 4 wins and 4 losses. About the only good news surrounding Spartan football was that Robaire Smith and Paul Edinger earned All-American honors for 1998. Although it could have been worse, the 1998 season was not what Nick Saban or Spartan fans were expecting. The off-season would be an uncomfortable time for Coach Saban. He had eight long months to explain why things were not going as well as expected with his football program.

Lloyd Carr's Wolverines kept things going in the right direction with two road wins over Iowa (12-9) and Northwestern (12-6). A Homecoming Day win over Indiana (21-10) pushed the Wolverines to a record of 4 wins and 0 losses in the Big Ten Title chase. Michigan was half-way to their second straight conference championship. The Wolverines won three more games over Minnesota (15-10), Penn State (27-0) and Wisconsin (27-10) which gave them a perfect record of 7-0 heading into their annual battle with Ohio State. The bad news was that Michigan lost at OSU (31-16). The good news was that the Wolverines still earned a share of the conference championship since their record of 7-1 matched those of Wisconsin and Ohio State. The Maize and Blue footballers finished their season on a positive note with a win over Arkansas (45-31) in the Citrus Bowl. Michigan ended the 1998 season with a record of 10 wins and 3 losses. All things considered; it was a good season for Lloyd Carr's team. Michigan stalwart Jon Jansen was the only Wolverine to earn All-American honors in 1998.

Game #92: October 9, 1999 at Spartan Stadium in East Lansing

BACKGROUND INFORMATION:

Lloyd Carr was back for season number five in 1999. If Carr's first two seasons fell below expectations, the second two probably exceeded them. Michigan had won a national championship and two conference titles in the last two years and nobody in Ann Arbor wanted it to stop! The Wolverines were loaded with talent on both sides of the ball. Yes, expectations would be high again for Coach Carr's football team. After all, he was coaching at Michigan! Once again, the pollsters thought that Michigan would be an excellent football team in 1999 and they started the season off at number-seven in the press polls.

The Wolverines started well in 1999 since Carr's seventh ranked footballers won their first five games and rose to number three in the weekly polls. For the second time in three years, it looked like Michigan was ready to climb another tall mountain. This time Michigan State was early in the schedule. The Wolverines would have to journey to enemy territory and win another big game in East Lansing. Tighten up your chin-straps men. This was going to be another bitter "Big Boy" football battle!

Fifth-year Coach Nick Saban was getting tired of making excuses for his football team and his program. Spartan supporters were getting restless in East Lansing. It looked like 1999 would be a "make or break" year for Saban and his football team. Nobody who wore Spartan colors was going to settle for anything less than a Big Ten championship. Saban knew it and so did his coaches and his football team. This team had to deliver in a BIG way or else!

The Spartans opened the 1999 season just like Michigan did! Michigan State won their first two home games against Oregon (27-20) and Eastern Michigan (51-7). Then, the Spartans won two straight road games against Notre Dame (23-13) and Illinois (27-10). A dominating 49-3 win over Iowa put the MSU footballers at 5 wins and 0 losses for the first time since 1966! Whoa, life was good again in East Lansing! Ah, but would it stay that way? Third-ranked Michigan was coming to town and everyone was wondering if those dastardly Wolverines would ruin another MSU football season. Could the eleventh ranked Spartans pull off another upset over the favored Wolverines?

GAME SUMMARY: UM 31 MSU 34

The ninety-second series game turned out to be another "upset" as MSU defeated third-ranked, Michigan. Both offenses were flying high on this day and the defenses were on their heels for most of the game. Once again, some key players stepped up to make BIG plays for both teams, but MSU ended up with more of them, which is why they won this titanic football struggle.

Michigan State took the lead midway through the first quarter on a 1-yard touchdown run by Tico Duckett. Paul Edinger kicked the extra-point. The Spartans were up 7-0 after one quarter of football. Early in the second quarter, Michigan kicker Hayden Epstein got the Wolverines on the board with a 56-yard field goal to make it 7-3. (*Detroit News*, 10/10/1999, Page 54)

MSU's Edinger matched Epstein's score with a 39-yard field goal of his own to make it 10-3 Spartans. With just over three minutes to go in the half, Michigan struck quickly with an 81-yard scoring pass from Drew Henson to Marcus Knight. Wolverine Jeff Del Verne kicked the extra-point, and the game was tied at 10-10. Spartan Paul Edinger finished the first half scoring with his second field goal (43-yards). It was 13-10 in favor of MSU at the half. (*Detroit News*, 10/10/1999, Page 54)

The Spartans dominated the third quarter and put fourteen more points on the board. Quarterback Bill Burke threw two scoring passes. One to Gari Scott for 19-yards and another 15-yard touchdown to Plaxico Burress. The Spartans led 27-10 at the end of the third quarter. Tom Brady led a furious Michigan comeback, but it fell short. Brady led a nice drive that ended with a 2-yard scoring run by Anthony Thomas. Del Vern's extra point made it 27-17 in favor of MSU with just over fourteen minutes to play. Burke and the Spartans responded quickly to Michigan's tally with a 14-yard touchdown run by Dawan Moss. Edinger made the extra point kick, and the Spartan lead grew to 34-17 with twelve minutes to play. Brady threw two more touchdowns (19-yards to David Terrell and 8-yards to Aaron Shea), but Michigan ran out of time. The Spartans had another "Upset Win" over the "upset" Wolverines. (*Detroit News*, 10/10/1999, Page 54)

MSU's simple game plan—throw the ball all over the place and run just enough to keep the Michigan defense off-balance—worked to perfection. Michigan State quarterback Bill Burke set a team record with 400 passing yards. He had 21 completions out of 36 pass attempts. Burke also threw two touchdown passes and no interceptions. Quarterback reliever Tom Brady also played well. He completed 30 of 41 passes for 285 yards and two touchdowns. Plaxico Burress was the BIG difference in the game. He grabbed 10 passes for 255-yards and seemed to make every big third down catch that MSU needed him to make. Yes, it was another BIG win for the Spartans and a BIGGER loss for the Wolverines. (*Detroit News*, 10/10/1999, Page 54)

Team	1st	2nd	3rd	4th	Final
UM	0	10	0	21	31
MSU	7	6	14	7	34

SERIES UPDATE:

Nick Saban's second series win gave him an overall record of 2 wins and 3 losses against the Wolverines. Even better, the Paul Bunyan Trophy was back in East Lansing for a longer stay this year. For the record, the Wolverine series advantage now stood at 60 wins, 27 losses, and 5 ties. The Spartans decreased Michigan's advantage in the Paul Bunyan Trophy series to 27 wins 18 losses, and 2 ties. Michigan State ended the decade of the Nineties with 4 victories and 6 defeats against Michigan. Yes, Spartan fans started talking trash as soon as the game was over. It was not going to stop for another year! Go Green! Go White!

SERIES MILESTONES:

The 1999 UM vs MSU series game was memorable for many reasons. First, it turned out to be Nick Saban's last series game. He is the only man in series history to win his first and last series game. Again, he finished with 2 wins and 3 losses in five series games. Second, both Michigan and Michigan State finished the Big Ten season with exact records of 6 wins and 2 losses and tied for second place in the conference. It was the first time that the Mitten State's Big Ten teams had ever tied for second place at the end of a Big Ten season. Of course, Bill Burke's 400-yards of passing yards set a series record. Plaxico Burress also set new series standards for receptions (10) and receiving yards (255).

SEASON SUMMARIES:

Michigan's conference championship hopes took a hit with the loss to MSU. They took a bigger hit the next week with a Big House loss to Illinois (35-29). Lloyd Carr pulled his team together and they won their last four conference games against Indiana (34-31), Northwestern (37-3), Penn State (31-27) and OSU (24-17). An overtime win over Alabama (35-34) in the Orange Bowl gave the Wolverines a final record of 10 wins and 2 losses in 1999.

As I already mentioned, Michigan finished in a tie for second place with MSU with a record of 6 wins and 2 losses. Nose tackle Rob Renes and Guard Steve Hutchinson both earned All-American honors for Michigan in 1999.

Michigan State's huge win over Michigan put them at 6-0 for the season and 3-0 in the Big Ten. They were in the driver's seat with five conference games to go. Unfortunately, a road trip to Purdue was the next game on the schedule. The Spoilermakers lived up their name again and beat MSU by a score of 52-28. Okay, the Spartans were not undefeated in the conference, but they were still in the race. The only problem was that they had to go to Madison to play the Badgers. The good news was that the Spartans scored ten points. The really bad news was that Wisconsin scored forty! Coach Saban got his team back-on-track in week nine against Ohio State and the Spartans won 23-7. Michigan State finished strong with two wins over Northwestern (34-0) and Penn State (35-28) to end the regular season at 9 wins and 2 losses.

Nick Saban did not take any time to celebrate his best season. He was too busy looking for another job. He signed on to coach at Louisiana State University and he was long gone by early December. Assistant Coach Bobby Williams was named MSU's twenty-first football coach on December 5, 1999. The Nick Saban Era at Michigan State ended abruptly. He saved his best for last and gave MSU fans their first nine-win season since 1987. Saban's final record at MSU was 34 wins and 24 losses. His teams won just over fifty-eight percent (.585) of their games. Bobby Williams did an excellent job of winning the hearts and minds of his players. The Spartans beat a strong Florida team (37-34) in the Citrus Bowl on January 1, 2000. The Bobby Williams Era was off to an excellent start. Maybe he would be the guy to take the Spartan's back to "the good old days!"

DECADE AND SERIES SUMMARIES:

The last decade of the Twentieth Century turned out to be a true rivalry period in the Michigan vs Michigan State football series. The Wolverines "won" the Nineties, but it was the closest margin of victory so far. The Maize and Blue footballers won six of the ten games in the decade which means that the Spartans lost four. There were a few blowouts in the Nineties, but many of the games were close, very close!

Decade and Series Summary 1898 to 1999

Time Frame	UM Won-Lost-Tied	MSU Won-Lost-Tied
1990-1999	6-4-0	4-6-0
1898-1999	60-27-5	27-60-5

The Spartans lost some more ground in the Nineties, but not a lot. Michigan now held their biggest margin ever, in the annual football matchups. Things would have to change in the next decade or Michigan might have to buy a house for Paul Bunyan in Ann Arbor! Okay, it was not quite that bad, but things had to get better in East Lansing.

BIG TEN SUMMARY:

Now, it's time to take a closer look at the numbers and reflect on how the Wolverines and Spartans compared in Big Ten play from 1990 to 1999. First, Gary Moeller's tenure was exceptionally good, especially the first three years. His Big Ten record was 30-8-2. Coach "Mo" won almost seventy-eight percent (.775) of his conference games. He also won, or shared, three Big Ten Championships in five years. Lloyd Carr's performance was also noteworthy in the last five years of the Nineties. He posted a record of 31 wins and 9 losses which worked out to the same winning percentage (.775) as Gary Moeller. Coach Carr's teams won two Big Ten Titles between 1995 and 1999.

Big Ten Summary 1990 to 1999

Statistical Area	UM	MSU
Number of Head Coaches	2	2
Games Played	80	80
Wins	61	41
Losses	17	30
Ties	2	1
Winning Percentage	.775	.519
Winning Seasons	10	5
Losing Seasons	0	2
Even Seasons	0	3
Big Ten Championships	5	1

The Spartans were inconsistent in conference play during the Nineties. George Perles posted a winning conference record of 18-14-0 from 1990 to 1993. He started the decade by earning a share of the conference championship in 1990. Then, everything fell apart for Coach Perles. By the time he left, all Big Ten wins in 1994 were wiped from the record book because of the NCAA penalties against the MSU football program. Officially, the Big Ten record book reflects a final record of 18 wins and 22 losses for George Perles.

Nick Saban's five year stay in East Lansing resulted in three winning conference seasons and two that were even. Coach Saban's record during this time worked out to 23 wins, 16 losses and 1 tie. His winning rate in the Big Ten was almost fifty-nine percent (.587). The "Saban Years" put the Spartan football program in a better place by the time he left in 1999.

For the third straight decade, Michigan had the edge in all "good" categories on the Big Ten Summary Chart. The Wolverines earned twenty more conference wins in the Nineties than the Spartans. Unfortunately, Michigan State had twenty-one more losses during this time. The Maize and Blue footballers posted ten winning conference seasons compared to five for the Green and White. Finally, Michigan won five conference championships during this decade and the Spartans earned one. The Wolverines continued to be the best Big Ten team in Michigan for the last decade of the Twentieth Century.

PROGRAM SUMMARIES:

The 1990s continued to be notable for Michigan, but not for Michigan State. The Wolverines were ranked a lot because they won a lot. Michigan posted an outstanding record of 93 wins, 26 ties and 3 ties in the Nineties. That body of work resulted in a winning rate of just under seventy-eight percent (.774) and one national championship. Once again, the Wolverine football program achieved at an extremely high level for another decade. More importantly, the future continued to look bright for Michigan football as the Twenty-first Century approached.

Program Summaries 1990 to 1999

Statistical Area	UM	MSU
Number of Head Coaches	2	2
Games Played	122	117
Wins	93	57
Losses	26	58
Ties	3	2
Winning Percentage	.774	.496
Winning Seasons	10	4
Losing Seasons	0	3
Even Seasons	0	3
National Championships	1	0
All-American Selections	22	5

After fixing the football mess that he inherited in East Lansing, George Perles made one of his own. Yes, the first season of the 1990s was about as good as it gets. The Spartans won eight games and earned a share of the Big Ten Title. Then, the wheels started to wobble and eventually fall off the MSU football bus. Two straight losing seasons and a 6-6-0 effort in 1993 made life difficult for the Spartan football leader. Finally, everything crashed when MSU President M. Peter McPherson decided that George Perles had to go!

President McPherson fired Perles late in the 1994 season. Later, an investigation into the MSU Athletic Department revealed some NCAA infractions that caused the Spartans to forfeit five wins in 1994. The official record reads 0 wins, 11 losses and 0 ties for the final season of the Perles Era at Michigan State. Sadly, the first five years of the decade ended at 22 wins, 34 losses and a winning rate that was just under forty percent (.393).

Nick Saban was hired to clean up the mess that George Perles left for him. Coach Saban did a commendable job in his five year stay in East Lansing. Saban had things going in the right direction when he bolted to LSU. His Spartans posted a record of 35 wins, 24 losses, and 1 tie during his tenure. Of course, he went on to bigger things in December 1999. Bobby Williams replaced Nick Saban and promptly won a bowl game to start the 21st Century with a perfect record of 1-0-0. Coach Williams was hoping that he could keep Michigan State football moving forward especially when they played Michigan!

CHAPTER 13

Little Brother Gets Ticked Off 2000 to 2009

T he first day of the twenty-first century, arrived right on time on January 1, 2000. It cascaded across the globe from east to west amid dire predictions of widespread computer glitches and massive technological failures. Fortunately, everything went smoothly on day one! Once again, a new century and a new decade caused people to wonder what the future might be like in the 21st Century. Of course, a lot of the future would be much like the past. However, changes, some big and some small, would become an integral part of American life starting on January 1, 2000. Advances in telecommunications continued to shrink the entire world. Telephone and internet communications were now taking place at lighting speed. Job growth continued in the high-tech fields. More and more people were working in industries that did not exist twenty-years ago. Of course, terrorism and global wars were still grabbing everyone's attention just about daily on the television. There was lots of good news in the new world, but there was also plenty of bad. The Twenty-First Century had a truck load of challenges ahead. One area of American life was going to be less challenging. College football continued to grow in popularity and revenue continued to stream into the coffers of the NCAA. Television rights were generating billions of dollars to shore up the "entertainment" divisions of all major colleges in the country.

Game #93: October 21, 2000 at Michigan Stadium in Ann Arbor

BACKGROUND INFORMATION:

The NCAA rules committee made two changes to increase player safety in 2000. First, they limited the ability of "two on one" blocks. Second, crackback blocks below the waist by offensive players were put on the "no-no" list. (*USA Today CFE,* Page 572)

Bobby Williams, the first African American Head Coach in MSU football history, entered his first full season in East Lansing with a perfect record of 1 win and 0 defeats since he won his first game against Florida in the Citrus Bowl. The fans obviously liked what they saw in game one, but what would a full season of Bobby Williams mean for Spartan football?

285

Coach Bobby Williams had to find a quarterback and another All-American receiver since Plaxico Burress left early for the NFL. He still had some promising talent on offense, defense, and special teams. The problem for MSU fans is that they just did not know what to expect from the 2000 edition of the Michigan State Spartans.

MSU started fast in 2000. They won their first three games against Marshall (34-24), Missouri (13-10), and Notre Dame (27-21). So far, so good for Coach Williams. Unfortunately, the Spartans dashed any hope for an undefeated season with three consecutive losses to Northwestern (37-17), Iowa (21-16), and Wisconsin (17-10). Just like that, they were heading into Michigan Week with a record of 3 wins and 3 losses. Would Williams have his Spartans ready for their visit to Ann Arbor on October 21, 2000?

Lloyd Carr was back for his sixth season in 2000. Michigan football was still in good hands with Coach Carr in charge. He was doing things just the way Bo and Wolverine Nation liked it. He had already won two Big Ten Championships and one national Championship. Life was good in Ann Arbor. Coach Carr had plenty of excellent players coming back on both sides of the ball. Once again, the pollsters figured that Carr would have another excellent football team in 2000. As it turned out, they were correct.

Sixth ranked Michigan began the 2000 season with a big win over Bowling Green (42-17). The Rice Owls suffered a similar fate in game two since they lost (38-7) to the Wolverines. Game three did not go as well for the Maize and Blue. Michigan traveled to California to play UCLA. Unfortunately, Carr's footballers lost the Bruins (23-20). Michigan started the Big Ten season with two straight wins over Illinois (35-31), and Wisconsin (13-10). A trip to Lafayette, Indiana did not go well since the Wolverines lost to Purdue (32-31). Michigan's record dropped to 4 wins and 2 losses half-way through the season. Carr's footballers tuned-up for their MSU series game with a 58-0 win over Indiana in week seven. It looked like the offense was playing well and the defense was getting better. The sixteenth-ranked Wolverines appeared capable enough to avenge their defeat in 1999.

GAME SUMMARY: MSU 0 UM 14

Game #93 of the in-state gridiron gathering was a stark contrast to the 1999 game. The defenses were "large and in charge" for most of this game, especially Michigan's. The Wolverines posted their first series shutout since 1985.

It was an impressive performance by Carr's defenders. The Michigan offense was good enough to put fourteen points on the board and that was all they needed. Michigan running back Anthony Thomas led the Wolverines with 25-carries and 175-yards. More importantly, he scored the only two touchdowns of the game. Quarterback Drew Henson also played well for Michigan. He completed 17 of 31 passes for 138-yards and had no interceptions. It was another nice win for the Wolverines and another disappointing loss for the Spartans. (*Chicago Tribune*, 10/22/2000, Page 119)

Once again, the team that won the rushing part of the game also claimed victory. Michigan runners pounded the turf for 188-yards compared to only 63-yards for the Spartans. Michigan State earned more first downs (22 to 19) and passed for 292-yards compared to Michigan's 138-yards. (*Chicago Tribune*, 10/22/2000, Page 119) Yes, MSU could have won this game. All they had to do was score fifteen lousy points. That pretty much sums up the game.

Team	1st	2nd	3rd	4th	Final
MSU	0	0	0	0	0
UM	7	0	7	0	14

SERIES UPDATE:

Michigan's series advantage grew again. The Wolverines now owned 61 victories, 27 losses, and 5 ties. The Maize and Blue won the first game of the 21st Century and went up by a count of 1-0-0 for the new decade. The Paul Bunyan Trophy series still favored the Wolverines who now owned a record of 28 wins, 18 losses, and 2 ties since 1953.

SERIES MILESTONES:

Series game number ninety-three had the biggest crowd in the history of the series. The Big House saw 111,514 football fans pass through the turnstiles. This Ann Arbor gathering broke the previous high by 276 people. Bobby Williams became the first African American Head Coach in series history. The 2000 contest between Michigan and Michigan State was his first series game and his first series loss. Lloyd Carr improved his series record to 4 wins and 2 losses.

SEASON SUMMARIES:

The Spartans bounced back after the Michigan loss with a 14-10 win over Illinois. Ohio State defeated MSU in Columbus (27-13). The Green and White defeated Purdue 30-10 in week ten. The MSU footballers lost their final game at Penn State (42-23). Year one of the Bobby Williams Era ended at 5 wins and 6 losses. Michigan State posted a record of 2 wins and 6 losses in Big Ten play that put them in a tie for 9th place. No Spartans played well enough to earn All-American honors in 2000. Obviously, MSU fans were hoping for more in 2000, but the final record was about what many expected. The simple fact was that Bobby Williams had a lot of work to do in East Lansing.

Michigan failed to use the momentum of their win over MSU the next week at Northwestern. The Wildcats won a shootout over the Wolverines by a score of 54-51. Michigan's chances for a conference championship took a big hit in Evanston. Now, they would need to win their remaining games and get some help. As it turned out, that is exactly what happened.

Michigan did what they had to do and defeated Penn State (33-11) and Ohio State (38-26) to finish at 6 wins and 2 losses in conference play. They shared the Big Ten Title with Northwestern and Purdue. A victory in the Citrus Bowl gave Michigan a final record of 9 wins and 3 losses for the 2000 season. Steve Hutchinson and David Terrell earned first team All-American honors for their stellar play in 2000.

Game #94: November 3, 2001 at Spartan Stadium in East Lansing

BACKGROUND INFORMATION:

(Note-Both Michigan and Michigan State had their playing schedules altered by the tragic events of September 11, 2001. The nation was in mourning when the weekend of September 15th approached. All college and professional sporting events were cancelled for that weekend. Many schools were able to adjust their season slates, but some of the scheduled games were never played. It was a tragic time in America.)

Lloyd Carr earned a share of his third Big Ten Championship in six years in 2000. Once again, there were some rough spots in the season, but Carr's calm demeanor helped his players regroup and finish strong. The 2001 season was expected to be another winning season in Ann Arbor. The only question was, "How many games would the Wolverines win this year?" One area of concern for Coach Carr's seventh season was his offense. The 2000 team scored the most points in his six-year tenure (404). However, quality lineman like Steve-Hutchinson, Jeff Backus, and Mo Williams were gone. Finding someone to fill the shoes of running back Anthony Thomas was also a big concern.

The good news in Ann Arbor was that John Navarre gained a lot of experience in his freshman year and he would be back for his second full season as Michigan's quarterback. Of course, there was still plenty of talent on the Michigan Football Roster. Nobody was shedding any tears for Lloyd Carr's football team. In fact, Michigan was ranked number twelve in the country which meant that they could be surprisingly good.

The Wolverines began the season with a solid win over Miami of Ohio (31-13). A week two road trip to Seattle did not go as well. Michigan lost to Washington (23-18). The Maize and Blue footballers finished their non-conference schedule with a win over Western Michigan (38-21). It looked like Coach Carr's team was ready for the Big Ten season. The Wolverines rolled to four straight conference wins over Illinois (45-20), Penn State (20-0), Purdue (24-10) and Iowa (32-26. Sixth-ranked Michigan owned a record of 6 wins and 1 loss. More importantly, they were undefeated going into their annual blood battle against MSU.

Bobby Williams was back for his second full season in 2001. His first season was not a complete disaster, but Spartan fans wanted more than five wins—a lot more! Coach Williams thought that he made some progress in year one. He was hoping to do the same in his second year at the Spartan helm. No one was picking MSU to win the conference championship in 2001, but improvements were expected. Nobody really knew what to expect from the Spartans in 2001, but it promised to be another interesting season in East Lansing.

The 2001 model of the Michigan State football team rolled off the assembly line and promptly defeated Central Michigan (35-21) and Notre Dame (17-10). The Spartans lost a tough one to Northwestern in week three (27-26). Fortunately, they bounced back to defeat Iowa (31-28). They split the next two games—losing to Minnesota (28-19) and winning against Wisconsin (42-28). MSU was inconsistent in the first six weeks of the season, but still had a winning record of 4 wins and 2 losses. Once again, they would be the underdogs to Michigan in their own stadium. Would the home field advantage give MSU an edge in this critical series game?

GAME SUMMARY: UM 24 MSU 26

The ninety-fourth game in series history was one more classic in-state hate battle. Another standing room only crowd (75,262) showed up to cheer their Spartans to victory over the "enemy team" from Ann Arbor. As always, the Spartans were "fired-up" and looking to play well against the hated Wolverines.

Michigan State scored first when Charles Rogers caught a 17-yard touchdown pass from Jeff Smoker and the PAT kick made it 7-0. Michigan responded with a 57-yard field goal by Hayden Epstein. The Wolverines were on the board, but still trailed 7-3 at the end of the first quarter. Michigan took their first lead in the second quarter on 14-yard scoring pass from John Navarre to Marquise Walker. The touchdown and Epstein's extra point made it 10-7 Michigan. Hard running T.J. Duckett pounded into the Wolverine end zone a few minutes later and Rayner's kick made it 14-10 in favor of the Spartans. Michigan scored again on another touchdown from Navarre to Walker and it was 17-14 after the extra point kick. That is how the first half ended. (*C-Tribune*, 11/4/2001, Page 34)

Both defenses stiffened their spines in the third quarter. The only score of the period came on a 27-yard field goal by Spartan kicker Dave Rayner. It was all tied up (17-17) heading into the final fifteen minutes of play. Both defenses held their ground until Rayner connected on a 17-yard field goal to make it 20-17 Spartans with about 7-minutes to play. Later, Michigan recovered a fumble by Jeff Smoker and the Wolverines scored on a Navarre's third touchdown pass of the day to Jermaine Gonzalez (20-yards). Hayden Epstein's PAT kick made it 24-20 Michigan with 2:28 left to play. Spartan quarterback Jeff Smoker lined his offense up for what he hoped would be a game winning drive. It turned out to be one of the most unusual drives in the history of the series. (*C-Tribune*, 11/4/2001, Page 34)

Smoker was sacked early in the drive and a fourth down pass was incomplete. However, a costly facemask penalty gave MSU four more downs. So, the drive continued. The Spartans gained 17-yards on their own with a key pass from Smoker to Herb Haygood. Smoker was sacked again, but Michigan was penalized for too many men on the field. The Spartans had new life, but now they were battling the Wolverines and the clock!

MSU faced a fourth down and needed at least four yards to continue the drive. Smoker hit Duckett for 8-yards and the Spartans still had a chance, but the clock was running. Smoker spiked the ball with 17-seconds remaining. The ball now sat on the 3-yard line. Jeff Smoker tried to run the ball into the end zone, but he only gained one yard. He frantically lined his team up to spike the ball and he did! The clock showed one-second to play. (*C-Tribune*, 11/4/2001, Page 34)

At this point things got crazy. Michigan coaches screamed that Smoker's "spike" was tardy. According to the Maize and Blue, and ABC television broadcaster, Brent Musburger, the game was over. Frank Beckman, Michigan's radio announcer also weighed in a little stronger by calling the controversial play "Criminal." None of these opinions mattered. What mattered was that there was one second and one play left in the game. If Michigan stopped the Spartans from scoring a touchdown, the game was over. If MSU scored, they would win. It was just that simple. Well, the Spartans did score on a 2-yard pass from Jeff Smoker to T. J. Duckett and that was it.

One of the most controversial endings in college football was in the history books. The Spartans defeated Michigan (26-24) and the "Clock gate" game went down in history. (*C-Tribune*, 11/4/2001, Page 34) Michigan fans blamed the loss on Spartan timer Bob Stehlin. According to Wolverine fans, "Spartan Bob" stopped the clock before Smoker's spike. Ultimately, the Big Ten carefully reviewed the controversial play and determined that the Spartan timer had acted correctly. There was no apologetic phone call from Chicago about the way the game ended. The bottom line about this game is that Michigan really shot themselves in the foot with two huge penalties on the final drive. Ultimately, the Spartans, given the extra chances, found a way to win.

Team	1st	2nd	3rd	4th	Final
UM	3	14	0	7	24
MSU	7	7	3	9	26

SERIES UPDATE:

Oh boy, this was a game for the ages! It was an absolute bitter pill for the Wolverines to swallow, but the Spartans loved it! Michigan still held a big advantage in the series, but that did not take the sting out of this painful defeat. The Wolverines now owned a series record of 61 wins, 28 losses, and 5 ties. Michigan and Michigan State were even in the first decade of the Twenty-first Century at 1 win and 1 loss. The Spartans still trailed in the Paul Bunyan Trophy series with 19 wins, 28 losses, and 2 ties, but Paul Bunyan was not going back to Ann Arbor for another year! Time to brag about beating Michigan. Life was good in East Lansing and Bobby Willliams was a hero, along with Spartan Bob! Go Spartans!

SERIES MILESTONES:

There were some notable milestones that came out of this game. First, Bobby Williams earned his first series win in his first series game in East Lansing. Yes, playing at home is a particularly good thing, especially when you are the underdog! Second, it was the 25th series game ever played in Spartan Stadium and certainly the most controversial! Also, T. J. Duckett became the first Spartan to rush for over two-hundred yards against the Wolverines (211-yards). The Michigan defense set a record with twelve sacks in the game, but they could have used one more. Finally, Hayden Epstein's first quarter field goal 57-yards) was the longest in Michigan football history.

Image 12 Sparty, and everyone else in Spartan Nation, was happy after MSU's victory over Michigan in 2001. Photo taken by Carol Gallagher, September 2021.

SEASON SUMMARIES:

Carr's Wolverines put the MSU loss behind them and won the next two conference games against Minnesota (31-10), and Wisconsin (20-17) to stay in the conference race. A season ending loss to Ohio State (26-20) gave Michigan a record of 6 wins and 2 losses in the conference which earned them a second-place finish. Michigan played in the Citrus Bowl for the second straight year which was good. Unfortunately, they lost to Tennessee (45-17) which was not good. The Wolverines finished the 2001 season with a final record of 8 wins and 4 losses. Larry Foote and Marquise Walker earned All-American honors for their outstanding play.

Michigan State may have exerted way too much effort in beating Michigan because they had nothing left in the tank for the next three games. They lost to Indiana (37-28), Purdue (24-14), and Penn State (42-37). The Spartans ended the regular season with a 55-7 win over Missouri. MSU finished year two of the Williams Era with a 44-35 victory over Fresno State in the Silicon Valley Football Classic Bowl Game. MSU's modest two-game winning streak at the end of the season gave Bobby Williams a winning season with 7 wins and 5 losses. The Spartans posted a record of 3 wins and 5 losses in the Big Ten and earned a tie for 8th place. MSU's Herb Haygood earned All-American honors for the 2001 season.

Game #95: November 2, 2002 at Michigan Stadium in Ann Arbor

BACKGROUND INFORMATION:

The NCAA made the 2002 season a year of faster play on the field with a "clock experiment." The offense now had twenty-five seconds to snap the ball after it was spotted following a first down, out of bounds play, a penalty, or a change of possession. (*USA Today CFE*, Page 600)

Speaking of the clock, the Big Ten also made a change in their game timing policy after the infamous "Clock gate" incident at the end of the 2001 UM vs MSU game in East Lansing. Now, all conference games would be officially timed by a neutral official on the field, instead of someone from the home team. It was a year too late as far as Lloyd Carr was concerned.

The good news for Bobby Williams was that he was back for his third season in 2002. His Spartans posted a winning record in his second season and he defeated the hated Wolverines in his second try. Coach Williams also won his second straight bowl game in December 2001. Yes, he was making progress with his football rebuild in East Lansing. As always, the burning questions were about his 2002 team and how good they would be in the upcoming season. The best news for Williams was that starting quarterback, Jeff Smoker, was back for his final year. Williams had plenty of returning talent, but nobody thought that it was enough to compete for the conference championship. Of course, Williams was hoping to prove the doubters wrong!

Michigan State's 2002 season started with two easy wins over Eastern Michigan (56-7) and Rice (27-10). Weeks three and four were against tougher competition. The California Bears came to East Lansing and clawed the Spartans up and down the field. The final score of 46-13 went in favor of the visitors. Notre Dame came to town for game number four and the Williams footballers played better, but not good enough to win. The Irish left town with a 21-17 victory over the Green and White. The Spartans finished their non-conference schedule with a record of 2 wins and 2 losses.

Coach Smith's footballers won their conference opener over Northwestern (39-24). The Spartans had a record of 3 wins and 2 losses heading into October. They were looking to get on a win streak and head into the Michigan game with some positive momentum. Unfortunately, it did not work out that way. Michigan State lost their first three games in October to Iowa (44-16), Minnesota (28-7), and Wisconsin (42-24). Williams suspended star quarterback Jeff Smoker for the last five games of the season which helped explain the big loss to the Badgers. Without his starting quarterback, Williams knew that the trip to Ann Arbor could be ugly. As it turned out, it was!

The Wolverines began the 2002 season with all the typical questions about who was going to replace some of the stars who graduated. Lloyd Carr lost many key starters. Fortunately, he had some very good players coming back. Quarterback John Navarre was back to run he Michigan offense and the defense had All-American cornerback Marlin Jackson. It looked like Michigan would be ready to compete for another Big Ten Championship along with Ohio State and Iowa.

Thirteenth-ranked Michigan began the 2002 season with an "upset" win over eleventh-ranked Washington in Ann Arbor. Michigan rose to #7 in the country and pounded Western Michigan (35-12) in week two. The first road game of the season was at Notre Dame and it did not go well. The 20th ranked Irish sent Michigan home with their first loss (25-23). The Maize and Blue footballers slipped down to the fourteenth ranking, but they did not slip against Utah, at least not totally. The Wolverines defeated the Utes (10-7). Now, it was time for the Big Ten season to begin and Michigan was ready! Carr's footballers won their first three conference games against Illinois (45-28), Penn State (27-24) and Purdue (23-2). Even though the Maize and Blue rose back up to #8 in the country, it did not intimidate Iowa. The Hawkeyes completely ruined Homecoming Day (34-9). Michigan had a record of 6 wins and 2 losses heading into MSU Week. The big question was "Which Wolverine team would show up on Saturday November 2, 2002?"

GAME SUMMARY: MSU 3 UM 49

The underdog Spartans gave the favored, and 15th-ranked, Wolverines all they could handle for the first four minutes of this game. After a short drive, MSU took a 3-0 lead on a 39-yard field goal with eleven minutes to play in the first quarter.

Unfortunately for Michigan State, that was as good as it would get for the rest of the day! Fullback B.J. Askew scored on a 2-yard run five minutes later and Adam Finley's kick made it 7-3. John Navarre gave Michigan the lead with a 1-yard touchdown and the PAT kick made it 14-3 at the end of the first quarter.

Navarre hooked up with Ron Bellamy on a 39-yard touchdown pass and the Finley's point-after-touchdown kick upped the score to 21-3 at halftime. *C-Tribune,* 11/3/2002, Page 35)

Michigan scored 28-unanswered points in the second half—fourteen in each quarter. John Navarre threw his second and third touchdowns of the game to Bennie Joppru (12-yards) and Ron Bellamy (47-yards) in the third quarter. Michigan led 35-3 after forty-five minutes of play. The Wolverines finished off the Spartans, and the game, with touchdown runs by Askew (1-yard) and Tim Bracken (5-yards) in the final quarter. Michigan's offense scored in every quarter and the defense did not allow a touchdown all day. The Maize and Blue offense rolled up 441-yards (188 rushing and 253-passing). The Spartans were limited to a total of 237-yards. MSU rushed for 59-net yards and gained 178-yards through the air. It was not enough! *(C-Tribune,* 11/3/2002, Page 35)

There is no doubt that the drive back to East Lansing was somber and quiet. Things got worse the next day when MSU Athletic Director, Ron Mason, announced that he had fired Bobby Williams. Veteran Offensive Coordinator Morris Watts was named interim coach for the final three games of the 2002 season. There was a lot going on with the Spartan football program on November 3, 2002 Unfortunately, none of it was good. It appeared that Coach Williams had lost control of his team. He had to go. The Michigan State Football program was officially a "mess."

Team	1st	2nd	3rd	4th	Final
MSU	3	0	0	0	3
UM	14	7	14	14	49

SERIES UPDATE:

Once again, Michigan posted another win over Michigan State. The Wolverine series advantage grew to 62 wins, 28 losses, and 5 ties. Michigan went up by a margin of 2-1 in the new decade. The Maize and Blue's trophy game advantage grew to a margin of 29 wins, 19 losses, and 2 ties. Let the bragging begin in Ann Arbor! Go Blue!

SERIES MILESTONES:

As it turned out, there were quite a few milestones in series game number ninety-five. First, it was the first time that a coach was relieved of his duties after a series loss. Second, it was the last series game for Bobby Williams. He finished his brief stint in East Lansing with a series record of 1 win and 2 losses. His overall record ended with 16 victories and 17 defeats. Third, it was another record-breaking series crowd in Ann Arbor. A total of 111, 542 showed up for this game which was twenty-eight more people than the record crowd in 2000. Finally, it was the fiftieth game since MSU joined the Big Ten Conference in 1953.

SEASON SUMMARIES:

Lloyd Carr's Wolverines kept on winning after the Michigan State game and kept themselves in the hunt for the Big Ten Championship chase. They beat Minnesota (41-24) and Wisconsin (21-14) and headed into the last game with a shot at winning a share of the championship. The only problem was that OSU does not like to share, especially with Michigan. The Buckeyes won a close game in Columbus (14-9). The Wolverines had to settle for second place in the Big Ten. Michigan ended the season on a positive note with a bowl victory over Florida (38-30). Michigan's final record in 2002 was 10 wins and 3 losses. The Wolverines finished the conference season with a record of 6 wins and 2 losses. Marlin Jackson earned All-American honors for the second straight season and Bennie Joppru was selected for the first time.

To their credit, the Spartans bounced back from a tough loss and a tougher week. MSU defeated Indiana (56-21). Unfortunately, Morris Watts ran out of magic and the MSU footballers lost their final two games to Purdue (45-42) and Penn State (61-7). It was an ugly ending to a disastrous football season in East Lansing. The Spartans finished the final season of the Williams Era with a record of 4 wins and 8 losses. They won 2 and lost 6 in the Big Ten and finished in 8th place. The only good news was that MSU's talented receiver, Charles Rogers, earned All-American honors for the Spartans. It was not that good because Rogers decided to leave early for the NFL. Wow, what a crazy season in East Lansing! You cannot make this stuff up, but you still do not believe it when you read it on the page!

Game #96: November 1, 2003 at Spartan Stadium in East Lansing

BACKGROUND INFORMATION:

Player safety issues continued to change the game of college football in 2003. More restrictions were placed on below the waist blocks by players flanked outside the "box." However, the "halo" rule that previously protected punt return specialists with a two-yard safety zone was dropped. Interesting! (*USA Today CFE*, Page 615)

As usual, Lloyd Carr entered the 2003 season with high expectations and a national ranking of #4 to match those expectations. Michigan was loaded with talent! John Navarre was back to lead the offense that was expected to be explosive. Chris Perry would be the featured running back and Braylon Edwards was expected to catch a lot of passes. The defense was an elite collection of talent. Grant Bowman, Carl Diggs and Leon Hall were ready to stuff opponents on offense starting with game one.

Michigan kicked off the 2003 season with three big wins over Central Michigan (45-7), Houston (50-3) and Notre Dame (38-0). Third-ranked Michigan traveled to Oregon (#22) for their final non-conference game and returned with a 31-27 loss to the Ducks. Oregon was running a "Spread Offense" and the Wolverines could not figure out how to defend it. Michigan did find a way to shut down Indiana and defeated the Hoosiers (31-17). Carr's ninth-ranked team went to Iowa for game number six and that did not go well since the #23 Hawkeyes beat Michigan (30-17).

Then the Wolverines went on a small roll and won three straight games against Minnesota (38-35), Illinois (56-14), and Purdue (31-3). Michigan was right in the middle of the Big Ten Championship race. As usual, the next game against MSU was another BIG game for the eleventh ranked Wolverines.

Once again, there was a new man on the sidelines, but nobody in the Big Ten knew much about John L. Smith. They heard that he was quite a character who liked to live on the "wild side." He rode motorcycles, ran with the bulls in Spain, and climbed mountains. Yes, he liked to live life to the full. How that would translate into building a winning football program in East Lansing was anybody's guess. One of the first things that Coach Smith did in his new job was reinstate quarterback Jeff Smoker. Now, Smith had a quarterback. He also had many skilled players coming back on offense and defense. He had some talent to work with. The question was, "Could he do anything with the talent that he inherited?

Coach Smith did quite a bit with the talent that he had on his first-year roster. His Spartans posted two nice wins against Western Michigan (26-21), and Rutgers (44-28) before losing to Louisiana Tech (20-19). MSU finished the non-conference season with a solid win over Notre Dame (22-16) in South Bend. Smith's footballers showed that they were ready for the Big Ten season since they won their first four conference games. Iowa, Indiana, Illinois, and Minnesota all went down to the improved Spartans. Michigan State had a record of 7 wins and 1 loss heading into the annual "blood battle" with Michigan. They were the ninth-ranked team in the country and MSU could not wait to play the Wolverines in Spartan Stadium. This promised to be one of best series games in a long, long time! Time for the coaches to teach their players how to tighten up their chinstraps—this was going to be the most physical game of the season in East Lansing!

GAME SUMMARY: UM 27 MSU 20

The ninety-sixth game in the UM vs MSU blood-letting event was played on a cloudy day. The temperature was forty-nine degrees at kickoff. A crowd of 75, 129 fans showed up to watch the festivities. Both defenses played well in the first fifteen minutes which resulted in a scoreless first quarter.

The Wolverines thought they could run the ball on the Spartan defense and they did! They marched 55-yards in fourteen plays. Chris Perry put the Wolverines in the lead with a 1-yard touchdown run. Garrett Rivas kicked the PAT and Michigan was up 7-0. MSU put together a 74-yard drive but had to settle for a 20-yard field goal by Dave Raynor. It was 7-3 in favor of Michigan with seven-minutes to play in the first half. The Wolverines scored with one-minute remaining in the half when John Navarre connected on a 40-yard scoring pass to Braylon Edwards. Michigan missed the extra point kick. The Maize and Blue led 13-3 at halftime. (*Detroit News*, 11/2/2003, Page 37)

The third quarter was even with Michigan scoring on a 26-yard pass from Navarre to Andy Mignery. Michigan State scored their first touchdown when Jeff Smoker hooked up with Agim Shabaj for a 73-yard scoring play. Michigan led 20-10 after forty-five minutes of play.

The Wolverines increased their lead to 27-10 when John Navarre threw a 16-yard scoring pass to Braylon Edwards and Rivas made the extra-point kick. The Spartans scored the last ten points of the game, but they ran out of time. (*Detroit News*, 11/2/2003, Page 37)

Yes, it was official. The eleventh ranked Wolverines "upset" the Spartans and about seventy thousand Green and White fans. It was another painful defeat for Michigan State and their new coach. Michigan's plan to run the ball worked out well for the Maize and Blue. Chris Perry set a Michigan record with 51-carries. His workhorse effort produced 219-yard valuable yards. His early touchdown gave Michigan a lead that they never surrendered. John Navarre's 223-passing yards kept the Spartan defense off balance for much of the game. Meanwhile, MSU was held to 39-yards rushing (yes, you read it right!), but did get 254-passing yards from Jeff Smoker. Each team threw an interception and Michigan lost a fumble that was returned for a 65-yard touchdown. (*Detroit News*, 11/2/2003, Page 37) Both teams played as hard as they always do against each other. However, Michigan played a little bit better.

Team	1st	2nd	3rd	4th	Final
UM	0	13	7	7	27
MSU	0	3	7	10	20

SERIES UPDATE:

Another game was in the Mitten State pigskin series history book. Michigan continued to be large and in-charge, despite the presence of a new coach at Michigan State. The Wolverine series advantage now stood at an imposing 63 victories, 28 defeats, and 5 ties. Coach Carr's footballers increased their Twenty-First Century edge to 3 wins, and 1 loss. The Wolverines upped their record to 30 wins, 19 losses, and 2 ties in the Paul Bunyan Trophy series. Michigan kept the "bragging rights" for another year. Once again, losing to the team from Ann Arbor was getting old again in East Lansing.

SERIES MILESTONES:

Series Game #96 marked the first series game for John L. Smith and his first loss. It was also the first series game played on natural grass in East Lansing since 1968. Michigan became the first series team to win 30 trophy games since Paul Bunyan went up for grabs in 1953. Finally, it was the first time three consecutive series games were played in the month of November.

SEASON SUMMARIES:

Michigan kept rolling after their win over MSU. The Wolverines played their second straight road game at Evanston and hammered Northwestern (41-10). Carr's footballers beat OSU 35-21 to end the Big Ten season in first place with a record of 7 wins and 1 loss. Michigan's six game winning streak came to a sudden halt in the Rose Bowl with a loss to Southern California (28-14). The Wolverines ended the season with a final record of 10 wins and 3 losses. Chris Perry earned All-American Honors in 2003.

John L. Smith saw his Spartans suffer two more defeats after losing to Michigan. Road losses at Ohio State (33-23) and Wisconsin (56-21) put the Spartans at 7 wins and 4 losses with one game remaining. Fortunately, Smith's Spartans won their last conference game against Penn State (41-10). Coach Smith's big year ended with a disappointing loss to Nebraska (17-3) in the Alamo Bowl. Michigan State's record in year one of the John L. Smith Era ended at 8 wins and 5 losses. John L. Smith's Spartans won 5 games and lost 3 in the conference and finished in a tie for fourth place. Interestingly, Coach Smith's eight wins was the most by a first -year coach in Michigan State Football history. His breakout season also earned him coach of the year honors in the Big Ten. Kick returner Deandre Cobb earned All-American honors in 2003.

Game #97: October 30, 2004 at Michigan Stadium in Ann Arbor

BACKGROUND INFORMATION:

The Big Ten Conference voted to experiment with video replay to assist the on-field game officials. One official was assigned to the press box to make all final decisions regarding replays. It was a brave new video world in the Big Ten in 2004. (*USA Today CFE*, Page 632)

The John L. Smith Era started well in East Lansing. His first year exceeded the expectations of most "experts." Of course, everyone in Spartan Nation was hoping for more than eight wins in 2004. Smith set the "bar" high in 2003. It was not unreasonable to expect nine or more wins in 2004. Like Coach Carr, one of Coach Smith's biggest challenges in 2004 was to find a quarterback to replace Jeff Smoker. Smith had some promising underclassmen who appeared ready to take over Smoker's duties. Coach Smith also had some strong players returning on offense and defense. Michigan State had the potential to be a strong team in 2004, but only time would tell.

The Spartans did not get off to a good start in 2004. They lost at Rutgers (19-14), won against Central Michigan (24-7), and lost to Notre Dame (31-24). The bad news was that they had a non-conference record of 1 win and 2 losses. The good news was that they were undefeated in conference play. Smith's footballers won their first conference game against Indiana (30-20) but lost the next game to Iowa (38-16). MSU went on a modest two-game winning streak when they defeated Illinois (38-25) and Minnesota (51-17). The Spartans had 4 wins and 3 losses heading into Michigan Week. Once again, MSU was the underdog at Ann Arbor. However, they had plenty of upsets against the Wolverines. Why not do it again?

The University of Michigan football team kicked off season #125 in 2004. Once again, the Wolverines were picked to compete, again, with Ohio State for the Big Ten Championship in 2004. Writers were no longer calling the Big Ten the "Big Two" (Michigan and Ohio State) and the "Little Eight." However, the Wolverines and the Buckeyes were still winning more than their fair share of conference titles. Michigan had plenty of starters returning for Lloyd Carr's tenth season, but one of them was not quarterback John Navarre. Coach Lloyd Carr had to find a quarterback, but just about every other position had experienced players. Michigan started the season as the eighth-ranked team in the country. It was time to play some football.

Carr's talented team began the season with a big win over Miami of Ohio (43-10). Game two at Notre Dame ended in a 28-20 loss to the Irish. Michigan finished the non-conference portion of their 2004 schedule with a 24-21 win over San Diego State. Michigan looked like a championship contender once conference play began. The Wolverines won their first five Big Ten games and only two were close. The Maize and Blue had a record of 7 wins and 1 loss and a #12 ranking heading into MSU Week. It was time for the annual Mitten State pigskin brawl. Game on!

GAME SUMMARY: MSU 37 UM 45

The ninety-seventh game of the series was like so many of the previous rivalry games. It was hard-hitting and full of big plays on offense and defense. The record gathering of 111, 609 watched both teams play at a high level on a warm (low 70s), but cloudy day in Ann Arbor.

Michigan State scored early on a 72-yard run by Deandra Cobb. Dave Raynor's extra-point made it 7-0 in favor of the visitors. Michigan responded with an 80-yard drive that Mike Hart finished with a 7-yard scoring run. Garrett Rivas made the PAT for Michigan and the score was tied with seven minutes to play in the first quarter. Drew Stanton scored on a 5-yard run and Raynor's kick gave MSU a 14-7 lead at the end of the first fifteen minutes of play. Both teams scored on field goals in the second quarter. Michigan State got a 22-yarder from Raynor and Michigan's Garrett Rivas split the uprights from 34-yards out. The Spartans led 17-10 at halftime. (*Detroit News*, 10/31/2004, Page 40)

Neither team scored in the third quarter, but the Spartans scored first in the final period. Dave Raynor booted his second field goal (19-yards) and MSU increased their lead to 20-10. Five minutes later, Deandra Cobb bolted 64-yards to the end zone and MSU led 27-10 with Raynor's PAT kick. Three minutes later Garrett Rivas brought the Wolverines a little closer with a 24-yard field goal. MSU still led by a score of 27-13. The Wolverine defense got the ball back after a three and out and Chad Henne finished a 62-yard drive with a scoring pass to Braylon Edwards (36-yards). Rivas kicked the point-after-touchdown and it was now 27-20 Spartans with six-minutes to play. *(C-Tribune, 11/3/2002, Page 35)*

Michigan State failed to get a first down on their last drive and the Wolverines got the ball back with just under three-minutes to play. Two plays later, Henne threw another scoring pass to Braylon Edwards and the Rivas kick made it 27-27 with only a few minutes to play. Neither team scored before the clock expired. The first series game in history was going to overtime. (*Detroit News*, 10/31/2004, Page 40)

Michigan scored first in the first overtime thanks to a 34-yard field goal by Rivas. Michigan State countered with a 23-yard field goal by Dave Raynor. At the end of the first overtime, the score was tied at 30-30. In the second overtime, MSU scored on a 3-yard run by Jason Teague and Raynor's PAT kick made it 37-30. Michigan came right back with a Henne touchdown pass to Jason Avant (5-yards) and the Rivas extra point tied the score (37-37) at the end of the second overtime. Michigan scored on their possession in the third overtime on a 24-yard scoring pass from Chad Henne to Braylon Edwards. Michigan converted the two-point attempt to take their first, and only, lead of the game at 45-37. That is how it ended!

Wow, it was an exhausting game for everyone. Players, coaches, officials, and fans gave this game everything that they had. It was a shame that someone had to lose, but the overtime rule in 1996 guaranteed that someone would lose this great game. It was a great win for Michigan and one of the most painful defeats ever for the Spartans!

Team	1st	2nd	3rd	4th	OT1	OT2	OT3	Final
MSU	14	3	0	10	3	7	0	37
UM	7	3	0	17	3	7	8	45

SERIES UPDATE:

Michigan increased their series advantage 64 wins, 28 losses, and 5 ties. The Wolverines added another win to their decade advantage which now stood at 4 wins and 1 loss. The Maize and Blue footballers improved their trophy series record to 31 wins, 19 losses, and 2 ties. It is hard to know what John L. Smith was thinking, but it probably was not good. Michigan had "bragging rights" again and it was killing his recruiting in the great State of Michigan!

SERIES MILESTONES:

The biggest milestone of the day was the gigantic crowd of 111, 609. Thanks to ninety-five people, it was another record-breaker. Of course, the first overtime game in series history was a big event in series history. The fact that it went three overtimes, made it three times better! The UM vs MSU overtime series classic was also the first overtime game ever played in the history of Michigan Stadium. Of course, John L. Smith was still looking for his first series win since he slipped to 0-2-0 against hated Michigan. Both quarterbacks, Spartan quarterback Drew Stanton and Michigan's Chad Henne both started their first series game. They both played well.

SEASON SUMMARIES:

Coach John L. Smith's job did not get any easier after losing to Michigan. He had to get his team ready to play Ohio State. The Spartans were not as ready as they should have been. Final Score: MSU 19 OSU 32. Michigan State bounced back with a big win (49-14) over Wisconsin before ending the season with two straight losses to Penn State (37-14) and Hawaii (41-38). The Spartans ended year two of the John L. Smith Era with a final record of 5 wins and 7 losses. It was a step back for the program. The Green and White footballers posted 4 wins and 4 losses in the Big Ten which earned them a tie for 5th place. Spartan punter, Brandon Fields, was the only MSU player to earn first team All-American honors in 2004.

After defeating the Spartans, Michigan kept on winning with a victory over Northwestern (42-20). The Wolverines had a shot at winning the conference championship against Ohio State in the last game of the season. However, the bad news was that the Buckeyes prevailed (37-21). The good news was that both teams finished with identical conference records of 7 wins and 1 loss and shared the Big Ten Title in 2004. Michigan ended the season on a bad note with a painful Rose Bowl loss to Texas (38-37) and finished at 9 wins and 3 losses. Four Wolverines earned All-American honors (Marlin Jackson, Dave Baas, Braylon Edwards, and Ernest Shazor) for their stellar play in 2004.

Game #98: October 1, 2005 at Spartan Stadium in Lansing

BACKGROUND INFORMATION:

Another "off-the-field" event took place between the bitter rivals when WJR got into a contract dispute with officials at Michigan. Eventually, the radio station dropped the Wolverines in favor of the Spartans. Just another "off the field" rivalry event that added a little more fuel to the raging fire that is UM vs MSU!

The 2005 season was Michigan's 100th year of Big Ten play. It was also season number eleven for Lloyd Carr. which was great news for Michigan but not for the Spartans. After losing his first game to MSU, Carr won eight of the next ten games. Michigan was on a three-game series winning streak. Michigan State fans were not happy with the Lloyd Carr Era. Once again, Michigan, along with Ohio State and Penn State, was among the favorites to compete for the conference championship in 2005. Coach Carr had plenty of excellent players coming back. A ten-win season was not hard to imagine for the fourth-ranked Wolverines.

The Maize and Blue footballers began the 2005 season with a solid win over a rising Northern Illinois team (33-17). Things did not work out so well the next week against Notre Dame. The rude guests from South Bend left Ann Arbor with a 17-10 upset victory over Michigan. The Wolverines ended their non-conference season with 55-0 romp over Eastern Michigan. Carr's team had a record of 2 wins and 1 loss heading into Big Ten play. Fourteenth-ranked Michigan traveled to Madison for their first conference game and came home on the short end of a 23-20 score. The un-ranked Wolverines had a record of 2 wins and 2 losses heading into Michigan State Week. Worse yet, MSU was ranked #11 and the game was going to be played in East Lansing. Things were not looking good for Lloyd Carr's football team.

John L. Smith's third season in East Lansing was a critical time in his tenure. He went from Big Ten Coach of the Year in 2003 to the Green and White "Doghouse" in about twenty-four months! The 2005 season was going to be watched carefully by everyone associated with Michigan State Football. Coach Smith absolutely had to have a winning season, or else!

Coach Smith's players knew what was going on and they came out of the gate with four straight wins to start the 2005 season. The offense, led by Drew Stanton, was on fire! Unfortunately, the defense showed some cracks in the first four games, but MSU was able to overcome their defensive imperfections early in the 2005 season. After defeating Kent State (49-14), Hawaii (42-14), Notre Dame (44-41), and Illinois (61-14), the Spartans were 4-0 for the first time since 1966. The eleventh-ranked MSU footballers were more than ready to face the Wolverines in Spartan Stadium on October 1, 2005.

GAME SUMMARY: UM 34 MSU 31

For the first time since 1968, Michigan State (#11) was ranked at the start of series game number ninety-eight, but not Michigan. It was another typical edition of the intense in-state football series. There were bone-crunching blocks and teeth-rattling tackles on just about every play. The mothers of the players feared for the safety of their sons! Time for another intense, and nasty, football game between two bitter rivals.

Barry Gallagher

The underdog Wolverines scored first on a 2-yard pass from Chad Henne to Jason Avant. Garrett Rivas kicked the point and Michigan led 7-0 with seven minutes remaining in the first quarter. Less than two-minutes later, Mario Manningham streaked into the end zone with a 43-yard pass from Henne. The Rivas extra point made it 14-0 with seven minutes to play in the first period. *(Lansing State Journal [LSJ]*, 10/2/2005, Page 32)

Drew Stanton led Michigan State on a nice drive that ended with a 4-yard touchdown run by Stanton. John Goss kicked the extra point, and the score was 14-7. Michigan scored early in the second quarter on a 5-yard scoring pass from Henne to Brian Thompson. Garrett Rivas kicked his third extra-point and Michigan led 21-7. Michigan State came back to score fourteen unanswered points on a 1-yard plunge by Jehuu Caulcrick and a 61-yard touchdown pass from Drew Stanton to Kerry Reed. Spartan kicker John Goss made both PATs and the score was tied at 21-21. Garrett Rivas closed out the first half scoring on a 20-yard field goal with 9-seconds remaining. The half ended with Michigan ahead by a score of 24-21. It was time for both coaches to have a focused discussion with their defenses! (*LSJ*, 10/2/2005, Page 32)

Michigan State tied the score (24-24) early in the third quarter on a 26-yard field goal by Goss. The rivals were even heading into the final quarter. Would someone win the game in the next fifteen minutes or would there be another overtime? Mike Hart put Michigan back in front with a 1-yard scoring run. Rivas kicked the extra-point and Michigan pushed the lead to 31-24. Michigan was driving with about six-minutes to go when defensive tackle Domata Peko picked up a Chad Henne fumble and rambled 74-yards to pay dirt. Goss kicked another extra point and the score was tied again at 31-31. Michigan had a chance to win the game with one minute to play, but Rivas missed a medium range field goal attempt. (*LSJ*, 10/2/2005, Page 32)

For the second year in a row, this bitter rivalry game would be decided in overtime. Unlike 2004, this game only took one overtime to determine the winner. Michigan earned the victory when Garret Rivas redeemed himself on a 35-yard field goal. It was another BIG win for the Wolverines and a HUGE loss for the Spartans. Not much else to say about this one. As the sports announcers say, "both teams played their hearts out, but somebody had to lose." It turned out to be a BIG win for Michigan. Not only did the Maize and Blue footballers win the game, but they also won for the fourth straight season. It was another uplifting series win for the Wolverines and another shattering loss for the Spartans.

Team	1st	2nd	3rd	4th	OT	Final
UM	14	10	0	7	3	34
MSU	7	14	3	7	0	31

SERIES UPDATE:

After ninety-eight years, any series win is to be celebrated. All series wins are celebrated even more when it happens to be an "upset" win in the other guy's stadium. Michigan's 2005 series win was one to remember for Wolverine fans everywhere! The Maize and Blue advantage against Michigan State continued to grow. Michigan now owned 65 series wins, 28 losses, and 5 ties. Coach Carr's footballers now had five victories in six games in the new decade. The Wolverine lead in the trophy series now stood at 32 wins, 19 losses, and 2 ties after fifty-three battles for Paul Bunyan.

302

If Coach John L. Smith had ever seen the Paul Bunyan Trophy up close, it was a brief encounter. Spartan players and fans were probably wondering when they would ever see Paul Bunyan back in their trophy room. Yes, it was frustrating for Smith and his Spartans. MSU would have to wait until 2006 for their next shot at the Wolverines.

SERIES MILESTONES:

Yes, the ninety-eighth game of the series was in the record books. It was the first series overtime game in East Lansing. It was also the first time that back-to-back overtime series games were played by Michigan and Michigan State.

SEASON SUMMARIES:

After the close win in East Lansing, the Wolverines lost on Homecoming Day to Minnesota (23-20). With only a slim chance to win the conference title, Michigan won the next four games over Penn State (27-25), Iowa (23-20), Northwestern (33-17), and Indiana (41-14). Unfortunately, the Wolverines lost their final game of the regular season to Ohio State (25-21). Michigan ended the season with a conference record of 5 wins and 3 losses. The third-place Wolverines were invited to the Alamo Bowl to play Nebraska. Michigan's disappointing season ended with a 32-28 defeat at the hands of the Cornhuskers. Michigan's final record of 7 wins and 5 losses was the worst campaign in the eleven-year tenure of Lloyd Carr. For the first time in the new Millennium, no Wolverine players earned first team All-American honors in 2005.

After losing to the Wolverines, Michigan State lost two more games to Ohio State (35-24) and Northwestern (49-14). The Spartans ended their three-game losing streak with a 46-15 win over Indiana. With three games to go, MSU had a record of 5 wins and 3 losses. They had a chance for a winning season and a bowl game. Unfortunately, the Spartan defense fell apart and MSU went on a three-game losing streak. Smith's footballers finished the season with a record of 5 wins and 6 losses. No Spartans earned first team All-American honors in 2005. It was another disappointing season in East Lansing. Spartan Nation was losing patience with the quirky coach named John L. Smith.

Game #99: October 7, 2006 at Michigan Stadium in Ann Arbor

BACKGROUND INFORMATION:

The NCAA wanted to put an end to four-hour college football games. The rules experts attempted to shorten games with a few initiatives. The game clock now started when the ball was kicked, instead of when it was received. It also started on the "ready for play" signal after a change of possession. Another move was designed to give coaches a chance to contest a "questionable call." Now coaches had one "challenge" per game. The play would be reviewed by video replay. If the reviewed play was upheld, the "losing" coach lost one timeout. As it turned out, the challenge process actually slowed down more games. The gains that were made with the speeding up of play were often lost because of the challenge review process. Oh well, at least they tried! (*USA Today CFE*, Page 664)

Unfortunately, the John L. Smith Era at MSU was in a downward spiral in year four. Two straight losing seasons will do that to a coach and his program. It was going to take a championship season to save his job, but nobody in Spartan Nation believed that would happen. There was a ton of negative energy surrounding the Michigan State football program. Most "experts" figured that MSU would release Coach Smith from his contract, and everybody would move on. As it turned out, that is exactly what happened in East Lansing in 2006.

John L. Smith knew that the 2006 series game against Michigan would be the biggest game of his MSU tenure. A win over the Wolverines could be a job-saver. A blow-out loss could be the end of the line—just like it was for Bobby Williams. I am sure that Coach Smith believed that his team had the talent to play with and defeat Michigan. However, it would take the best game of the season to accomplish that feat! The unpredictable Spartans kicked off the 2006 season with three straight wins over Idaho (21-17), Eastern Michigan (52-20), and Pittsburgh (38-23). A loss to Notre Dame (40-37) snapped the streak. MSU opened the Big Ten season with a Homecoming Day loss to Illinois (23-20). Ouch! Michigan State had a record of 3 wins and 2 losses heading into Michigan Week. Nobody knew what to expect from the Spartans in Week Six.

Coach Lloyd Carr posted another winning season in 2005, but he was not happy about the final record. The good news was that the Wolverines won seven games. The bad news was that they lost five games, including the last two games of the season. Overall, things were looking good for Michigan in 2006. Carr had plenty of experienced players returning on offense, defense, and special teams. The sportswriters thought that Michigan would be strong again in 2006 because they ranked the Wolverines at number fourteen to start the season. If Carr's team could stay healthy, they could be another championship team in year twelve of his Michigan coaching tenure.

The Michigan Wolverines had a perfect start to the 2006 football season. Coach Carr's team won all three nonconference games against Vanderbilt (27-7), Central Michigan (41-17), and Notre Dame (47-21). They also won their first two Big Ten games against Wisconsin (27-13) and Minnesota (28-14). After five games the Wolverines were undefeated (5-0) and ranked #6 in the country. It looked like they were ready for Michigan State!

GAME SUMMARY: MSU 13 UM 31

Game number ninety-nine in the annual Mitten State pigskin mauling was good news for the Wolverines and bad news for the Spartans. This game was basically over at halftime, but Coach Smith's team did not quit!

Michigan opened the scoring with about nine minutes to play in the first quarter. Chad Henne tossed a touchdown pass to Adrian Arrington (13-yards) and Garrett Rivas kicked the extra point to give UM a 7-0 lead. The Wolverines scored again in the second quarter on another Henne scoring pass to Mario Manningham (41-yards). Rivas kicked the extra point and added a 24-yard field goal to give Michigan a 17-0 lead at halftime. (*DFP*, 10/8/2006, Page 52)

Carr's offense put the game out of reach in the third quarter with two more touchdowns. Manningham caught a 27-yard pass from Henne and Brandon Minor scored on a 40-yard run. Garrett Rivas kicked both extra points. Michigan State's Jehuu Calcrick put the Spartans on the board with a 1-yard run. The third quarter ended with Michigan in front by a score of 31-7. Drew Stanton scored MSU's final points on a 2-yard run to make it 31-13 in favor of Michigan. (*DFP*, 10/8/2006, Page 52)

Once again, the Wolverines were the better team on this day. The Michigan defense shut down MSU's offense and the UM offense scored plenty of points. The Spartans were outplayed on both sides of the ball. It was a great day for the Maize and Blue, but not for anyone wearing Green and White!

Team	1st	2nd	3rd	4th	Final
MSU	0	0	7	6	13
UM	7	10	14	0	31

SERIES UPDATE:

Michigan's victory gave the Wolverines their fifth straight series win. This win increased their series advantage to 66 wins, 28 losses, and 5 ties. Lloyd Carr's team pushed their decade record to 6 wins and 1 loss. Finally, the Maize and Blue's trophy series record now stood at 33 victories, 19 defeats, and 2 ties. Michigan retained Paul Bunyan and Mitten State "bragging rights" for another year. Yes, Spartan fans were sick of it, but there was nothing they could do about it until 2007. Go Blue!

SERIES MILESTONES:

There was only one noteworthy item to mention about the ninety-ninth game in series history. It turned out to be the last series game for Coach John L. Smith. Unfortunately, he ended with a record of 0 wins and 4 losses against Michigan. Three of his losses were by seven points or less and two were overtime games. Oh, what might have been. Time to dust off the "Help Wanted" ad for the next MSU football coach.

SEASON SUMMARIES:

The fourth year of the John L. Smith Era really went south after the loss to Michigan. The Spartans lost the next game to Ohio State (38-7) but managed to defeat Northwestern (41-38) a week later. MSU was sitting on a record of 4 wins and 4 losses with four games to play. It was still possible to salvage a winning season, but it was not meant to be. Smith's footballers lost the last four games of the season and only one game was close. MSU ended the season with a final record of 4 wins and 8 losses. Unfortunately, no Spartan played well enough to earn All-American honors in 2006. It was an ugly end to Coach Smith's time in East Lansing. John L. Smith posted a final record of 22 wins and 26 losses at Michigan State. His final Big Ten record finished at 12 wins and 20 losses. It was time to find a new football coach.

Meanwhile, down in Ann Arbor, Michigan was beating everybody they played! The Wolverines defeated Penn State (17-10), Iowa (20-6), Northwestern (17-3) Ball State (34-26) and Indiana (24-3). It was time for the first #2 Michigan vs #1 Ohio State battle in the history of "The Game." Yes, both teams were undefeated heading into this titanic contest. Sadly, Bo Schembechler died the day before the game which really took a toll on the Wolverine players and coaches. Michigan gave it their best shot, but future Heisman winner Troy Smith and the Buckeyes prevailed (42-39).

Michigan's best season since 1997 ended on a sad note (Bo's death) and two bad notes—OSU loss and a Rose Bowl loss. The Wolverines finished with a final record of 11 wins and 2 losses. They tied for second place in the Big Ten with a record of 7 wins and 1 loss. Leon Hall, Jake Long and LaMarr Woodley all earned first team All-American honors for their outstanding play in 2006.

Game #100: November 3, 2007 at Spartan Stadium in East Lansing

BACKGROUND INFORMATION:

The NCAA rules committee flip-flopped on a timing issue. Once again, the clock started when a kickoff was received, not kicked. In another change, the kickoff position was moved back from the 35-yard line to the 30-yard line. (*USA Today CFE*, Page 683)

Coach Lloyd Carr was back for his thirteenth season in 2007. So far, his coaching career at Michigan was a series of winning seasons (12 straight), many Big Ten Championships (five) and a national championship (1997). Chad Henne, Jake Long and Mike Hart were back for one more year. There was plenty of talent at just about every key position. Once again, the Wolverines were expected to compete with the Buckeyes along with Penn State and Iowa for the conference title.

Fifth ranked Michigan's first game in 2007 turned out worse than anyone could have predicted. Oh boy, what a shocker! Appalachian State University brought their "Spread Offense" to the Big House and left with the biggest upset in the history of Michigan Stadium! Michigan lost to the Mountaineers 34-32. Wow, nobody saw this coming, especially Lloyd Carr. Michigan dropped completely out of the rankings after their game one debacle.

The Wolverines traveled to Oregon the next week and saw the "Spread Offense" again. This one was a blur as the Ducks whacked Michigan 39-7. Yes, Carr's team was having trouble defending the "Spread." Worse yet, the high-powered Wolverine offense was stuck in low gear. Coach Carr got things going in a better direction with a big win over Notre Dame (38-0). Tenth ranked Penn State was next. Michigan played better and defeated PSU (14-9). The Wolverines went on a roll and won five straight over Northwestern (28-16), Eastern Michigan (33-22), Purdue (48-21), Illinois (27-17), and Minnesota (34-10). Michigan now had 7 wins and 2 losses. Coach Carr's football team was back in the rankings at number twelve. The best news was that they were undefeated in conference play at 5-0. It was time for a late season encounter with their bitter rivals in East Lansing. As always, there would be a lot on the line in this game.

Mark Dantonio was hired to replace John L. Smith on November 27, 2006. He enjoyed a successful run at Cincinnati. Now, he was ready to step up to the challenge of leading a Big Ten program. The good news was that he was the twenty-fourth head coach in Spartan football history. The bad news was that he was the fifth one in the last twelve years! Dantonio coached for Nick Saban for five years and Bobby Williams for one season. Coach "D" also spent three years at Ohio State under Jim Tressel. As defensive coordinator, he helped the Buckeyes win the 2002 national championship.

Coach Dantonio was familiar with MSU football and he knew what a championship football program looked like. The big question was, "Could Mark Dantonio bring Spartan football back to the championship level that it enjoyed in the 1950s and 1960s?" Coach Dantonio was all business all the time. He brought a serious, determined approach to his football program. Mark Dantonio showed his true colors right out of the gate in 2007. After learning that Michigan lost their season opener to Appalachian State, he told a reporter that he was going to observe a "moment of silence" for the poor Wolverines. Nobody in Ann Arbor thought his remark was humorous, especially Michigan's Mike Hart. Yes, things between Coach "D" and the "arrogant ones" in Ann Arbor were off to a "chippy" start.

The 2007 Spartans won all their non-conference games over UAB (55-18), Bowling Green (28-17), Pittsburgh (17-13), and Notre Dame (31-14). The Green and White footballers were 4-0 and looked strong on both sides of the ball. However, no one was getting too excited in East Lansing. Remember, John L. Smith started with four straight wins in 2005. Then, he lost six of the last seven games. As always, the Big Ten schedule would quickly separate the contenders and the pretenders. Unfortunately, Dantonio's team looked more like pretenders than contenders after they lost their first two conference games to Wisconsin (37-34) and Northwestern (48-41). Coach Mark Dantonio won his first Big Ten game and his first Homecoming Game on the same day when his Spartans defeated Indiana (52-27). The euphoria ended quickly with two straight losses to Ohio State (24-17) and Iowa (34-27). MSU's record through nine games was 5 wins and 4 losses. Now it was time for the biggest game of the year in East Lansing. The hated invaders from Ann Arbor were coming to town and the Spartans were the underdogs. Would Mark Dantonio become the second Spartan coach to win his first game against Michigan?

GAME SUMMARY: UM 28 MSU 24

Mitten State series Game #100 was another college football classic. As usual, every play featured ferocious blocks and bone-crunching tackles. The annual fall "Michigan Bowl" football game had grown to be one of the highlights of the college football season. All the "nasty" history, and the great games surrounding this heated rivalry, made this a must watch game.

The underdog Spartans put together a 56-yard drive on their first possession and took a 3-0 lead on Brett Swenson's field goal (36-yards). Michigan responded with a 62-yard drive of their own. It ended with an 11-yard scoring pass from Chad Henne to Mario Manningham. K.C. Lopata's PAT gave Michigan a 7-3 lead at the end of the first quarter.

The Wolverines scored the only points of the second quarter on another touchdown pass from Henne to Carson Butler (5-yards). Lopata's second PAT kick made it 14-3 in favor of Michigan at halftime. (*DFP*, 11/4/2007, Page 51) Michigan State made some excellent adjustments on defense and shut down the Maize and Blue offense in the third quarter. Meanwhile, the Spartan offense put together a 75-yard drive that ended with a touchdown run by Jehuu Caulcrick (1-yard). Swensen's extra point closed the gap to 14-10 with Michigan still in the lead.

The Spartans appeared to take control of the game in the fourth quarter with two touchdowns. Brian Hoyer threw a 5-yard scoring pass to Kellen Davis and Caulcrick scored on another 1-yard run. Brett Swensen's PATs gave MSU a 24-14 lead with just over seven minutes to play in the game. (*DFP*, 11/4/2007, Page 51)

Then, freshman Chad Henne and the Michigan offense took charge of the game for the last few minutes of play. Henne led the Wolverine offense on a 79-yard drive that ended with a 14-yard touchdown reception by Greg Matthews. Lopata's extra point closed the gap to 24-21. The Michigan defense held and turned the ball back to Henne's offense. The senior quarterback went to work and took the Wolverines on an eight-play drive that covered 54-yards. The final play was a winner when Henne connected on a 31-yard touchdown pass to Mario Manningham. Lopata kicked his fourth extra point and Michigan led 28-24 with just over two-minutes to play. Michigan State had one final possession to win the game. Unfortunately for MSU, they could not move the ball. The Wolverines held on for a hard-fought 28-24 victory. What a game! (*DFP*, 11/4/2007, Page 51)

Yes, it was another crushing defeat for MSU and their rookie coach. The "century game" against the hated Wolverines turned out much closer than most people thought it would. The Spartans were an improved team. They were in this game all the way. However, some fourth quarter defensive breakdowns and some Wolverine "luck" were too much to overcome.

Team	1st	2nd	3rd	4th	Final
UM	7	7	0	14	28
MSU	3	0	7	14	24

SERIES UPDATE:

After 100 years, Michigan was "large" and "in-charge" of the Mitten" State's annual "blood-letting" event. For the record, the Wolverines now owned 67 wins, 28 losses, and 5 ties. Michigan's advantage in the first decade of the 21st Century grew to 7 wins and 1 loss. After a short day's stay in East Lansing, Paul Bunyan was headed back to Ann Arbor for a longer visit. Michigan's trophy series advantage increased to 34 wins, 19 losses, and 2 ties. Things were about as bad as they could be for MSU fans.

SERIES MILESTONES:

The series "century" game had many milestones and one bomb that was dropped after the game and heard around the college football world! Of course, game #100 was the biggest milestone of the day. It was also the first game for Coach Mark Dantonio and his first loss. This memorable series game was also the last for Coach Lloyd Carr. He finished his career with a series record of 10 wins and 3 losses. Yes, Spartan fans were glad to see him go!

Of course, this was the game where the "little brother" comment was officially "born" thanks to Michigan running back Mike Hart. Mark Dantonio did not find it humorous. Coach "D" promised that it was not over that day. In fact, he promised that it would never be over. With steam practically coming out of both ears, Dantonio warned Michigan Nation that "Pride comes before the fall." The rivalry was now intensely personal for Coach Mark Dantonio. Series game number one-hundred and the words of Mike Hart raised the intensity level of this already uber-intense series to an all-time high, if that is possible. And, yes, Mark Dantonio and his Spartans were officially "ticked off" which would not be a good thing for Wolverine Nation!

SEASON SUMMARIES:

Michigan rose to the number thirteen after their win over MSU. However, it did not matter to Wisconsin. The Badgers ambushed the Wolverines in Madison and sent them home with their first conference loss (37-21). Ohio State extended UM's losing streak to two games with a 14-3 win at the Big House. Fortunately, the Wolverines sent Coach Carr out on a winning note with a victory over Florida in the 2008 Capital One Bowl. Lloyd Carr's final season ended with a record of 9 wins and 4 losses. Offensive lineman Jake Long was Lloyd Carr's last All-American player.

Lloyd Henry Carr ended his Michigan coaching career with a final record of 122 wins and 40 losses. His winning percentage was just over seventy-five percent (.753) for all games and just under seventy-eight percent (.779) in the Big Ten. He won the national championship in 1997 and won or shared five conference championships. It was an outstanding run for the former "interim" head coach at Michigan. Of course, the BIG question was "Who was the best man to lead the Michigan football team in 2008?"

The bad news for the Spartans was that they lost a game they probably should have won against the Wolverines. The good news was that MSU got it together and won the last two games of the regular season against Purdue (48-3) and Penn State (35-31). Even though they finished with a conference record of 3 wins and 5 losses, the Spartans earned a bid to the Champs Sports Bowl, but lost to Boston College (24-21). The first season of the Mark Dantonio Era ended at 7 wins and 6 losses. It was Michigan State's first winning season since 2003. Of course, Dantonio's post game comments about Mike Hart and Michigan caused his Green and White stock to soar! Wow, if he could back up his strong words with some wins, life could really be good again in East Lansing.

Game #101: October 25, 2008 at Michigan Stadium in Ann Arbor

BACKGROUND INFORMATION:

The NCAA made three changes for the 2008 season. First, they adopted a forty-second ready-for-play clock like the NFL. Again, the goal was to speed up play and reduce the overall length of games. Second, there was a renewed effort to reduce excessive player celebrations and taunting. Players who crossed the sportsmanship "line" would be flagged for unsportsman-like conduct. (*USA Today CFE*, Page 709) Third, a "targeting" penalty was created to keep players from making forcible contact with the crown of the helmet or making forcible contact to the head or neck area of an opponent. Targeting calls would earn a fifteen-yard penalty

Michigan State was a much better team in year one of the Mark Dantonio Era in East Lansing. Coach "D" stamped his name, his work ethic, and his values all over the MSU football program. Personal responsibility and accountability were the new "by-words" in the Duffy Daugherty Football Building. The Spartans played hard for 60-minutes in 2007 and were in every game that they did not win. The largest margin of defeat was seven points in losses to Northwestern, Ohio State, and Iowa. They lost the Michigan game by four points and two more by three points (Wisconsin and Boston College). MSU scored a lot of points. Unfortunately, they gave up way too many. If former Defensive Coordinator Mark Dantonio could tighten up his defense, things could really turn around quickly in East Lansing.

Michigan State kicked off the 2008 season with a tough loss at California (38-31). Dantonio's Spartans opened their home season with a 42-10 win over Eastern Michigan. MSU won their last two non-conference games against Florida Atlantic (17-0) and Notre Dame (23-7). Michigan State had a record of 3 wins and 1 loss heading into conference play. The Spartans earned a nice win in Bloomington (42-29) and won two more games against Iowa (16-13) and Northwestern (37-20). Coach Dantonio's mentor, Jim Tressel, brought his OSU Buckeyes to East Lansing and left with a 45-7 win over MSU. Ouch! Michigan State had a record of 6-2 heading into Michigan Week. Mark Dantonio was preparing his team for his first trip to Ann Arbor. Yes, Coach Dantonio was intent on starting Michigan's prideful fall as soon as possible!

The search for Lloyd Carr's successor was awkward to say the least. LSU Coach Les Miles turned a cold shoulder to his alma mater and other high-profile coaches (like Jim Harbaugh) did not want any part of the football drama in Ann Arbor. Highly qualified coaches were not exactly lining up to be the next Wolverine football coach. Finally, Athletic Director Bill Martin turned to West Virginia, the place that gave Michigan a legend named Fielding H. Yost. Would Rich Rodriguez of West Virginia University be the right man for the job? Rodriguez was considered an offensive minded coach who was famous for his "Spread Offense." He had never been an assistant at Michigan or in the Big Ten. He was an "outsider" when he arrived in Ann Arbor. Of course, none of that would matter if he won a lot of games, would it?

The 2008 Michigan football team began the season as an un-ranked team for the first time since 1985. Utah certainly did not think much about Rich Rodriguez and his football team. The Utes came to Ann Arbor and left with a 25-23 victory. Game two went better for the Wolverines, but not great. Nobody was impressed with a 16-6 win over Miami of Ohio.

A road trip to South Bend did not end well since the Irish beat Michigan by a score of 35-17. Just when thousands of fans were thinking about jumping off the top of Michigan Stadium, the Maize and Blue footballers upset #9 Wisconsin (27-25). Michigan had a record of 2 wins and 2 losses heading into conference play. The Wolverines stumbled out of the gate and lost their first three Big Ten games. Would Rich Rodriguez have his team ready to compete with an angry bunch of "little brothers" from East Lansing?

GAME SUMMARY: MSU 35 UM 21

The good news was that Michigan had the home field advantage for this series game. The bad news was that it did not really matter because the Spartans were determined to earn their first Big House victory since 1990. Playing at home helped the Wolverines because they were in the game for the first three quarters. Then, the angry Spartans put the pedal to the metal and sped away with a big win over the hated men in Maize and Blue.

Michigan State scored first on a 61-yard touchdown pass from Brian Hoyer to Blair White early in the first quarter. Brett Swenson kicked the extra point and the Spartans led 7-0. The Wolverines tied the game on a 19-yard scoring pass from Steve Threat to Brandon Minor and a successful PAT by K.C. Lopata made it 7-7 at the end of the first quarter. The Spartans regained the lead on a 64-yard run by Javon Ringer and Swenson's second extra point made it 14-7. Michigan responded again with another touchdown by Minor (2-yard run). Lopata's second extra point made it 14-14 at halftime. (*DFP*, 10/25/2008, Page 51)

Michigan took their first lead of the game on a 2-yard run by Threat. Lopata's third PAT made it 21-14 in favor of the Wolverines. The Spartans responded with a long drive that ended with a touchdown pass from Hoyer to Charlie Gantt. Swenson's third extra point tied the game. It was 21-21 at the end of the third quarter.

The Spartan offense took over the game late in the fourth quarter. Javon Ringer scored on a 3-yard run that finished an 82-yard drive. Swenson's kick made it 28-21 MSU. Michigan State iced the game with about three minutes to play. Hoyer threw his third touchdown pass to Josh Rouse. Brett Swenson kicked his fifth and final extra point to give the Spartans a 35-21 lead and that is how the game ended. (*DFP*, 10/25/2008, Page 51)

Michigan State was the better team in this game. They won the first down battle by a margin of 22 to 13. The Spartans totaled 473-yards of offense compared to 252-yards for the Wolverines. The Green and White runners pounded out 167-yards, but the Maize and Blue men only managed 84-yards. Brian Hoyer threw for 306-yards while Steve Threat could only connect for 168-yards for Michigan. (*DFP*, 10/25/2008, Page 51)

Team	1st	2nd	3rd	4th	Final
MSU	7	7	7	14	35
UM	7	7	7	0	21

SERIES UPDATE:

Another game was in the history books, but this one ended differently than most recent games. Yes, Michigan still held a BIG series lead. However, one BIG game can make a BIG difference when you have not beaten your rival in six seasons. Michigan still had a dominating series margin (67-29-5), but Spartan victory #29 was so sweet! Michigan State now had a record of 2 wins and 7 losses in the first decade of the new Millennium. The best news was that MSU took the Paul Bunyan Trophy and "bragging rights" home with them. The Green and White footballers now had a trophy record of 20 wins, 34 losses, and 2 ties. Go Spartans!

SERIES MILESTONES:

As always, there were some notable items to mention from series Game #101. First, Coach Mark Dantonio posted his first series win in his second attempt. It was even better since it came in Ann Arbor. Second it was also Michigan State's twentieth win in the Paul Bunyan Trophy games. Third, it was MSU's first series win in Ann Arbor since 1990. Fourth, Rich Rodriguez became the fifth consecutive Wolverine coach to lose his first game to Michigan State. Finally, the fired-up Spartans broke series protocol and changed series tradition when they charged the Michigan side of the field in search of Paul Bunyan. Michigan Equipment Manager Jon Falk was unpacking the famous trophy for his trip to the MSU locker room. The Green and White footballers were in no mood for a locker room party as series teams did in the past. No, the Spartans found their "prize" and paraded to the "Spartan" end of the field to show off their bounty and celebrate with their fans! It was a wild, joyful scene for Michigan State.

SEASON SUMMARIES:

The Spartans just kept on winning (Wisconsin- 25-24) and winning (Purdue-21-7) before losing the last game of the regular season to Penn State (49-18). MSU earned a bid to the Capitol One Bowl and finished the season with a loss to Georgia (24-12). The good news was that Mark Dantonio's team ended the 2008 season with a final record of 9 wins and 4 losses. They posted a winning record of 6 victories and 2 losses in the Big Ten which was good enough for third place. Javon Ringer became the first Spartan to earn first team All-American honors since 2004. It was an impressive season for Coach "D" and his team.

Coach Rich Rodriguez and his Wolverines continued to struggle after their loss to Michigan State. They lost to Purdue (48-42) and beat Minnesota (29-6). Rich Rod's team finished the season with losses to Northwestern (21-14) and Ohio State (42-7). Yes, it was a "record setting" season in Ann Arbor, but not in a good way. Michigan lost nine games in a single season for the first time in their long and illustrious history. They ended the season with a final record of 3 wins and 9 losses. They posted a dismal record of 2 wins and 6 losses in the Big Ten. Yes, Rich Rodriguez was off to a rocky start in Ann Arbor.

To put things in perspective, you must go back a few years to see what some other Michigan football coaches did in their first season. Bo Schembechler arrived in 1969 and lost two regular season games in his first year. However, he did not lose his ninth regular season game until the fifth game of his tenth season in Ann Arbor.

Gary Moeller did not lose his ninth regular season game until the third game of his fifth season at Michigan. Lloyd Carr understood what he was supposed to do. Coach Carr did not lose his ninth regular season game until the eleventh game of his fourth season. I doubt that Rich Rodriguez knew about these kinds of expectations and standards. Coach Rodriguez did not come close to measuring up to the Michigan Standard in his first year. No doubt about it, the biggest room in Schembechler Hall at the end of the 2008 season was definitely the "room for improvement."

Game #102: October 3, 2009 at Spartan Stadium in East Lansing

BACKGROUND INFORMATION:

There were no new rules changes in 2009, but the NCAA did advise game officials to protect "defenseless" players from helmet-to-helmet hits. (*USA Today CFE*, Page734)

Rich Rodriguez was doing his best to weather the storm that hung over his program after the 2008 season. He had a chance to recruit more players for his "Spread Offense" and some for his porous defense. The program was still a work in progress, Coach "Rich Rod" was confident that he could turn things around and silence most of his critics. All he had to do was win, just win! For the second straight year, the Wolverines were un-ranked at the start of the football season. Nobody in the press was expecting much from Michigan in 2009. As it turned out, the Maize and Blue rolled through the non-conference schedule in impressive fashion. They beat Western Michigan (31-7), Notre Dame (38-34) and Eastern Michigan (45-17). The Wolverines opened Big Ten play with a high scoring win over Indiana (36-33). The good news was that Rich Rod's offense was averaging over thirty-points per game. The bad news was that the defense was giving up way too many points. Michigan rose to #22 in the country, but everyone knew that the Wolverines would have to play much better against MSU to continue their winning ways.

Coach Mark Dantonio's first two teams won 16 games and he was looking to win some more in 2009. It looked like his football "culture" was taking hold. His coaching staff was working hard to make his program competitive with the best in the Big Ten. Some people were even talking about championships, but most experts thought that the Spartans were one or two years away from such lofty conversations. The pollsters certainly were not convinced yet. None of the major polls had MSU ranked in the top twenty-five teams at the start of the 2009 season. Of course, Dantonio and his staff were intent on proving them wrong! As expected, Michigan State began the season with an easy win over Montana State (44-3). The Spartans were not expected to lose to Central Michigan, but that's exactly what happened. Once again, the rude Chippewas came to East Lansing and left town with a 29-27 upset win over Sparty.

I am sure that all the fine folks in Ann Arbor gave Dantonio's Spartans a "moment of silence" for their disappointing loss. Or maybe not! Michigan State journeyed to South Bend the next week and came back with another loss (33-30) to Notre Dame. Obviously, the non-conference part of the 2009 football schedule did not go well (1 win and 2 losses).

Maybe things would get better in conference play. Or maybe not! MSU traveled to Madison to play the Badgers and returned home with another defeat. Yes, the Spartans were in this one, but still lost a tough one to Wisconsin (38-30). Mark Dantonio's team was off to a miserable start. Would they be able to get in the win column against #22 Michigan?

GAME SUMMARY: UM 20 MSU 26

The Wolverines were favored to win Game #102, but not by much. Everyone expected a close game and that is what they got. Both defenses played better than they had all season. Michigan's much maligned defenders helped set up the first score of the game with a first quarter interception.

Jason Olesnavage kicked a 36-yard field goal to convert that turnover into a 3-0 Wolverine lead. Michigan State responded with a nice drive that ended with a Larry Caper touchdown run (1-yard). Brett Swenson made the extra point and MSU led 7-3 at the end of the first quarter. Both teams traded field goals in the second quarter. Olesnavage kicked a 42-yarder for Michigan and Swenson booted a 26-yarder on the last play of the half. The Spartans took a 10-6 lead to the locker room at halftime. (*DFP*, 10/4/2009, Page 53)

Michigan State scored the only points of the third period on a 24-yard field goal by Swenson. It was 13-6 in favor of the Spartans with fifteen minutes to play. Dantonio's footballers took the biggest lead of the game on a 15-yard run by Glenn Winston in the first minute of the final quarter. Swenson kicked the PAT and MSU led 20-6 with fourteen minutes to play. Freshman quarterback Tate Forcier led the Wolverines to their first touchdown with a 60-yard touchdown pass to Darryl Stonum. Olesnavage's extra point kick closed the score to 20-13. Michigan's defense held the Spartans and Michigan had a chance to tie the game. With minutes remaining, Forcier took his offense on a drive that ended with a 9-yard scoring pass from Forcier to Roy Roundtree. Jason Olesnavage booted the extra point to tie the game at 20-20 and that is how the fourth period ended. (*DFP*, 10/4/2009, Page 53)

For the third time in the last six games, the bitter rivals went to overtime to determine a winner. As it turned out, Michigan got the ball first in overtime and the Spartan defense held. All MSU needed was a field goal to win, but Larry Capers wanted more. He broke multiple tackles on his way to a game winning 23-yard run and that was it! Michigan State defeated Michigan (26-20) for the second straight season. (*DFP*, 10/4/2009, Page 53) The Spartans were ready to party because Michigan was going home without Paul Bunyan! Go Green! Go White!

As usual, Game #102 was hard-hitting and teeth rattling all the way. Michigan State controlled the ball for much of the game and outgained the Wolverines by a margin of 417-yards to 251-yards. Once again, the team that won the rushing game won the football game The Spartans rushed for 197-yards compared to only 28-yards for Michigan. I am certain that plenty of blood was left on the Spartan Stadium turf that day, but Rich Rod's team left more.

Team	1st	2nd	3rd	4th	OT	Final
UM	3	3	0	14	0	20
MSU	7	3	7	6	6	26

SERIES UPDATE:

After the win, Michigan State improved their series standing. The Spartans now owned 30 wins, 67 losses, and 5 ties. MSU ended the decade with 3 wins and 7 losses. More importantly, they pushed their series record to 21 wins, 34 losses, and 2 ties. Michigan State players and fans would enjoy "bragging rights" for another year. Even worse, there was nothing the Wolverines could do about until the next decade!

SERIES MILESTONES:

Game number one-hundred and two marked the last game of the first decade of the new Millennium. After two straight overtime losses, it was MSU's first overtime series win. Of course, it was the second straight series loss for Michigan. The Spartans also recorded their thirtieth series victory. It was also the first time that Coach Dantonio recorded two consecutive series victories. Mark Dantonio won his first series game in Spartan Stadium in his second attempt. Finally, both teams finished the season with losing records which was the first time that such an unusual event took place in the long history of both schools.

SEASON SUMMARIES:

Michigan dropped out of the rankings the next week. They went to Iowa to try to get back in the win column. The Hawkeyes failed to cooperate and sent the Wolverines back to Ann Arbor to dissect a 30-28 loss. The Maize and Blue footballers took their frustrations out on hapless Delaware State and pounded the Hornets (63-6). Unfortunately for Michigan, there were no more "breaks" in the schedule. Rich Rod's team lost the last five games of the season because the defense allowed about thirty points per game. The offense only scored an average of eighteen points a game over this stretch. The Wolverines were "in deficit" (by about 12 points a game) towards the end of the season. It is not the kind of math a team needs to win football games.

Michigan finished the 2009 season with a final record of 5 wins and 7 losses which was an improvement from 2008. However, no one in Ann Arbor was celebrating. Team #130 set a Maize and Blue record for Big Ten futility with 1 win and 7 losses. The Rich Rodriguez Era was not going well in Ann Arbor. Now, in addition to losing too many games, the Wolverines were being investigated by the NCAA for violating practice rules. It was not a good time to be a Wolverine or a Wolverine fan!

Coach Dantonio's Spartans used the momentum of the Michigan victory to win the next two games over Illinois (24-14) and Northwestern (24-14). [Note – This is not a misprint. Both wins were by the same exact score.] Unfortunately, MSU ran out of football magic and lost three of the last five games to finish with 6 wins and 6 losses.

The Spartans ended the Big Ten season at 4 wins and 4 losses. The good news was that Coach "D's" team earned a spot in the Valero Alamo Bowl. The bad news is that they lost a shootout to Texas Tech (41-31) on January 2, 2010.

That was it for year three of the Mark Dantonio Era. A losing season (6-7) was not expected by anyone in East Lansing, but it happened. It was time to go back to the drawing board and figure how to get the Spartans back on the winning side of the ledger. The good news was that linebacker Greg Jones earned first team All-American honors and Paul Bunyan was staying in East Lansing for another year!

DECADE AND SERIES SUMMARY:

Lloyd Carr's Wolverines dominated the Spartans from 2000 to 2007 by winning seven of eight games. Of course, Carr's departure and the arrival of Mark Dantonio changed things. Michigan State won the last two games of the decade and Dantonio was determined to win more in the next ten years—a lot more!

Rich Rodriguez was having a tough time in Ann Arbor and very few people thought that he would make it past his four-year contract. Since both teams ended the decade with losing seasons, it was hard to forecast what might happen in the next ten years. The only certainty was that the series would continue to be as nasty and intense as any rivalry in college football. Bring on Decade Two of the 21st Century!

Decade and Series Summary 1898 to 2009

Time Frame	UM-Won-Lost-Tied	MSU-Won-Lost-Tied
2000-2009	7-3-0	3-7-0
1898-2009	67-30-5	30-67-5

BIG TEN SUMMARY

Let us take a quick look at how the Wolverines and Spartans fared in Big Ten play from 2000 to 2009. The first decade of the new Millennium was outstanding for Michigan, especially for the first eight years. Of course, the last two years were not. The Spartans had too much turmoil in the coaching ranks from 2000-2009 to seriously compete in the Big Ten. Remember, they had four different coaches in ten years. This not a good way to build a winner in one of America's toughest football conferences.

The Wolverines were the best Big Ten team in Michigan during the first decade of the 21st Century. They were not great, but they were very good for the first eight years of the decade before things slipped. Lloyd Carr won plenty of conference games and claimed three conference championships. Of course, Rich Rodriguez took the Wolverines to the bottom of the Big Ten in two short years which skewed Michigan's overall performance. The numbers on the chart below tell a complete story about the state of Big Ten Football in the Mitten State from 2000 to 2009.

Big Ten Summary 2000 to 2009

Statistical Area	UM	MSU
Number of Head Coaches	2	4
Games Played	80	80
Wins	53	32
Losses	27	48
Ties	0	0
Winning Percentage	.663	.400
Winning Seasons	8	2
Losing Seasons	2	6
Even Seasons	0	2
Big Ten Championships	3	0

Michigan State's football fortunes in the Big Ten almost went into bankruptcy in the first decade of the 21st Century. Bobby Williams was not the answer in East Lansing. Morris Watts was not either. John L. Smith gave Spartan fans a glimmer of hope in 2003. Unfortunately, things went downhill in the next three years and Smith was gone. Mark Dantonio was making progress with his first nine-win season and two wins over Michigan. Spartan fans were hoping that Coach "D" would keep beating Michigan and other teams too!

PROGRAM SUMMARIES:

Michigan was a consistent winner from 2000 to 2008, but not from 2008-2009. Coach Lloyd Carr won a ton of games in his final eight years at Michigan. In fact, he posted a record of 73 wins and 27 losses during this time. That worked out to an impressive winning percentage of seventy-three percent. Unfortunately, Rich Rodriguez only won eight of twenty-four games from 2008 to 2009. Michigan football was in trouble at the end of the decade. Despite the late drop off in performance, all Wolverine numbers were still better than those of Michigan State for the decade.

The Michigan State football program underachieved from 2000 to 2009. The Spartans could not build a consistent winner because of all the coaching changes and everything that goes with hiring and firing and hiring and firing. Every fan in East Lansing knew that MSU football was struggling. The BIG question on everyone's mind was "Would Coach Dantonio be around long enough to really rebuild the MSU football program?"

Michigan and Michigan State had the same problem on December 31, 2009. Football in Ann Arbor and East Lansing was hard to watch unless you had a bag over your head. Okay, the Spartans were not that bad to watch in 2008 and 2009, but the Wolverines were. Both UM and MSU needed football "makeovers." Only time would tell if Rich Rodriguez and Mark Dantonio could lead their football teams to better places starting in 2010. It promised to be another interesting decade of Mitten State football.

Program Summaries 2000 to 2009

Statistical Area	UM	MSU
Number of Head Coaches	2	4
Games Played	124	122
Wins	81	60
Losses	43	62
Ties	0	0
Winning Percentage	.653	,492
Winning Seasons	8	4
Losing Seasons	2	6
Even Seasons	0	0
National Championships	0	0
All-American Players	16	6

CHAPTER 14

Little Brother Humbles "little blue" 2010 to 2019

C ollege football continued to grow and garner more attention, and dollars, than ever before. The television folks pushed games and times into almost every day of the week during "college football season" Saturday was the standard day for broadcasting college football games, but special "games" were now showing up on Tuesdays, Wednesdays, Thursdays, and Fridays. In the western time-zones, fans could watch college football from 10:00 am until past midnight every Saturday from early September until the first week of December. However, oversaturation did not appear to be a problem in 2010. The networks just kept broadcasting games to anyone, and everyone, who would watch them. Yes, college football was still a BIG DEAL in America, especially for the networks!

Game #103: October 9, 2010 at Michigan Stadium in Ann Arbor

BACKGROUND INFORMATION:

Mark Dantonio's Spartans underachieved in 2009—period! However, he got a "free pass" from MSU Nation for beating Michigan for the second straight season! Coach Dantonio knew he had to tighten up his defense and shore up his running game. He thought that his passing game and special teams would be highly effective in 2010. As it turned out, he was right. Coach Dantonio knew that his team would be good in his fourth season, but he did not know how good. He thought that his team, if it stayed healthy, could be good and maybe compete for the Big Ten Championship. Not too many "experts' thought he could pull that off, not quite yet!

The Michigan State Spartans began the 2010 season on a mission to prove that 2009 was a fluke. They won their first two non-conference games against Western Michigan (38-14) and Florida Atlantic (30-17) but got a lot of attention in week three with an overtime win over Notre Dame (34-31). Unfortunately, the Notre Dame game victory proved to be a little too exciting for Coach Dantonio. He suffered a mild heart attack after the game and did not coach for two weeks. Fortunately, his coaching staff kept everything going in the right direction. A win over Northern Colorado (45-7) put the Spartans at 4 wins and 0 losses at the end of the non-conference portion of their schedule.

A powerful Wisconsin team give MSU their stiffest test of the season in week five. However, the Spartans passed the test with a 34-24 win over the Badgers. Michigan State looked like they were good enough to compete for a Big Ten championship. The seventeenth ranked Spartans appeared ready to defend the Paul Bunyan Trophy on October 9, 2010. Mark Dantonio was back on the sidelines with his Spartans when they went to Ann Arbor in week six. This game was always "personal" for Coach "D" and he had to be there!

Year number three of the Rich Rodriguez Era was overshadowed by the negative energy produced by the NCAA findings about Michigan's failure to follow basic practice protocols. Two straight losing seasons did not help the situation either! Rich Rodriguez was a man on the "hot-seat" in 2010. He was fighting for his coaching life in Ann Arbor. He had three recruiting classes under his belt, but his best players were still young. Most "experts" felt that he was still two years away from putting a competitive team on the field. Unfortunately, nobody thought that he would be around that long. Bottom line—Rich Rodriguez would have to put together an outstanding season to survive at Michigan. No pressure, right?.

The good news was that the Michigan Stadium "make-over" was finally complete. Michigan began the season against Connecticut in a much more modern "Big House." The Wolverines played well on September 4, 2010 and defeated Connecticut (30-10). They went to Notre Dame in week two and returned to Ann Arbor with a BIG win over the Irish (28-24). The Rodriguez "Spread Offense" warmed up in week three as the Maize and Blue footballers defeated Massachusetts (42-37). Bowling Green had no answer for Rich Rod's "Spread" and lost (65-21) to Michigan. The Wolverines kept on winning in their first Big Ten game of the season against Indiana. Michigan went to Bloomington and won (42-35). It was only the second conference road game win in the three-year tenure of Coach Rodriguez. After five games the Wolverines went from being un-ranked to #18 in the country. The offense, with a kid named Denard Robinson running the show, was often spectacular, but the defense, was not! Michigan would find out how good they were when the seventeenth ranked Spartans came to town.

GAME SUMMARY: MSU 34 UM 17

The one-hundred and third game of the series was one to remember for the Spartans and another one for the Wolverines to forget! Michigan scored first on a 34-yard field goal by Seth Broekhuizen and it was 3-0 Michigan after one quarter. The Spartans "woke-up" and took the lead in the second quarter on a 61-yard run by Edwin Baker.

Dan Conroy's PAT kick made it 7-3 MSU. The Wolverines came back to take the lead on a 12-yard scoring pass from Denard Robinson to Martell Webb. Broekhuizen's extra-point kick made it 10-7 in favor of Michigan with seven-minutes to play in the half. La'Veon Bell busted loose for a 41-yard touchdown run and Conroy's kick gave the Spartans a 14-10 lead with just over four minutes remaining in the first half. Dan Conroy finished the first half scoring with a 38-yard field goal and the Spartans went to the locker room with a 17-10 lead over their hated rivals. (*DFP*, 10/10/2010, Page 57)

Kirk Cousins and the Spartans took the second half kickoff straight to the end zone. Cousins connected on a 41-yard touchdown pass to Mark Dell with just over twelve minutes remaining in the quarter. Conroy's third extra point expanded the MSU lead to 24-10. Eight minutes later, the Spartans scored again on an 8-yard run by Larry Caper. Michigan State now led 31-10 with Conroy's extra-point conversion. The third quarter ended with MSU in the lead (31-10). Denard Robinson gave Michigan fans some hope when he scored on a 4-yard run in the first minute of the final quarter. Seth Broekhuizen made the extra point and the score was 31-17. The Spartan defense shut the Wolverines down for the rest of the game. Dan Conroy kicked his second field goal (28-yards) to close out the scoring. (*DFP*, 10/10/2010, Page 57)

"Little brother" did it again and Michigan State earned a hard-fought 34-17 victory over Michigan. The Spartans were better on offense, defense, and special teams. It was another complete victory for the Green and White. Dantonio's footballers rolled up 536-yards of offense (249 rushing and 287 passing) and totaled 24 first downs. Meanwhile, the Wolverine offense underperformed with 377-yards of offense (162 rushing and 215 passing). Michigan managed to earn nineteen first downs in this game but came up short in the points department. Once again, the only thing better than a rival win is a victory in his bigger, better football stadium. (*DFP*, 10/10/2010, Page 57)

Team	1st	2nd	3rd	4th	Final
MSU	0	17	14	3	34
UM	3	7	0	7	17

SERIES UPDATE:

Michigan State's series record improved to 31 wins, 67 losses, and 5 ties. They took the lead in the second decade of the Twenty-first Century by a margin of 1-0. Paul Bunyan would get back on the bus with the Spartans and remain in East Lansing for another year. After fifty-eight trophy games, the Green and White now owned a record of 22 wins, 34 losses, and 2 ties. Mark Dantonio's footballers earned their third consecutive win over Rich Rodriguez and his Wolverines. A Spartan "three peat" had not happened since the Duffy Daugherty Era in the mid-1960s. Michigan fans were not happy. Of course, Spartan loyalists were dancing in the streets and bragging a lot! Go Green! Go White!

SERIES MILESTONES:

Game #103 turned out to be the third and last game for Michigan's Rich Rodriguez. He finished with a series record of 0 wins and 3 losses. His career record of 8 wins and 16 losses produced a "winning" percentage of .333 which was/is the lowest in Michigan Football History. The game was also another record breaker in the attendance department. The new and improved Big House had room for 113,.065 onlookers. It broke the old series record set in 2002 by a whopping margin of 1,456 people. It was also the first time that both teams were undefeated heading into the battle for Paul Bunyan since 1999. Finally, it was MSU's twentieth series win in Ann Arbor.

SEASON SUMMARIES:

Mark Dantonio's Spartans kept on winning after they beat Michigan. They defeated Illinois (26-6) and Northwestern (35-27) to run their streak to eight consecutive wins. Iowa put an end to the winning with a 37-6 defeat of the Spartans. MSU was still in the hunt for the conference championship, but they would have to win their last three games and get some help. As it turned out, that is exactly what happened. The Green and White footballers defeated Minnesota (31-8), Purdue (35-31), and Penn State (28-22) to close out the regular season with a record of 11 wins and 1 loss. Better yet, they finished the conference season with a record of 7 wins and 1 loss which tied them with Wisconsin for the Big Ten Title. The Spartans earned a bid to the Capital One Bowl to play Alabama, but that did not go well. The Crimson Tide rolled over MSU (49-7). Coach Dantonio's fourth team ended with a final record of 11 wins and 2 losses. He became the first Spartan coach to win eleven games in one season. Yes, it was a break-out year for the Green and White.

The good news for Michigan was that they still had a record of 5 wins and 1 loss after the MSU game. The bad news was that they still had six Big Ten games to play. Michigan did not win a lot of conference games in the first two years of the Rodriguez Era and 2010 was no different. Coach Rodriguez tried to pick his team up for their next game against Iowa.

The offense played well enough to win, but the defense allowed way too many points and the Hawkeyes left town with a win (38-28). Michigan lost the next game to Penn State (31-41) to make it three straight losses. Michigan beat Illinois in triple overtime (67-65) and then defeated Purdue (27-16). The Wolverines were 7-3 with two games to go. Unfortunately, they lost to Wisconsin (48-28) and Ohio State (37-7) to finish the regular season with a record of 7 wins and 5 losses. Michigan set another dubious record in 2010 when they allowed 458 points for the season. The first, and only, Wolverine team to accomplish that feat—ugh! Michigan earned a bid to the Gator Bowl but lost to Mississippi State (52-14). There is no way Rich Rodriguez could survive this disappointing season. And, as a matter of fact, he did not. Athletic Director Dave Brandon fired him in early January 2011. It was time to find a new leader of the Michigan Wolverine football program.

Game #104: October 15, 2011 at Spartan Stadium in East Lansing

BACKGROUND INFORMATION:

There was some BIG news in the Big Ten in 2011. The conference welcomed Nebraska as the twelfth member and reorganized too. Now, the Big Ten would have a championship game like some of the other top conferences. To do this, the twelve conference teams were divided into two divisions—Leaders and Legends. Michigan and Michigan State were both assigned to the Legends Division and would compete for the division championship and the right to play in the Big Ten Conference Championship game in December. Yes, the days of co-championships in the Big Ten were over!

The Michigan Football Program planned to change re-tool their offense in 2011. The Spread Offense was going to give way to good old Michigan "Smash Mouth" football. At least, that was Brady Hoke's plan. However, Hoke faced the problem that Rich Rodriguez had when he started at Michigan. Rodriguez had the offense he wanted to run, but he did not have all the right players in years one and two. After getting some of the "right" players, he got fired. Brady Hoke was a fan of the running game and suffocating defenses. Everything sounded great, but the question was "What are you going to do until you get the players you need to run your systems?" Fortunately, Coach Hoke had a guy named Denard Robinson who was good enough and almost strong enough to carry Hoke's offense for the first two and one-half years of his tenure.

Unlike Rodriguez, Brady Hoke had a Michigan "pedigree" having coached at Michigan from 1995 to 2002 as an assistant. He knew the words to the "Victors", and he had an unabashed love and respect for the Michigan Football tradition. Coach Hoke also had some quirky ideas and habits which eventually became the subject of ridicule by some fans and the media. Brady Hoke knew about Michigan's rivalries. In fact, he wanted to take the rivalry "thing" to a new level. Hoke borrowed an idea that OSU's John Cooper used—with bad results. Coach Hoke did Cooper one better by installing two "Count Down Clocks" in Schembechler Hall to remind his players about how many days remained until the next game against Michigan State and Ohio State. That is some of the background about the arrival of the Brady Hoke Era at Michigan in 2011. The Wolverines started well under their new coach. In fact, they started very well! The Wolverines won their first four non-conference games against Western Michigan (34-10), Notre Dame (35-31), Eastern Michigan (31-3), and San Diego State (28-7).

The undefeated Maize and Blue footballers won their first two Big Ten games against Minnesota (58-0) and Northwestern (42-24) to run their winning streak to six straight games. It was an impressive start! Michigan went from being unranked to #11 on the Monday prior to the annual showdown with the Spartans. The 2011 edition of the annual "Backyard Brawl" promised to be something special!

Mark Dantonio continued to enjoy his time in East Lansing. His Spartans had an amazing run in 2010 and they had many excellent players returning in 2011. One of them was quarterback Kirk Cousins. With Cousins leading the offense and a pair of strong running backs, the MSU offense was formidable. Fortunately for Coach "D," the defense was even better. Oh, by the way, his special teams were, well, "special."

There was no reason to think that the 2011 edition of the Michigan State Spartans would not compete for the Big Ten Championship again. Michigan State began the season as the 17th ranked team in the country. The Spartans charged out of the gate in 2011 with wins over Youngstown State (28-6) and Florida Atlantic (44-0). However, their modest two-game win streak came to a halt at Notre Dame (31-13). Coach Dantonio got his team rolling again with wins over Central Michigan (45-7) and Ohio State (10-7). It was time for the fifth edition of the "Little Brother" vs "little blue." Coach Dantonio did not need any countdown clocks to fire his team up for this game. All he needed to do was remind his players about how much he hated Michigan and guys like Mike Hart. This matchup was now very, very personal for Mark Dantonio. His players always seemed to step up a little bit more for Michigan, now that Coach D was running the Spartan football show. The underdog Spartans (#23) waited impatiently for #11 Michigan's arrival on October 15, 2011.

GAME SUMMARY: UM 14 MSU 28

Another capacity crowd of 77,515 showed up at Spartan Stadium for series game #104 Michigan scored first in this game when quarterback Denard Robinson dashed for a 15-yard touchdown. Brendan Gibbons made the extra-point, and it was 7-0 with about seven minutes to play in the first quarter. Michigan State tied the game a few minutes later when Edwin Baker rammed into the end zone for a 1-yard score. Dan Conroy's PAT kick made it 7-7 and that is where the score remained until the third quarter. (*Lansing State Journal* [*LSJ*], 10/16/2011, Page 32)

Kirk Cousins put the Spartans in front on a 10-yard scoring pass to Keshawn Martin at the 11-minute mark of the third stanza. Again, Conroy converted the extra point and MSU led (14-7). Cousins and Martin hooked up again on a 13-yard touchdown pass and it was 21-7 in favor of the Spartans after forty-five minutes of play. With about nine minutes to play, Michigan closed the gap to 21-14 when Denard Robinson connected with Roy Roundtree on a 34-yard scoring pass and Gibbons converted the kick. Michigan was moving the ball and pushing hard to tie the score when Isaiah Lewis picked off a Robinson pass and took it 39-yards for a "pick-six." Dan Conroy closed out the scoring with his fourth extra-point of the day. MSU led 28-14 and that is how the game ended. (*LSJ*, 10/16/2011, Page 32)

Just like 2010, the Spartan defense stepped up to slow down Denard Robinson and the Michigan offense. The Wolverines only produced 250 yards of offense (82-net yards rushing and 168-yards passing). Michigan won the first down battle (20-16) but lost the touchdown battle (4-2) and that was the difference in the game. Michigan State's offense scored plenty of points and gained enough yards (333) to control the ball and the game for over thirty-minutes of playing time. The Spartans converted 7 of 14 third down plays while Michigan only made 3 of 15 attempts. (*LSJ*, 10/16/2011, Page 32)

Of course, it was another fiercely contested game with plenty of hard tackles and bone-crunching blocks. Yes, it was another "Big Boy" football game in the Mitten State, but the Spartans were the better team for the fourth consecutive season. Michigan fans were not thrilled with the outcome, but Spartan fans were fired-up! Obviously, Brady Hoke's "Countdown Clock" did not work for this game. The Wolverines would have to do something different in 2012 if they hoped to get back on the winning side of the ledger against Sparty.

Team	1st	2nd	3rd	4th	Final
UM	7	0	0	7	14
MSU	7	0	14	7	28

SERIES UPDATE:

There is no doubt that the Spartan players, coaches, and fans thoroughly enjoyed their decisive win over Michigan. There was so much to celebrate! Yes, Michigan still held a healthy advantage in the series with a record of 67 wins, 32 losses, and 5 ties. However, the Spartans pushed their decade lead to 2-0 with their impressive win. Dantonio's team won the Paul Bunyan Trophy for the fourth consecutive season. Michigan State's record in the "Big Ten Years" improved to 23 wins, 34 losses, and 2 ties.

SERIES MILESTONES:

There were two important series milestones for game number one-hundred and four. First, it was the first game for Coach Brady Hoke and his first loss. Like Bump Elliott, Bo Schembechler, Gary Moeller, Lloyd Carr and Rich Rodriguez, Hoke became the sixth straight Wolverine coach to lose his first series game to the Spartans. Second, it was the first time that both teams competed as members of the Big Ten's Legends Division. Finally, Dantonio's fourth consecutive win allowed him to share this distinction with Charlie Bachman, Biggie Munn, and Duffy Daugherty.

SEASON SUMMARIES:

The Wolverines bounced back from their loss at MSU and earned a Homecoming Day victory over Purdue (36-14). Things did not go as well at Iowa the next week. The Hawkeyes sent U of M home with a loss (24-16). The Wolverines had a record of 7 wins and 2 losses with three games to play. They were probably out of the division championship race, but still had plenty to play for. Coach Hoke kept his team focused and the Wolverines won two more games against Illinois (31-14) and Nebraska (45-17) to set up a big game against Ohio State. Michigan defeated the Buckeyes (40-34).

Michigan finished the regular season with a record of 10 wins and 2 losses. Much to the chagrin of the Spartans, the Wolverines earned a bid to a BCS bowl to play Virginia Tech in the Sugar Bowl. Hoke's footballers ended their magical year with a 23-20 overtime win to end the season with a final record of 11 wins and 2 losses. Michigan center Dave Molk earned All-American honors in 2011.

Michigan State followed up their victory over Michigan with another big win against Wisconsin (37-31). Maybe they thought that they had everything under control. An embarrassing loss at Nebraska (24-3) brought the Spartans back to earth. Coach Dantonio got his team back on track and they finished season with four straight wins over Minnesota (31-24), Iowa (37-21), Indiana (55-3) and Northwestern (31-17). MSU ended the regular season with a record of 10 wins and 2 losses and a ranking of #11.

The Spartans won the Legends Division Championship and earned the right to play Wisconsin for the Big Ten Championship. Sadly, MSU could not beat the Badgers twice in the same season. Wisconsin defeated the Spartans 39-42 to win the first Big Ten Championship game in December 2011. Before the Big Ten championship game, the Wolverines (who lost to MSU) got the bid to the Sugar Bowl, not Sparty. Yes, Mark Dantonio had steam coming out of his ears and his nostrils when he spoke about the lack of respect that the bowl folks showed for his players and his program. Once again, the "arrogant ones" from Ann Arbor were given something that he felt MSU deserved. One more reason for Spartan fans to dislike Michigan.

Oh, by the way, MSU played in the Outback Bowl and defeated Georgia in triple overtime (33-30) to finish with 11 wins, 3 losses, and a Legend's Division Championship. Defensive tackle Jerel Worthy earned first team All-American honors for the Spartans. Coach Dantonio was probably feeling a lot like comedian Rodney Dangerfield. Both men always seemed to be battling for respect, no matter what they accomplished. Yes, the rivalry continued to be very, very personal for Mark Dantonio and his Spartans.

Game #105: October 20, 2012 at Michigan Stadium in Ann Arbor

BACKGROUND INFORMATION:

Michigan State was looking forward to defending their Legends Division title in 2012. They also wanted to get back to the championship game and finish the job in the new season. Mark Dantonio was still fighting for respect for his program and his players. No matter how well they played and no matter what they accomplished, the Michigan "shadow" always seemed to darken the fall skies in East Lansing.

The only thing Coach "D" could do about it was to continue to beat Michigan and everybody else too. Someday, if Michigan State kept on playing better than Michigan, they would get the respect they deserved and would finally be able to step out of Michigan's shadow! That was Coach Dantonio's mindset for the 2012 season. Win as many games as possible, especially the Wolverine encounter in Ann Arbor! Pretty simple plan, right?

Coach Dantonio's footballers started well in 2012 with two wins over Boise State (17-13) and Central Michigan (42-7). Unfortunately, they lost to Notre Dame for the second straight season (20-3). The Spartans came back in week four and defeated Eastern Michigan (23-7). Ohio State stopped the one-game win streak by invading Spartan Stadium and escaping with a narrow 17-16 victory. Dantonio's team split the next two games—winning at Indiana (31-27) and losing on Homecoming Day to Iowa (19-16). After seven games, MSU had a record of 4 wins and 3 losses. The unranked Spartans had to get ready for another BIG GAME in the BIG HOUSE. A win against hated Michigan could save Michigan State's season.

Brady Hoke really could not have done much more in his first season. He joined Fielding H. Yost, as only the second Michigan football coach to win 11 games in his first season. One of Hoke's "rival clocks" worked since Michigan beat OSU for the first time since 2003. His Wolverines also won Michigan's first Sugar Bowl game in January 2012. Of course, Wolverine fans were disappointed that Brady could not beat Sparty. And, a Big Ten Championship and a National Championship would have been nice too.

Oh, by the way, how in the heck did he lose to Iowa, are you kidding me? Overall, most people were happy with the first year of the Brady Hoke Era. However, as Hoke himself stated in his first press conference, "This is Michigan!" Yes, the bar continued to be extremely high for Brady Hoke. He had to live up to the monstrous expectations or face the consequences. The biggest question surrounding the start of the 2012 season was, "What would Brady Hoke's team do for an encore?" Well, like I wrote in the first part of this paragraph, it was clear what Coach Hoke had to do in year two. He had to win 10 or 11 games, win the Legends Division, beat Notre Dame, MSU and OSU and compete for the Big Ten Title. Yes, those were high expectations, but remember, "This is Michigan!"

The eighth ranked Wolverines had one of the toughest non-conference games in history in 2012. They kicked off the season against second-ranked Alabama in Arlington, Texas. It turned out to be a wake-up call about how the "Big Boys" really play college football. Alabama dominated the undermanned Wolverines by a final score of 41-14. Worse yet, it really was not as close as the score indicated. Maybe thoughts about a National Championship would have to wait for a few years. Michigan was clearly not in the same "league" as the Crimson Tide. Things went better in weeks two and three as the Wolverines defeated Air Force (31-25) and Massachusetts (63-13). Coach Hoke took his footballers to South Bend and got another gut-punch from the Irish. The offense forgot to get off the bus and Michigan lost (13-6). It was ugly! The bad news was that the Wolverines had a record of 2 wins and 2 losses in non-conference play. The good news was that they were undefeated in the Big Ten. Hoke's team started fast in conference play with wins over Purdue (44-13) and Illinois (45-0). Michigan was ranked #23 heading into MSU week. The MSU Countdown Clock showed "six days." It was time to figure out a way to beat the invaders from East Lansing.

GAME SUMMARY: MSU 10 UM 12

Game number one-hundred and five in the "blood series" was one to remember for Michigan and one to regret for Michigan State. Both defenses were "dialed-up" for this game. Every block and every tackle registered a reading on the Richter Scale. Wow, the boys were really hitting hard in this game. The teams battled to a scoreless tie in the first quarter. It was obvious after 15-minutes of play that points would be extremely hard to come by in this game. Michigan opened the scoring early in the second quarter on a 24-yard field goal by Brendan Gibbons. Michigan State took the ensuing kickoff down the field on a long drive that ended on a missed field goal (38-yards) by Dan Conroy. Michigan still led 3-0 with about five minutes to play in the half. The Wolverines drove the ball into Spartan territory before the drive stalled. Michigan's "long kicker," Matt Wile, nailed a 48-yard field goal to send the Wolverines to the locker room with a 6-0 halftime lead. (Lansing State Journal [LSJ], 10/21/2012, Page 45)

The Spartan offense made some halftime adjustments that produced immediate results in the third quarter. After the Wolverines punted on their opening possession, Andrew Maxwell marched the Spartans down the field and finished the drive with a 2-yard scoring pass to tight end Paul Lang. Dan Conroy's PAT kick made it 7-6 and that is how the third quarter ended. Michigan took advantage of a Jordan Kovacs interception to put more points on the board with just over thirteen-minutes to play. Brendan Gibbons kicked his second field goal of the game (21-yards) to give Michigan the lead at 9-7. (*LSJ*, 10/21/2012, Page 45)

Michigan State responded with a 90-yard drive that ended with a 19-yard field goal by Dan Conroy. MSU led 10-9 with just over five minutes to play in the game. Both teams failed to produce anything on their next possessions. Michigan got the ball with three minutes to go and Denard Robinson got them into position for a late field goal attempt. Brendan Gibbons kicked a 38-yard game winner with nine seconds to play. (*LSJ*, 10/21/2012, Page 45) Michigan won by a final margin of 12-10. Whew, what a game!

Obviously, both teams lost the same amount of blood in this game since neither team dominated. The statistical battle in this game was just as close as the final score. Both teams had 16 first downs. Michigan won the "rushing game" by a margin of 51-yards (163 to 112). MSU won the "passing game" with 192-yards compared to 163 passing yards for Michigan. Each team punted seven times and had one pass interception. (*LSJ*, 10/21/2012, Page 45) Remarkably, there were no fumbles in this ferocious game. So, once again, the team that rushed for the most yards won the game. This has been the formula for success in this game (and just about every other game) going back to 1898. Some things just never change!

Team	1st	2nd	3rd	4th	Final
MSU	0	0	7	3	10
UM	0	6	0	6	12

SERIES UPDATE:

Michigan regained possession of the Paul Bunyan Trophy after four long years. The Wolverines increased their series advantage to 68 wins, 32 losses, and 5 ties. The Maize and Blue earned their first win of the second decade of the 21st Century, but MSU still had the advantage at 2 wins and 1 loss. Michigan still held the advantage in the Paul Bunyan Trophy years with a record of 35 victories, 23 defeats, and 2 ties. The Spartans probably missed having Paul Bunyan with them on the trip back to East Lansing, but "little brother" promised to take good care of him for the next year! Go Blue!

SERIES MILESTONES:

There were four milestones that emerged from this game. First, Michigan's BIG WIN was the 900th in the history of the Michigan Football Program. Thus, the Wolverines became the first, and only, team to achieve that many victories in the history of college football. The fact that it took place against the Spartans made it even better. Second, the gigantic crowd of 113, 833 broke the series record that was set in 2010. Third, Brady Hoke got his first series win in his second game so that was a "monkey" off his back. Finally, this game marked the sixtieth "Paul Bunyan Trophy game" in series history.

SEASON SUMMARIES:

The Spartans bounced back from their tough loss in Ann Arbor and won a thriller at Wisconsin (16-13). Unfortunately, inconsistency on offense and defense continued to plague the Green and White. MSU lost to Nebraska (28-24) and Northwestern (23-20) before winning their final game at Minnesota (26-10). Michigan State finished the regular season with 6 wins and 6 losses. The Spartans earned a bid to the Buffalo Wild Wings Bowl and defeated Texas Christian University (17-16). MSU ended with a final record of 7 wins and 6 losses. Michigan State running back Le'Veon Bell earned All-American honors in 2012.

Brady Hoke's Wolverines ran out of luck in week eight at Nebraska. Denard Robinson was knocked out of the game with an injury and Michigan eventually lost to the Cornhuskers (23-9). Fortunately, Devin Gardner stepped up for Michigan. He led the Wolverine offense to three impressive wins over Minnesota (35-13), Northwestern (38-31) and Iowa (42-17). Michigan was still in the hunt for the Legends Division Title. In order to win it, Coach Hoke's team had to defeat OSU, in Columbus. The Wolverines came up short and lost to the #4 Buckeyes (26-21). The promising season ended on a low note when Michigan lost to South Carolina (28-33) in the Outback Bowl. Coach Hoke's second season ended with a final record of 8 wins and 5 losses. They won six of eight conference games and finished second in the Legends Division. Michigan tackle Taylor Lewan was the only Wolverine to earn All-American honors in 2012.

Game #106: November 2, 2013 at Spartan Stadium in East Lansing

BACKGROUND INFORMATION:

Brady Hoke's status at Michigan slipped a few notches after his team underperformed in 2012. Yes, his team did beat Sparty for the first time in five years, but he also lost to Notre Dame and Ohio State. Once again, the Wolverines failed to win the Big Ten Championship or even the Legends Division for that matter. They did finish #24 in the final Associated Press football poll, but again, "This is Michigan." The sad fact was that Michigan was losing ground to Ohio State with every tick of the countdown clock. Coach Hoke had to get things back on track or he would have to put up a Hoke Era "countdown clock" in his office. Unfortunately, Michigan fans have the patience of a rattle snake when it comes to losing football. There was no pressure here. Well, okay, there was a lot of pressure here, for sure! The good news was that Hoke had a lot of talent coming back in 2013. The big issue was about his offensive line that still was not moving people the way he promised when he arrived in 2011.

For the second time in three years, Hoke's footballers began the season with five straight wins. They rolled through the non-conference season with victories over Central Michigan (59-9), Notre Dame (41-30), Akron (28-24) and Connecticut (24-21). The offensive line was still inconsistent, but the Wolverines kept winning and defeated Minnesota (42-13) to open Big Ten play. Penn State snapped Michigan's win streak with a 43-40 overtime win (4 OTs) over the Wolverines. The Brady Bunch bounced back with a high-scoring win over Indiana (63-47). Now, Michigan's defense was really getting exposed. Things were getting interesting heading into MSU week. Could the twenty-third ranked Wolverines pull it together and play well against the Spartans?

Michigan State fans were hoping that year seven of the Mark Dantonio Era would be lucky for the football team. Although MSU had another winning season, most Green and White fans were disappointed in MSU's final record of 7 wins and 6 losses. Coach "D" knew that he needed to solidify his quarterback situation and tighten things up on defense, especially pass defense. Of course, winning would solve a lot of other problems that people were complaining about. Mark Dantonio focused on starting fast and getting his team to play consistent football.

Michigan State began the 2013 football season with a solid 26-13 win over a surprisingly strong Western Michigan team. They also won the next two nonconference games against South Florida (21-6) and Youngstown State (55-17). Unfortunately, the Spartan's failed to pass their first "road test" at Notre Dame. Once again, the Irish sent MSU home to ponder another defeat (17-13). Maybe that loss was a "wake up" call because the Spartans went on a four-game win streak to start the Big Ten season. MSU defeated Iowa (26-14), Indiana (48-28), Purdue (14-0), and Illinois (42-3) to tune-up for the Michigan game in early November. The Spartans were ranked #22 in the nation with their record of 7 wins and 1 loss. Once again, everything would be on the line in East Lansing when Michigan came to town. Would Dantonio's Spartans be able to stay unbeaten in the conference and win back Paul Bunyan?

GAME SUMMARY: UM 6 MSU 29

Series Game #106 between the bitter rivals from Ann Arbor and East Lansing was humbling for the Wolverines, but not for the Spartans! The pre-game hype helped raise the intensity level to an all-time high. This game was another hard-hitting battle from the first play until the last!

The Wolverines drew first blood in the first quarter when Matt Wile booted a 49-yard field goal. MSU came right back and evened the score at 3-3 when Michael Geiger nailed a 44-yard kick. The score remained tied (3-3) at the end of the first quarter. Geiger made his second field goal (44-yards) to put MSU in front 6-3. With three minutes to play in the half, Brendan Gibbons evened the score at 6-6 with a 39-yard field goal. Michigan State came back with a late drive that ended with a 14-yard pass from Conner Cook to Bennie Fowler. Geiger's PAT conversion with 23-seconds to play made it 13-6 Spartans at halftime. (*Chicago Tribune [C-Trib.]*, 11/3/2013, Page 25)

Both defenses made good adjustments at halftime. The offenses had more trouble moving the ball in the third quarter. Michigan State managed to put three more points on the board when Michael Geiger connected on his third field goal from 35-yards out. The Spartans led 16-6 at the end of forty-five minutes of play. Michigan's offense could not get anything going in the game and tried to pass their way to victory late in the game. Unfortunately, MSU's pressure was too much to overcome. Meanwhile, the Green and White footballers were running the ball down the throats of the Wolverine defenders. It got ugly for Michigan in the final quarter as MSU added two more touchdowns and one more extra point. Michigan State won by a final score of 29-6. It was a dominant effort for the Spartans! (*C-Trib.*, 11/3/2013, Page 25)

Once again, the numbers told the story of this game. Michigan State earned 19 first downs while the Wolverines only earned 12. The Spartans rolled up 142-net rushing yards and added 252-yards through the air. Michigan was held to -48 (minus 48) net rushing yards. (Yes, you read it right!). The only good news was that the Wolverines totaled 216 passing yards, but it was not enough. (*C-Trib.,* 11/3/2013, Page 25) Once again, a strong running game and a strong running defense were the keys to victory. Michigan State used both "keys" to defeat the hated Wolverines. Go Spartans!

Team	1st	2nd	3rd	4th	Final
UM	3	3	0	0	6
MSU	3	10	3	13	29

SERIES UPDATE:

Michigan State halted Michigan's recent series "win streak" at one game. The Spartans now had a series record of 33 wins, 68 losses, and 5 ties. Yes, Michigan was still on the winning side of the Paul Bunyan Trophy ledger with a record of 35-24-2. The Spartans increased their "decade" advantage to 3 wins and 1 loss. MSU players, coaches and fans would enjoy the highly coveted "bragging rights" for the next year.

SERIES MILESTONES:

There was only one milestone to note about this game. The minus 48 rushing yards by Michigan was their worst in series history. Of course, this meant that it was the best showing by a Spartan run defense in series history! The crowd of 76, 306 was not even close to the East Lansing record of over 80,000 people. Other than some more lost blood, there was nothing else to note about this game.

SEASON SUMMARIES:

Michigan's football season continued to go in the wrong direction after the loss in East Lansing. The Wolverines returned home and lost to Nebraska (17-13). Michigan played poorly for most of the game at Northwestern. Fortunately, they eked out a 27-19 win in triple overtime. Hoke's Wolverines lost the last two games of the regular season to Iowa (24-21) and Ohio State (42-41) to end the regular season at 7 wins and 5 losses.

The Wolverines had a chance to end the season on a positive note with a win in the Buffalo Wild Wings Bowl but lost to Kansas State (31-14). Season number three of the Brady Hoke Era finished at 7-6. Michigan's tackle and Co-Captain Taylor Lewan earned All-American honors for the second straight season.

Michigan State continued to play well after their decisive win over Michigan. In fact, they were perfect as they closed out the regular season with wins over Nebraska (41-28), Northwestern (30-6), and Minnesota (14-3). The Spartans earned their second berth in the Big Ten Championship Game and this time, they defeated Ohio State (34-24). Michigan State ended the regular season with a sterling record of 12 wins and 1 loss.

Dantonio's Spartans represented the Big Ten in the 100th Rose Bowl Game and defeated Stanford (24-20). MSU finished with a final record of 13 wins 1 loss, a Legends Division title, a Big Ten Championship, and a Rose Bowl Championship. As it turned out, Mark Dantonio's seventh season was a "lucky" one for him and Spartan Nation. Actually, MSU was not that "lucky" in 2013—they were really good! Two Spartans Darqueze Dennard and Mike Sadler earned All-American honors for MSU in 2013.

Game #107: October 25, 2014 at Spartan Stadium in East Lansing

BACKGROUND INFORMATION:

For the second time in four years, the BIG news in the Big Ten in 2014 was all about the conference realignment. This was necessary because the Big Ten added two more teams (Rutgers and Maryland) to the conference. The new divisions were titled East and West. It was based mostly on geography in contrast to the Leaders and Legends which really did not make a lot of sense anyway. Michigan and Michigan State both landed in the Eastern Division which made total sense.

Brady Hoke was feeling the heat as he started his fourth year at the Wolverine helm. After starting off like Fielding Yost (11 wins) in 2011, he dropped all the way to Rich Rodriguez status with his record of 7 wins and 6 losses in 2013. Wins were down for the second straight season and everybody was starting to doubt Brady Hokes' abilities as a head coach. Brady knew he was on the "hot seat" in 2014. He did not make any excuses or blame anybody, he just tried to stay positive and get things moving in the right direction again. He did fire his old friend Al Borgess to get more production out of this offense, but everything else remained the same. It was hard to say what it would take for Brady Hoke to keep his job at Michigan, but it was going to take something closer to 2011.

Coach Hoke knew he had to avoid something that happened to Lloyd Carr in 2007. He had to beat Appalachian State in the first game of the 2014 season. Hoke's footballers made it look easy with a big win over the Mountaineers (52-14). Notre Dame would offer a much bigger challenge. The Irish announced that they were ending the rivalry series for the immediate future and Brady implied that Notre Dame was "chicken" and afraid to play Michigan. Well, Brady was not even eating chicken when he left South Bend. The Wolverines lost to the Irish (31-0) and Coach Hoke was eating "crow" the next day. That one hurt! Michigan managed to rebound from the Notre Dame beat down and defeated Miami of Ohio (34-10).

Things really got ugly in the next three weeks as the Wolverines lost three straight games. First, Michigan lost to Utah (10-26). Then, they opened the conference season with another taste of "humble pie" after losing to Minnesota (30-14). To make matters worse, quarterback Shane Morris suffered a concussion during the game and was able to go back on the field for another play. Are you kidding? Athletic Director Dave Brandon threw Hoke under the bus with the way he and his department mishandled the entire affair. Meanwhile, Hoke took his team to New Jersey and lost to Rutgers (26-24).

With his program in chaos about medical issues, an anemic offense, who the starting quarterback was and was not, it was hard to focus on winning football games. Somehow, Michigan "willed" a win over Penn State (18-13), but it was ugly. With a record of 3 wins and 4 losses, Brady Hoke had to get his team ready for another trip to East Lansing. Yes, for the first time in the one-hundred and seven-year history of the series, Michigan was going to play back-to-back games in a Michigan State stadium. The unranked Wolverines were big underdogs to the Spartans in this one. It had the potential to get out of hand, early!

Coach Mark Dantonio had plenty to celebrate in 2013. He was the first coach in Spartan Football History to win thirteen games and he was sitting on top of the world. Of course, everyone in Spartan Nation was expecting more of the same in 2014. The only thing that is harder than creating a winning football program is sustaining it. That was the challenge that Mark Dantonio had in his eighth season. He had to keep a good thing going. The media was starting to show MSU some of the respect that Dantonio had been working for since he took over at MSU in 2007. The Spartans began the season as the eight-ranked team in the country. It was time to play some more winning Spartan Football!

Michigan State opened the 2014 season against an FCS opponent from Jacksonville State. As expected, the Spartans went about their business and sent their guests home with a loss (45-7) and a nice check. Things got tougher in week two with a road game against Oregon. The Spartans stayed with the high-flying Ducks for most of the game, but Oregon pulled away in the final quarter to secure a 46-27 victory. Michigan State won their last two non-conference games against Eastern Michigan (73-14) and Wyoming (56-14). Coach Dantonio's footballers began the defense of their conference title with three consecutive wins over Nebraska (27-22), Purdue (45-31), and Indiana (56-14). The eighth-ranked Spartans at 7 wins and 1 loss appeared more than ready to host the Wolverines in the annual blood-letting event.

GAME SUMMARY: UM 11 MSU 35

The one-hundred and seventh game of the "in-state-hate" football series was not much of a game if you are a Wolverine fan. It was another decisive victory for the Spartans. Michigan State scored first, last, and added more in between as the out-manned Wolverines struggled to stay in the game. The Spartans took a 7-0 lead early in the first quarter when Jeremy Langford finished a 75-yard drive with a 2-yard scoring run and a Michael Geiger extra point. Michigan came back late in the second quarter to cut the lead to 7-3 on a 48-yard field goal by Matt Wile. The Spartans got the ball back with about three minutes to play in the half. They pushed down the field on a 73-yard drive that ended on another short run by Jeremy Langford. Michael Geiger kicked his second extra point and MSU led 14-3 at halftime. (*Chicago Tribune [C-Trib.]*, 10/26/2014, Page 90)

The Spartans kept the Wolverines off the scoreboard in the third quarter and added fourteen points to increase their lead to 28-3 at the end of forty-five minutes of football. Devin Gardner led Michigan on a short drive and De'Veon Smith scored on a 1-yard run, but it was too little, too late. Even with the two-point conversion, Michigan still trailed 28-11 with just over three minutes to play.

Michigan State got the ball back and kept running the ball through the Wolverine defense. Michigan could not stop MSU, but the rules did. When you score a touchdown, you must give up the ball. Jeremy Langford's third touchdown and Mike Geiger's fifth extra-point made it 35-11 Spartans. It was finally over! (*C-Trib.*, 10/26/2014, Page 90)

As usual, the team that won the rushing game won the football game too. The Spartans rolled up 219-yards on the ground and limited the Wolverines to just 61-net rushing yards. Michigan State passed for 227-yards and limited Michigan to just 125-yards. MSU totaled 22 first downs and limited Michigan to just 13. (*C-Trib.*, 10/26/2014, Page 90)

Bottom line—it was a dominating win by Michigan State. They continued to be the best team in the Mitten State and one of the top teams in the Big Ten. Michigan was losing ground. Nobody knew when things would get better in Ann Arbor. Things did not look good for Brady Hoke's future in Ann Arbor.

Team	1st	2nd	3rd	4th	Final
UM	0	3	0	8	11
MSU	7	7	14	7	35

SERIES UPDATE:

Michigan State's win kept Paul Bunyan in East Lansing for another season. MSU drew a little closer in the trophy series and improved their record to 25 wins, 35 losses, and 2 ties. The Spartans still trailed Michigan in the overall series with 34 wins, 68 losses, and 5 ties. However, Mark Dantonio was doing his best to reduce the gap because it was still very personal for Coach "D." The Green and White improved their decade advantage to 4-1.

SERIES MILESTONES:

As usual, game number one-hundred and seven had some interesting series milestones. First, it was the first time in series history that back-to-back games were played in East Lansing. Second, it was also the first game on record where one team used a metal stake to gain a little motivational advantage. As it turned out, the tactic backfired on the Wolverines. Coach Hoke apologized for his player's inappropriate pre-game behavior. However, "Stake Gate" added another interesting twist to the rivalry and showed how desperate things had become in Ann Arbor. Finally, it turned out to be Brady Hoke's last game since he was fired at the end of the season. He finished with a series record of 1 win and 3 losses. His overall record ended at 31 wins and 20 losses. He also had a winning record in the Big Ten (18-14), but it was not good enough to keep the job he loved! As Hoke often said, "This is Michigan." Unfortunately, Brady Hoke's best effort was not good enough in Ann Arbor.

SEASON SUMMARIES:

Michigan put the embarrassing loss to MSU behind them and focused on beating Indiana. The Wolverines got back on the winning side of the scorebook with a 34-10 victory over the Hoosiers. The "Brady Bunch" went to Northwestern in week ten and barely defeated the Wildcats (10-9). With two games to play, Michigan had a record of 5 wins and 5 losses. A winning season and a possible bowl game were still within reach. Ultimately, it was not in the cards. The Wolverines lost an ugly game to Maryland (23-16) and got blown out by the Buckeyes (42-28) to finish the season and Hoke's Michigan coaching career on a low note. The Maize and Blue footballers ended with a final record of 5 wins and 7 losses and went 3-5 in the Big Ten. There was no bowl game for the Wolverines in 2014 and there were no All-Americans either. It was a sad ending for Coach Hoke because he really loved Michigan. Time to move on!

Coach Brady Hoke said he would have "walked to Ann Arbor" (from San Diego, California?) when he found out he was hired to be the head Football coach at Michigan. It was right up there with the "best things" of Coach Hoke's life. Sadly, December 2, 2014 was probably one of the worst days for Brady because that is the day that he walked out of Schembechler Hall. Season four of the Hoke Era was a nightmare in so many ways. Everything that could go wrong, did go wrong in 2014. It is hard to imagine things went so far south in such a rapid manner, but it happened. Dave Brandon resigned in November after the fallout from the Shane Morris "Concussion Mess." Michigan Man Jim Hackett was lured out of retirement to clean up the "Brandon Mess" and find Michigan's next football coach. Would Michigan finally get the man they wanted?

Mark Dantonio's Spartans should have saved some points from their victory over Michigan because they came up short the next week against Ohio State. The Buckeyes won a shootout (49-37) at Spartan Stadium. The Spartans finished strong with three consecutive wins over Maryland (37-15), Rutgers (45-3) and Penn State (34-10). MSU placed second in the Big Ten's East Division but earned an invitation to the Cotton Bowl Classic to play #4 Baylor. Dantonio's footballers defeated the Bears (42-41) in one of the most exciting games of the 2014 bowl season. Michigan State ended with a final record of 11 wins and 2 losses in 2014. Center Jack Allen and safety Kurtis Drummond earned All-American honors for the Spartans.

Game #108: October 17, 2015 at Michigan Stadium in Ann Arbor

BACKGROUND INFORMATION:

Spartan fans were probably sad to see ready Hoke leave so soon since he had lost three of four game against the Green and White! Oh well, they still had Coach Dantonio. How bad could it be? Jim Harbaugh was certainly getting plenty of hype about his football team. However, hype does not win football games. Michigan State was expected to field another strong football team in 2015. Coach Dantonio had plenty of talent on both sides of the ball. Once again, expectations were high in East Lansing, regardless of what was going on in Ann Arbor.

Michigan State bolted out of the gate in 2015. They won all four non-conference games against Western Michigan (37-24), #5 Oregon (31-28), Air Force (35-21) and Central Michigan (30-10). So far, so good. The #2 Spartans extended their perfect start to 6 wins and 0 losses with two straight Big Ten wins. Even though MSU was winning, they were not winning enough "style" points for their close victories and dropped five places in the rankings. The seventh ranked Spartans were as ready as they were going to be for their series matchup in Ann Arbor. Coach Dantonio's team was chomping at the bit when the MSU team bus arrived at Michigan Stadium. However, as Coach "D" explained in the Fox documentary, *Divided We Stand*, he kept his team in place for an extra ten seconds before he allowed anyone to get off the busses. Dantonio told his team that they would get those seconds back during the game. Oh boy, Coach "D" was using a Jedi mind trick on his football team. Would it really work?

Interim Athletic Director Jim Hackett accomplished what he was asked to do. First, he cleaned up the "mess" that was left by Dave Brandon. Second, and more important, he hired Jim Harbaugh to be the next football coach at Michigan. Third, he stayed around long enough for Michigan to hire Warde Manual and then he left. It was shortest, yet one of the most impactful, tenures of any Michigan Athletic Director. Finally, Jim Harbaugh was back in Ann Arbor and everyone in Wolverine Nation was thrilled. Michigan could not afford to "miss" on another football coaching hire and Hackett nailed it. Coach Harbaugh was ready for a "homecoming" and he hit the ground running. Yes, he hit the ground running extremely fast! The hiring of Jim Harbaugh gave Michigan Football instant "credibility." Harbaugh's track record as a college and professional coach put him in a unique position.

Jim Harbaugh started using his "name" immediately to put together an elite recruiting class. Harbaugh's energy and incredible work ethic rippled throughout Schembechler Hall. It resembled what happened in December 1968 when a guy named Schembechler showed up in Ann Arbor. Of course, the BIG difference was everybody knew Jim Harbaugh's name. There was no "Jim Who" stuff this time around! The big question in Ann Arbor was "How much of an impact would he have in his first year?" Well, just like Bo, Jim Harbaugh had a big impact on the Michigan Wolverine Football team in 2015. Yes, it was a BIG impact!

Although improvements were expected in Michigan Football in 2015, none of the football polls pegged Harbaugh's Wolverines at the start of the season. Unranked Michigan began the Jim Harbaugh Era with a tough road contest at Utah. Michigan could not overcome some careless interceptions by quarterback Jake Ruddock and the Maize and Blue came home with a loss (24-17). Yes, it was a tough game to lose, but Harbaugh did not push any panic buttons. Instead, Harbaugh, and his Wolverines, put the pedal to the metal. Michigan won the next three non-conference games against Oregon State (35-7), UNLV (28-7), and # 22 Brigham Young (31-0).

Whoa—the Wolverines were 3-1 heading into the conference season. Harbaugh's footballers kept the streak alive with two straight Big Ten shutout wins over Maryland (28-0) and Northwestern (38-0). Jim Harbaugh had everything going in the right direction. The offense was clicking, the defense was sticking, and the special teams were playing well. It was time for the 12th ranked Wolverines to wage another bitter battle with 7th ranked Michigan State. Oh boy, this would be a fun game to watch!

GAME SUMMARY: MSU 27 UM 23

Series game number one-hundred and eight proved to be one of the most memorable games in the long and storied history of the "blood" series. Both teams were having excellent seasons, but this was the BIGGEST game of the season, so far. Coaches Harbaugh and Dantonio were facing off for the first time. It promised to be a special Mitten State matchup.

The defenses won the first quarter since it was 0-0 at the end of the first quarter. Michigan opened the scoring early in the second quarter when Sione Houma scored on a 2-yard run. Kenny Allen's extra point made it 7-0. Later in the quarter, the Spartans capitalized on a targeting penalty on Joe Bolden. LJ Scott scored two plays later an 11-yard run and Michael Geiger tied the game (7-7) with his extra point. Late in the second quarter, Allen kicked a 38-yard field goal that gave Michigan a 10-7 lead at halftime. (*C-Trib.*, 10/18/2015, Page 12)

Michigan received the second half kickoff and drove straight down the field. Sione Houma finished the drive with his second touchdown (1-yard run). Allen's extra point made gave Michigan a 17-7 lead. The Spartans scored three minutes later a Connor Cook to Macgarrett Kings 30-yard pass play. Geiger's second extra point reduced Michigan's advantage to 17-14. Kenny Allen's second field goal (21-yards) extended Michigan's advantage to 20-14 at the end of the third quarter. Early in the fourth quarter, Allen's third field goal game the Wolverines a 23-14 advantage. Michigan State responded twenty-nine seconds later when Cook connected with Trevon Pendelton on a 74-yard pass play. It was originally called a touchdown, but later ruled down at the 1-yard line. LJ Scott scored on the next play and Geiger's PAT closed the gap to 23-21 (*C-Trib.*, 10/18/2015, Page 12)

The last nine minutes of the game, again, were dominated by the defenses. Both teams squandered their remaining possessions and it looked like time would run out on the Spartans. With ten seconds remaining in the game, Michigan had the ball and the lead. All they had to do was execute a successful fourth down punt. Of course, that did not happen! Punter Blake O'Neill fumbled a low snap, the ball popped into the air as he tried to punt it away and landed in the hands of a Spartan special team player. MSU freshman Jalen Watts-Jackson caught O'Neill's fumble and ran the ball into the endzone as time expired. (*C-Trib.*, 10/18/2015, Page 12) Final Score: Michigan State 26 Michigan 23

Michigan State's final "drive" of the game (a fumble "six") took about ten seconds. The Spartans trailed for 59 minutes and 50 seconds, but they made those last 10 seconds count, MSU led for one second, but that is all they needed to win the game. You cannot make this stuff up! I still do not know how Mark Dantonio came up with his "10 second scenario," on the team bus but it worked out well for MSU. What a nightmare for Wolverine fans. What a miracle for Spartan Nation. What a game!

Team	1st	2nd	3rd	4th	Final
MSU	0	7	7	13	27
UM	0	10	10	3	23

SERIES UPDATE:

Michigan State's HUGE WIN allowed them to chip away again at Michigan's series advantage. Here is what the series numbers looked like after 108 games: Michigan State 35 wins, Michigan 68 wins, and 5 ties games. The Spartans now owned 26 victories, 35 losses, and 2 ties in the Paul Bunyan Trophy games. Mark Dantonio improved his series record to 7 wins and 2 losses. Finally, Michigan State's record in the second decade of the 21st Century improved to 5 wins and 1 loss. Paul Bunyan's "day trip" was over. Time to go home! Spartans Will! Spartans Did!

SERIES MILESTONES:

Jim Harbaugh's first start against MSU in 1984 ended badly for him and the Wolverines. He broke his arm and Michigan lost at home to the hated Spartans. Coach Jim Harbaugh's first series game was even more bizarre. The Wolverines were ten seconds away from an "upset" of #7 MSU. Those last ten seconds were unbelievable and shocking for Harbaugh and his team. Of course, Spartan fans were thrilled beyond belief. This game was special for many reasons which made it the most watched 3:30 pm start game in the history of ESPN. (*Reaching Higher,* Page 116) There were many other notable milestones in this game.

First, it was Jim Harbaugh's first series game and his first series loss. The shocking defeat made him the seventh straight Wolverine coach to lose his first game to MSU dating back to Bump Elliott. Second, the victory extended Mark Dantonio's series record to 7-2 and gave him his 100th career coaching victory (including his time at Cincinnati). Third, the improbable win also made Dantonio the first Spartan coach to defeat three different Wolverine coaches (Rodriguez, Hoke, and Harbaugh) in their first series meeting. Fourth, Michigan punter Blake O'Neill set a record for the longest series punt when he launched an 80-yarder in the first half. Of course, his fumble at the end of the game will go down in Wolverine infamy. Finally, this game was the first series tussle to be decided on a last-second fumble recovery (fumble six) at the end of the game. This game always causes me to ask, "How did Coach "D" know that the last ten seconds of the game would be so important?"

SEASON SUMMARIES:

Mark Dantonio's Spartans defeated Indiana (52-26) after their miraculous win over Michigan. Then, they met their match at Nebraska. The unranked Cornhuskers defeated Sparty (39-38) and ended the dreams of an undefeated season. Michigan State bounced back with three straight wins and earned a spot in their third Big Ten Championship game in six years. The Spartans won the title with a gutty win over Iowa (16-13). That victory gave MSU a berth in the College Football Playoffs against top-ranked Alabama. Once again, the Crimson Tide rolled the Spartans again (38-0). Despite the crushing loss to Alabama, nobody in East Lansing shed any tears at the end of the 2015 season. The Spartans finished with a final record of 12 wins and 2 losses, a win over Michigan, a Big Ten Championship and the #6 ranking in the country. Coach Dantonio had done it again! He proved that ten-win seasons are nice, but a twelve-win season and a Big Ten Championship are even better.

Harbaugh's Wolverines rebounded from their MSU loss and won four straight games. They lost the final game of the season to Ohio State. Michigan ended the season on a positive note with a big win over Florida (41-7) in the Citrus Bowl. Jim Harbaugh's first season finished with a record of 10 wins and 3 losses. His team posted a Big Ten record of 6 wins and 2 losses. Two Michigan players, tight end Jake Butt and defensive back Jourdan Lewis earned All-American honors in 2015. Overall, Coach Harbaugh's first year in Ann Arbor was a huge improvement over 2014. Most Michigan fans were happy about Wolverine football again. However, as Brady Hoke would say, "This is Michigan." Harbaugh would have to do more in the future to satisfy the spoiled Wolverine fans.

Game #109: October 12, 2016 at Spartan Stadium in East Lansing

BACKGROUND INFORMATION:

Mark Dantonio and Jim Harbaugh had successful seasons in 2015. However, both men shared a problem in 2016. Coach Dantonio lost three-year starter Connor Cook and Coach Harbaugh lost Jake Rudock who was stellar as a graduate transfer. Job #1 for both coaches was to find a QB in Spring drills and get him ready for the 2016 season.

James Joseph Harbaugh entered his second season on the sidelines in Ann Arbor in 2016. He won ten games (including a bowl game) in his first year, but he did not defeat Michigan State or Ohio State. Yes, the biggest room in Schembechler Hall was the "room for improvement." One improvement was the hire of a guy named Don Brown as Defensive Coordinator. Harbaugh was hoping that Wilton Speight would continue to improve as his starting quarterback. Michigan also improved the "look" of their uniforms thanks to Nike. Interim Athletic Director Jim Hackett signed a new deal with Nike before he left. It stipulated that Michigan would be the first college football program to wear Jordan brand uniforms. Yes, there was a lot of "new" and "improved" in Ann Arbor in August 2016. Michigan opened the season as the seventh ranked team in the country. However, after seven games, it appeared that they were better than that! The Wolverines were undefeated at 7-0 and ranked #2 in the country as MSU week approached.

Spartan fans had reason for optimism in 2016 because Mark Dantonio was back for his tenth season. Thanks to Coach Dantonio's successful track record, expectations continued to be high for MSU football. Unfortunately, the Spartans lost a ton of starters on both sides of the ball from the twelve-win 2015 team. The MSU coaching staff would have to do an incredible job to post another winning season in East Lansing. Sophomore Tyler O'Connor earned the right to lead the Spartan offense in 2016. He had some big shoes to fill, and the defense was in a "makeover" mode. There were a lot of uncertainty heading into the first game. Michigan State started fast with wins against Furman and #17 Notre Dame. Then, things got ugly as MSU lost five straight games which included four consecutive Big Ten defeats. It did not look like the unranked Spartans would be able to defend the Paul Bunyan Trophy against the hated invaders from Ann Arbor.

GAME SUMMARY: UM 32 MSU 23

Mitten State Game #109 was set for an early afternoon kickoff (1:00 pm EST) in Spartan Stadium. Second ranked Michigan took the field in their new Nike Jordan Brand road uniforms as the favorite. Yes, the Wolverines looked good, but would they play as good as they looked on paper and in their new uniforms?

Michigan State opened the scoring in the first quarter on a 5-yard run by LJ Scott. Michael Geiger's extra point gave the Spartans a 7-0 lead. Michigan answered on their next possession with a long drive that ended on a 3-yard scoring run by Jabrill Peppers. Kenny Allen's extra point tied the game at 7-7 and that is how the first quarter ended. (*Lansing State Journal* [*LSJ*], 10/30/2016, Page 43)

Early in the second quarter, Michigan took the lead (14-7) on a 1-yard touchdown run by De'Veon Smith and another Allen extra point. MSU closed the gap to 14-10 after a 52-yard field goal by Geiger. Kenny Allen matched Geiger's kick with a 23-yard field goal of his own that extended the Michigan lead to 17-10. Michigan scored three times in final minute of the first half on Smith's second touchdown (5-yards), Allen's third extra point, and Allen's second field goal. Michigan was in control with a 27-10 lead at halftime. (*LSJ*, 10/30/2016, Page 43)

Both defenses made all the right adjustments at halftime which resulted in a scoreless third quarter. Early in the final period of play, Michigan put together a short drive that ended with Allen's third field goal (45-yards). The Wolverine lead grew to 30-10 and things were looking bad for the home team. Michigan State's offense went to work and scored two late touchdowns and one extra point to reduce Michigan's lead (30-23). The only problem was that there was only one second left on the clock after the final Spartan touchdown. Once again, there was a scoring play that resulted from a fumble at the end of the game. Michigan defender Jabrill Peppers scooped MSU's botched two-point conversion attempt and sprinted to the Spartan end zone for a two-point defensive conversion that sealed Michigan's 32-23 win. (*LSJ*, 10/30/2016, Page 43)

The Wolverines actually won the game with their 20-point outburst in the second quarter. The Spartans made a valiant effort in the last few minutes of the game, but it was too late. Michigan's victory was their first win in Spartan Stadium since 2007. It was also the first Wolverine win over Sparty since 2012. Yes, it was time for Paul Bunyan to spend some time in Ann Arbor after a long absence from the Tree City.

Team	1st	2nd	3rd	4th	Final
UM	7	20	0	5	32
MSU	7	3	0	13	23

SERIES UPDATE:

Jim Harbaugh's first series win evened his record at 1-1 and dropped Mark Dantonio's record to 7-3. For those of you who are keeping score at home, the Wolverine series advantage now stood at 69 wins, 35 losses, and 5 ties. Michigan's advantage in the Paul Bunyan Trophy games grew to 36 wins, 26 losses, and 2 ties. More importantly, Paul was on the UM bus for a happy trip back to Ann Arbor. Go Blue!

SERIES MILESTONES:

The 2016 version of the "Backyard Brawl" did not end as dramatically as 2015, but there were some milestones to mention. First, it was Coach Harbaugh's first win in his second attempt. It was also his first win in Spartan Stadium. Second, the two-point conversion by Jabrill Peppers was also the first one ever recorded in the series. Finally, the Pepper's play made it the first time in series history that two consecutive games ended on a scoring play that resulted from a fumble. You cannot make this stuff up!

SEASON SUMMARIES:

The Wolverine victory improved their record to 8 wins and 0 defeats for the first time since Lloyd Carr's did the same thing in 2006. It was also the first time that Michigan was 5-0 in the Big Ten since 2007. The Wolverines added another victory to their record with a win against Maryland (59-3). The winning streak came to a sudden end with a last second loss at Iowa (14-13). Michigan bounced back with a 20-10 victory over Indiana which put them at 10 wins and 1 loss heading into Ohio State Week.

Unfortunately, Harbaugh's footballers lost to the Buckeyes and Florida State (2017 Orange Bowl) to end the season with 10 wins and 3 losses. Michigan finished as the tenth ranked team in the country. Jake Butt and Jourdan Lewis repeated as All-Americans in 2016 and Jabrill Peppers earned that distinction for the first time. Again, it was a good season, but Harbaugh and Wolverine Nation wanted more.

After the home loss to Michigan, the Spartans lost three of their last four games. The only highlight was a 49-0 victory over Rutgers. MSU ended the season with a record of 3 wins and 9 losses. They fell from Big Ten Champs to Big Ten chumps. Of course, no one dared to talk about firing Mark Dantonio. Instead, he got a second "free pass" for the 2016 season. Everyone started to focus on the 2017 season as soon as the clock zeroed out at Beaver Stadium on November 26, 2016. Yes, Coach Dantonio's elite program took a big hit in his tenth season in East Lansing. It was time to move forward and get the Spartan football train back on the right track.

Game #110: October 7, 2017 at Michigan Stadium in Ann Arbor

BACKGROUND INFORMATION:

Mark Dantonio was a man on a mission in 2017. He was doing everything in his power to put the memory of the 2016 season in the rear-view mirror. Yes, season eleven of the Dantonio Era had to be different. It was hard to tell exactly what would be different since Coach "D" retained his entire staff. He did change some of the coaching responsibilities, but things looked the same, not different in the Spartan Football Building. Loyalty is a word that meant everything to Coach Dantonio. He did not fire anybody. Instead, he chose to get his coaches and players focused on winning more football games. Unfortunately, Dantonio dismissed four key players for sexual misconduct in early 2017. The loss of these players left a void that would have to be filled with some unproven players. The task of putting together another winning season just got harder, a lot harder!

The Spartans began the 2017 season with two straight home wins. They dropped to 2-1 after losing to Notre Dame. They bounced back with a win at Iowa (17-10). Michigan State was in a good place heading into Michigan Week. Of course, Mark Dantonio would have his Spartans ready to play in Ann Arbor. Coach "D" had a record of 3 wins and only 1 loss in Ann Arbor. The Big House was his second football home. Yes, recent history led even the most ardent Michigan football fan to be wary of the upcoming game against unranked and disrespected MSU. One thing was certain about Game #110—the Spartans and their "chippy" coach would be ready to play on October 7, 2017.

Year three of the Jim Harbaugh Era promised to be better than the first two seasons and they were not exactly terrible. Of course, Coach Jim Harbaugh had not defeated Ohio State and the Big Ten Championship drought now sat at twelve seasons. The biggest question surrounding the 2017 season was "Would the Wolverines stop the "no championship" streak at twelve seasons?" As usual, Michigan had plenty of talent on their roster, but so did the best teams in the Big Ten's Eastern Division. It was going to be another challenging fall, but that was life in the Big Ten in the 21st Century. The eleventh ranked Wolverines kicked off the 2017 season with an impressive win over seventeenth ranked Florida (33-17). Harbaugh's team rolled to a 4-0 start and a number eight ranking by the time they hit a bye week on September 30, 2017. Michigan had an extra week to prepare for the Mitten State rivals from East Lansing.

GAME SUMMARY: MSU 14 UM 10

Jim Harbaugh entered his third series game with a record of 1 win and 1 loss. He was planning to earn his first series victory in the Big House in his second attempt. Harbaugh knew it would not be easy even though Michigan was favored to win. Prior to the game, he told reporters that, "I do not care what you see on film from Sparty a week ago, two weeks ago, three weeks ago. When they (MSU) see Maize and Blue, it brings a fire inside them. (*DFP*, 10/8/2017, Page 53) Yes, this was going to be another "Backyard Brawl" to remember. Coach Dantonio and his Spartans probably figured that they had the favored Wolverines right where they wanted them—at home and primed for another upset!

Seventh ranked Michigan scored first on a 30-yard Quinn Nordin field goal midway through the first quarter. The Spartans responded with a score of their own a few minutes later. Brian Lewerke finished a drive with a 14-yard touchdown run. Matt Coghlin's extra point-kick, gave MSU a 7-3 lead after one quarter. The weather conditions worsened in the second quarter as heavy rain and high winds provided some formidable opposition to every player on the field. Halfway through the second quarter, Brian Lewerke made some key plays with his legs and his right arm. His biggest play of the game turned out to be 16-yard scoring pass to Madre London. Coghlin's second extra point gave MSU a 14-3 lead and that is how the first half ended. (*DFP*, 10/8/2017, Page 53) It looked like the Wolverines would have an uphill climb against the Spartans and the weather in the second half.

Michigan successfully battled the weather and the Spartans for most of the third quarter, but only scored once. Fullback Khalid Hill finished an impressive drive with a 1-yard touchdown run. Nordin's extra point brought the Wolverines closer at 14-10. As it turned out, that was all the scoring for the rest of the game. Both teams squandered their opportunities. Michigan had the ball last and had a chance to win the game. Just like 2015, the game came down to the final play. Could Michigan end the game on a miracle play like Michigan State did two years ago? No, they did not! Backup quarterback John O'Korn's final pass to the end zone was incomplete and that was it! Final Score: MSU 14 UM 10. (*DFP*, 10/8/2017, Page 53)

Yes, Michigan State earned another hard-fought victory over Michigan. The weather was a big factor in the game, but both teams had to play in it. It affected the "quality" of play, but not the "intensity!" The slippery ball and the aggressive MSU defense caused five turnovers that the Wolverines could not overcome. The Michigan defense limited the Spartan offense to two conversions on fourteen third-down plays. Worse yet, the MSU offense only gained sixty yards in the second half. Ultimately, it was not a problem since Sparty already had fourteen points on the scoreboard. Once again, the only thing better than a rival win, is an upset rival win in The Big House.

Coach Mark Dantonio and his Spartans did it again. For the fourth time in five visits, MSU defeated mighty Michigan in the Big House and abducted Paul Bunyan. The "upset" wins in Ann Arbor were becoming very upsetting for the locals. Why "little brother" kept winning against the Wolverines was puzzling to all members of Maize and Blue Nation. Oh well, they would have to wait a year for another shot at Dantonio and his Spartans.

Team	1st	2nd	3rd	4th	Final
MSU	7	7	0	0	14
UM	3	0	7	0	10

SERIES SUMMARY

Michigan State's upsetting upset victory in Ann Arbor improved their record to 36 wins, 69 losses, and 5 ties. Paul Bunyan was back on the bus with his suitcase since he would be staying in East Lansing for another year. After sixty-five trophy games, the Spartans owned a record of 27 wins, 36 losses, and 2 ties. MSU's decade advantage grew to a record of 6 wins and 2 losses.

SERIES MILESTONES:

Game #110 turned out to be another tough loss for Jim Harbaugh. His series record dropped to 1 win and 2 losses with both defeats coming in The Big House. This was the first time in series history that a Michigan football coach lost his first two home games to the dastardly Spartans. This game was also the first prime time night game in the history of Michigan vs Michigan State football. Finally, the weather limited attendance, but the record shows that 112,432 fans showed up in the wind and rain. Yes, that makes it the largest crowd ever to attend a series game in "nasty" weather!

SEASON SUMMARIES:

Michigan State's victory over Michigan got the attention of the pollsters. The Spartans jumped into the rankings at #21 and traveled to Minnesota where they played like a ranked team (sort of) and defeated the Gophers (30-27). MSU kept the streak going with a home win over Indiana (17-9). The modest four game win streak came to an end after an agonizing triple overtime loss at Northwestern (39-31). Dantonio did not have time to feel sorry for himself or his team. He had a week to get his Spartans ready to host #7 Penn State. As it turned out, Dantonio's team was more ready that James Franklin's team and MSU won a close one (27-24). Things did not go as well at Ohio State the next week. The Buckeyes clobbered the Spartans (48-3)—ouch! Wow, Mark Dantonio's team was down, but not out. Michigan State got off the mat and won their last two conference games against Maryland (17-7) and Rutgers (40-7).

The Green and White footballers earned a trip to the 2017 Holiday Bowl and ended the season on a positive note with a victory over Washington State (42-17). The Spartans finished the 2017 season with a final record of 10 wins and 3 losses. Yes, Coach Dantonio turned things around in East Lansing after the dreadful season in 2016. Despite their disappointing loss to MSU, Michigan still had a record of 4 wins and 1 loss. Coach Harbaugh used the short memory trick on his team and got them ready for a trip to Bloomington, Indiana. The Wolverines won a tough game against the Hoosiers (27-20). Unfortunately, things did not go as well the next week in Happy Valley. Penn State played like the second ranked team in the country, because they were. Michigan was overmatched in this game and lost to PSU (42-13). The next three games went better since the Wolverines defeated Rutgers, Minnesota, and Maryland. Only two obstacles remained in Jim Harbaugh's quest for a third consecutive ten-win season. Thanks to some very rude hosts in Madison and Columbus,

Michigan lost the last two regular season games to Wisconsin and Ohio State. The good news was that the Maize and Blue footballers earned a trip to the Outback Bowl in January 2018. The bad news was that they lost to South Carolina (26-19). The unranked Wolverines ended the season with a final record of 8 wins and 5 losses. Defensive tackle Maurice Hurst earned All-American honors in 2017. Of course, the crazy rumors about Jim Harbaugh leaving for the NFL began as soon as the season ended. Even more ridiculous was the talk about his firing. It made for a lot of "off-season noise." Actually, Coach Harbaugh was not going anywhere. He was going to hit the recruiting trail harder than ever and work and work to put a better team on the field in 2018.

Game #111: October 20, 2018 at Spartan Stadium in East Lansing

Season number four of the Jim Harbaugh Era was going to be interesting in 2018. As always, there was plenty of talent on offense, defense, and special teams. However, there were some new faces in town to help Michigan win more football games. Harbaugh hired a new strength, Ben Herbert, to reduce the odds that his Wolverines would be pushed around the field by the likes of Iowa, Michigan State, Wisconsin, and Ohio State. He also hired veteran Jim McElwain to coach his talented, but young, wide receivers. Sherrone Moore was his new tight ends coach. When Offensive Coordinator Tim Drevno left, Jim Harbaugh opted not to replace him. Instead, Michigan would have an offense by committee with everyone on the offensive staff having input. Apparently, passing game coordinator Pep Hamilton would call most of the plays. Only time would tell if this approach would really work, especially in the BIG games where a few key play calls often determine the victor.

Fourteenth ranked Michigan opened the season at twelfth ranked Notre Dame in a high-profile night game. Don Brown's defense gave up some big plays and Shea Patterson and the offense by "committee" could not get rolling. It all added up to a disappointing loss to the Irish (24-17). Three straight home games helped get the Wolverines on a winning path. They defeated Western Michigan (49-3), SMU (45-20) and Nebraska (56-10). Northwestern proved to be a stiffer test to open Big Ten play, but the Wolverines defeated the Wildcats (20-17). Michigan was now 4-1, but they wanted more. Two more wins over Maryland (42-21) and Wisconsin (38-13) increased their record (6-2) and their ranking (#6). Were the Wolverines ready for another rescue Paul Bunyan trip in East Lansing?

Mark Dantonio was back for his twelfth season in 2018. His successful track record in East Lansing made it hard not to expect more of the same in the upcoming season. In addition to his "history," Coach Dantonio also had nineteen returning starters from his 2017 team. Yes, things looked promising at the MSU football building. Dantonio knew he had a talented football team and the Associated Press pollsters agreed. The Spartans began the season as the eleventh ranked football team in the country according to the first AP poll.

Michigan State won their opener in East Lansing against Utah State (38-31). Their unimpressive victory dropped them to the fifteenth spot by the time they kicked off game two at Arizona State. The fired-up Sun Devils were ready to rumble, but Sparty was not. MSU went home on the short end of a 16-13 score. The Spartans responded with two straight wins over Indiana (35-21) and Central Michigan (31-20).

345

Homecoming Day did not end happily since the Spartans lost to unranked Northwestern (29-9). Dantonio's football team bounced back with a huge win at #8 Penn State (21-17). Michigan State appeared ready to do battle with #6 Michigan. Bring on the Wolverines!

GAME SUMMARY: UM 21 MSU 7

Once again, the annual "pigskin pounding" between Michigan and Michigan State had plenty of drama before, during and after the game. In 2018, Michigan players described the middle portion of their schedule as the "Revenge Tour." This was because they were focused on defeating teams that beat them in 2017. The Spartans were the second stop on the "tour" since Michigan already defeated Wisconsin. The fireworks for series Game #111 began early with a pre-game face off between the locked-arm Spartans and some Wolverines who were stretching in the middle of the field. MSU's intimidating "walk-on" ritual had been going on for much of the Mark Dantonio Era. This time it backfired when Devin Bush got "clothes-lined" by the Green and White. The irate Bush kicked up the big "S" in the middle of the field. After the incident, Michigan rallied around their star linebacker. Instead of psyching-out the Wolverines, "Clothesline Gate" unified the Michigan team and made them more determined than ever to beat MSU in East Lansing. It also cost MSU $10,00.00 after the Big Ten fined the Spartans for being on the field during Michigan's "warm-up time."

Both defenses showed up for the first quarter which meant that both offenses had trouble moving the ball. The first quarter ended in a scoreless tie. In the second quarter, Michigan drove twenty-nine yards from their own sixteen-yard line before a driving rain forced both teams to go to their locker rooms. After the unscheduled delay, the Wolverine offense drove fifty-five more yards to the end zone. Nico Collins caught a 6-yard scoring pass from Shea Patterson and Quinn Nordin's extra point made it 7-0. Michigan held their narrow lead until halftime. (*LSJ*, 10/21/2018, Page 9C)

Michigan State's offense got a huge lift late in the third quarter when the Spartan defense forced and recovered a fumble at the Michigan seven-yard line. A well-executed trick play from Darrell Stewart Jr. to quarterback Brian Lewerke put six points on the scoreboard and Matt Coghlin's PAT kick tied the game at 7-7. The Wolverines responded on the next drive when Patterson connected on a 79-yard pass/run play to Donovan Peoples-Jones. Nordin's second extra point put Michigan back in the lead at 14-7. Michigan's defense had the MSU offense locked down. Midway through the final quarter, the Wolverine offense went on another 84-yard drive that took almost seven minutes of precious game time. Ben Mason's 5-yard blast with five minutes to play increased UM's lead to 20-7. Quinn Nordin's extra point ended the scoring. Final Score: Michigan 21 Michigan State 7. (*LSJ*, 10/21/2018, Page 9C)

The hard-fought Wolverine victory ended a seventeen-game road losing streak to ranked opponents. Harbaugh's footballers got a huge monkey off their back in addition to winning a rival road game. The final score did not reflect Michigan's dominance in this game. The Maize and Blue defenders limited the Spartan offense to 15-rushing yards and 94-yards of offense for the entire game. Shea Patterson completed 14 of 25 passes for 212-yards and two touchdowns. Karan Higdon rushed 33 times for 144-yards. The Wolverines won the time of possession statistic by a margin of 41 minutes to only 19 minutes for Sparty. (*LSJ*, 10/21/2018, Page 9C)

Michigan's balanced attack allowed them to control the game but did not produce an excessive number of points. In the end, Michigan scored enough points to win a BIG game. Paul Bunyan was re-captured on the field by a jubilant band of Wolverines and Phase II of the Wolverine "Revenge Tour" was accomplished successfully. Hail to the Victors!

Team	1st	2nd	3rd	4th	Final
UM	0	7	7	7	21
MSU	0	0	7	0	7

SERIES UPDATE:

Coach Jim Harbaugh left East Lansing with his second series win. His record was even again at 2-2 versus Michigan State and Mark Dantonio. For the record, the Wolverine series advantage stood at 70 wins, 36 losses, and 5 ties. Michigan's record in the Paul Bunyan Trophy years grew to 36 wins, 26 losses, and 2 ties. The Wolverine win was their 21st in East Lansing and improved their series road winning percentage to almost sixty-three percent (.629). Mark Dantonio's rival record slipped to 8 wins and 4 losses.

SERIES MILESTONES:

Of course, the game was as nasty as ever with plenty of hard hitting and hard feelings to go around. After the game, Coach Harbaugh called the "Clothesline" incident "Bush League" and commended his team for staying focused on the game, instead of Sparty's bad behavior. The Wolverine victory made Jim Harbaugh the first Michigan coach to win his first two games in East Lansing. Another series mark may have been Michigan's stifling defense on third down. MSU went zero for twelve (as in 0-12) in third down conversions which must be some sort of record. Of course, the Maize and Blue became the first series team to win seventy games. Finally, Michigan became the first series team to score touchdowns after two 84-yard drives in the same game.

SEASON SUMMARIES:

Michigan's victory pushed their record to 7 wins and 1 loss. It also pushed them up to a number five ranking in the polls. The Wolverines were on a roll and they kept on rolling for the next three weeks. Victories over #14 Penn State (42-7), Rutgers (42-7) and Indiana ((31-20) raised their record (10-1) and their ranking (#4) heading into Columbus, Ohio. The Wolverine "Revenge Tour was three for three in 2018. The only "unfinished" business was a desperately needed victory over Ohio State. As it turned out, Ohio State did not want to be a part of the Wolverine tour. Don Brown's defense could not cover the short pass over the middle or just about any other play that OSU ran. It was a very, very long day for the Wolverines. Final Score: OSU 62 Michigan 39. Harbaugh's team was invited to play in the 2018 Peach Bowl and that did not end well either. The University of Florida watched the OSU film and learned their lessons well. The Wolverines lost to the Gators (41-15) and that was it! Jim Harbaugh's fourth season ended with a record of 10 wins and 3 losses. Linebacker Devin Bush joined a long, long line of Wolverines who called themselves All-Americans in 2018.

Despite another winning season, Michigan lost to Notre Dame and Ohio State. Harbaugh's program also failed to deliver a Big Ten Championship or a bowl victory. Yes, fans in Ann Arbor were wondering if Coach Harbaugh was ever going to finish the job he was hired to do. Once again, the biggest room in Schembechler Hall on December 29, 2018 was still the "room for improvement." Jim Harbaugh and his staff still had a lot of work to do if they were ever going to beat the Buckeyes and win a Big Ten Title. I am sure they started working on those improvements in early January 2019.

As expected, the Spartan loss to Michigan was disappointing to everyone in East Lansing. Dantonio's teams had been beating the Wolverines on a regular basis. Now losses to UM were no longer expected. Of course, there is no crying in baseball or football. Another game loomed on the horizon. Time to suck it up and get ready for Purdue. Fortunately, Sparty sucked it up and defeated the Boilermakers (23-13). MSU's next challenge took them to Maryland where they beat the Terrapins (24-3). The Spartans still had a lot to play for, but they could not beat Ohio State or Nebraska in the next two weeks. Dantonio's team defeated Rutgers (14-10) to end the regular season at 7 wins and 5 losses. The Green and White footballers earned an invite to the Red Box Bowl to play Oregon. Unfortunately, the Spartans were in no mood to party on December 31, 2018 after losing to the Ducks (7-6). That final score (7-6) was also MSU's final record for season twelve of the Dantonio Era. A season that began with high hopes, high rankings and high expectations fizzled out in the middle and again at the end. Mark Dantonio's football team would have to be much better in 2019 or things might have to change in East Lansing. Time to get back to work!

Game #112: November 16, 2019 at Michigan Stadium in Ann Arbor

BACKGROUND INFORMATION:

One item to note was the 150th Anniversary year of college football in 2019. Yes, a long time ago two teams (Princeton and Rutgers) got together for a crazy game called football.

Mark Dantonio was back for season thirteen in 2019. Although he never talked about it publicly, he accomplished a lot in his first twelve seasons. His record of 107 wins and 51 losses put him in position to pass Duffy Daugherty (109-69-5) and become the winningest coach in MSU football history. Passing Duffy was probably not a big priority for Coach "D" and his staff. They were focused on scoring more points, allowing less, and winning more games. If they did those things, it would be another winning season in East Lansing.

Eighteenth ranked Michigan State kicked off the 2019 season with two straight wins. MSU slipped to 2-1 after another upsetting upset loss to unranked Arizona State (10-7). Dantonio's Spartans bounced back with a big win at Northwestern (31-10). It was win #110 for Coach "D" at MSU. He was now the winningest coach in the history of Aggie/Spartan football. The Spartans ended September with a shootout victory over Indiana (40-31) and a record of 4 wins and 1 loss. October's record looked difficult since Sparty would face a top ten team for three straight weeks. Welcome to life in the Big Ten in 2019.

The twenty-fifth ranked Spartans traveled to Columbus to face #4 Ohio State. The Buckeyes sent their guests home with a loss (34-10). Things turned out even worse in Madison since the Badgers blasted MSU (38-0). Things improved slightly when the Dantonio's team hosted Penn State. The Spartans still lost, but at least they scored (28-7). Michigan State lost every game in October and finished the month with an overall record of 4 wins and 4 losses. Spartan Nation was hopeful that November would be a better month. That did not happen either. Illinois upset the favored Spartans in East Lansing by a score of 37-34. Coach Dantonio's football team arrived in Ann Arbor with a record of 4 wins and 5 losses. Everyone in East Lansing figured that the Spartans had the Wolverines right where they wanted them. The fifteenth ranked Wolverines were favored to win in The Big House. Another perfect opportunity for an upset, right?

Jim Harbaugh was back for the 2019 season which was an accomplishment. Both Rich Rodriguez and Brady Hoke failed to make it to their fifth year. Yes, this was progress in Ann Arbor! The good news was that Jim Harbaugh had won a lot of games in Ann Arbor (47 to be exact). However, he was still winless against rivals like Notre Dame (0-1) and Ohio State (0-4). Harbaugh was only even against Sparty (2-2). As Brady Hoke used to say, "This is Michigan" and Coach Harbaugh's body of work to date was less than satisfying for Wolverine Nation. Then, there was the matter of no Big Ten Championships. Yes, Michigan's "no championship" streak was at fourteen straight seasons—the longest title draught in program history! Coach Harbaugh's team could end that streak as soon as December 7, 2019. But only IF his Wolverines could defeat OSU and only IF Michigan could win the Big Ten Championship game in Indianapolis. Those were two BIG IFs. Would team #140 be ready for all the challenges of the 2019 season?

The seventh ranked Wolverines kicked off the season with a 40-21 victory over Middle Tennessee State University. One week later, they defeated Army 24-21 in overtime and went into a bye week schedule to prepare for a tough game at Wisconsin. The Badgers played like they were on their own "revenge tour" in 2019 since they embarrassed the Wolverines (35-14). Harbaugh's team rebounded nicely with three straight wins over Rutgers (52-0), Iowa (10-3) and Illinois (42-25). Another potential "revenge tour" game lurked in Happy Valley. Michigan had not won at Penn State since 2015 and it did not happen in 2019. The seventh ranked Nittany Lions defeated the sixteenth ranked Wolverines 28-21. Two more wins over #8 Notre Dame (45-14) and Maryland (38-7) pushed Michigan's record to 7 wins and 2 losses. Just like 2017, Harbaugh and his staff had an extra week to prepare for another visit from the Spartans. Wolverine fans were wondering "Would Coach Harbaugh finally win a home game against Mark Dantonio and his Spartans?"

GAME SUMMARY: MSU 10 UM 44

The last series game of the second decade of the 21st Century promised to be another colossal collision between two football foes who were going in different directions. Michigan was headed towards another winning season while Michigan State was trying to salvage their season with another upset win against the hated Wolverines.

Michigan State scored first in the sixty-seventh battle for the Paul Bunyan Trophy. Brian Lewerke completed a 1-yard scoring pass to tight end Max Rosenthal. Matt Coghlin's extra point gave MSU a 7-0 lead at the end of one quarter. Then, Michigan's defense went to work and so did Shea Patterson. Patterson engineered three straight scoring drives in the second quarter. Hassan Haskins scored on a 1-yard run, Patterson tossed a 5-yard scoring pass to Nick Eubanks and Quinn Nordin converted two extra points and kicked a 28-yard field goal. The Wolverines led 17-7 at halftime. (*DFP*, 11/17/2019, Page 5D)

Michigan's defense continued to keep MSU out of the end zone in the third quarter. Shea Patterson threw an 18-yard touchdown to Donovan Peoples-Jones. Quinn Nordin made the extra point and traded field goals with MSU's Coghlin. The Wolverines led 27-10 at the end of the third quarter. Harbaugh's football team owned the fourth quarter and made sure that there were no magical Spartan comebacks in this game. Shea Patterson tossed two more scoring passes (22-yards to Nico Collins and 39-yards to Corneilus Johnson). Nordin added two more extra points and a 33-yard field goal to seal Michigan's victory margin at 44-10. (*DFP*, 11/17/2019, Page 5D)

Michigan was clearly the better team on this November day. The Maize and Blue defenders were a big story all day long, but the offense was good too. Don Brown's defense held Michigan State to 54-yards rushing and 220-yards of total offense. They limited Brian Lewerke to 17 completions on 30 attempts and only 166-yards. Shea Patterson's stat line looked much different. He completed 24 of 33 passes for 384-yards, 4 touchdowns and no interceptions. (*DFP*, 11/17/2019, Page 5D)

As expected, both teams lost some blood in this game, but Sparty lost more. I am sure that Mark Dantonio was "steamed" again when Shea Patterson threw a 39-yard touchdown pass on third down with only two minutes remaining in the game. Nothing like rubbing it in, right? Of course, all is fair in love, war and rivalry football games!

Team	1st	2nd	3rd	4th	Final
MSU	7	0	3	0	10
UM	0	17	10	17	44

SERIES UPDATE:

Michigan's dominant victory raised their series advantage to 71 wins, 36 losses, and 5 ties. Paul Bunyan remained in Ann Arbor for the second straight season which had not happened since 2006-2007. After sixty-three trophy games, the Wolverines had the most trophy wins at 38 wins, 27 losses, and 2 ties. Despite the loss to UM, Dantonio's Spartans still won the decade with a record of 6 wins and 4 losses.

SERIES MILESTONES:

The Mitten State blood-letting contest of 2019 turned out to be a one-sided contest. Michigan had several milestones to note, but the Spartans only had one. First, Jim Harbaugh won his first rival game in The Big House in his third attempt. Second, the big win also gave Harbaugh the advantage over Mark Dantonio (3 wins to 2 losses) in their very "personal" series rivalry. Third, Shea Patterson set a Wolverine record for the most passing yards against MSU (384). Shea Patterson also tied the UM record with four touchdown passes against the Spartans. Fourth, Michigan's victory was also #50 for series games played in Ann Arbor, which is a lot of games. Finally, it was the largest margin of defeat (34 points) that Coach Dantonio ever experienced in a rivalry game.

Unfortunately, Coach "D" saved his worst for last. As it turned out, this was his last series game since he retired in February 2020. Mark Dantonio finished his rival battles with a final record of 8 wins and 5 losses. He raised the intensity level of the Mitten State football rivalry to an all-time high, along with a little help from Mike Hart!

SEASON SUMMARIES:

Michigan State's loss at Michigan extended their losing streak to five games. Things improved after the Spartans defeated Rutgers (27-0). MSU finished the season on a two-game winning streak after they defeated Maryland (19-16). The Green and White footballers ended the regular season with a record of 6 wins and 6 losses. The Spartans earned a bid to the Pinstripe Bowl and made the most of it with a 27-21 victory over Wake Forest. Coach "D's" thirteenth season ended at 7 wins and 6 losses. Unfortunately, the 2019 season was another disappointment for Dantonio and Spartan Nation. I am certain that Coach Dantonio's spirits rose a little in mid-January 2020 when he accepted a 4.3 million longevity bonus from Michigan State.

A few weeks later, a former staffer sued Coach Dantonio and MSU for "wrongful termination." There were also some ugly allegations about NCAA recruiting violations that Dantonio flatly denied. On February 4, 2020, Mark Dantonio announced that he was retiring from his coaching position. Of course, he left with the title of "Winningest Coach" in Michigan State University football history. Coach "D" posted an overall record of 114 wins and 57 losses (.666) in East Lansing. He also finished with a Big Ten record of 69 wins and 39 losses (.638) and three Big Ten Championships. Dantonio took his Spartans to twelve bowl games and broke even at 6 wins and 6 losses. Mark Dantonio's work was done. He was looking forward to slowing down after thirteen years in East Lansing.

Michigan's win over MSU raised their record to 8 wins and 2 losses. It also bumped them up to the thirteenth poll position heading into a road trip to Indiana. The Wolverines kept rolling and left Bloomington with a 39-14 victory over the Hoosiers. Once again, the stage was set for "The Game" in Ann Arbor. Maize and Blue fans were not happy when OSU left town with another dominating win over Michigan (56-27).

The Wolverines continued their post-season pattern of going to a bowl game and losing it. Alabama showed the Wolverines how the "Big Boys" in the SEC played football and helped them end another season on a losing note (39-14). Michigan finished the season with a final record of 9 wins and 4 losses. The good news was that UM enjoyed another winning season, played in another bowl game, and added another All-American player in La Vert Hill. The bad news was that the championship drought continued and so did the losing to Ohio State—ugh!

DECADE AND SERIES SUMMARY:

Mark Dantonio's Spartans dominated the Wolverines for most of the decade. Even though MSU lost in 2018 and 2019, they still posted a record of 6 wins and 4 losses. Coach "D" feasted on Rich Rodriguez (1 win and 0 losses) and Brady Hoke (3 wins and 1 loss) from 2010 to 2014. Things finally turned in Michigan's favor (3-2) from 2015 to 2019. The Mitten State football rivalry continued to provide some of the most intense football games of the decade.

Decade and Series Summary 1898 to 2019

Series Years	UM Won-Lost-Tied	MSU Won-Lost-Tied
2010-2019	4-6	6-4
1898-2019	71-36-5	36-71-5

BIG TEN SUMMARY:

Now, it is time to take a closer look at some key statistics about how Michigan and Michigan State fared in the Big Ten from 2010 to 2019. There are similarities in the wins and losses for both teams since they each had seven winning seasons. Both schools won at the rate of sixty percent or better. There are two big differences between Michigan and Michigan State in the second decade of the 21st Century. First, Mark Dantonio gave MSU ten years of stability during the decade while Michigan had three different head coaches. Just like every other decade, program stability is a good thing. It really is the foundation of a winning football program.

Big Ten Summary 2010 to 2019

Statistical Area	UM	MSU
Number of Head Coaches	3	1
Games Played	84	84
Wins	53	56
Losses	31	28
Winning Percentage	.631	.667
Winning Seasons	7	7
Losing Seasons	3	3
Even Seasons	0	0
Big Ten Championships	0	3

That brings us to the second difference between the programs from 2010 to 2019. Coach Dantonio's program stability allowed him to win more games and achieve a slightly higher conference winning percentage It also produced three Big Ten Championships compared to zero for Michigan. Yes, Michigan failed to win, or tie, for at least one Big Ten Title in a decade for the first time since 1898. Michigan State's championships were the biggest difference between the two programs in this decade. That is why Michigan State was the best Big Ten team in the Mitten State from 2010 to 2019.

PROGRAM SUMMARIES:

Michigan and Michigan State won many games in the second decade of the 21st Century, but the Spartans won a few more. Both teams were consistent winners during this decade with two exceptions. Brady Hoke's last team finished at 5 wins and 7 losses which is why he is no longer coaching at Michigan. Mark Dantonio's only losing season came in 2016 when the Spartans ended a miserable campaign at 3 wins and 9 losses.

When you look at the numbers on the chart below, you see a lot of good for the Wolverines and the Spartans. The biggest differences in the programs can be found in line one and line ten. Michigan's coaching merry-go-round did not lead to a dominating decade. Line ten, the All-American line, looks like a good news line for Michigan. I think the opposite. Michigan seemed to have the best talent for most of the decade, but those four and five-star players did not produce more wins than Sparty. Coach Dantonio and his staff had less "star" talent, but MSU won the decade. The second decade of the new Millennium saw a lot of good football and some excellent seasons as well from both teams. Brady Hoke's first team in 2011 set the bar high with 11 wins and 1 loss. Unfortunately, Hoke could not achieve anything close to that in his final three seasons. Jim Harbaugh posted three 10 wins seasons in the last five years of the decade.

Program Summaries 2010 to 2019

Statistical Area	UM	MSU
Number of Head Coaches	3	1
Games Played	129	132
Wins	85	92
Losses	44	40
Winning Percentage	.659	.697
# Winning Seasons	9	9
# Losing Seasons	1	1
# Even Seasons	0	0
National Championships	0	0
All-American Players	12	4

Michigan State's performance from 2010 to 2016 was as good as any team in the country except Alabama, Clemson, and Ohio State. Coach Dantonio's teams won 65 games during that period including 13 in 2013, 12 in 2015 and 11 in 2010, 2011 and 2014. The last four years did not go as well with one 10-win season (2017) and one 3-win season (2016) and two back-to-back 7-win seasons in 2018 and 2019.

When it was all said and done, Michigan State had the winningest and most stable program in the Mitten State from 2010 to 2019. The Spartans were strong in the first half of the decade and Michigan was not. Jim Harbaugh had a mess to clean up when he arrived in Ann Arbor in 2015. He worked hard to turn things around at Michigan, but he made some good progress. The bottom line was that the Spartans had bragging rights for the decade and Michigan did not! This decade was one of the closest in series history. It was going to be fun to see what would happen with both programs in 2020 and beyond!

CHAPTER 15

A Covid-19 Season 2020

Covid-19 killed over 650,000 Americans and millions around the world. It was the most devastating pandemic to hit the world in over one hundred years. Of course, the loss of so many lives was only part of the story. Economies in every country took huge hits and millions of people lost their jobs. Entire industries such as airlines, hotels and restaurants were brought to their knees by this pernicious virus. Professional and college sports were totally shut down at the start of the pandemic. The National Basketball Association and the National Hockey League both attacked the problem of resuming their seasons with caution. Surprisingly, both leagues were able to finish their seasons safely. Major League Baseball was the next sport to come alive during the pandemic. Once again, they were able to overcome some setbacks and keep their players safe. The season ended when the Los Angeles Dodgers won the World Series Championship in October 2020.

Getting the professional sports up and running was one thing, but college sports was a much different problem. The NCAA shut down all college sports in March 2020. National basketball tournaments for men and women were both cancelled along with all spring sports. The Covid-19 illness and death numbers increased during the summer and things looked bad for a resumption of fall sports. Initially, all major college conferences looked at what was happening and most determined that opting out would be the best choice in the fall of 2020. However, the Southeast Conference, the Atlantic Coast Conference and some independents like Notre Dame and Army decided they could have safe seasons. The college football season was delayed, but the schools who committed to playing were determined to make it work. Eventually, the Big Ten came on board, but only for a short time. They published a revised schedule which they promptly cancelled. After great outcries from players, coaches, parents, and fans the Big Ten decided that they could make a season work. Finally, an eight-game conference only playing schedule was developed. The Big Ten football season began on the weekend of October 23 and 24, 2010.

Game #113: October 31, 2020 at Michigan Stadium in Ann Arbor

BACKGROUND INFORMATION:

Mark Dantonio's abrupt departure in February 2020 was a shocker for most Spartan fans. Those who knew him best may have seen some signs, but the timing was not great. MSU Athletic Director Bill Beekman really had to hustle to find a suitable replacement. Luke Fickell, Cincinnati's Head Coach, was the top target, but he rejected the Spartan offer immediately. Now, the awkward search was on. All open positions had already been filled in January 2020. Beekman had to dig deep. Finally, the Spartans went after former a MSU assistant named Mel Tucker. Coach Tucker just finished his first season at Colorado. He was not looking to bail out on the Buffaloes.

Mel Tucker also rejected Michigan State is first offer. However, what Tucker did not know was that the fine folks in East Lansing decided to put all their eggs in one BIG basket. Yes, it was a lot of eggs and a whole bunch of money. As it turned out, money talks and all that money "spoke" to Tucker. The MSU offer allowed Mel Tucker to double his salary to about 5.5 million dollars per year when he said "Yes" to the Spartans. Bill Beekman got a good man despite the challenging circumstances of a late hire. Tucker hit the ground running. He hired a staff and did some recruiting. By March, Coach Tucker was settled in nicely in East Lansing, and getting ready for the upcoming season. The big question was, Would the Spartans even be able to play in 2020?"

Of course, Michigan State was able to play like the rest of the Big Ten. Coach Tucker's team opened the new season at home against Rutgers on October 24, 2020. Thanks to Covid-19, it was the latest season opener in Spartan football history. Unfortunately, it was also one of the most disappointing. The Scarlet Knights ruined Coach Tucker's debut since they left East Lansing with a 38-27 win over Sparty. Things looked bad for MSU since a ranked Wolverine squad was waiting in Ann Arbor for the 113th game in series history. Of course, this was a familiar scenario for the Spartans. No matter how bad things were going, Michigan State was always "ready" to play Michigan. The question was, "Would the Wolverines be "ready" for "little brother?"

Once again, year six of the Jim Harbaugh Era promised to be another interesting season. The Maize and Blue roster was a little thin thanks to the loss of many talented players. Some of Harbaugh's best players left for a variety of reasons: grad transfers, early losses to the NFL and Covid-19 opt-outs. Despite all that, the pollsters still thought that the Wolverines were good since they were ranked in both polls (16th in the AP and 15th in the Coaches). This was going to be Harbaugh's "youngest" and most inexperienced team. How they would develop and play in Michigan's Football System was anybody's guess.

Michigan opened the season at Minnesota in what was expected to be a difficult challenge for the Wolverines. The Wolverines started slowly against the Gophers but finished strong! When it was over, the scoreboard read 49-42 in favor of the Maize and Blue. Harbaugh's team did not play perfectly, but a win is a win. It looked like they were more than ready for Mel Tucker and his winless Spartans.

GAME SUMMARY: MSU 27 UM 24

Series Game #113 was another "upset" win for Michigan State and a another "upsetting" loss for Michigan. It certainly did not matter that the Wolverines were favored by three touchdowns. Of course, none of those points were on the scoreboard when the game began. As usual, every point had to be earned and MSU earned more!

Michigan State opened the scoring on a 30-yard touchdown pass from Rocky Lombardi to Ricky White. Matt Coghlin's extra point gave MSU a 7-0 lead. The Wolverines answered a few minutes later when Blake Corum finished a drive with an 8-yard touchdown run. After Quinn Nordin's extra point, the game was tied at 7-7 and that is how the first quarter ended. Lombardi drove the Spartans to another score when he tossed his second touchdown pass to Connor Heyward (2-yards). Coghlin's second extra point made it 14-7 in favor of MSU with five minutes to play in the second quarter. Michigan responded again and rolled up enough yards for Nordin to kick a 23-yard field goal. The Spartans led 14-10 at halftime. (*LSJ*, 11/1/2020, Page 8B)

Michigan State scored on their first possession of the second half when Coghlin booted a 27-yard field goal. His kick extended the MSU lead to 17-10. The Wolverines responded again and tied the game (17-17) on Corum's second touchdown and Nordin's second extra point. The Spartans took another lead with about four minutes to play in the quarter on a 51-yard Coghlin field goal. MSU led 20-17 with fifteen minutes to play. (*LSJ*, 10/21/2018, Page 9C)

Early in the fourth quarter, Michigan State upped their lead to 27-17 thanks to Lombardi's third TD pass (13-yards to Heyward) and Coghlin's third extra point. Both defenses played well in the final part of the fourth quarter. Although Michigan managed to score with about two minutes to play, (2-yard run by Hassan Haskins and Nordin's PAT) it was not enough. Oh boy, "little brother" did it again and Michigan State earned a hard-fought 27-24 victory over Michigan. (*LSJ*, 11/1/2020, Page 8B)

Bottom line, the Spartans were better on offense, defense, and special teams. It was another complete victory for the Green and White football team. Of course, it was even better since it took place in The Big House! The Spartans played better than everyone thought. Well, everyone but Mel Tucker, his staff, and his players. Maybe MSU was looking ahead to Michigan when they lost to Rutgers. They looked like a completely different, and scarry, team on Halloween!

Yes, it was an awfully close game statistically and on the scoreboard. Despite all the numbers, the game came down to one BIG PLAY! It was not a touchdown, a field goal, or a long run. Spartan linebacker Antquan Simmons, who led both teams in tackles with 11 takedowns, tipped what looked like a sure touchdown pass late in the second quarter. The third down-play prevented a touchdown and resulted in a field goal for Michigan. It was a critical four-point swing that eventually proved to be the difference in the game since the Wolverines lost by three points.

Wow, little things can often make a BIG difference! Yes, both teams shed some blood in this game and probably in equal measure. However, the Wolverines shed some tears after this game was over because this one really hurt. Remember, a MSU vs UM rivalry loss is like losing four times because you: 1) lost a game 2) lost a Big Ten game and 3) lost the Paul Bunyan Trophy, 4) lost bragging rights for another year. Yes, rival games are bliss when you win and torture when you lose. The first ever Halloween matchup in series history turned out to be a sad "trick" for Michigan, and a happy "treat" for Michigan State! Go Green! Go White!

Team	1st	2nd	3rd	4th	Final
MSU	7	7	6	7	27
UM	7	3	7	7	24

SERIES UPDATE:

Michigan State's series win total improved to 37 but remained at 71 losses, and 5 ties. They took the lead in the third decade of the Twenty-first Century by a margin of 1 win and 0 losses. Paul Bunyan got on the bus with the Spartans and would remain in East Lansing for most of the next twelve months. After sixty-eight trophy games, the Green and White now owned a record of 28 wins, 38 losses, and 2 ties.

SERIES MILESTONES:

Series game number one-hundred and thirteen was the first game of the third decade of the 21st Century. It was also the first time that the Mitten State rivals ever played on Halloween Day. Mel Tucker's upset win over the team "down the road" gave him a record of 1-0 versus Harbaugh and Michigan. It was only the second time that an Aggie/Spartan coach ever defeated a Wolverine team in his first attempt. He joined Nick Saban as the only two men to accomplish this feat. Jim Harbaugh's series record dropped to 3 wins and 3 losses. Finally, this game set a new attendance "low" for the series and for Michigan Stadium. Thanks to Covid-19, only 615 people attended this game.

SEASON SUMMARIES:

Unfortunately, the Spartans failed to capitalize on their upset win in Ann Arbor. Instead, they lost two straight games to Iowa (49-7) and Indiana (24-0). MSU's fifth game of the season against Maryland was canceled due to Covid on November 21, 2020. Once again, things did not look good for the Spartans since #8 Northwestern was their next foe. Guess what? Tucker's football team sprung another surprise and sent the Wildcats home with a 29-20 loss. Michigan State had a record of 2 wins and 3 losses with two games to play. A winning season was possible, but it did not happen. MSU lost to Ohio State (52-12) and Penn State (39-24). They were scheduled to play Maryland during Champions Week, but Covid-19 won that game too! Fort the first time in Spartan football history, two scheduled games against the same team were both cancelled in the same season.

When it finally over, the Green and White footballers ended 2020 with a record of 2 wins and 5 losses. It was the worst season since 1982 when Muddy Waters posted a record of 2 wins and 9 losses. Yes, as bad as things were, they could have been worse. Mel Tucker's first season in East Lansing ended on a low note. The Spartans finished at the bottom of the Big Ten East Division. Yes, there were some positives about Mel Tucker's first season like the upset wins over Michigan and Northwestern. However, there was plenty of work to do in the weight room and on the recruiting trail. You must start somewhere and that is what Coach Tucker did. He started, albeit late. Now, the only way to go is up!

The wounded Wolverines took the MSU loss extremely hard. Of course, they should have! This was a game they were favored to win. Instead of bouncing back with a better effort against Indiana, they lost to the Hoosiers (38-21). Just when it looked like things could not get worse, they got worse. The Badgers came to down and whacked Michigan 49-11. Things went better at Rutgers. It took two overtimes, but the Wolverines beat the Scarlet Knights 48-42.

Maybe things were looking up. Harbaugh's footballers had a record of 2 wins and 3 losses with three games to play. They had a chance for another winning season in Ann Arbor. Unfortunately, Penn State and Covid-19 had other plans. The Nittany Lions ruined Senior Day when they defeated the Wolverines (27-17). Michigan did not play the final two games of the season (Ohio State and Iowa) because of the pandemic. Jim Harbaugh's team ended 2020 with a record of 2 wins and 4 losses. And, for the first time in Michigan football history, the Wolverines failed to win a home game. Wow! It was the worst season since 1958 when Bennie Oosterbaan's Wolverines ended the season with a record of 2 wins, 6 loss and 1 tie.

Unfortunately, Michigan football was a BIG disappointment in year six of the Jim Harbaugh Era. There is no way to sugarcoat what happened in Ann Arbor in 2020. Michigan lost many good players for a variety of reasons before the season began. However, after the Minnesota game, they were out-coached and out-played every week for the rest of the season. All Wolverine weaknesses were thoroughly exploited by every opponent. Unfortunately, Michigan rarely returned the favor. Instead, they incurred way too many penalties and receivers dropped too many catchable passes in key situations. Meanwhile, the defense allowed too many yards and lots of points. Don Brown's defenders rarely came up with a big play when needed. Yes, it was a painful Wolverine football season. Of course, there were some highlights, but way too many lowlights in the 2020 football season.

The sad fact was that Jim Harbaugh and his assistant coaches continued to draw elite salaries but did not come close to delivering elite results. One of the best things that did not happen in 2020 was the season finale at Ohio State. Yes, the greatest rivalry game in college football did not happen. If the game were played, I am certain that they would have suffered their worst loss ever to the hated Buckeyes. The season ended badly, but another crushing loss to OSU would have been awful.

The 2020 college football season was unusual in so many ways. When you look back, it is amazing that the season happened at all. The Big Ten Conference and all member schools were careful in their approach to the Covid season. Although there were some cases in almost every program, the season was completed. The good news is that Covid vaccines are being administered to millions of Americans. The bad news is that Covid variants continue to cause problems where vaccination rates are low. The future is really hard to forecast right now in America and around the world.

Both Michigan and Michigan State have plenty of work to do in 2021. Losing seasons have a way of creating laser-like focus and fixing things that need to be fixed. Hopefully, our two favorite college football teams will be able to complete their 2021 seasons as scheduled. If that happens, the bitter rivals will meet again on October 30, 2021 in East Lansing.

MORE MITTEN STATE FOOTBALL HISTORY COMING IN 2021:

As I write the final pages of this book, no one knows what college football will look like in 2021. Hopefully, things will be better and all teams can play a full season in front of real fans. NFL Hall of Fame coach Bill Parcells, once said, "You are your numbers." What he meant by this is that a football coach can be known as a great strategist, a good game manager, and a great practice coach. When all is said and done, the bottom line is this: "Does the coach win and win within the rules?"

Let us take a final look at the numbers for the Michigan and Michigan State football programs as of December 31, 2020.

Program Area	UM	MSU
First Football Season	1879	1896
Total Wins	964	710
Total Losses	348	470
Total Ties	36	44
Winning Percentage	.728	.598
National Championships	11	6
Heisman Winners	3	0
All -Americans (Consensus)	83	31
Big Ten Championships	42	9
Bowl Games	48	29
Bowl Wins	21	13
Bowl Winning Percentage	.438	.448

When you talk about the Michigan and Michigan State football programs it is always interesting to look at the numbers. Of course, the Wolverines started playing seventeen years sooner than the Aggies/Spartans. Yes, they have won more games. They have won more games than any other program in the history of college football.

MSU has always been at a disadvantage when being compared to Michigan, but that's life in Mitten State football. Every number on the previous chart favors the Wolverines except one. The Spartans are slightly better than Michigan at bowl game winning percentage (.448 to .438). Although most of the numbers favor the Wolverines, Michigan State keeps coming after the Maize and Blue. There is no doubt in my mind that Mel Tucker knows about these numbers. He also knows that there is nothing that he can do to change all that history. The only thing that Coach Tucker can do is work to improve upon his current series record of 1 win and 0 losses.

As we look to the future of the Michigan vs Michigan State football rivalry it is interesting to note the results so far in the 21st Century. I think that the rivalry is nastier and more competitive than ever. Michigan owns a razor thin advantage in the first twenty-one games of the 21st Century. Check out the numbers below:

Series Summary 2000 to 2020

Series Years	UM Won-Lost	MSU Won-Lost
2000-2020	11-10	10-11

The numbers do not lie. This is the closest twenty-one-year period in series history. The Mitten State pigskin series continues to be one of the greatest rivalries in all of college football. I think it will remain that way for a long, long, long time

Image 13 This is how two elevators were decorated at the Chicago Hilton and Towers Hotel for the Big Ten Kickoff Luncheon in 2014. The Spartans rose to greater heights in the Big Ten Conference than Michigan from 2010 to 2019. Which program will rise the highest in 2021 and beyond? Photo from Barry Gallagher, Private Collection.

Appendix A – Michigan vs Michigan State Decade Summaries

Decade	Year(s)	# Games	A2 Games	EL Games	UM	MSU
1	1898	1	1	0	1-0-0	0-1-0
2	1900-09	3	2	1	2-0-1	0-2-1
3	1910-19	10	8	2	8-2-0	2-8-0
4	1920-29	10	9	1	10-0-0	0-10-0
5	1930-39	10	10	0	4-4-2	4-4-2
6	1940-49	8	7	1	8-0-0	0-8-0
7	1950-59	10	8	2	2-7-1	7-2-1
8	1960-69	10	5	5	2-7-1	7-2-1
9	1970-79	10	5	5	9-1-0	1-9-0
10	1980-89	10	5	5	8-2-0	2-8-0
11	1990-99	10	5	5	6-4-0	4-6-0
12	2000-09	10	5	5	7-3-0	3-7-0
13	2010-19	10	5	5	4-6-0	6-4-0
14	2020-	1	1	0	0-1	1-0
Totals	123	113	76	37	71-37-5	37-71-5

Appendix B – Michigan Coaches vs Michigan State

Coach	Year(s)	Overall	%	Vs MSU	%
Ferbert	1896-1899	24-3-1	.875	1-0-0	1.000
Yost	1901-1923, 1925-1926	165-29-10	.888	16-2-1	.868
Little	1924	6-2-0	.750	1-0-0	1.000
Wieman	1927-1928	9-6-1	.600	2-0-0	1.000
Kipke	1929-1937	46-26-4	.639	3-4-2	.389
Crisler	1938-1947	71-16-3	.816	8-0-0	1.000
Oosterbaan	1948-1958	63-33-4	.656	4-6-1	.409
Elliott	1959-1968	51-42-2	.548	2-7-1	.250
Schembechler	1969-1989	194-48-5	.802	17-4-0	.809
Moeller	1990-1994	44-13-4	.771	3-2-0	.600
Carr	1995-2007	122-40	.763	10-3	.769
Rodriguez	2008-2010	15-22	.405	0-3	.000
Hoke	2011-2014	31-20	.607	1-3	.250
Harbaugh	2015-2020	49-22	.690	3-3-0	.500

Appendix C – Michigan State Coaches vs Michigan

Coach	Year(s)	Overall	Win %	Vs UM	Win %
Keep	1897-98	8-5-1	.607	0-1-0	.000
Bemies	1899-1900	3-7-1	.318	N/A	N/A
Denman	1901-1902	7-9-1	.441	0-1-0	.000
Brewer	1903-1910*	58-23-7	.699	0-4-1	.100
Macklin	1911-1915	29-5-0	.853	2-3-0	.400
Sommers	1916	4-2-1	.643	0-1-0	.000
Gauthier	1918	4-3-0	.571	0-1-0	.000
Clark	1920	4-6-0	.400	0-1-0	.000
Barron	1921-22	6-10-2	.389	0-2-0	.000
Young	1923-1927	18-22-1	.451	0-5-0	.000
Kipke	1928	3-4-1	.438	0-1-0	.000
Crowley	1929-1932	22-8-3	.712	0-2-2	.250
Bachman	1933-1946	70-34-10	.658	4-8-0	.333
Munn	1947-1953	54-9-2	.846	4-3-0	.571
Daugherty	1954-1972	109-69-5	.609	10-7-2	.578
Stolz	1973-1975	19-13-1	.591	0-3-0	.000
Rogers	1976-1979	24-18-2	.568	1-3-0	.250
Waters	1980-1982	10-23-0	.303	0-3-0	.000
Perles	1983-1994	68-67-4	.504	4-8-0	.333
Saban	1995-1999	34-24-1	.585	2-3-0	.400
Williams	1999-2002	16-17-0	.485	1-2-0	.333
Watts	2002	1-2-0	.333	0-0-0	N/A
Smith	2003-2006	22-26-0	.458	0-4-0	.000
Dantonio	2007-2019	114-57-0	.667	8-5-0	.615
Tucker	2020-Present	2-5	.286	1-0-0	1.000

Bibliography

Borton, John and Paul Dodd. *Wolverines Handbook: Stories, Stats and Stuff About Michigan Football.* Wichita: The Wichita Eagle and Beacon Publishing Company, 1996

Boyles, Bob, and Paul Guido. *The USA Today College Football Encyclopedia.* New York: Sky Horse Publishing, 2011

Changelis, Angelique. *100 Things Michigan Fans Should Know and Do Before They Die.* Chicago: Triumph Books, 2009.

Clarke, Kim, Editor *Always Leading, Forever Valiant: Stories of the University of Michigan, 1817-2017.* Ann Arbor: University of Michigan Press, 2017.

Emmerich, Michael. *100 Things Michigan State Fans Should Know and Do Before They Die:* Chicago: Triumph Books, 2016.

Geelhoed, E. Bruce. *Bump Elliott, the Michigan Wolverines and Their 1964 Championship Football Season.* Jefferson, NC: McFarland & Company, Inc., Publishers, 2014

Green, Jerry. *The University of Michigan Football Vault: The History of the Wolverines.* Atlanta: Whitman Publishing, LLC, 2008

Grinczel, Steve. *Michigan State Football: They Are Spartans.* Charleston: Arcadia Publishing, 2003

Herget, James E. *American Football: How the Game Evolved.* Lexington, KY: Create Space, 2013

Madej, Bruce with Greg Kinney, Mike Pearson, and Rob Toonkel. *Michigan: Champions of the West.* Champaign: Sports Publishing, 1997

Michigan Daily. *Michigan Football: From the Pages of the Michigan Daily.* Chicago: Triumph Books, 2012.

Ours, Robert. *College Football Encyclopedia: The Authoritative Guide to 124 Years of College Football.* Rocklin, CA: Prima Publishing, 1994.

Perry, Will. *The Wolverines: The Story of Michigan Football.* Huntsville, AL: Strode Publishing, 1974

Scheller, William. *The University of Michigan Story: Hail to the Victors.* New York: Universe Publishing, 2008

Bibliography – Continued

Stabley, Fred W. *The Spartans: Michigan State Football*. Tomball, TX: Strode Publishing, 1988.The State News, *Reaching Higher: Mark Dantonio and the Rise of Michigan State Football*. Chicago: Triumph Books, 2016

Thomas, David A. *Michigan State College: John Hannah and the Creation of a World University 1926-1969*. East Lansing: Michigan State University Press, 2008.

Watterson, John Sayle. *College Football: History, Spectacle and Controversy*. Baltimore: The Johns Hopkins University Press, 2000.

Widder, Keith R. *Michigan Agricultural College: Evolution of a Land-Grant Philosophy.*
East Lansing: Michigan State University Press, 2005

Young, David. J. *Arrogance and Scheming in the Big Ten: Michigan State's Quest for Membership and Michigan's Powerful Opposition*. Grand Rapids: DJY Publishing, 2011.

Young, David. J. *The Student and the Professor: John Hannah, Ralph Aigler, and the Origin of the Michigan State-Michigan Rivalry*. Grand Rapids: DJY Publishing, 2015.

Acknowledgements

Appreciation and gratitude are important parts of the book publishing process. This book is no exception. I thank God for my life and I thank God for my wife. My beloved Carol is the most important person in my life. I could not have written this book without her constant love and support. She is the most understanding and loving person I know. I am so fortunate to have shared the best portion of my life with this amazing woman. She always keeps me grounded and has always supported me in my work. Thank you, my darling!

Second, I am so blessed to have the love and support of our five children. Even though I have fathered Army Mules, Spartans, Broncos, and Xavier Musketeers, they still love me even though I love the Michigan Wolverines! Thank you, Mike, Mark, Wendy, Marty, and Matthew! I love you and your families so much.

Third, I am forever indebted to Bill LeMonnier for inspiring me to explore the depth of the UM vs MSU football rivalry. His remarks in the *Chicago Tribune* in July 2014 caused me to go on a seven-year journey that resulted in the writing and publication of this book. I am grateful to have finally met Bill and for the Foreword that he wrote for this book. Thank you Bill for all the stories you shared and for your great Foreword!

Fourth, thank you to Chuck Romano and my granddaughter, Erin, for their great work on the book cover. My cousin, Joe Gallagher, read the entire manuscript and offered many helpful comments that greatly improved the final product. I am also indebted to Tracy Atkins from Book Design Templates for her outstanding work on the interior design of this book. Thank you everyone, for your contributions to this book!

Fifth, I am grateful to the Bentley Historical Library at The University of Michigan. The Bentley Library is an amazing repository of the history of The University of Michigan. The incredible collection of football records, pictures and documents helped me greatly in researching and writing his book. Greg Kinney, Diana Bachman, and Caitlin Moriarty helped me at every turn. Thanks Greg, Diana, and Caitlin—you are absolutely the best at what you do!

Sixth, I always take time to thank my high school Creative Writing teacher, Mr. Richard Hill. He taught me some important things about writing that I still practice today. Most importantly, he instilled a passion for writing that I carry with me over fifty-years later! Mr. Hill is also a die-hard Michigan Wolverine Fan and graduate of The University of Michigan. Thank you, Mr. Hill and Go Blue!

Finally, although there was no single book that documented the complete history of the Michigan vs Michigan State football rivalry, there is plenty of information available. I am grateful to all the authors I have cited in my bibliography. I enjoyed reading their books and appreciate their contributions to this book. Of course, I am grateful to all the newspaper columnists who documented the history of every series game from 1898 to 2020. I could not have completed this book properly without all their outstanding articles about Wolverine and Aggie/Spartan football. Thank you, authors, and journalists!

Photographs and Images Permissions

Thank you to the Bentley Historical Library at The University of Michigan for permission to use the images listed below.

Page	BHL #	Description	Credit	Collection
9	BL016139	Ferry Field	Benham and Allen	UM, Athletic Dept.
16	BL010061	Checkerboard	Unknown	UM, Athletic Dept.
44	N/A	1918 Poster	BHL	Program Covers
59	N/A	1924 M. S. C. Dedication	BHL	Program Covers
95	BL007212	T. Harmon/Helmets	Ivory Photo	UM, Athletic Dept.
116	BL006718	Fritz Crisler	UM, Athletic Dept. Records	UM, Athletic Dept.
135	BL008857	Paul Bunyan Trophy and Governor Williams	Michiganensian	Michiganensian
182	BL009543	Highsmith -1969	Bob Kalmbach	UM, Athletic Dept.
202	BL015219	Striped Football 1975	Bob Kalmbach	UM, Athletic Dept.
248	BL018975	Fab Five	Bob Kalmbach	UM Athletic Dept./ News and Information
269	BL017781	Saban 1995	Bob Kalmbach	UM Athletic Dept.

ABOUT THE AUTHOR

Photo Courtesy of Mike Tanner, Saint Mike's Photography

Barry Gallagher is a graduate of Eastern Michigan University where he earned a bachelor's degree in Secondary Education and a master's degree in Educational Administration. From 1973 to 1983 he worked as a teacher, coach, school administrator, and served in the U. S. Army Reserve. In 1983 he went on active duty served in various positions as a Military Police Officer and Human Resources Officer. Gallagher retired as a Colonel in 2003. Barry is the author of two books on *Wolverine football: Michigan Football's Greatest Era* and *The Legend of Bo Schembechler*. He is the author of four other books.

If you enjoyed this book, it would be great if you could leave a positive review on Amazon. It is amazingly easy to do, and I would really appreciate it. Thank You!

How to contact Barry Gallagher:

E-Mail: PowerGroup@comcast.net

Website: www.gobluefootballhistorian.com